Iran's Weapons of Mass Destruction

The Real and Potential Threat

Anthony H. Cordesman and Khalid R. Al-Rodhan

THE CSIS PRESS

Center for Strategic
and International Studies
Washington, D.C.

Significant Issues Series, Volume 28, Number 3
Printed on recycled paper in the United States of America
Cover design by Robert L. Wiser, Silver Spring, Md.
Cover photograph: Satellite image showing the nuclear facility at Bushehr, Iran
© Digital Globe/Reuters/Corbis

10 09 08 07 06   5 4 3 2 1

ISSN 0736-7136
ISBN-13: 978-0-89206-485-4
ISBN-10: 0-89206-485-4

Library of Congress Cataloging-in-Publication Data
Cordesman, Anthony H.
    Iran's weapons of mass destruction : the real and potential threat / Anthony
H. Cordesman and Khalid R. Al-Rodhan.
        p. cm. — (Significant issues series ; v. 28, no. 3)
    Includes bibliographical references.
    ISBN-13: 978-0-89206-485-4 (pbk. : alk. paper)
    ISBN-10: 0-89206-485-4 (pbk. : alk. paper)
        1. Weapons of mass destruction—Iran. 2. Iran—Strategic aspects.
    3. Iran—Politics and government—1997–   .   I. Al-Rodhan, Khalid R.
    II. Title. III. Series.
    U793.C665 2006
    358'.30955—dc22
                                            2006013513

CONTENTS

TABLES, FIGURES, AND MAPS

Tables

Figures

Maps

ACKNOWLEDGMENTS

The authors relied heavily on the work of William D. Sullivan, research assistant and program coordinator for the Office of the Arleigh A. Burke Chair in Strategy at CSIS. The authors would also like to thank two research interns, William Elliott and Nikos Tsafos, for researching earlier drafts of this book.

James Dunton, Roberta Howard Fauriol, Donna Spitler, Divina Jocson, and Ashorkor Tetteh of the CSIS Press deserve special recognition for their tireless work to edit and publish this book on short notice and amid ongoing developments in Iran's nuclear program.

This book would have been impossible to write without the comments, corrections, and suggestions of many policymakers, arms controls experts, and government officials from the United States, Europe, and the Middle East. The authors relied on many sources, particularly reports by the International Atomic Energy Agency (IAEA), the International Energy Agency (IEA), the Energy Information Administration (EIA), GlobalSecurity.org, the Institute for Science and International Security (ISIS), the Federation of American Scientists (FAS), the International Institute for Strategic Studies (IISS), and the Nuclear Threat Initiative (NTI). Although the analysis relies heavily on the work of these agencies, press reports and news articles were also used extensively in researching this book.

Map of Iran

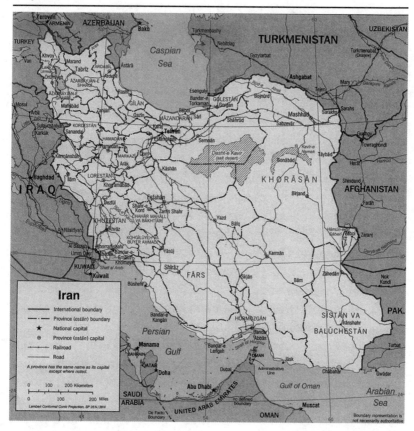

Source: CIA, Map of Iran, 2001, available at http://www.lib.utexas.edu/maps/middle_east_and_asia/iran_pol01.jpg.

CHAPTER ONE

INTRODUCTION

There is no simple or reliable way to characterize Iran's ability to acquire weapons of mass destruction and the means to deliver them. Iran is clearly attempting to acquire long-range ballistic missiles and cruise missiles, but it has never indicated that such weapons would have chemical, biological, radiological, or nuclear (CBRN) warheads. Iran has never properly declared its holdings of chemical weapons, and the status of its biological weapons programs is unknown.

There have been strong indications of an active Iranian interest in acquiring nuclear weapons since the time of the shah, Mohammad Reza Pahlavi, and strong indications that Ayatollah Ruhollah Khomeini revived such efforts after Iraq invaded Iran and began to use chemical weapons. There is, however, no reliable history of such efforts or "smoking gun" that conclusively proves their existence.

The Iranian leadership has consistently argued that its nuclear research efforts are designed for peaceful purposes, although various Iranian leaders have made ambiguous statements about acquiring weapons of mass destruction and Iranian actions strongly suggest that the country is trying to acquire nuclear weapons. Whether such deniability is plausible or not is highly questionable. Still, Iran has been able to find some alternative explanation for even its most suspect activities, and there is no present way to disprove its claims with open source material.

The EU3 (the United Kingdom, Germany, and France) have actively negotiated with Iran to bring a halt to such suspect activities, but Iran has consistently refused to reach meaningful agreements with the EU3 despite the incentives it has been offered. At times, Iran has refused Russian offers to provide nuclear fuel on a much cheaper basis than it can possibly produce such fuel. The fact that the United States has supported such negotiations could mean that Iran's compliance would eliminate the threat of U.S. and Israeli military action or preemption.

Much more is involved than the issue of whether Iran does or does not have the bomb. Iranian efforts to acquire nuclear weapons interact with the ongoing struggle to prevent proliferation of weapons of mass destruction (WMDs) in the Middle East. Israel has nuclear weapons; Syria has a chemical and biological weapons program; and there is uncertainty regarding Egypt's WMD program. In addition, Pakistan and India are both nuclear powers. The region as a whole is drifting into further proliferation and a nuclear Iran may expand the efforts to go beyond the usual suspects. It remains uncertain how key countries such as Saudi Arabia, Jordan, Egypt, and Turkey would respond to a nuclear-armed Tehran.

Any crisis over Iranian proliferation could have a major impact on the evolving balance of power in the region. The United States, the UK, Iraqi Sunnis, and many regional powers have expressed their concerns about Iran's involvement in Iraq's internal affairs. Key Arab states, such as Saudi Arabia and Jordan, have expressed their anxiety about the creation of a new Shi'ite block that could include Iran, Iraq, Syria, and Lebanon and that could redefine the balance of power in the region across sectarian lines.

THE PROBLEM OF UNCERTAINTY VERSUS CREDIBILITY

A long chain of indicators suggest that Iran *is* proliferating. Iran's missile development programs make sense only if the missiles are equipped with CBRN warheads. There have been numerous confirmed disclosures of suspect Iranian activity. Iran's nuclear program has been under intense scrutiny by the International Atomic Energy Agency (IAEA) in recent years, and the IAEA reports disclose a pattern of activity that makes little sense unless it is tied to a nuclear weapons program.

Yet the data on Iranian nuclear weapons efforts remain uncertain. The summary reporting by the IAEA has not stated that there is decisive evidence that Iran is seeking such weapons, even though the detailed disclosures in IAEA reporting since 2002 strongly indicate that it is likely that Iran is continuing to covertly seek nuclear technology. Neither the United States nor its European allies have yet released detailed white papers on their intelligence analysis of Iranian efforts, and there have been several press reports that the U.S. intelligence community believes that its knowledge of the Iranian nuclear program is less than adequate to make the case for where, when, and how the Iranians will acquire a nuclear weapon.[1]

Under the terms of the Nuclear Non-Proliferation treaty (NPT), which it is a signatory to, Iran does have the right to acquire a full nuclear fuel cycle for peaceful purposes, and the Iranian government has found ways to justify all of its activities to date as research, or related to nuclear power, or minor mistakes, or the result of importing contaminated equipment. It has claimed that its concealed and secret efforts are the result of its fears that the United States or Israel might attack what it claims are legitimate activities.

In fact, however, Iran may have advanced to the point where it can covertly develop nuclear weapons even if it agrees to the terms proposed by the EU3 and Russia and appears to comply with IAEA inspection. As the experience of the United Nations in Iraq has shown all too clearly, there are severe limits to even the most advanced inspection regime. Iran might well be able to carry out a covert research and development effort, make major advances in weapons development, and improve its ability to produce fissile material. It might well acquire a "breakout" capability to suddenly make weapons or be able to produce small numbers of weapons without detection.

The problems in addressing Iran's capabilities go beyond the ability to determine the facts. Since 2002, the Bush administration and the EU3 have consistently argued that Iran's efforts to acquire nuclear weapons are real and must be stopped. The ability of the United States, the IAEA, and the EU3 to halt the Iranian nuclear program is complicated, however, by the mistakes the United States and the UK made in characterizing Iraq's efforts to acquire weapons of mass destruction.

The United States in particular has problems in convincing the international community that Iran is a grave threat to global security. Credibility is a precious commodity, and one sometimes worth more than gold.

It is also impossible to deny that Iran is being judged by a different standard because of its regime association with terrorism, its efforts to export its Shi'ite revolution, and its reckless political rhetoric. There is nothing wrong with a "dual standard." Nations that present exceptional risks require exceptional treatment. The fact remains, however, that Iran was under missile and chemical attack from Iraq, and it seems to have revived its nuclear programs at a time that Iraq was already involved in a major effort to acquire biological and nuclear weapons. In addition, three of Iran's major neighbors—India, Israel, and Pakistan—have already proliferated. It also must deal with the presence of two outside nuclear powers: Russia near its northern border and the United States in the Gulf.

The situation is further confused by an increasingly thin line between the technology needed to create a comprehensive nuclear fuel cycle for nuclear power generation and dual-use technology that can be used to covertly develop nuclear weapons. A nation can be both excused and accused for the same actions. This can make it almost as difficult, if not impossible, to conclusively prove Iran's guilt as to prove its innocence, particularly if its programs consist of a large number of small, dispersed efforts and larger "dual-use" facilities.

Some efforts at proliferation have been called a "bomb in the basement"—programs to create a convincing picture that a nation has a weapon without any open testing or formal declaration. Iran seems to be trying to develop a "bomb in a fog"—to keep its efforts both covert and confusing enough that there will be no conclusive evidence that will catalyze the UN into cohesive and meaningful action or justify a U.S. response. Such a strategy must be made more overt in the long run if it is to make Iran a credible nuclear power, but the long run can easily stretch out for years: Iran can break up its efforts into smaller, research-oriented programs or pause them; focus on dual-use nuclear efforts with a plausible rationale; permit even intrusive inspection; and still move forward.

UNCERTAIN OPTIONS FOR DEALING WITH UNCERTAIN PROLIFERATION

The options for dealing with Iranian proliferation are as uncertain as the nature of Iran's actions. Some observers have argued that it may be impossible for the United States, the West, or the international community to stop Iran from acquiring nuclear capabilities. In this case, some have argued, the cost of action may be far greater than the cost of inaction. This argument is based on the lack of credible military or diplomatic options for the international community.

Foreign policy specialists have argued that, looking at the energy market, one can conclude that the global economy cannot afford further disruption of oil supply. European experts such as Michael Emerson of the Center for European Policy Studies have argued, "The success of sanctions is doubtful. A military strike isn't on the table from a European perspective. The alternatives to success are dire."[2]

Other experts have argued that there are no good or lasting military options. They feel that too little is known about Iran's nuclear facilities to target them effectively, that many are dispersed or hardened, and that Iran could reconstitute a better hidden and more covert program and step up its biological weapons efforts. They argue that military options, even if they did slow down Iran's efforts, would unify Iranian support for a nuclear program and push Iran toward a higher level of risk taking. They also argue that Iran could respond asymmetrically to military attacks by indirect attacks on energy facilities and exports in the Gulf, pushing Afghanistan and Iraq toward further instability and increasing support for violent Palestinian militant movements and Hezbollah, as well as returning to an aggressive effort to build support from outside Shi'ites and other Islamists.

There definitely are no perfect or risk-free options, and there may not even be any particularly good ones, but there are options.

The Problem of Sanctions

International censure is a useful tool in diplomacy, but only if a nation is sensitive to such censure and willing to negotiate. Sanctions can have more impact, but a determined proliferator may choose to ride them out, and it is unclear whether there are reliable enforcement mechanisms to stop Iran from moving ahead on its nuclear weapons research and bringing important aspects of development to the prototype or production-ready stage.

Broad economic sanctions can hurt a population more than a regime, and they can be exploited as attacks on a nation. Iraq under Saddam Hussein is a case in point—regime loyalists exploited UN sanctions and made billions while Iraqi civilians suffered both economically and sometimes physically, from lack of medicines and malnutrition. Even if the UN could agree on sanctions for Iran—and then enforce them with the integrity and concern for the people it lacked in dealing with the sanctions on Iraq and administering the Iraqi "oil for food" program—the end result could cause humanitarian suffering and strengthen the hand of the regime by allowing it to charge that the West was attacking Iran and thus exploit nationalist resentment.

Technical sanctions might slow the inflow of technology and fissile materials, but Iran may well have moved beyond the point where it needs overt imports of technology and equipment. Many dual-use imports would almost certainly continue, and firms in nations like China, North Korea, and Pakistan would probably continue to be covert suppliers. This particular technological genie is probably out of the bottle, at least in Iran.

Sanctions on Iran's petroleum exports, and on its imports of petroleum products, might put serious pressure on the regime. Such sanctions would affect Iran's entire economy, however, and have a serious humanitarian impact. They also would almost certainly raise the price of petroleum products throughout the world, not only by cutting Iranian exports but because they would lead to a higher "risk premium" on all Gulf exports due to the fear of war.

It is equally worth remembering that any effective economic or diplomatic sanctions would have to mean stopping Iran's oil revenues from being diverted into rebuilding its military and WMD capabilities. Stopping energy exports from Iran, however, can do grave damage to the global economy. The energy market is tight, with virtually no spare capacity. In 2005–2006, OPEC's total oil production spare capacity was 1.0–1.6 million barrels a day (mmbpd); and in 2005, the U.S. Energy Information Administration (EIA) estimated that Iran produced 4.1 mmbpd—nearly 5 percent of the world's total oil supply and 11 percent of OPEC's oil production capacity.[3]

During the current war in Iraq, Saudi Arabia and other countries covered the shortages in exports due to instability in Venezuela and Nigeria and disruptions caused by Hurricanes Katrina and Rita. In a tight world oil market, however, there is no way to make up for oil production capacity of 3.9–4.2 mmbpd (or average production levels of 4.1 mmbpd) and average export levels of 2.1 mmbpd. Sanctioning some 5 percent of the world's oil supply may well lead to massive smuggling and violation. In addition, those sanctions almost certainly will have a greater effect on the price of oil than a 5 percent increase. Estimates about the global economic impact of disruptions in Iranian oil supply differ, but virtually all estimates agree that energy prices will increase to unprecedented levels, including exceeding the $100 per barrel mark.

These problems scarcely rule out sanctions. However, they show that sanctions have clear drawbacks as well as advantages. It is also all too possible that even if sanctions did appear to work to the extent that Iran complied with the terms proposed by Russia and the EU3, it could still carry out a covert research and development effort, make major advances in weapons development, and improve its ability to produce fissile material. If it had months (or years) to conceal its existing efforts while it was under sanctions, Iran would be even more able to acquire a covert "breakout" capability to suddenly make weapons of mass destruction or produce small numbers of weapons without detection. "Building a bomb in a fog" may be difficult, but it is far from impossible.

The Problem of Military Options

In addition to the lack of effective diplomatic mechanisms to enforce sanctions, many experts believe that there are no military options with lasting effectiveness. Besides the military targeting issues discussed throughout this analysis, they argue that the United States is preoccupied in Iraq; and while the presence of more than 130,000 U.S. troops in Iraq may seem a deterrent to Iran, the difficulties the United States faces in Iraq make a military conflict all too unlikely.

Efforts to hold Iraq together and forge an inclusive government with support from Sunni Arabs, Shi'ite Arabs, Kurds, and other minorities are already tenuous. For one thing, Iran has great influence with several leading political groups and militias among Iraq's Shi'ites. Moreover, the division between Shi'ites and Sunnis in Iraq is fueled by terrorist elements such as Abu Musab al-Zarqawi who wish to recast the war against the West as a war also against the Shi'ites. Efforts by al-Zarqawi to start an Iraqi civil war and his declaration against the Shi'ites, along with the fear of a spillover of Iraq's insurgency into neighboring states, compound the ongoing struggle against terrorism. In addition, Iran has had long-term relations with extremists and militant groups such as Hezbollah and with dissident groups in Bahrain, Saudi Arabia, and Kuwait.

The mix of proliferation and asymmetric warfare is changing the nature of threat in the region. Saddam Hussein is gone, yet Iran's possible nuclear weapons, the asymmetric capabilities of its Islamic Revolutionary Guards Corps (IRGC), the threat from transnational terrorist groups such as al-Qa'ida, and the ongoing internal stability issues in the Middle East complicate the strategic options for regional powers and key power projectors such as the United States, the UK, and NATO.

Afghanistan remains equally fragile and has its own Shi'ite factions. Iran can tighten its relations with Syria (with a governing Alawite minority elite) and exploit Lebanon's Shi'ites and its own ties to Hezbollah. Iran also has links to Shi'ite movements in Bahrain and Yemen and to other non-Sunni groups in the Gulf. Its submarines, mine warfare capabilities, 20,000-man naval branch of the IRGC, and strategic position near the Strait of Hormuz and main shipping channels in the Gulf enable it to indirectly or covertly attack or threaten the world's key source of oil exports.

At the same time, Iran is a highly vulnerable state. Its air force and surface-to-air missile systems are largely worn, and most elements are obsolete or obsolescent. The fact that targeting cannot be perfect does not mean that many known, probable, and possible facilities cannot be destroyed at great cost to Iran. Iran's key conventional military assets, bases and facilities for its asymmetric forces, and military production and missile facilities are all hostages to a high-level U.S. attack. Such an attack might not halt Iran, but it would certainly slow its efforts. It is also unclear what a few covert nuclear weapons would be worth over time in the face of massive U.S. military, deterrent, and retaliatory superiority, the deployment of antiballistic missiles into the region, and the buildup of other Gulf defenses.

The wild card remains the Israeli response. Israel has argued that Iran must not be permitted to acquire nuclear weapons, but has also argued that the problem is an international, not an Israeli, problem. The election in 2005 of Mahmoud Ahmadinejad to the presidency in Iran and his statements about wiping Israel off the map, however, make Iran's nuclear program an existential threat to Israel. Iran has also made its position clear: an attack by Israel on Iranian nuclear facilities will be met with total retaliation. Iran's minister of defense, General Mostafa Mohammad Najjar, has been quoted as saying, "Any attack against Iran's peaceful nuclear facilities will meet a swift and crushing response from the armed forces."[4] Iran's foreign minister, Manouchehr Mottaki, expressed a similar sentiment, asserting that Iran would respond to such an attack "by all means" at its disposal.[5]

Notes

[1] Dafna Linzer, "Iran Is Judged 10 Years from Nuclear Bomb," *Washington Post*, August 2, 2005, sec. A-1.

[2] Matthew Schofield, "Analysts: Iran Will Make Atomic Bomb," *Miami Herald*, January 30, 2006, available at http://www.mercurynews.com/mld/miamiherald/news/world/13744571.htm.

[3] Energy Information Administration (EIA), *Short-Term Energy Outlook* (Washington, D.C.: EIA, January 2006), table 3a, available at http://www.eia.doe.gov/emeu/steo/pub/3atab.html.

[4] Ali Akbar Dareini, "Iran Says It Will Resist 'Bully' Nations," Associated Press, February 1, 2006.

[5] Ewen MacAskill and Simon Tisdall, "Iran's Message to the West: Back Off or We Retaliate," *Guardian*, February 2, 2006, available at http://www.guardian.co.uk/iran/story/0,,1700266,00.html.

CHAPTER TWO

IRAN'S MOTIVATION FOR ACQUIRING WEAPONS OF MASS DESTRUCTION

Iran has consistently denied the existence of nuclear weapons programs since the time of the shah. But Iran has been equally consistent in acknowledging a nuclear research power program and in insisting it needs nuclear power for peaceful purposes. The result has been that Iran has always been able to point to nuclear power as the rationale for its activities, and to try to explain any weapons-related activity as research. It has sometimes moved from "plausible deniability" to "implausible deniability," but it has always had an excuse.

This excuse raises two questions about Iran's motives. The first is how serious Iran is about nuclear power. Many question Iran's motives in seeking power reactors and ask why Iran needs nuclear energy when it has the second-largest reserves of oil and gas in the world. In 2004, Iran was estimated to have 132.5 billion barrels of oil (11.1 percent of the world's proven oil reserves) and 970.8 trillion cubic feet (Tcf) of natural gas (15.3 percent of the world's proven gas reserves).[1]

Iran has the potential to dominate the global gas markets, if it invests and attracts foreign investment in its energy sector. The Iranian government answers by saying that nuclear power is Iran's sovereign right, and that it needs to diversify its energy sources. But it has never made a convincing case in terms of investment and cost, national need, or alternative national needs for the money it is investing in acquiring nuclear "energy." It has also determinedly refused offers of cheaper reactor fuel from nations like Russia.

The second set of questions concerns Iran's motives for seeking nuclear weapons. One can only speculate about such motives for a nation that has denied an interest in such weapons for more than 30 years. The case for Iranian nuclear weapons, however, seems more convincing from an Iranian perspective than the case for nuclear power.

KEY MOTIVES

There are many possible reasons why Iran would want to acquire nuclear weapons, as well as chemical and biological weapons. While it is impossible to determine Iranian motives with absolute precision, it seems likely that they include a mix of the following factors:

- **National pride.** Many Iranians believe that it is their right to acquire nuclear weapons. Some Iranian officials have stated that 95 percent of the population believes that Iran has the right to acquire nuclear capabilities.[2] While this number is likely exaggerated, the fact is that nuclear weapons provide a unique level of military status and prestige, and could potentially make Iran something approaching a regional superpower and restore its place as a major player in regional affairs. The need to gain that status and prestige began during the time of the shah, before the revolution.

- **Strategic posture in the region.** The ability to use long-range missiles and the possession of nuclear weapons could be used not only to deter the United States and Iran's neighbors, but also to intimidate and pressure Iran's neighbors to support its policies and/or to deter interference in limited military operations by Iran in areas like Iraq or the Gulf.

- **The legacy of Iraq.** Iran has already been attacked by Iraq with missiles and chemical weapons. It saw Iraq seek to develop biological and nuclear weapons to strike it. Saddam may be gone, but Iran may wish to make sure that it cannot be threatened again without the capabilities to retaliate massively against such threats.

- **Instability in the Gulf and the region and conventional military inferiority.** Iran's conventional forces have never been rebuilt since its defeat in the Iran-Iraq War. Iraq may be gone, but Saudi Arabia and even the United Arab Emirates have outpaced Iranian in modernization. Nuclear forces may be expensive, but conventional forces are even more so. To put this challenge in perspective, during 1997–2004 Iran was able to order only $2.3 billion worth of new arms agreements, while Saudi Arabia ordered $10.5 billion, Kuwait $3.1 billion, and the UAE $12.0 billion. Even a small nation like Oman spent $2.5 billion during the same period.

- **Deterrence of the United States and U.S. discussions of military action and regime change.** The example of the U.S. invasion of Iraq and U.S. dominance of the conventional military balance in the Gulf are key factors. President Bush has described Iran as part of the "axis of evil." In addition, many in the United States have attacked Iran for its support of Hezbollah, Hamas, and other enemies of Israel and have called for preemptive strikes on Iran's nuclear facilities. The U.S. invasion of Iraq, as apposed to North Korea, has also shown that having nuclear weapons can balance out conventional inferiority. Iran believes it must be able to retaliate against any U.S. or regional attack that threatens its regime or the defeat of its conventional forces.

- **Deterrence to Israel.** It is an open secret that Israel has nuclear weapons. Most estimates show the Israelis to have 100–200 warheads. In addition, Israel's conventional armed forces are superior to Iran's aging military equipment. Iran and neighboring states have argued that one cannot ask Iran to give up its ambition for nuclear weapons without demanding the same of Israel. The potential threat posed by a hostile Israel, with its own long-range strike systems and nuclear weapons, has also forced Iran to expand its WMDs and delivery capabilities.

- **Nuclear "sandwich."** Iran is "surrounded"—by Pakistan and India to the east, Israel to the northwest, Russia to the northeast, and the United States in the Gulf. Thus Iran is virtually encircled by nuclear-equipped armies, and it feels that it needs to balance that with its own weapons. As will be analyzed in depth in subsequent chapters, the problem of WMD proliferation goes beyond Iran and the Middle East.

- **The example set by other nations.** India, Pakistan, and North Korea possess a deterrent against conventional aggression due to their nuclear arsenal. The confrontation between Pakistan and

India, while it has heated in the past, has been limited to diplomatic and sometimes low-level conflict at worst. Iran may feel that nuclear weapons could immunize it against conventional attacks and reduce its chances of being preempted the same way Iraq was.

■ **Lessons from recent conflicts.** These conflicts include the Iran-Iraq War (1980–1988), the Gulf War (1990–1991), the Afghanistan War (2001–present), and the Iraq War (2003–present). Iraq's extensive use of chemical weapons against Iran and its use of conventionally armed ballistic missiles against Iranian cities during the Iran-Iraq War proved to Iran that it must build up its deterrence capabilities. The Gulf, Afghanistan, and Iraq Wars showed Iran the impact of U.S. conventional superiority. In addition, one of the lessons of the Gulf War was that the use of missiles by Iraq against targets in Saudi Arabia and Israel was effective but required either arming them with WMDs or increasing their accuracy to hit their targets.

■ **The threat of Sunni Islamic extremism.** Many neo-Salafi Sunni Islamic extremists attack Shi'ites and other sects of Islam as anything from apostate to polytheist. Iran may see a long-term threat these extremists will come to dominate neighboring states, and see Iran as a religious enemy. It may also feel a nuclear Iran will be too powerful for such movements to directly attack.

■ **The cause of Shi'ite Islamic extremism.** Iran's new political leadership seems to have revised some of the rhetoric about Iran's serving as an example for Islam and as a natural leader in the region. Although there is little evidence Iran is seeking to create what King Abdullah of Jordan has called a "Shi'ite crescent," Iran may well see itself as a defender of Ayatollah Khomeini's religious revolution and the Shi'ite sect and as a nation that could export its beliefs with more credibility and safety if it were a nuclear power.

There is no way to determine what combination of these motives will drive Iran's behavior, and it is dangerous to assume that Iran has (or has had) fixed plans for proliferation or the use of the forces it develops. Iran faces so much opposition to acquiring such weapons that it is forced to proliferate on a target-of-opportunity basis and constantly adapt its approaches to acquiring weapons and delivery systems. Even if it has force plans, it will almost certainly change them over time and, necessarily, its doctrine, war plans, and targeting.

At the same time, it is equally dangerous to assume that Iran's actual behavior in a war or crisis will be based on such motives and will lead Iran to behave as a "rational bargainer." Iran has not acted aggressively in the past in military terms, and the ruling elite have been cautious about taking risks. History provides warning after warning, however, that behavior can change radically, and take unpredictable risks, in the face of a major crisis. The history of the West in the twentieth century is filled with such examples and is ample proof that this takes place regardless of nation and culture.

NATIONAL STATEMENTS ABOUT TEHRAN'S WMD PROGRAMS

The Iranian leadership has never announced its motives and ambitions for building Iran's WMD program; rather, it has denied its existence. The clerical establishment has been equally consistent in its public statements about Iran's nuclear intentions. For example, Ayatollah Ali Khamenei was quoted on August 19, 2005, as saying that "our governments and myself have said numerous times that we are not seeking nuclear weapons. The uranium enriched in Iran is only enriched 3 to 4 percent, whereas for a nuclear bomb uranium must be enriched 94 to 95 percent."[3]

Even so, successive Iranian governments have issued public statements about Iran's right to nuclear technology. The government of President Mahmoud Ahmadinejad has made this right a central argument. President Ahmadinejad has stated that it is Iran's inalienable right to have access to nuclear technology for "peaceful purposes." In his speech to the sixteenth session of the United Nations General Assembly on September 17, 2005, President Ahmadinejad outlined his government's policy on the nuclear issue in depth and again claimed that Iran opposed nuclear proliferation:

> Allow me, as the elected President of the Iranian people, to outline the other main elements of my country's initiative regarding the nuclear issue:

1. The Islamic Republic of Iran reiterates its previously and repeatedly declared position that in accordance with our religious principles, pursuit of nuclear weapons is prohibited.

2. The Islamic Republic of Iran believes that it is necessary to revitalize the NPT and create the above-mentioned ad-hoc committee so that it can combat nuclear weapons and abolish the apartheid in peaceful nuclear technology.

3. Technically, the fuel cycle of the Islamic Republic of Iran is not different from that of other countries which have peaceful nuclear technology. Therefore, as a further confidence building measure and in order to provide the greatest degree of transparency, the Islamic Republic of Iran is prepared to engage in serious partnership with private and public sectors of other countries in the implementation of [a] uranium enrichment program in Iran. This represents the most far-reaching step, outside all requirements of the NPT, being proposed by Iran as a further confidence building measure.

4. In keeping with Iran's inalienable right to have access to a nuclear fuel cycle, continued interaction and technical and legal cooperation with the IAEA will be the centerpiece of our nuclear policy. Initiation and continuation of negotiations with other countries will be carried out in the context of Iran's interaction with the Agency. With this in mind, I have directed the relevant Iranian officials to compile the legal and technical details of Iran's nuclear approach, based on the following considerations:

4.1. International precedence tells us that nuclear fuel-delivery contracts are unreliable and no legally binding international document or instrument exists to guarantee the delivery of nuclear fuel. On many occasions such bilateral contracts have either been suspended or stopped altogether for political reasons. Therefore, the Islamic Republic of Iran, in its pursuit of peaceful nuclear technology, considers it within its legitimate rights to receive objective guarantees for uranium enrichment in the nuclear fuel cycle.

4.2. In its negotiations with the EU3, Iran has tried in earnest to prove the solid and rightful foundations of its nuclear activity in the context of the NPT, and to establish mutual trust. The selection of our negotiating partners and the continuation of negotiations with the EU3 will be commensurate with the requirements of our cooperation with the Agency regarding non-diversion of the process of uranium enrichment to non-peaceful purposes in the framework of the provisions of the NPT. In this context, several proposals have been presented which can be considered in the context of negotiations. The Islamic Republic of Iran appreciates the positive contribution of South Africa and H.E. President Mbeki personally in the resolution of the nuclear issue and cognizant of South Africa's active role in the IAEA Board of Governors would welcome its active participation in the negotiations.

4.3. The discriminatory approaches regarding the NPT that focus on the obligations of state-parties and disregard their rights under the Treaty should be discontinued.

As the President of the Islamic Republic of Iran, I assure you that my country will use everything in its power to contribute to global tranquility and peace based on the two maxims of spirituality and justice as well as the equal rights of all peoples and nations. My country will interact and cooperate constructively with the international community to face the challenges before us.[4]

Some other statements have been somewhat more ambiguous, although they too have rejected the option of nuclear weapons. On June 19, 2004, Hasan Rowhani, the secretary general of the Iranian Supreme National Security Council, was quoted as following:

The decision made by the Islamic Republic of Iran not to possess weapons of mass destruction, including nuclear weapons, goes back to many years and not only the near past. Therefore, even during the eight-year war Iraq imposed on us and although Iraq used chemical weapons against Iran, we did not seek the production of nuclear, chemical, or biological weapons . . . .

Our decision not to possess weapons of mass destruction is strategic because we believe that these weapons will not provide security for Iran. On the contrary, they will create big problems. Iran exerted huge efforts during the past few years to build bridges of confidence with the states of the region. We absolutely do not want to blow up these bridges by mobilizing our resources to produce weapons of mass destruction. We are confident that our possession of these weapons will force these countries to seek the support of big powers. Consequently, regional security will worsen. This will not serve our national security. Therefore, our efforts focused and continue to focus on building bridges of confidence with the states of the region before focusing on the possession of weapons of mass destruction.[5]

Similar statements have been made since the early days of the Islamic Republic. In October 1991, for example, Ayatollah Mohajerani, then Iran's deputy president, was quoted as saying that Iran should work with other Islamic states to create an "Islamic bomb." On the other hand, in February 1997, President Ali Akbar Hashemi Rafsanjani, when asked if Iran intended to acquire nuclear weapons, was quoted as saying, "Definitely not. I hate this weapon."[6]

Iran has also consistently emphasized two key issues. First, that it needs to diversify its energy resources. Second, that Iran's abandonment of nuclear weapons must be tried to a nuclear-free Middle East. For example, On October 5, 1997, Iran's foreign minister, Kamal Kharrazi, summarized Tehran's position on these two issues as follows:

We are certainly not developing an atomic bomb, because we do not believe in nuclear weapons . . . . We believe in and promote the idea of the Middle East as a region free of nuclear weapons and other weapons of mass destruction. But why are we interested to develop nuclear technology? We need to diversify our energy sources. In a matter of a few decades, our oil and gas reserves would be finished and therefore, we need access to other sources of energy . . . . Furthermore, nuclear technology has many other utilities in medicine and agriculture. The case of the United States in terms of oil reserve is not different from Iran's. The United States also has large oil resources, but at the same time they have nuclear power plants. So there is nothing wrong with having access to nuclear technology if it is for peaceful purposes.[7]

The Iranian media have been equally consistent in making such denials. In 1996 the Iranian government-run Voice of the Islamic Republic of

Iran described such charges as "baseless" and referred to various articles about the transfer of weapons-related technology as "a propaganda ploy by Western media affiliated to the Zionist regime." It stated that "Iran's efforts to reach nuclear energy are centered around the axis of the creation of electricity, which is required for the country's developing industry, and using this energy for medical and agricultural objectives," and that the IAEA found that Iran's nuclear programs "respect all the technical and legal aspects of non-proliferation." In contrast, it continued, "the Zionist regime has more than 200 nuclear warheads."[8]

THE BALANCE OF POWER IN THE REGION

Iran has roughly the same possible motives for making such denials, however, that it has for acquiring nuclear weapons. Iranian CBRN capabilities would raise major mid-term and long-term challenges to the southern Gulf states, Iraq, Israel, and the West in terms of deterrence, defense, retaliation, and arms control.

As long as outside nations fail to act decisively, Iran can continue to disguise most of the necessary research and development effort to develop improved enrichment and weapons design and manufacture technology regardless of the limits placed on it by IAEA inspection, agreements with Europe, or possible actions by the UN Security Council. This could include the ballistic testing of weapons and warheads with the same weight, size, and balance as real weapons, and the use of complex simulation and testing with nuclear weapon designs that substitute material with lower levels of enrichment for plutonium-239 (Pu-239) or highly enriched uranium (HEU) but otherwise are workable in every respect.

Iran's strategic posture in the region has long been a source of concern to the United States and many regional leaders, especially following revelations about Iran's involvement in Iraqi internal affairs by using its intelligence and Islamic Revolutionary Guards Corps assets to help Iraq's Shi'ites—particularly Islamist Shi'ite groups. Sunni countries in the Middle East are concerned about what King Abdullah II of Jordan in 2004 called the forming of a "Shi'ite crescent." He argued that an alliance was forming between Iran and Iraq and could extend to include Syria and Lebanon, and that Iran is working for a Shi'ite dominated "Islamic republic in Iraq."[9]

The director of the U.S. Defense Intelligence Agency (DIA), Vice Admiral Lowell E. Jacoby, summarized U.S. concerns on March 17, 2005, in testimony to the U.S. Senate Armed Services Committee:

> Iran is important to the United States because of its size, location, energy resources, military strength, and antipathy to U.S. interests. It will continue support for terrorism, aid insurgents in Iraq, and work to remove the United States from the Middle East. It will also continue its weapons of mass destruction and ballistic missile programs. Iran's drive to acquire nuclear weapons is a key test of international resolve and the nuclear nonproliferation treaty.
>
> Iran's long-term goal is to see the United States leave Iraq and the region. Another Iranian goal is a weakened, decentralized, and Shi'a-dominated Iraq that is incapable of posing a threat to Iran. These goals and policies most likely are endorsed by senior regime figures.
>
> Tehran has the only military in the region that can threaten its neighbors and Gulf stability. Its expanding ballistic missile inventory presents a potential threat to states in the region. As new longer-range MRBMs [medium-range ballistic missiles] are fielded Iran will have missiles with ranges to reach many of our European allies. Although Iran maintains a sizable conventional force, it has made limited progress in modernizing its conventional capabilities. Air and air defense forces rely on out-of-date U.S., Russian, and Chinese equipment. Ground forces suffer from personnel and equipment shortages. Ground forces equipment is also poorly maintained.
>
> We judge Iran can briefly close the Strait of Hormuz, relying on a layered strategy using predominately naval, air, and some ground forces. Last year it purchased North Korean torpedo and missile-armed fast attack craft and midget submarines, making marginal improvements to this capability.[10]

Saudi Arabia has openly expressed its concerns about Iran's role in a Shi'ite-dominated Iraq. The Saudi foreign minister, Prince Saud al-Faisal has said, "We fought a war [the Gulf War] together to keep Iran out of Iraq after Iraq was driven out of Kuwait. Now we are handing the whole country over to Iran without reason."[11]

The Saudi leadership has also been clear about the consequences of a nuclear Iran. Prince Saud al-Faisal has been quoted as saying that a nuclear Iran "threatens disaster in the region." The Kingdom, however, has stressed that the problem of proliferation goes beyond Iran's ambition. The Saudi minister of interior, Prince Nayef al-Saud, has argued that Iran's nuclear program "has peaceful aims." Moreover, Prince Nayef has said that the problem is not with Iran's ambition but with the double standard in the West's position toward Israeli nuclear capabilities. "This puts a question mark not only before the Arabs but also before the whole world . . . and this gives justification for every country to think of having nuclear weapons," he has said.[12]

Senior Saudi officials have said that Saudi Arabia has examined its options for responding to an Iranian nuclear threat, including an effort to acquire its own nuclear weapons, but that it has rejected such an option. Experts, however, argue that a nuclear Iran would lead the Kingdom to reexamine its strategic and military postures in the region to deal with a shift in the balance of power in the Gulf and protect its neighboring Gulf Cooperation Council (GCC) states.

The fear of a nuclear Iran has also reached beyond regional powers. Even non-state Sunni actors have expressed concerns about Iranian nuclear ambitions. The Egyptian Muslim Brotherhood, for example, has argued that a nuclear Iran might make the prediction of Jordan's King Abdullah in December 2004 a reality. Their spokesman, Essam El-Erian, was quoted as saying, "If Iran developed a nuclear power, then it is a big disaster because it already supports Hezbollah in Lebanon, Hamas in Palestine, Syria and Iraq, then what is left? . . . We would have the Shi'ite crescent that the Jordanian king warned against."[13]

Leaders in the region have also stressed the need for a more comprehensive counterproliferation strategy that must include Israel's nuclear arsenal and the overall problem of WMD proliferation. For example, the Saudi foreign minister, Prince Saud al-Faisal, has argued that "Iran is always mentioned but no one mentions Israel, which has [nuclear] weapons already. . . . We wish the international community would enforce the movement to make the Middle East a nuclear-free zone."[14]

The Arab League has taken a similar position regarding Iran's nuclear threat, arguing that it should be tied to a "Nuclear-Free Middle East." Iran's nuclear ambitions, the League argues, are tied to Israel's possession of nuclear capabilities. Mohamed ElBaradei, director general of the IAEA, has also argued that Israel's nuclear weapons "served as an incentive for countries to arm themselves with equal or similar weapons capacity."[15]

The official policy of the United States has been to support the idea of a nuclear-free Middle East, but U.S. reports have regularly omitted mention of Israel's nuclear arsenal. Some proliferation experts have argued that such an effort to discuss Iran's nuclear programs without discussing the overall nuclear balance in the Middle East is counterproductive. George Perkovich of the Carnegie Endowment for International Peace, for example, has said that the aim of the United States "should be to create a security environment, and you can't do that if you don't recognize publicly that Israel has nuclear weapons."[16]

The United Nations has followed a somewhat similar track. On February 4, 2006, the IAEA resolution referring Iran to the UN Security Council emphasized the need for the regional halt to the development of nuclear weapons. The resolution stated that "a solution to the Iranian issue would contribute to global nonproliferation efforts and to realizing the objective of a Middle East free of weapons of mass destruction, including their means of delivery."[17]

These positions may help explain why Iran's neighbors have not played a major role in the negotiations about its nuclear program thus far. Their position—that a nuclear Iran is dangerous, but that Tehran cannot be blamed for wanting nuclear weapons unless the world deals with Israel's nuclear arsenals—is unlikely to change in the near future. And they are likely to continue to hold an ambiguous strategic posture for the sake of keeping good relations with Iran.

As for their response to a nuclear-armed Iran in the Gulf, Iran's neighbors have three options: to acquire their own WMD and missile capabilities to deter Iran; to develop a missile defense shield; and/or to ask the United States or Pakistan to extend their nuclear deterrence to include them.

Saudi Arabia and Iran's smaller Gulf neighbors can respond with accelerated efforts to deploy theater missile defenses—although such

Table 2.1
Iran's CBRN Efforts in a Global Context: Nations with Weapons of Mass Destruction (WMDs)

Country	Type of Weapon of Mass Destruction		
	Chemical	Biological	Nuclear
East-West			
Britain	Production capability	Production capability	Deployed
France	Production capability	Production capability	Deployed
Germany	Research	Research	Research
Russia	Stockpiled	Production capability	Deployed
Sweden	None	None	Production capability
United States	Dismantling	Production capability	Deployed
Middle East			
Algeria	Development?	Research	Research
Egypt	Stockpiled	Development?	Research
Iran	Deployed	Development	Development
Iraq	Destroyed	Destroyed	Destroyed
Israel	Production capability	Production capability	Deployed
Libya	Dismantling	Dismantling	Dismantling
Syria	Deployed	Development?	Research
Yemen	None?	None	None
Asia and South Asia			
China	Destroyed?	Production capability?	Deployed
India	Deployed?	Deployed?	Deployed
Japan	Research	Research	Research
North Korea	Deployed	Deployed	Deployed?
Pakistan	Research?	Production capability?	Deployed
South Korea	Dismantling?	Research	Research
Taiwan	Stockpiled?	Production capability?	Production capability
Thailand	Production capability?	None	None
Vietnam	Production capability?	None	None
Other			
Argentina	None	None	Research
Brazil	Research	Research	Research
South Africa	Terminated	Terminated	Terminated

Sources: Adapted by the authors from the Monterrey Institute of International Studies, Nuclear Threat Initiative (NTI), and GlobalSecurity.org.

Note: Where published assessments are uncertain or conflicting reports raise questions about a state's capabilities, the term used is followed by "?"

(continued)

Table 2.1 *(continued)*

Definitions:

Deployed: Has nuclear, biological, or chemical (NBC) weapons integrated in military forces and ready for use in the event of conflict.

Stockpiled: Has produced significant quantity of NBC weapons, but these are not stored in proximity to military units that would employ them.

Production capability: Able to produce significant quantity of fissile nuclear material or CB agents, but not known to have done so.

Development: Engaged in laboratory- or pilot-scale activities to develop production capability for fissile material or CB agents.

Research: Engaged in dual-use research with peaceful civilian applications, but that can also be used to build technical capacity and/or infrastructure necessary for NBC development and production.

Dismantling: Is removing NBC weapons from deployment to storage areas and is destroying agents and munitions.

Terminated: Produced NBC weapons, but subsequently ended and dismantled program.

None: No confirmed open-source evidence of capability.

---

systems seem more likely to be "confidence builders" than leakproof. This course of action would almost certainly lead the United States to consider counterproliferation strikes on Iran and to work with its southern Gulf allies on developing an adequate deterrent. Given the United States's rejection of biological and chemical weapons, this raises the possibility of creating a major U.S. theater nuclear deterrent, although such a deterrent could be sea- and air-based and deployed outside the Gulf. If the United States failed to provide such a deterrent and/or missile defenses, it seems likely that the southern Gulf states would be forced to accommodate Iran or else seek their own weapons of mass destruction.

Iran's WMD program, however, must be understood as a global phenomenon that requires a global response. Proliferation is not confined to Iran, the Gulf, or the Middle East. It is a problem that reaches all continents, and existing nonproliferation treaties, sanctions, and incentives have not prevented the spread of WMD, as table 2.1 shows. Chemical, biological, radiological, and nuclear technology is easily accessible, even through open source materials, and many dual-use technologies can be ordered over the Internet. Existing mechanisms, including the Chemical Weapons Convention (CWC), Biological Weapons Convention (BWC), and the Nuclear Nonproliferation Treaty, are outdated; they do not have meaningful enforcement or incentive mechanisms and are just starting to think of ways to stop proliferation of WMDs to non-state actors, particularly transnational terrorist organizations.

Notes

[1] BP, *Statistical Review of World Energy 2005* (London: BP PLC, June 2005), pp. 4, 20.

[2] "Iran Determined to Continue Civilian Nuclear Program," *BBC Monitoring International Reports,* June 24, 2005, available through LexisNexis.

[3] Stefan Smith, "Iran Regime 'Solid' in Pursuing Nuclear Drive: Khamenei," Agence France-Presse, August 19, 2005.

[4] Speech by Mahmoud Ahmadinejad to the United Nations General Assembly, September 17, 2005, available at http://www.un.org/webcast/ga/60/statements/iran050917eng.pdf.

[5] Quoted in an interview on Al Jazeera television station. Partial transcript is available from the *CBW Conventions Bulletin,* no. 65 (September 2004), available at http://www.casa.susx.ac.uk/Units/spru/hsp/CBWCB65.pdf.

[6] Rafsanjani was answering a question from Mike Wallace of CBS News's *60 Minutes* on March 23, 1997; the transcript is available at http://www.iranian.com/Feb97/Opinion/CBS.html.

[7] Interview, "Iranian Minister: U.S. Can't 'Divide and Rule,'" *Washington Post,* October 5, 1997, sec. C-04.

[8] "Iran Rejects Steel Smuggling Allegation," United Press International, August 14, 1996.

[9] Robin Wright and Peter Baker, "Iraq, Jordan See Threat to Election from Iran," *Washington Post,* December 8, 2004, available at http://www.washingtonpost.com/wp-dyn/articles/A43980-2004Dec7.html.

[10] Lowell E. Jacoby, "Current and Projected National Security Threats to the United States" (statement for the record by the director of the Defense Intelligence Agency [DIA] to the U.S. Senate Armed Services Committee, March 17, 2005).

[11] Robert Gibbons, "Saudi Says U.S. Policy Handing Iraq over to Iran," Reuters, September 21, 2005, available at http://in.today.reuters.com/news/newsArticle.aspx?type=worldNews&storyID=2005-09-21T030042Z_01_NOOTR_RTRJONC_0_India-216835-1.xml.

[12] P. K. Abdul Ghafour, "Naif Raps West on N-Policy," *Arab News* (Jeddah, Saudi Arabia), February 2, 2006, available at http://www.arabnews.com/?page=1&section=0&article=77201&d=2&m=2&y=2006.

[13] Michael Slackman, "Iran the Great Unifier? The Arab World Is Wary," *New York Times,* February 5, 2006.

[14] Walter Pincus, "Push for Nuclear-Free Middle East Resurfaces," *Washington Post,* March 6, 2005, sec. A-24.

[15] Ibid.

[16] Ibid.

[17] International Atomic Energy Agency (IAEA), *Implementation of the NPT Safeguards Agreement in the Islamic Republic of Iran: Resolution Adopted on 4 February 2006,* February 4, 2006, available at http://www.iaea.org/Publications/Documents/Board/2006/gov2006-14.pdf.

CHAPTER THREE

IRAN'S CHEMICAL WEAPONS

Nuclear weapons are only one of the weapons of mass destruction that Iran may be developing or have in inventory. Iran's efforts to acquire chemical weapons (CW) and biological weapons (BW) raise many additional questions, and Iran's statements regarding the use of chemical and biological weapons are no more reassuring than its statements regarding the use of nuclear weapons.

IRAN'S CHEMICAL WARFARE CLAIMS

Iran is formally committed to avoiding the development, possession, and use of both chemical and biological weapons. Tehran signed the Chemical Weapons Convention in 1972 and ratified it in 1973. It signed the Biological Weapons Convention in 1993 and ratified it in 1997.[1] In the past, Iranian leaders have been quoted arguing that using biological or chemical weapons is immoral and against their religious convictions, legal agreements, and international treaties.

In 2005, Iran's ambassador to the United Nations in Geneva, Mohammad Reza Alborzi, stated in a speech to the Chemical Weapons Convention Conference that Iranian policy is "not to resort to these weapons."[2] Outside experts argue, however, that those convictions and legal framework did not prevent Iran from moving ahead with its nuclear program. Iran also learned from the Iran-Iraq War that religion and morality sometimes provide little deterrence against the use of chemical weapons and that such weapons can inflict serious damage on the battlefield.

Iran has pursued chemical weapons since it first came under chemical attack by Iraq early in the Iran-Iraq War. According to the World Health Organization (WHO), as many as 25,000 Iranians were killed by the Iraqi chemical attacks during the war and more than 100,000 received treatment against chemical agents.[3] It remains unclear, however, whether Iran retaliated with its own chemical weapons.

Iran seems to have used chemical weapons on several occasions, but the evidence is uncertain. While there is no disagreement that Iraq used chemical agents during the eight years of the Iran-Iraq War, Iran has denied it used such weapons against Iraq. Most experts, however, believe that Iran did use chemical agents against Iraqi forces in the 1980s. These almost certainly included chemical artillery rounds captured from Iraq and may well have included some Iranian-made weapons.[4]

In addition, while the work of the IAEA has revealed a lot about Iran's nuclear program since 2002, there has been far less public and international discussion of Iran's chemical and biological program. The Organization for the Prohibition of Chemical Weapons (OPCW) has conducted only very limited inspections of "declared Iranian chemical facilities." There has been no inspection of possible biological weapon facilities.[5]

HISTORY OF IRAN'S CW PROGRAM

Iran has bought defensive as well as offensive capabilities. Iran purchased large amounts of chemical defense gear from the mid-1980s onward. It also obtained stocks of non-lethal CS gas (a form of tear gas), although it quickly found that such agents had limited military impact as they could only be used effectively in closed areas or very small open areas.

Acquiring poisonous chemical agents was more difficult. Iran had no internal capacity to manufacture poisonous chemical agents when Iraq first launched its attacks with such weapons. And although Iran seems to have made limited use of chemical mortar and artillery rounds as early as 1985—and possibly as early as 1984—these rounds were almost certainly captured from Iraq.

Iran had to import much of the necessary equipment and supplies covertly, and it took several years to get substantial amounts of production equipment and the necessary feedstock. Iran sought aid from European firms like Lurgi to produce large "pesticide" plants, and it began to try to obtain the needed feedstock from a wide range of sources, relying heavily on its embassy in Bonn to manage the necessary deals. Although Lurgi did not provide the pesticide plant it sought, Iran did obtain substantial support from other European firms and feedstock from many other Western sources.

By 1986–1987, Iran had developed the capability to produce enough lethal agents to load its own weapons. The director of the U.S. Central Intelligence Agency (CIA) and informed observers in the Gulf made it clear that Iran could produce blood agents like hydrogen cyanide, phosgene gas, and/or chlorine gas. Iran was also able to weaponize limited quantities of blister (sulfur mustard) and blood (cyanide) agents beginning in 1987, and had some capability to weaponize phosgene gas and/or chlorine gas.

These chemical agents were produced in small batches and evidently under laboratory-scale conditions, which enabled Iran to load small numbers of weapons before any of its new major production plants went into full operation. These gas agents were loaded into bombs and artillery shells, and were used sporadically against Iraq in 1987 and 1988.

Reports regarding Iran's production and research facilities since that time are highly uncertain:

- Iran seems to have completed a major poison gas plant at Qazvin, about 150 kilometers west of Tehran. This plant is reported to have been completed between November 1987 and January 1988. Although supposedly a pesticide plant, the facility's true purpose seems to have been poison gas production using organ phosphorous compounds.

- It is impossible to trace all the sources of the major components and technology Iran used in its chemical weapons program during this period. Mujahedin-e Khalq (MEK) sources claim that Iran set up a chemical bomb and warhead plant operated by the Zakaria Al-Razi chemical company near Mahshar in southern Iran, but it is unclear whether these reports are true.

- Reports that Iran had chemical weapons plants at Damghan and Parchin that began operation as early as March 1988 and may have begun to test-fire Scuds with chemical warheads as early as 1988–1989 are equally uncertain.

- Iran established at least one large research and development center under the control of the Engineering Research Center of the Construction Crusade (Jahad e-Sazandegi), and had established a significant chemical weapons production capability by mid-1989.

- Debates took place in the Iranian parliament, or Majlis, in late 1988 about the safety of Pasdaran gas plants located near Iranian towns, and Ali Akbar Hashemi Rafsanjani, then speaker of the parliament, described chemical weapons as follows: "Chemical and biological weapons are poor man's atomic bombs and can easily be produced. We should at least consider them for our defense. Although the use of such weapons is inhuman, the war taught us that international laws are only scraps of paper."[6]

Post Iran-Iraq War estimates of Iran chemical weapons production are largely speculative, but various U.S. and European experts have made the following estimates:

- U.S. experts believe Iran was beginning to produce significant amounts of mustard gas and nerve gas by the time of the August 1988 cease-fire in the Iran-Iraq War, although its use of chemical weapons remained limited and had little effect on the fighting.

- Iran's efforts to equip plants to produce V-agent nerve gases seem to have been delayed by U.S., British, and German efforts to limit technology transfers to Iran, but it may have acquired the capability to produce persistent nerve gas during the mid-1990s.

- Production of nerve gas weapons started no later than 1994.

- Iran began to stockpile cyanide (cyanogen chloride), phosgene, and mustard gas weapons after 1985. Recent CIA testimony indicates that production capacity may approach 1,000 tons annually.

- On August 2, 2002, the National Security Council's director for the Near East indicated that Iran is producing and stockpiling blister, blood, and choking agents.

- The Defense Department's 2001 report *Proliferation: Threat and Response* suggests that, in addition to producing and stockpiling blister, blood, and choking agents, Iran has weaponized these agents for use with artillery shells, mortars, rockets, and bombs. The report also states that Iran is continuing its research on nerve agents.

- Iran's weapons seem to include bombs and artillery. Shells include 155 mm artillery and mortar rounds. Iran also has chemical bombs and mines. It may have developmental chemical warheads for its Scud missiles. It may also have a chemical package for its 22006 RPV (remotely piloted vehicle), but this is doubtful.

- There are reports that Iran has deployed chemical weapons on some of its ships. Training for Iranian naval forces suggests that these forces are preparing for the possibility of operating in a contaminated environment.

- Iran has increased chemical defensive and offensive warfare training since 1993.

Iran has sought to buy more advanced chemical defense equipment, and it has sought to buy specialized equipment on the world market to develop an indigenous capability to produce advanced feedstock for nerve weapons. The following illustrate some of the open-source materials regarding these efforts:

- CIA sources indicated in late 1996 that China might have supplied Iran with up to 400 tons of chemicals for the production of nerve gas.

- A 1996 report indicated that Iran obtained 400 metric tons of chemicals for use in nerve gas weapons from China—including carbon sulfide.

- Another report indicated that China supplied Iran with roughly 2 tons of calcium hypochlorite in 1996 and delivered another 40,000 barrels in January or February of 1997. Calcium hypochlorite is used for decontamination in chemical warfare.

- Iran placed several significant orders with China that were not delivered. Razak Industries in Tehran and Chemical and Pharmaceutical Industries in Tabriz ordered 49 metric tons of alkyl dimethylamine, a chemical used in making detergents, and 17 tons of sodium sulfide, a chemical used in making mustard gas. The orders were never delivered, but they were brokered by Iran's International Movalled Industries Corporation (Imaco) and China's North Chemical Industries Co. (Nocinco). Both brokers have been linked since early 1995 to other transactions affecting Iran's chemical weapons program, and Nocinco has supplied Iran with several hundred tons of carbon disulfide, a chemical used in nerve gas.

- Another Chinese firm, identified publicly only as Q. Chen, seems to have supplied glass vessels for chemical weapons.

- The United States imposed sanctions on seven Chinese firms in May 1997 for selling precursors for nerve gas and equipment for making nerve gas—although the United States made it clear that it had "no evidence that the Chinese government was involved." The Chinese firms were members of the Nanjing Chemical Industries Group and Jiangsu Yongli Chemical Engineering and Import/Export Corporation. Cheong Yee Ltd., a Hong Kong firm, was also involved. The precursors included thionyl chloride, dimethylamine, and ethylene chlorohydril. The equipment included special glass-lined vessels, and the Nanjing Chemical Industries Group completed construction of a production plant in Iran to manufacture such vessels in June 1997.

- Iran sought to obtain impregnated alumina (aluminum oxide), which is used to make phosphorus oxychloride—a major component of the nerve agents VX and GB (sarin)—from the United States.

- Iran has obtained some equipment from rogue Israelis. Nahum Manbar, an Israeli national living in France, was convicted in an Israeli court in May 1997 for providing Iran with $16 million of production equipment for mustard and nerve gas from 1990 to 1995.

- The CIA reported in June 1997 that Iran had obtained new chemical weapons equipment technology from China and India in 1996.

- India is assisting in the construction of a major new plant at Qazvin, near Tehran, to manufacture phosphorous pentasulfide, a major precursor for nerve gas. The plant is fronted by Meli

Agrochemicals, and the program was negotiated by Dr. Mejid Te-
hrani Abbaspour, a chief security adviser to Rafsanjani.

- A number of reports indicate that China has provided Iran with
  the ability to manufacture chemical weapons indigenously and
  has provided precursors since at least 1996.[7]

- A recent report by German intelligence indicates that Iran has
  made major efforts to acquire the equipment necessary to produce sarin (GB) and tabun (GA), using the cover of purchasing
  equipment for pesticide plants that Iraq used for its Sa'ad 16 missile development plant in the 1980s. German sources note that
  three Indian companies—Tata Consulting Engineering, Trans-
  pek, and Rallis India—have approached German pharmaceutical and engineering concerns for such equipment and technology
  under conditions where German intelligence was able to trace the
  end user to Iran.

- The United States cited two Indian companies, Sabero Organics
  and Sandya Organics, as supplying Iran with additional feedstocks for chemical weapons in January 2006.[8]

ASSESSING IRAN'S CW CAPABILITIES

The various claims and counter assertions about Iran's current capabilities are as hard to substantiate as they are to rebut. Open sources
are limited and conflicting, and Iranian claims go unchecked. Outside
governments have provided some useful summary assessments of Iranian chemical weapons programs, but few details.

Official Estimates of Iranian Capability

The CIA has reported that Chinese entities were still trying to supply
Iran with CW-related chemicals between 1997 and 1998. The U.S.
sanctions imposed in May 1997 on seven Chinese entities for knowing-
ly and materially contributing to Iran's chemical weapons program
remain in effect. In addition, the CIA estimated in January 1999 that
Iran obtained material related to chemical warfare from various
sources during the first half of 1998. It already has manufactured and
stockpiled chemical weapons, including blister, blood, and choking

agents and the bombs and artillery shells for delivering them. However, Tehran is seeking foreign equipment and expertise to create a more advanced and self-sufficient chemical warfare infrastructure.

The last unclassified U.S. formal assessment of this aspect of Iranian proliferation was released in 2001, and it provided only a broad summary:[9]

> Iran has acceded to the Chemical Weapons Convention (CWC) and in a May 1998 session of the CWC Conference of the States Parties, Tehran, for the first time, acknowledged the existence of a past chemical weapons program. Iran admitted developing a chemical warfare program during the latter stages of the Iran-Iraq war as a "deterrent" against Iraq's use of chemical agents against Iran. Moreover, Tehran claimed that after the 1988 cease-fire, it "terminated" its program. However, Iran has yet to acknowledge that it, too, used chemical weapons during the Iran-Iraq War.

> Nevertheless, Iran has continued its efforts to seek production technology, expertise, and precursor chemicals from entities in Russia and China that could be used to create a more advanced and self-sufficient chemical warfare infrastructure. As Iran's program moves closer to self-sufficiency, the potential will increase for Iran to export dual-use chemicals and related equipment and technologies to other countries of proliferation concern.

> In the past, Tehran has manufactured and stockpiled blister, blood and choking chemical agents, and weaponized some of these agents into artillery shells, mortars, rockets, and aerial bombs. It also is believed to be conducting research on nerve agents. Iran could employ these agents during a future conflict in the region. Lastly, Iran's training, especially for its naval and ground forces, indicates that it is planning to operate in a contaminated environment.

In mid-May 2003, the Bush administration released a statement to the Organization for Prohibition of Chemical Weapons in which the United States accused Iran of continuing to pursue production technology, training, and expertise from abroad. The statement asserted that Iran was continuing to stockpile blister, blood, choking, and some nerve agents. This was followed by an unclassified report released by the CIA in November 2003 stating that "Iran is a party to the

Chemical Weapons Convention (CWC). Nevertheless, during the reporting period it continued to seek production technology, training, and expertise from Chinese entities that could further Tehran's efforts to achieve an indigenous capability to produce nerve agents. Iran likely has already stockpiled blister, blood, choking, and probably nerve agents—and the bombs and artillery shells to deliver them—which it previously had manufactured."[10]

John R. Bolton, then the undersecretary of arms control and international security at the U.S. State Department, did report on Iran's chemical program in testimony to the House International Relations Committee's Subcommittee on the Middle East and Central Asia in 2005, but only in summary terms:[11]

> We believe Iran has a covert program to develop and stockpile chemical weapons. The U.S. Intelligence Community reported in its recent unclassified *Report to Congress on the Acquisition of Technology Relating to Weapons of Mass Destruction and Advanced Conventional Munitions*, also known as the "721 Report," that Iran continues to seek production technology, training, and expertise that could further its efforts to achieve an indigenous capability to produce nerve agents. A forthcoming edition of the 721 report is expected to state that "Iran may have already stockpiled blister, blood, choking, and nerve agents—and the bombs and artillery shells to deliver them—which it previously had manufactured."
>
> Iran is a party to the Chemical Weapons Convention (CWC). The CWC's central obligation is simple: no stockpiling, no development, no production, and no use of chemical weapons. The overwhelming majority of States Parties abide by this obligation. Iran is not, and we have made this abundantly clear to the Organization for the Prohibition of Chemical Weapons (OPCW). Although Iran has declared a portion of its CW program to the OPCW, it is time for Iran to declare the remainder and make arrangements for its dismantlement and for the destruction of its chemical weapons.

European assessments seem to agree with those of the U.S. Department of Defense and the CIA, but there have been only limited public reports. The German Federal Customs Administration published a report in November 2004 stating that "Iran has an emerging chemical industry. Its CW program obtains support, according to accounts received, from China and India. It probably possesses chemical agents such as sulphur mustards, Tabun, and hydrogen cyanide, possibly also sarin and VX. Iran is attempting to acquire chemical installations and parts thereof, as well as technology and chemical precursors."[12]

Arms Control Estimates of Iranian Capability

Arms control efforts have not provided meaningful transparency, and ratifying the CWC has not guaranteed the end of Tehran's CW programs; it has meant only that if Iran is violating the treaty, it is an "illegal" activity.

Unfortunately, there have been no meaningful inspections or independent analysis of Iran's chemical weapons program. Iran did submit a statement in Farsi to the CWC secretariat in 1998, but it consisted only of questions about the nature of the required compliance. Iran has not provided the CWC with detailed data on its chemical weapons program, and it has also stridently asserted its right to withdraw from the convention at any time.

NGO Estimates of Iranian Capability

Some NGO reporting provides more detail. A study by the Monterey Institute indicates that a number of sites in Iran may be related to Iran's chemical warfare effort:[13]

- **Abu Musa Island:** Suspected location where Iran holds a large number of chemical weapons, principally 155 mm artillery shells, in addition to some weaponized biological agents.

- **Bandar Khomeini:** Allegedly the location of a chemical weapons facility, run by the Razi Chemical Corporation, established during the Iran-Iraq War to manufacture chemical weapons.

- **Damghan:** Either a chemical weapons plant or warhead assembly facility. Primarily involved in 155 mm artillery shells and Scud warheads.

- **Esfahan:** Suspected location of a chemical weapons facility, possibly operated by the Poly-Acryl Corporation.

- **Karaj:** Located about 14 kilometers from Tehran, site of an alleged storage and manufacturing facility for chemical weapons. Reports suggest that the facility was built with Chinese assistance.

- **Marvdasht:** Suspected to have been a manufacturing facility for mustard agents during the Iran-Iraq War, operated by the Chemical Fertilizers Company.

- **Parchin:** Site of at least one munitions factory and suspected of being a major chemical weapons production facility. Reports of uncertain reliability indicate that the plant was in operation no later than March 1988. In April 1997, a German newspaper reported that, according to the German Federal Intelligence Service, the factories at Parchin were producing primary products for chemical warfare agents.

- **Qazvin:** Site of a large pesticide plant widely believed to produce nerve gas.

- **Mashar:** Site of a warhead filling facility, according to allegations, of uncertain reliability, by Iranian opposition groups.

In January 2006, the Nuclear Threat Initiative summarized what is and is not known about the status of Iran's chemical weapons as follows:

Despite its acquisition of precursors from abroad, Iran is allegedly working to develop an indigenous CW production capability. The CIA believes that "Teheran is rapidly approaching self-sufficiency and could become a supplier of CW-related materials to other nations." As of 1996, the Department of Defense claimed that Iran had stockpiled almost 2000 tons of toxic chemical agents and was continuously working on expanding its CW program. Iran has several advanced research institutions employing various chemicals for a variety of reasons, including pesticide production, pharmaceutical research, and other medical studies. Iran has also conducted several military exercises to date that have included defensive chemical and biological weapons maneuvers.

Iran continues to deny any allegations that it is actively pursuing an offensive CW program. In 1996, it held the first regional seminar on the national implementation of the CWC in Tehran so that government authorities could familiarize themselves with their duties and obligations under the treaty. It also held a mock "trial inspection" at the Shahid Razkani chemical factory to allow inspectors to see how such a procedure was conducted. Iran submitted a declaration on its chemical facilities and its past CW stockpile, it has destroyed chemical weapons production equipment in the presence of OPCW inspectors, and it has undergone a number of OPCW inspections of its chemical industrial facilities. Iran continues to play an active role at the Organization for the Prohibition of Chemical Weapons (OPCW), is recognized as a member in good standing, and currently serves on its executive council. Although U.S. and Israeli intelligence agencies continue to insist Iran maintains a stockpile of chemical weapons, no challenge inspections of Iranian facilities have been requested, and none of the allegations made regarding the stockpiling of CW can be verified in the unclassified domain. However, Iran continues to retain a strong incentive for developing a defensive CW program.[14]

Iran's Possible War-fighting Capability

These factors make it almost impossible to know how Iran may use any chemical warfare capabilities it does possess. Iran does not overtly train its forces for offensive chemical warfare, and its current and future war-fighting capabilities are unknown.

Iran has stated its objection to the use of CBW in war on religious grounds—based on Ayatollah Khomeini's statements in the 1980s—and its legal obligation under international conventions. As noted earlier, most experts, however, believe that Iran at least used confiscated Iraqi chemical shells against Iraqi forces during the Iran-Iraq War. It had definitely instituted its own program to produce chemical weapons and may have used its weapons. The International Institute of Strategic Studies (IISS) pointed out in its 2005 study of Iran's weapons that "despite a similar record with respect to nuclear weapons and the NPT, Iran conducted undeclared nuclear activities in violation of the treaty for over 20 years. Whether Iran has carried [out] similar activities in violation of its CWC and BWC obligations cannot be determined definitively from the available public information."[15]

It seems likely that Iran retains at least some capability to make chemical weapons and that it may have inactive or mothballed facilities. There have been no public reports of active production, but such activity is possible. Iraq produced small lots of mustard gas weapons at the laboratory level before its major production facilities came online, and showed that it could produce at the batch level with relatively small and easy-to-conceal facilities. Iran's purchases also indicate that it could have a significant stock of precursors; and some less lethal weapons can be made out of refinery and petrochemical byproducts.

Any assessment of Iranian capabilities must also take into account that Iraq began to use chemical weapons against Iran in the early 1980s, and that Iran has had at least a quarter of a century in which to react to a real-world threat, six years of which were spent dealing with a nation seeking to acquire chemical, biological, and nuclear weapons to destroy it. Iranian military literature contains extensive reprints of Western and other literature on chemical, biological, radiological, and nuclear weapons, and Iran actively collects such literature on a global basis.

It seems clear that Iran has the technology base to produce mustard gas and nonpersistent nerve agents—including reasonably stable agents and binary weapons—and may have the technology to produce persistent nerve agents as well. It probably has had technical knowledge of "third-generation" and "dusty" agents. It has had the opportunity to reverse-engineer captured Iraqi weapons and may have received aid in weapons design from Russian, Chinese, and North Korean sources. It certainly has monitored UN reporting on the Iraqi chemical and biological programs, and may have acquired considerable detail on those programs, their strengths and weaknesses, and Iraq's sources abroad.

Iran almost certainly has the ability to make effective chemical artillery shells and bombs, as well as unitary rocket and missile warheads. It can probably design effective cluster bombs and warheads. It may have sprayers for use by aircraft, helicopters, and unmanned aerial vehicles (UAVs). Iran's ability to develop lethal missile warheads is far more problematic, however; the timing and dissemination problems are far more difficult and may be beyond Iran's current technical skills.

The history of Iranian experience with complex program management and systems integration has shown that Iran has serious problems in translating its technical expertise into practice. The knowledge of how to do things rarely leads to a similar capability to actually do them, particularly when programs remain concealed and are largely "mothballed" or have low levels of activity.

Testing chemical weapons presents serious problems when the test goes beyond static tests or relative crude measurements of how well given weapons disseminate the agent. It is particularly difficult in the case of missile warheads. Although it is possible to determine lethality in rough terms from residues, to do so requires repeated testing using actual weapons in a variety of real-world conditions. There are no reports of such testing, but, unlike most biological weapons, the operational lethality of chemical weapons can be safely tested against live animals. Again, there are no reports of such testing, but it is more than possible that they could be successfully concealed.

The history of actual chemical warfare, however, indicates that the results of such tests can be extremely unrealistic and that operational lethality has rarely approached anything like engineering and test predictions. The "scale-up" of individual weapons results into predictions of real-world results using large numbers of weapons has produced particularly misleading results. Moreover, as is the case with biological weapons, temperature, sunlight, wind, surface conditions, and a number of other external factors can have a major effect on lethality. These factors, coupled with the difficulty of measuring incapacity or deaths, also means that Iran and other users would have to carry out any chemical campaign with little ability to predict its actual lethality or conduct effective battle damage assessment. Such considerations might not be important, however, when the goal is terror, panic, area denial, or forcing an enemy to don protection gear, decontaminate, or accept casualties in addition to those from military operations.

At the same time, all of these factors combine to indicate that even if Iran does have plans and doctrine for using chemical weapons, and even if it has made serious efforts to estimate their lethality and effectiveness, such plans are unlikely to survive engagement with reality. Iran's past reports on its military exercises may be propaganda-driven,

Table 3.1
Scenarios for Iranian Covert or Proxy Use of Chemical, Biological, Radiological, and Nuclear Terrorism

- A radiological powder is introduced into the air conditioning systems of Cairo's high-rise tourist hotels. Symptoms are detected only over days or weeks, or public warning is given several weeks later. The authorities detect the presence of such a powder, but cannot estimate its long-term lethality and have no precedents for decontamination. Tourism collapses, and the hotels eventually have to be torn down and rebuilt.

- Parts for a crude gun-type nuclear device are smuggled into Israel or bought in the marketplace. The device is built in a medium-sized commercial truck. A physics student reading the U.S. Department of Defense weapons-effect manual maps Tel Aviv to maximize fallout effects in an area filled with buildings with heavy metals and waits for a wind maximizing the fallout impact. The bomb explodes with a yield of only 8 kilotons but with an extremely high level of radiation. Immediate casualties are limited but the long-term death rate mounts steadily with time. Peace becomes impossible, and security measures become Draconian. Immigration halts and emigration reaches crisis proportions. Israel as such ceases to exist.

- Several workers move drums labeled as cleaning agents into a large shopping mall, large public facility, subway, train station, or airport. They dress as cleaners and are wearing what appear to be commercial dust filters (or they have taken the antidote for the agent they will use). They mix the feedstocks for a persistent chemical agent at the site during a peak traffic period. Large-scale casualties result, and Draconian security measures become necessary on a national level. A series of small attacks using similar "binary" agents virtually paralyze the economy, and detection is impossible except to identify all canisters of liquid.

- Immunized terrorists visit a U.S. carrier or major U.S. Marine assault ship during the first hours of visitor's day during a port call in the Middle East. They are carrying anthrax powder in bags designed to make them appear slightly overweight. They slowly scatter the powder as they walk through the ship. The immediate result is 50 percent casualties among the ship's crew, its Marine complement, and the visitors who follow. The United States finds it has no experience with decontaminating a large ship where anthrax has entered the air system and is scattered throughout closed areas. After long debates about decontamination methods and safety levels, the ship is abandoned.

- A terrorist seeking to "cleanse" a nation of its secular regime and corruption—and trusting God to "sort out" the resulting casualties—introduces a modified culture of Ebola or a similar virus for which there is no effective treatment into an urban area. He scatters infectious cultures, and by the time it is detected, the attack has reached epidemic proportions. Medical authorities rush into the infected area without proper protection, causing the collapse of medical facilities and emergency response capabilities. Other nations and regions have no alternative but to isolate the nation or urban center under attack, letting the disease take its course.

- A terrorist group modifies the valves on a Japanese-manufactured remote-controlled crop-spraying helicopter that has been imported legally for agricultural purposes. It uses the aircraft at night or near dawn to spray a chemical or

(continued)

Table 3.1 *(continued)*

biological agent at altitudes below radar coverage in a line-source configuration. Alternatively, it uses a large home-built RPV with simple GPS (global positioning system) guidance. The device eventually crashes undetected into the sea or in the desert. Delivery of a chemical agent achieves far higher casualties than any conventional military warhead. A biological agent is equally effective, and the first symptoms appear days after the actual attack—by which time treatment is difficult or impossible.

■ A truck filled with what appears to be light gravel is driven through the streets of Tel Aviv or Cairo during rush hour or another peak traffic period. A visible powder does come out through the tarpaulin covering the truck, but the spread of the power is so light that no attention is paid to it. The driver and his assistant are immunized against the modified form of anthrax that is being released from behind the gravel or sand in the truck. The truck slowly passes through key areas of the city. Unsuspecting passersby and commuters not only are infected, but also carry dry spores home and into other areas. By the time the first major symptoms of the attack appear some 3–5 days later, anthrax pneumonia is epidemic and some septicemic anthrax has appeared. Some 40–65 percent of the exposed population dies and medical facilities collapse, causing serious, lingering secondary effects.

■ A terrorist group scatters high concentrations of a radiological or biological agent in various areas in a city, as well as trace elements into the processing intakes for the local water supply. When the symptoms appear, the terrorist group makes its attack known, but claims that it has contaminated the local water supply. The authorities are forced to confirm that water is contaminated, and mass panic ensues.

■ Immunized terrorists carry small amounts of anthrax or a similar biological agent onto a passenger aircraft like a B-747, quietly scatter the powder, and deplane at the regular scheduled stop. No airport detection system or search detects the agent. Symptoms do not appear until days later, and some 70–80 percent of those on the aircraft die.

■ Several identical nuclear devices are smuggled out of the former Soviet Union (FSU) through Afghanistan or Central Asia. They do not pass directly through governments. One of the devices is disassembled to determine the precise technology and coding system used in the weapon's PAL (permissive action link). This allows users to activate the remaining weapons. The weapon is then disassembled to minimize detection, with the fissile core shipped covered in lead. The weapon is successfully smuggled into the periphery of an urban area outside any formal security perimeter. A 100-kiloton ground burst destroys a critical area and blankets the region in fallout.

■ The same type of device is shipped to Israel or a Gulf area in a modified standard shipping container that is equipped with either detection and triggering devices that will set off the device as a result of local security checks or a GPS system that will set it off automatically when it reaches the proper coordinates in the port of destination. The direct explosive effect is significant, but "rain out" contaminates a massive local area.

■ Iran equips a freighter or dhow to spread anthrax along a coastal area in the Gulf. It uses a proxy terrorist group to launch an attack on Kuwait City and Saudi oil facilities and ports. Several days pass before the attack is detected, and the attacking group is never fully identified. The form of anthrax used is dry and

(continued)

Table 3.1 *(continued)*
Scenarios for Iranian Covert or Proxy Use of Chemical, Biological, Radiological, and Nuclear Terrorism

time-encapsulated to lead to massive prompt casualties and force time-consuming decontamination. Iran not only is revenged, but also benefits from the resulting massive surge in oil prices.

- A terrorist group scatters small amounts of a biological or radiological agent in a Jewish area during critical stages of the final settlement talks between Israel and the Palestinian Authority. Near panic ensues, and a massive anti-Palestinian reaction follows. Israeli security then learns that the terrorist group has scattered small amounts of the same agent in cells in every sensitive Palestinian town and area, and the terrorist group announces that it has also stored some in politically sensitive mosques and shrines. Israeli security is forced to shut down all Palestinian movement and carry out intrusive searches in every politically sensitive area. Palestinian riots and then exchanges of gunfire follow. The peace talks break down permanently.

- The Islamic Revolutionary Guards equip dhows to spread anthrax. The dhows enter the ports of Dubai and Abu Dhabi as commercial vessels—possibly with local or other southern Gulf registrations and flags. The attack is not detected for several days, and the resulting casualties include much of the population of Abu Dhabi as well as the UAE government. The UAE breaks up as a result, no effective retaliation is possible, and Iran achieves near hegemony over Gulf oil policy.

- A terrorist group attempting to drive Western influence out of Saudi Arabia smuggles a large nuclear device into Al Hufuf on the edge of the Ghawar oil field. It develops a crude fallout model using local weather data that it confirms by sending out scouts with cellular phones. It waits for the ideal wind, detonates the device, shuts down the world's largest exporting oil field, and causes the near collapse of Saudi Arabia.

- Alternatively, the same group takes advantage of the security measures the United States has adopted in Saudi Arabia and the comparative isolation of U.S. military personnel. Positioning itself in an area outside the security perimeter, it waits for the proper wind pattern and allows the wind to carry a biological agent over a Saudi airfield with a large U.S. presence. The United States takes massive casualties and has no ability to predict when the next attack might occur. It largely withdraws from Saudi Arabia.

- A seemingly ordinary freighter carrying fertilizer enters a Middle Eastern port and docks. In fact, the freighter has mixed the fertilizer with a catalyst to create a massive explosion, and it also carries a large amount of a chemical, radiological, and/or biological agent. The resulting explosion destroys the immediate target area and also scatters the chemical or biological weapon over the area.

- Extreme believers in Eretz Israel move a "cocktail" of radiological and persistent biological/chemical agents to the Temple Mount to contaminate the mosques. They use carefully designed devices that scatter very heavy matter over only a limited area, but they use explosives to ensure a high degree of contamination within the mosques. All prayer in the mosque area must be halted indefinitely, and there are significant casualties among the Islamic faithful in Jerusalem. The

(continued)

Table 3.1 *(continued)*

extremist Jewish group issues a statement demanding that the temple area be cleared of all non-Jewish religious activity, triggering mass violence.

■ A large terrorist device goes off in a populated critical economic or military assembly area—scattering mustard or nerve gas. Emergency teams rush in to deal with the chemical threat and the residents are evacuated. Only later does it become clear that the device also included a biological agent that not only killed most of the emergency response personnel, but also was quickly carried to a much wider area by the evacuees.

---

but some of Iran's conventional war-fighting exercises have a strong element of ideology and wishful thinking. This lack of demanding realism could lead military officers and civilian decisionmakers to make serious miscalculations based on the war they want to fight rather than the war they can fight.

Such considerations would have less impact if Iran chose to use proxies or covert means of attack to strike at high-value targets or for the purposes of terrorism and intimidation. The Islamic Revolutionary Guards Corps has conducted the kind of conventional exercises that could be adapted to such ends, and Iran has long supplied conventional weapons to movements like Hezbollah and Hamas.

The covert or proxy use of weapons of mass destruction cannot be ignored in assessing Iranian or any other form of proliferation. Table 3.1 presents a wide range of scenarios for delivering CBRN weapons that do not involve the use of military delivery systems or conventional weapons. Almost all of these scenarios can be adapted to some extent to make use of any given type of CBRN weapon, including the more lethal forms of chemical weapons.

But, as table 3.2 makes clear, chemical weapons are not capable of anything near the lethality of nuclear weapons or the most effective biological weapons. Like radiological weapons, their initial "terror" effect is likely to diminish quickly and do far more to provoke rather than intimidate or defeat. Iran's covert or overt use of chemical weapons would be a virtual license for its opponent to escalate to using weapons of mass destruction or to strike against high-value or civilian Iranian targets. It is also unclear that Iran could actually use such weapons either covertly or through proxies without coming under attack, regardless of whether evidence existed that it was directly responsible.

Table 3.2
Comparative Effects of Biological, Chemical, and Nuclear Weapons Delivered against a Typical Urban Target

With missile warheads

Assumes one Scud-sized warhead with a maximum payload of 1,000 kg; assumes that the biological agent would not make maximum use of this payload capability because this delivery system is inefficient. It is unclear this scenario is realistic.

	Area covered, km^2	Deaths, assuming 3,000–10,000 people per km^2
Chemical		
300 kg of sarin nerve gas with a density of 70 mg per m^3	0.22	60–200
Biological		
30 kg of anthrax spores with a density of 0.1 mg per m^3	10	30,000–100,000
Nuclear		
One 12.5 kt nuclear device achieving 5 lb. per in^3 of overpressure	7.8	23,000–80,000
One 1 Mt hydrogen bomb	190	570,000–1,900,000

(continued)

Only a bolt from the blue or a surprise covert or proxy attack would give it "plausible deniability," and Iran would then have to live with the risk of discovery over time.

Any broader military use of chemical weapons by Iran would present a number of problems:

- Chemical weapons individually are not lethal enough to have a major impact on ground battles. They take time to be effective and are best suited to relatively static battles, dominated by ground forces that do not have armored and protected vehicles and that cannot mass airpower effectively. This describes Iran and Iraq in 1980–1988. It does not describe the United States or most of Iran's opponents today. Airpower and seapower are largely immune to the kind of chemical attack Iran could launch,

Table 3.2 *(continued)*

With one aircraft delivering 1,000 kg of sarin nerve gas or 100 kg of anthrax spores

Assumes aircraft flies in straight line over the target at optimal altitude and dispenses the agent as an aerosol; assumes that the biological agent would not make maximum use of this payload capability because this delievery system is inefficient.

	Area covered, km^2	Deaths, assuming 3,000–10,000 people per km^2
Bright, sunny day		
Sarin nerve gas	0.74	300–700
Anthrax spores	46	130,000–460,000
Overcast day or night, moderate wind		
Sarin nerve gas	0.8	400–800
Anthrax spores	140	420,000–1,400,000
Clear, calm night		
Sarin nerve gas	7.8	3,000–8,000
Anthrax spores	300	1,000,000–3,000,000

Source: Adapted from Office of Technology Assessment, *Proliferation of Weapons of Mass Destruction: Assessing the Risks,* OTA-ISC-559 (Washington, D.C.: GPO, August 1993), pp. 53–54, available at www.anthrax.osd.mil/documents/library/proliferation.pdf.

Note: km^2 = square kilometers; kg = kilogram; mg = milligram; m^3 = cubic meter; kt = kiloton; Mt = megaton

with the possible exception of fixed, targetable area targets—many of which could only be denied for any significant time by large numbers of accurate attacks. Rapidly maneuvering ground forces would be a difficult target for Iran's much more static forces. Nations like the United States would have extensive amounts of detection, protection, and decontamination gear. They also would not have large, static rear area and support operations near the forward edge of the battle area (FEBA).

■ Iranian artillery tends to be slow moving and lacks the ability to rapidly target and switch fires. It relies heavily on static massed fires. This requires relatively short-range engagement against an equally slow moving or static opponent. In practice, Iran will probably face opponents that maneuver more quickly and have superior intelligence, surveillance, and reconnaissance (IS&R) assets. A repetition of the battlefield conditions of the Iran-Iraq War seems unlikely.

- Chemical weapons could be more effective as area weapons that forced enemy forces to abandon their positions, denied them the ability to use rear areas, or acted as a barrier to movement. In the Iran-Iraq War the tactical and maneuver effects of using chemical weapons were more important than their use as a killing mechanism. Again, however, chemical weapons tend to be most useful against relatively static opponents that do not have air superiority or supremacy.

- Iran has a number of potential long-range artillery rockets and missiles. A single chemical warhead, however, is more a terror weapon than a killing mechanism. Such systems have limited accuracy, and Iran has limited long-range targeting capability against mobile targets. The use of a few chemical rounds would be highly provocative and would justify massive escalation by an enemy. As such, it might do more to provoke than to terrify, intimidate, or damage. Iran might be able to use persistent nerve and mustard agents, however, to deny the use of a key facility like an air base, main supply facility, mobilization center, oil export facility, or desalination or power plants.

- Effective air strikes require a high level of confidence in the ability to penetrate enemy air defenses and also require good IS&R assets. In many cases, a chemical weapon would have only marginally greater lethality than a conventional precision-guided weapon or cluster weapon. Again, such use might do more to provoke than to terrify, intimidate, or damage.

- The use of chemical weapons against targets at sea presents significant targeting and meteorological problems that are certainly solvable, but do require exceptional planning and skill. Similarly, firing against coastal targets requires high volumes of CW fire or good meteorological data.

- Covert or proxy use presents serious problems in wartime. Plausible deniability is doubtful, and an opponent simply may not care whether it can prove Iran is responsible for any given use of CW.

- Operation lethality is dependent on an opponent's CW defense and decontamination facilities, level of depth, and speed of maneuver. Iran may be dealing with much more sophisticated opponents that the Iraq of the 1980s.

None of these problems and issues mean that Iran could not use chemical weapons effectively under some conditions. They might, however, deter Iran from stockpiling such weapons or using them except under the most drastic conditions. Iran has to understand that their use would tend to make Iran lose the political and information battle and give its opponent a license to escalate. While such concerns might well deter Iran under most circumstances, it is also important to understand that wars and drastic crises are not "most circumstances." One inherent problem in any such analysis is that even the most prudent decisionmaker in peacetime can panic, overreact, or drastically miscalculate in war.

Notes

[1] Arms Control Association, "Fact Sheet: Chemical and Biological Weapons Proliferation at a Glance," September 2002, available at http://www.armscontrol.org/factsheets/cbwprolif.asp.

[2] Quoted in International Institute for Strategic Studies (IISS), *Iran's Strategic Weapons Programmes: A Net Assessment,* IISS Strategic Dossier (London: IISS, 2005), p. 69.

[3] Ibid.

[4] Ibid.

[5] Ibid.

[6] FBIS Document, FBIS-NES, October 19, 1998.

[7] Shirly Kan, "China's Proliferation of Weapons of Mass Destruction" Congressional Research Service, March 1, 2002, CRS IB 9256.

[8] James Murphy, "Governments Support Firms Accused of Iran Arms Sales," *Jane's Defence Weekly,* January 11, 2006.

[9] Office of the Secretary of Defense, *Proliferation: Threat and Response,* U.S. Department of Defense, 2001, p. 36, available at: http://www.defenselink.mil/pubs/ptr20010110.pdf.

[10] CIA, *Unclassified Report to Congress on the Acquisition of Technology Relating to Weapons of Mass Destruction and Advanced Conventional Munitions,* November 2003, available at http://www.cia.gov/cia/reports/721_reports/pdfs/721report_july_dec2003.pdf.

[11] John R. Bolton, "Iran's Continuing Pursuit of Weapons of Mass Destruction" (testimony before the U.S. House International Relations Subcommittee on the Middle East and Central Asia, June 24, 2004), available at http://www.state.gov/t/us/rm/33909.htm.

[12] IISS, *Iran's Strategic Weapons Programmes*, p. 67.

[13] Merav Zafary, "Iranian Biological and Chemical Weapons Profile Study," Center for Nonproliferation Studies, Monterey Institute of International Studies, February 2001.

[14] Nuclear Threat Initiative, "Iran: Chemical Overview," revised January 2006, available at http://www.nti.org/e_research/profiles/Iran/Chemical/#fnB15.

[15] IISS, *Iran's Strategic Weapons Programmes*, pp. 82–83.

CHAPTER FOUR

IRAN'S BIOLOGICAL WEAPONS

Any analysis of Iran's biological weapons effort must be even more speculative than analysis of its chemical weapons standing. In 1997, the U.S. Department of Defense asserted that the Iranian biological weapons program "is in the research and development stage, [but] the Iranians have considerable expertise with pharmaceuticals, as well as the commercial and military infrastructure needed to produce basic biological warfare agents."[1]

The Defense Department updated its findings in 2001 as follows:

- Iran has a growing biotechnology industry, significant pharmaceutical experience, and the overall infrastructure to support its biological warfare program. Tehran has expanded its efforts to seek considerable dual-use biotechnical materials and expertise from entities in Russia and elsewhere, ostensibly for civilian reasons. Outside assistance is important for Iran, and it is also difficult to prevent because of the dual-use nature of the materials and equipment being sought by Iran and the many legitimate end uses for these items.

- Iran's biological warfare program began during the Iran-Iraq war. Iran is believed to be pursuing offensive biological warfare capabilities and its effort may have evolved beyond agent research and development to the capability to produce small quantities of agent. Iran has ratified the BWC.[2]

Since that time, the United States has not significantly updated its unclassified estimates except to state that such research and development efforts continue. The problem is knowing whether such statements are a suspicion, a strong probability, or a fact. Iran does have extensive laboratory and research capability, as well as steadily improving industrial facilities with dual-use production capabilities. Whether it has an active weapons development program, however, is a controversial matter.

The reality is that many nations now have the biotechnology, industrial base, and technical expertise to acquire biological weapons. Not only does most civil technology have "dual use" in building weapons, but the global dissemination of biological equipment has made control by supplier nations extremely difficult. Even when such controls do still apply to original sellers, they have little or no impact on the sellers of used equipment, and a wide range of sensitive equipment is now available for sale to any buyer on the Internet.

This makes it almost impossible to disprove a nation's interest in biological weapons. Moreover, there is little meaningful distinction between a "defensive" and an "offensive" capability. Nations can claim to be conducting defensive research, acquiring key gear for defensive purposes, and practicing "defensive" training and maneuvers.

So far, Iran has not demonstrated any such "defensive" activities. But there is an active debate over whether it has a biological weapons program.

POSSIBLE EARLY INDICATORS THAT IRAN MIGHT HAVE A BW PROGRAM

There is a long history of indicators that Iran *might* have some form of BW program. Reports first surfaced in 1982—during the Iran-Iraq War—that Iran had imported suitable types of biological cultures from Europe and was working on the production of mycotoxins—a relatively simple family of biological agents that require only limited laboratory facilities for small-scale production. Many experts believe that the Iranian biological weapons effort was placed under the control of the Islamic Revolutionary Guards Corps, which is known to have tried to purchase suitable production equipment for such weapons.

U.S. intelligence sources reported in August 1989 that Iran was trying to buy two new strains of fungus from Canada and the Netherlands that could be used to produce mycotoxins. German sources indicated that Iran had successfully purchased such cultures several years earlier.

Some Iranian universities and research centers may be linked to biological weapons programs. The Imam Reza Medical Center at Mashhad University of Medical Sciences and the Iranian Research Organization for Science and Technology in Tehran were identified as the end users for this purchasing effort, but it is likely that the true end user was an Iranian government agency specializing in biological warfare.

Since the Iran-Iraq War, various reports have surfaced that Iran may have conducted research on more lethal active agents like anthrax, hoof-and-mouth disease, and biotoxins. Iranian groups have repeatedly approached various European firms for equipment and technology that could be used to work with these diseases and toxins.

Unclassified sources of uncertain reliability have identified a facility at Damghan as working on both biological and chemical weapons research and production, and these sources believe that Iran may be producing biological weapons at a pesticide facility near Tehran.

Reports also surfaced in the spring of 1993 that Iran had succeeded in obtaining advanced biological weapons technology in Switzerland and containment equipment and technology from Germany. According to these reports, this led to serious damage to computer facilities in a Swiss biological research facility by unidentified agents. Similar reports indicated that unidentified agents had destroyed German bio-containment equipment destined for Iran. More credible reports by U.S. experts indicate that Iran might have begun to stockpile anthrax and botulinum in a facility near Tabriz, and that it can now mass manufacture such agents and has them in an aerosol form. None of these reports, however, can be verified.

THE UNCERTAIN NATURE OF IRAN'S BW PROGRAM SINCE THE MID-1990s

In 1996, the CIA reported, "We believe that Iran holds some stocks of biological agents and weapons. Tehran probably has investigated both toxins and live organisms as biological warfare agents. Iran has the technical infrastructure to support a significant biological weapons program with little foreign assistance." It also reported that Iran has "sought dual-use biotech equipment from Europe and Asia, ostensibly for civilian use" and that Iran might be ready to deploy biological weapons. Beyond this point, little unclassified information exists regarding the details of Iran's effort to "weaponize" and produce biological weapons.

Continuing Alarms and Excursions

Iran announced in June 1997 that it would not produce or employ chemical weapons including biological toxins. However, the CIA reported in June 1997 that Iran had obtained new dual-use technology from China and India during 1996.

The CIA reported further in January 1999 that Iran continued to pursue dual-use biotechnical equipment from Russia and other countries, ostensibly for civilian uses, and that Iran may have some limited capability for biological deployment. In 2001, an allegation by the former director of research and development at the Cuban Center for Genetic Engineering and Biotechnology surfaced claiming that Cuba had assisted the Iranian bioweapons program from 1995 to1998. The authenticity of the director's claims has not been established.[3]

A report produced in 2003 by the Iranian insurgent group Mujahedin-e Khalq, or MEK, asserted that Iran had started producing weaponized anthrax and was actively working with at least five other pathogens, including small pox. The MEK was the same organization that produced early evidence of Iran's noncompliance with the terms of the Nuclear Nonproliferation Treaty. Iran issued a vehement denial of these charges in a May 16, 2003, press release. The accuracy of either set of statements remains uncertain.

The Possible Role of Outside Suppliers

Russia has been a key source of biotechnology for Iran. Russia's world-leading expertise in biological weapons also makes it an attractive target for Iranians seeking technical information and training on BW agent production processes. This has led to speculation that Iran may have the production technology to make dry storable and aerosol weapons. This would allow it to develop suitable missile warheads, bombs, and covert devices.

In testimony in 2000 to the Senate Committee on Foreign Relations, John A. Lauder, the director of the Nonproliferation Center at the CIA, made the following assertions:

- Iran is seeking expertise and technology from Russia that could advance Tehran's biological warfare effort. Russia has several government-to-government agreements with Iran in a variety of scientific and technical fields.

- Because of the dual-use nature of much of this technology, Tehran can exploit these agreements to procure equipment and expertise that could be diverted to its BW effort.

- Iran's BW program could make rapid and significant advances if it has unfettered access to BW expertise resident in Russia.[4]

The CIA reported in November 2003 that "even though Iran is part of the Biological Weapons Convention (BWC), Tehran probably maintained an offensive BW program. Iran continued to seek dual-use biotechnical materials, equipment, and expertise. While such materials had legitimate uses, Iran's biological warfare (BW) program also could have benefited from them. It is likely that Iran has capabilities to produce small quantities of BW agents, but has only a limited ability to weaponize them."[5] John R. Bolton, then the undersecretary of arms control and international security at the U.S. State Department, included that portion of the report in his testimony to the House International Relations Committee in 2004. He continued:

- Because BW programs are easily concealed, I cannot say that the United States can prove beyond a shadow of a doubt that Iran has an offensive BW program. The intelligence I have seen suggests that this is the case, and, as a policy matter therefore, I believe we have to act on that assumption. The risks to international peace and security from such programs are too great to wait for irrefutable proof of illicit activity: responsible members of the international community should act to head off such threats and demand transparency and accountability from suspected violators while these threats are still emerging. It would be folly indeed to wait for the threat fully to mature before trying to stop it.

- Iran is a party to the Biological Weapons Convention (BWC) and the 1925 Protocol for the Prohibition of the Use in War of Asphyxiating, Poisonous, or Other Gases, and of Bacteriological Methods of Warfare. Like the CWC, the central obligation of the

BWC is simple: no possession, no development, no production and, together with the 1925 Protocol, no use of biological weapons. The overwhelming majority of States Parties abide by these obligations. We believe Iran is not abiding by its BWC obligations, however, and we have made this abundantly clear to the parties of this treaty. It is time for Iran to declare its biological weapons program and make arrangements for its dismantlement.[6]

ASSESSING IRAN'S BW CAPABILITIES

Iran's potential delivery systems for biological weapons include short-range cruise missiles, short-range air-launched tactical missiles, fighter aircraft, helicopters, drones, artillery shells, and rockets. Iran has the necessary technology and industrial base, the Iran-Iraq War gave it incentives to explore such weapons, and it has had more than a quarter century in which to act.

That said, there are simply too few facts and indicators to be able to assess the level of development in either Tehran's BW or CW programs. Simply possessing a suitable technology and industrial base is not reason enough to make even an informed guess. Any reasonable assessment of Iran's programs would require knowing its real-world capabilities to produce bioweapons and chemical agents. It would be equally important to know Iran's real-world capabilities and limitations for weaponizing chemical and biological agents.

The data that outside governments release on Iran's CW and BW programs are too general and vague to have great credibility. Moreover, they often seem to be overshadowed by a focus on Iran's nuclear research efforts and its missiles programs, which outside governments see as a more serious threat. One difficulty in assessing Iran's biological weapons programs stems from the fact that most of the claims against Tehran have been made by exile groups that have a vested interest in seeing the regime in Iran overthrown. The lesson of Iraq must not be forgotten: exile groups have ulterior motives and often deliberately lie or misstate rather than provide accurate information.

The uncertainties about whether Iran has a biological warfare program are further compounded by the uncertainties about what bio-

Table 4.1
Potential Biological Agents for State and Non-state Use

Lethal	Lethal/incapacitating	Incapacitating
Anthrax	Brucellosis	VEE, EEE, WEE
Bolivian hemorrhagic fever	Blastomycosis	Dengue fever
Ebola infection	Congo-Crimean hemorrhagic fever	West Nile encephalitis
Glanders	Diphtheria	Epidemic typhus
Lassa infection	Psittacosis	Legionellosis
Marburg infection	Japanese encephalitis	Murine typhus
Meliodosis	Monkeypox infection	Q fever
Plague	Omsk hemorrhagic fever	Rift Valley fever
Smallpox	Russian S/S encephalitis	Influenza A
Yellow fever	Tularemia	Scrub typhus/ Tsutsugamushi

Source: Adapted from Ken Alibek, "Biological Weapons/Bioterrorism Threat and Defense—Past, Present, and Future" (paper prepared for the ETH [Swiss Federal Institute of Technology] international conference on "Meeting the Challenges of Bioterrorism: Assessing the Threat and Designing Biodefense Strategies," Furigen, Switzerland, April 22–23, 2005).

Note: VEE = Venezuelan equine encephalitis; EEE = Eastern equine encephalitis; WEE = Western equine encephalitis

logical agent it might weaponize and how effective such a weapon can be. As table 4.1 shows, Iran could choose from a wide range of proven weapons, although anthrax is often suspected to be the weapon of choice. The list of possible biological agents also excludes the possibility that Iran could develop new, genetically engineered weapons—something that is likely, but not certain.

Biological weapons also can easily vary in lethality by several orders of magnitude, depending on how the weapon is made, delivered, and distributed. Laboratory testing is extremely uncertain, and large-scale human testing is almost impossible to carry out without detection. Moreover, there seems to be enough empirical evidence to suggest that human testing even under controlled conditions might have limited value under operational war-fighting conditions.

Possible War-fighting Capability

These factors make it almost impossible to know whether Iran has conducted meaningful biological weapons research or moved toward production and weaponization. They make it equally difficult to know how
Iran might use any BW capabilities it does possess. Although Iran has
collected a wide range of literature on BW and reprinted foreign articles
in some of its military journals, it does not overtly discuss any doctrine
of its own or train its forces for offensive biological warfare, and its current and future war-fighting capabilities are unknown.

As has been touched on earlier, Iran has stated its objection to the
use of both chemical and biological weapons in war on religious
grounds—based on Khomeini's statements in the 1980s—and its legal
obligation under international conventions. Most experts, however,
believe that Iran used at least some chemical weapons against Iraqi
forces. In addition, many Western societies and governments have
opposed CW and BW on moral and ethnical grounds and still gone
on to make them and use them.

What does seem likely is that *if* Iran has biological weapons, or has
the capability to create them rapidly, it would use a readily weaponiz-
able disease like anthrax. As table 4.2 makes clear, it does not take a
highly sophisticated biological weapon to have considerable potential lethality, even though the lethality data reflect the worst-case lethality of the agents shown. Table 4.3 shows that biological weapons,
like chemical weapons, also have very different levels of persistence
and value in area denial. It seems likely that Iran would avoid infectious agents out of fear it could lose control of the path of disease and
be subject to massive retaliation.

As is the case with chemical weapons, Iran has learned enough
about Iraq's BW programs to replicate them, and it may have acquired further knowledge from Russia, China, and/or North Korea.
It can probably design effective cluster warheads and line source
disseminators (flying aircraft in a straight line while disseminating
the agent) for use by aircraft, helicopters, and UAVs. Iran's ability to
develop highly lethal missile warheads is far more problematic. The
timing and dissemination problems are far more difficult and may be
beyond Iran's current technical skills.

Table 4.2
Area Coverage and Estimated Casualty Impact of Various Types of Biological Attacks
(maximum possible lethality)

Agent	Downwind area (reach in km)	Number of casualties	
		Dead	Incapacitated
Rift Valley fever	1	400	35,000
Tick borne-encephalitis	1	9,500	35,000
Typhus	5	19,000	85,000
Brucellosis	10	500	125,000
Q fever	20+	150	125,000
Tularemia	20+	30,000	125,000
Anthrax	20+	95,000	125,000

Source: George W. Christopher et al., "Biological Warfare, A Historical Perspective," *JAMA* 278, no. 5 (August 6, 1997).

Note: Assumes 50 kg of agent along a 2 km line upwind of a population center of 500,000.

Once again, however, Iran's past efforts at complex program management and systems integration have indicated that the country has serious problems with translating its technical expertise into practice. The knowledge of how to do things rarely leads to a similar capability to actually do them, particularly when programs remain concealed and are largely "mothballed" or have low levels of activity.

The effective weaponization of biological weapons is far more difficult than it is for chemical or nuclear weapons. Operational testing of the dispersal of biological agents is difficult and requires very extensive testing of each type of weapons system under a wide range of conditions. Animal testing would generally not be effective—although the development of anti-agriculture and anti-livestock weapons is a significant option. Selective human testing has uncertain value, and data based on epidemiology can be irrelevant to weaponized agents. The actual lethality of a given biological weapon can probably be determined only by actual use in an attack.

The delays in biological effects present obvious problems (and sometimes advantages), as there will be no way to determine how effective

Table 4.3
Lethality and Stability of Soviet Biological Weapons in the Late 1990s

Weapons type	Q_{50} in open air deployment (l or kg per km^2)	Stability
Liquid plague	3.5–4.5	1–2 hours in air
Dry tularemia	3.0–4.0	Several hours to one day in air
Old dry anthrax	15–20	Days and weeks in the air
New dry anthrax	4.5–5.0	Years on surfaces
Liquid anthrax	5.0–5.5	—
Dry brucellosis	3.5–4.5	Up to 2 days in air
Liquid glanders/ meliodosis	4.5–5.5	Several hours in air
Liquid smallpox	3.5–4.0	Up to 24 hours in air
Dry Marburg	−1.0 dry	30 minutes liquid in air, and several hours dry
Q fever	—	Several days in air
Glanders	—	Several hours in air
Liquid Ebola	—	30 minutes liquid in air, and several hours dry
Coccidioidomycosis	—	Days and weeks in air

Source: Adapted from Ken Alibek, "Biological Weapons/Bioterrorism Threat and Defense—Past, Present, and Future" (paper prepared for the ETH [Swiss Federal Institute of Technology] international conference on "Meeting the Challenges of Bioterrorism: Assessing the Threat and Designing Biodefense Strategies, Furigen, Switzerland, April 22–23, 2005).

Note: Q_{50} = amount of agent needed to infect 50 percent of the exposed population or troops evenly distributed over km^2. These calculations are based on a lethal dose (LD$_{50}$ of 10,000–20,000 spores for anthrax; 200–400 (up to 1,000?) bacterial cells for brucellosis; 100–200 [up to 1,000?] bacterial cells for glanders; 500–1,500 bacterial cells for plague; 10–100 bacterial cells for tularemia; 1–3 cells for Q fever; 1–10 virions for Ebola; 1–10 virions for Marburg; 5–10 virions (up to 50?) for smallpox; and 10–100 arthrospores for coccidioidomycosis).

l = liter; kg = kilogram; km^2 = square kilometer

a given weapon will be for days or weeks. A maneuvering enemy may not even know it is under attack for days, and the full effect in terms of killed and incapacitated might not be known for weeks. Much would depend on the detection and characterization capability and response capability of an enemy or target. Dealing with weapons whose effects they could only guess at, Iranian decisionmakers would be confronted with deciding what message—if any—to communicate to an enemy, as well as with the possibility that an enemy could panic or exaggerate the impact of an attack to the point where the level of escalation would have no limits.

It also seems unlikely that Iran has more than the most loosely conceived plans and doctrine for using such weapons, much less any meaningful way to estimate their lethality and effectiveness. A biological weapon whose real-world effect can vary from zero to that of a small nuclear weapon presents major challenges for any commander or leader, and the problem would be compounded by the time it would take before both Iran and its target began to have empirical battle damage data.[7] Any Iranian plan could not survive engagement with the reality of war fighting. Again, however, some of Iran's conventional war-fighting exercises have a strong element of ideology and wishful thinking, and a lack of demanding realism. As with chemical weapons, Iran's decisionmakers may focus on the war they want to fight rather than the war they can fight.

One way to get around these uncertainties would be for Iran to use proxies or covert means of attack to strike at very high-value targets or for the purposes of terrorism and intimidation. Once again, Iran's Islamic Revolutionary Guards Corps has conducted the kind of conventional exercises that could be adapted to such ends, and Iran has long supplied movements like Hezbollah and Hamas.

Iran's military use of biological weapons would present fewer problems in a large-scale or high-risk conflict than chemical weapons, although such use would scarcely be without problems:

- Biological weapons are not suited to tactical use in ground battles. At most, they are suited only for remote rear area and staging targets. At the same time, this physical limitation in some ways eases the problems in developing a suitable knowledge of enemy and own-force positions and reliable real-time meteorological data. Like nuclear weapons, the sheer scale of lethality makes biological weapons effective against both civil and military area targets.

- Biological weapons are best used against relatively static enemies or area targets. Iran will probably face opponents that maneuver more quickly and with superior intelligence, surveillance, and reconnaissance assets. A repetition of the battlefield conditions of the Iran-Iraq War seems unlikely.

- Biological weapons could be effective as area weapons that forced enemy forces to abandon positions, denied them the ability to use rear areas, or acted as a barrier to movement. BW tend to be most useful, however, against relatively static opponents that do not have air superiority or supremacy.

- Iran has a number of potential long-range artillery rockets and missiles. If Iran can develop effective biological warheads, a single warhead could be a highly effective killing mechanism or method of contaminating an area target. This would help compensate for the fact that many of Iran's systems have limited accuracy and that Iran has limited long-range targeting capability against mobile targets. Iran might be able to use persistent biological agents to deny the use of a key facility like an air base, main supply facility, mobilization center, oil export facility, or desalination or power plants.

- Effective air strikes require good IS&R assets and a high level of confidence in the ability to penetrate enemy air defenses. Unlike chemical weapons, however, even a single biological weapon could have enough lethality to destroy or cripple a large area target, and their use might do more to provoke than to terrify, intimidate, or damage.

- Like chemical weapons, the use of biological weapons against targets at sea would present significant targeting and meteorological problems. These probably are solvable, but do require exceptional planning and skill. Similarly, firing against coastal targets requires good "over-target" meteorological data.

- Covert or proxy use of BW presents serious problems in wartime. Plausible deniability is doubtful, and an opponent simply may not care if it can prove Iran is responsible for any given use of BW.

- Operational lethality is dependent on an opponent's BW defense and decontamination facilities, level of depth, and speed of maneuver. Iran may be dealing with much more sophisticated opponents that the Iraq of the 1980s.

As is the case with chemical weapons, none of these issues mean that Iran could not use biological weapons effectively. This would be particularly true if it has advanced to the point where it has dry, storable weapons with the kind of coated micropowders that are most lethal. Such weapons are comparable to small nuclear weapons and can have massive effects, no matter how well they are used in terms of tactical and strategic judgments.

Once again, the use of a CBRN weapon could cost Iran the political and information warfare battle and act as a license to its opponent to escalate. These factors *might* deter Iran under most circumstances, but wars and drastic crises are not "most circumstances." As stated earlier, one inherent problem in any such analysis is that even the most prudent decisionmaker in peacetime can panic, overreact, or drastically miscalculate in war.

Detecting Biological Weapons

Biological weapons offer Iran advantages that chemical weapons do not. They can serve as an alternative and backup to nuclear proliferation. As the scenarios in table 3.1 made clear, even relatively small amounts of highly lethal anthrax can be as lethal as a small nuclear weapon. In addition, the basic techniques for producing such weapons are well known, and even some of the most sophisticated equipment is now commercially available or sold without controls as used equipment. This includes some small adaptable reactors and milling/coating equipment.

There is no reason why biological weapons facilities cannot be disguised from most forms of technical collection or collocated with civil facilities that mask their technical nature. Many aspects of offensive and defensive research are so close in character to civilian biological and medical research that weapons efforts are difficult to distinguish and prove. This is particularly difficult if the effort is designed to produce only limited amounts for warhead or covert use, rather than large amounts for battlefield use or attacks on entire cities.

The chances of detection of a well-structured effort are near zero unless some human source or defector with inside knowledge makes the details available. Even then, there are no inspection arrangements under the Biological Weapons Convention, and biological weapons efforts are easy to rapidly disperse and dismantle. Modern proliferators are likely to use modular elements and computers without leaving the bulky paper trail of previous proliferators like Iraq.

A "quiet" proliferator might well pursue a successful biological weapons development and production effort without ever leaving enough evidence for outside nations and experts to do more than speculate. A "prudent" proliferator might well pursue biological weapons both as a backup to having to dismantle or delay a nuclear weapons program, and as a means of riding out sanctions or military strikes.

As the UN inspection effort showed in Iraq, it is almost impossible for even the best such effort to establish the level of BW activity in a country with some experience in concealment; the task is essentially as impossible as disproving a negative. A highly dispersed, modular biological weapons effort would be virtually impossible to fully target, and effective battle damage assessment would be impossible. Stockpiling biological weapons in a variety of facilities for defensive purposes would present even more problems. Both Russia and Iraq have also shown that nations are willing to take major risks in regard to biological weapons security and accidents if this means better concealment and deniability.

Notes

[1] Office of the Secretary of Defense, *Proliferation: Threat and Response*, U.S. Department of Defense, 1997, available at http://www.defenselink.mil/pubs/prolif97/.

[2] Office of Secretary of Defense, *Proliferation: Threat and Response*, U.S. Department of Defense, 2001, p. 36, available at http://www.defenselink.mil/pubs/ptr20010110.pdf.

[3] "Iran," *Jane's Sentinel Security Assessment: The Gulf States,* October 7, 2004, available at http://sentinel.janes.com/.

[4] John A. Lauder, "Russian Proliferation to Iran's Weapons of Mass Destruction and Missile Programs" (statement to the U.S. Senate Committee on Foreign Relations, October 5, 2000, available at http://www.cia.gov/cia/public_affairs/speeches/2000/lauder_WMD_100500.html).

[5] Director of Central Intelligence, *Unclassified Report to Congress on the Acquisition of Technology Relating to Weapons of Mass Destruction and Advanced Conventional Munitions: 1 July through 31 December 2003,* CIA, available at http://www.cia.gov/cia/reports/721_reports/pdfs/721report_july_dec2003.pdf.

[6] John R. Bolton, "Iran's Continuing Pursuit of Weapons of Mass Destruction" (testimony before the U.S. House International Relations Subcommittee on the Middle East and Central Asia, June 24, 2004, available at http://www.state.gov/t/us/rm/33909.htm).

[7] The importance of analyzing how lethal a given agent or weapon can be is even more crucial in assessing the risk posed by low-level attacks than the risk posed by high-level attacks. Anthrax probably qualifies as the most studied biological weapon, but it seems fair to say that the effectiveness of any given weaponization of the agent will be determined only when it is actually used, and that its real-world lethality could range from negligible to catastrophic. Furthermore, the weaponized version of anthrax is inhaled, while virtually all cases that occur in nature are cutaneous.

Although Iraq produced over 8,000 liters of concentrated anthrax solution before the Gulf War, there is little practical experience with anthrax as a human disease. Only 18 cases of inhalation were recorded in the United States between 1900 and 1978, 2 of which were the result of laboratory experiments. In contrast, some 2,000 cases of cutaneous anthrax are reported each year, 224 cases were reported in the United States during 1944–1994, and some 10,000 people died during an epidemic in Zimbabwe between 1979 and 1985. This helps explain why estimates of the lethality of weaponized inhalational anthrax have to be based on primate data, and why the range of uncertainty for a lethal dose of a 1–5 micron dry agent ranges from 2,500 to 55,500 spores. [Thomas V. Inglesby et al., "Anthrax as a Biological Weapon: Medical and Public Health Management," *Journal of the American Medical Association [JAMA]* 281, no. 18 (May 12, 1999): 1735–1745, 1736–1737; U.S. Army Center for Health Promotion and Preventive Medicine (USACHPPM), "The Medical NBC Battlebook," *USACHPPM Technical Guide* 244 (August 2002): 4–31.]

When Aum Shinrikyu tried to conduct anthrax attacks on Japanese and U.S. targets during the early 1990s, it succeeded in creating an effective aerosol, but grew anthrax from a nonvirulent strain and produced no casualties. [John A.

Gilbert, "Calibrating the Threat of Biological Attack" (paper prepared for the ETH [Swiss Federal Institute of Technology] international conference on "Meeting the Challenges of Bioterrorism: Assessing the Threat and Designing Biodefense Strategies," Furigen, Switzerland, April 22–23, 2005, p. 5.)]

At a more technical level, the Department of Defense "Medical NBC Battlebook" provides a source of data that scarcely eliminates the uncertainties surrounding lethality, disease effects, and medical impact, but which provides a reasonably authoritative picture of current medical thinking. The "Battlebook" does not give lethality data per se for anthrax, but shows a range of 8,000–50,000 spores for an infective dose. [USACHPPM, "The Medical NBC Battlebook."] The range of uncertainty for a key agent like anthrax is also illustrated in the World Health Organization (WHO) reporting on the risk of the use of such an agent in a "deliberate epidemic":

> Reported estimates of the dose required to infect 50% of a population of non-human primates in experimental studies of inhalational anthrax vary enormously, from 2500 to 760,000 spores, apparently reflecting differences in the many variables involved in such experiments. While doses lower than the LD50 produce correspondingly lower rates of infection, the very large number of experimental animals that would be required makes it impractical to determine doses that would infect only a small percentage of those exposed.
>
> The largest reported outbreak of human inhalational anthrax took place in 1979 in Sverdlovsk (Ekaterinburg), former Soviet Union. Of 66 documented fatal cases, all were more than 23 years in age, suggesting that adults might be more susceptible to inhalational anthrax than younger individuals might. The concomitant infection of sheep and cattle as far as 50 kilometers down wind of the apparent source points to the hazard of long-distance aerosol travel of infective spores.
>
> An outbreak of inhalational anthrax and cutaneous anthrax in the United States during October and November 2001 was caused by B. anthracis spores intentionally placed in envelopes sent through the post. Of the 11 reported inhalational cases, the probable date of exposure could be determined in six, and for these the median incubation period was 4 days (range 4–6 days). Prolonged antimicrobial prophylaxis administered to persons thought to be at greatest risk may have prevented cases from occurring later. All 11 inhalational cases received antimicrobial and supportive therapy and six survived. As in the Sverdlovsk outbreak, there was a lack of young persons among the inhalational cases, whose ages ranged from 43 to 94. [World Health Organization, "Annex 3: Biological Agents," in *Public Health Response to Biological and Chemical Weapons: WHO*

Guidance (Geneva: WHO, 2004), at http://www.who.int/csr/delibepidemics/biochemguide/en/index.html.]

These uncertainties lead to equally large uncertainties about detection and treatment, particularly since the Soviet experience in Sverdlovsk showed that cases occurred over a period of 2 to 43 days after exposure, and primate data indicate that weaponized spores can cause lethal effects 58 to 98 days after exposure. The diagnostics and postmortems at Sverdlovsk produced a wide range of symptoms and effects that made diagnosis difficult. If an attack was covert, it is also unlikely that the disease would be recognized quickly. The limited Soviet and Russian experience with the disease indicates that the first-stage symptoms are similar to those of flu, which could make initial diagnosis difficult. Even if a deliberate early effort is made to use diagnostic testing for anthrax, it would take 6–24 hours to confirm the disease, while the course of the disease normally lasts only three days before death occurs, presenting serious problems for organizing the proper response. A delay of even hours in administering antibiotics can be fatal. [Inglesby, "Anthrax as a Biological Weapon."]

Treatment presents further problems: there are no clinical studies of inhalational anthrax in human beings; a weaponized agent can be tailored to increase both its lethality and resistance to treatment; and rapid vaccination would not be practical even if the vaccine were known to be effective against the strain used in the weapon. The U.S. vaccine, which may or may not be effective against some strains of anthrax, normally is given in a six-dose series, and the United States does not regard the human live attenuated vaccine developed by the FSU as safe.

The communicability of a weaponized version of the disease is unclear, and containment and quarantine might be necessary. Serious problems could also arise in dealing with the dead, as cremation seems to be the only safe form of corpse disposal. [Inglesby, "Anthrax as a Biological Weapon"; USACHPPM, "The Medical NBC Battlebook."]

CHAPTER FIVE

"GUESSTIMATING" IRAN'S
NUCLEAR WEAPONS CAPABILITIES

There is more information available on Iran's nuclear programs than on its chemical and biological programs, but this scarcely eliminates major areas of uncertainty. Estimating Iranian nuclear capabilities is complicated by three key factors:

- First, the United States, the EU, and the UN all agree that Iran has the right to acquire a full nuclear fuel cycle for peaceful purposes under the Nuclear Nonproliferation Treaty, but there is no clear way to distinguish many of the efforts needed to acquire a nuclear weapon from such "legitimate" activities or pure research.

- Second, Iran has never denied that it carries out a wide range of nuclear research efforts. In fact, it has openly claimed that it is pursuing nuclear technology and has a "national" right to get access to nuclear energy. This has given it a rationale for rejecting Russia's offer to provide nuclear fuel but without giving Tehran the technology and the expertise needed to use it for weaponization purposes, and the United States agrees with this position.

- Third, it has never been clear whether Iran actually has a "military" nuclear program that is separate from its "civilian" nuclear research. U.S. and French officials have argued that they believe that Iran's nuclear program would make sense only if it had military purposes. Both governments have yet to provide evidence to prove these claims.

If Iran is a proliferator, it has shown that it is a skilled one highly capable of hiding many aspects of its programs, sending confusing and contradictory signals, exploiting the international inspection process, rapidly changing the character of given facilities, and pausing and retreating when expedient. It has also shown that denial can be a weapon, and that consistently finding an alternative explanation for all its actions, including concealment and actions that are limited violations of the NPT, can uphold some degree of "plausible deniability" for a long chain of ambiguous actions and events.

PROBLEMS IN ANALYZING IRAN'S WMD PROGRAM: A CASE STUDY

Iran also presents major problems in intelligence collection and analysis. The details of U.S., British, and other intelligence efforts to cover Iran remain classified. At the same time, studies of U.S. and British intelligence failures in covering Iraq have provided considerable insights into the difficulties of covering a nation like Iran. Background discussions with intelligence analysts and users reveal the following general problems in analyzing the WMD threat:

- The uncertainties surrounding collection of intelligence on virtually all proliferation and weapons of mass destruction programs are so great that it is impossible to produce meaningful point estimates. As the CIA has shown in some of its past public estimates of missile proliferation, the intelligence community must first develop a matrix of what is and is not known about a given aspect of proliferation in a given country, with careful footnoting or qualification of the problems in each key source. It must then deal with uncertainty by developing estimates that show a range of possible current and projected capabilities—carefully qualifying each case. In general, at least three scenarios or cases need to be analyzed for each major aspect of proliferation in each country— something approaching a "best," "most likely," and "worst case."[1]

- Even under these conditions, the resulting analytic effort faces serious problems. Security compartmentation within each major aspect of collection and analysis severely limits the flow of data to working analysts. The expansion of analytic staffs has sharply increased the barriers to the flow of data, and has brought into the process large number of junior analysts who can do little more than update past analyses and judgments. Far too little analysis is subjected to technical review by those who have actually worked on weapons development; and the analysis of delivery programs, warheads and weapons, and chemical, biological, and nuclear proliferation tends to be compartmented. Instead of a free flow of data and exchange of analytic conclusions, or "fusion" of intelligence, analysis is "stovepiped" into separate areas of activity. Moreover, the larger staffs get, the more stovepiping tends to occur.

- Analysis tends to focus on technical capability and not on the problems in management and systems integration that are often the real-world limiting factors in proliferation. This tends to push analysis toward exaggerating the probable level of proliferation, particularly because the level of technical capability is often assumed if all the necessary information is not available.

- Where data are available on past holdings of weapons and the capability to produce such weapons—such as data on chemical weapons feedstocks and biological growth material—the intelligence effort tends to produce estimates of the maximum size of the possible current holding of weapons and WMD materials. This tends to focus users on the worst case in terms of actual current capability, even though ranges are often shown and estimates are usually qualified with uncertainty. In the case of Iraq, this tendency was compounded by some 12 years of constant lies and disbelief that a dictatorship obsessed with record keeping would not have kept records if it had destroyed weapons and materials. The result was to assume that little or no destruction had occurred whenever UNSCOM, UNMOVIC, and the IAEA reported that major issues still affected Iraqi claims.

- Intelligence analysis has long been oriented more toward arms control and counterproliferation than war fighting, although the Defense Intelligence Agency and the military services have attempted to shift the focus. Dealing with broad national trends and assuming capability is not generally a major problem in seeking to push nations toward obeying arms control agreements or in pressuring possible suppliers. It also is not a major problem in analyzing broad military counterproliferation risks and programs. The situation is very different, however, in dealing with war-fighting choices, particularly issues like preemption and targeting. Assumptions of capability can lead to unnecessary preemption, overtargeting, inability to prioritize, and a failure to create the detailed collection and analysis needed to support warfighters down to the battalion level. This, in turn, often forces field commanders to rely on field teams with limited capability and expertise and to overreact to any potential threat or warning indicator.

■ Although the intelligence community does bring outside experts into the process, their function often is simply to provide advice in general terms rather than cleared review of the intelligence product. The result is often less than helpful. In addition, the use of cleared personnel in U.S. laboratories and other areas of expertise is inadequate and often presents major problems because those consulted are not brought fully into the intelligence analysis process and given all of the necessary data.

■ The intelligence community tends to try to avoid explicit statements about the shortcomings in collection and methods in much of its analysis and to repeat past agreed judgments on a lowest-common-denominator level—particularly in the form of the intelligence products that get broad circulation to consumers. However, attempts at independent outside analysis or "B-Teams" are not subject to the review and controls enforced on intelligence analysis, and the teams, collection data, and methods used are generally selected to prove given points rather than to provide an objective counterpoint to finished analysis.[2]

Few of these problems have been explicitly addressed in open-source reporting on Iran, and it is uncertain from the reporting on intelligence failures in the analysis of Iraq before the 2003 invasion that the intelligence community has covered these problems at the classified level.

Part of the overall problem lies with the user. Even at the best of times, policy-level and other senior users of intelligence tend to be intolerant of analysis that consists of a wide range of qualifications and uncertainties, and the best of times simply do not exist when urgent policy and war-fighting decisions need to be made. Users inevitably either force the intelligence process to reach something approaching a definitive set of conclusions, or else they make such estimates themselves.

Intelligence analysts and managers are all too aware of this reality. Experience has taught them that complex intelligence analysis—filled with alternative cases, probability estimates, and qualifications about uncertainty—generally goes unused or makes policymakers and commanders impatient with the entire intelligence process. In the real world, hard choices have to be made to provide an estimate that can actually be used and acted upon, and these choices must be either by the intelligence community or by the user.[3]

UNCERTAINTY AND CREDIBILITY OF SOURCES

If one looks at other sources of reporting on Iran, there have been many claims from many corners.

Opposition groups. Many claims come from opposition groups that are largely associated with Mujahedin-e Khalq, or MEK, which is designated a foreign terrorist organization by the U.S. State Department. Although their information has proved useful at times, some has been "too good to be true." For example, revelations about Iran's secret nuclear program by the National Council of Resistance of Iran (NCRI) did prove to be the trigger point for inviting the IAEA into Tehran for inspections. But its claim in September 2004 that Tehran had allocated $16 billion to building a nuclear bomb by mid-2005 was proved inaccurate.[4] And the January 2006 statements by the NCRI's former president, Alireza Jafarzadeh, about Iran's "5,000 centrifuges" were seen by many as an exaggeration or at least an unconfirmed allegation.[5]

Thus the source of claims must be taken into account. The NCRI is closely associated with MEK. MEK's motives are well known, and therefore its information must be considered with a certain level of skepticism. As a former CIA counterintelligence official said, "I would take anything from them with a grain of salt."[6]

The NCRI claimed that it relied on human sources for its information, including scientists and civilians working in Iranian facilities and locals living near the sites. In addition, the NCRI claimed at times that their sources were inside the Iranian regime and added, "Our sources were 100 percent sure about their intelligence."[7] But the NCRI provided no confirmation about its sources, and its information is considered by some in the United States and in European governments as less than credible.

"Walk-in" sources. U.S. officials have cited "walk-in" sources to prove the existence of an Iranian nuclear program. It is unclear who those sources are, but the United States insisted that they were not associated with the NCRI. In November 2004, U.S. officials claimed that a source provided U.S. intelligence with more than 1,000 pages of technical documents on Iranian "nuclear warhead design" and missile modifications to deliver an atomic warhead. In addition, it was reported that the documents included a "specific" warhead design based on implosion and adjustments, which was thought to be an attempt at fitting a warhead to Iranian ballistic missiles.[8]

According to the *Washington Post*, the "walk-in" source who provided the documents was previously unknown to U.S. intelligence. The same source was apparently the basis for the comments by Colin Powell, then secretary of state, on November 17, 2004, when he said, "I have seen some information that would suggest that they [Iran] have been actively working on delivery systems . . . . You don't have a weapon until you put it in something that can deliver a weapon . . . . I'm not talking about uranium or fissile material or the warhead; I'm talking about what one does with a warhead."[9]

Press reports indicate that the walk-in documents came from one source and lacked independent verification. The uncertainty about the source reportedly kept many in the U.S. government from using the information, and some were surprised when Secretary Powell expressed confidence in the information. Some saw it as a reminder of the problems in Secretary Powell's presentation to the UN regarding Iraqi WMDs, and they hoped that he had not made those remarks before the information was confirmed. Some U.S. officials went as far as saying that Powell "misspoke" when he was talking about the information.[10]

Other U.S. officials described the intelligence as "weak."[11] But other press reports claimed that the source, who was "solicited with German help," provided valuable intelligence that referred to a "black box," which U.S. officials claimed was a metaphor for a nuclear warhead design. One U.S. official was quoted by the *Wall Street Journal* as saying the documents represented "nearly a smoking gun," yet the same official claimed that this was not a definitive proof.[12]

Scientists in Iran. There are sources within Iran that have cooperated with the IAEA. According to IAEA reports, Iranian nuclear scientists were interviewed on specific questions. For example, in November 2003, the agency requested clarification on bismuth irradiation. It later reported that in January 2004 it "was able to interview two Iranian scientists involved in the bismuth irradiation. According to the scientists, two bismuth targets had been irradiated, and an attempt had been made, unsuccessfully, to extract polonium from one of them."[13]

But the credibility of those scientists depends on how much freedom they have to talk about specific issues, their level of involvement, and the nature of the questions posed to them. The nature of access and the type of information provided to the IAEA by Iranian scientists remain uncertain.

Independent intelligence. There is no obvious substitute for independent intelligence gathered by the United States, the EU, and regional powers. The IAEA and the UN do not have their own intelligence agencies. Rather, they have to rely on member states to provide them with the necessary information, including satellite images, electronic intercepts, human intelligence, and various other forms of information gathering and intelligence analysis. Still, the history of the U.S. and UK intelligence provided to UN inspectors in Iraq showed the limited ability of many intelligence agencies to get a full picture of a country's nuclear, biological, chemical, and missile programs.

KEY UNCERTAINTIES IN IRAN'S NUCLEAR DEVELOPMENTS

While Iran and Iraq are very different cases, much the same level of uncertainty exists about their nuclear programs. Almost no one believes that Iran has nuclear weapons, or is close to acquiring them, or presents a time-urgent threat. However, many believe that it is a matter of when, rather than if, Tehran acquires nuclear weapons. That is, once Iran acquires the capability to produce the materials needed for a nuclear fuel cycle, it would be capable of producing a full-fledged nuclear weapon.

As noted earlier, Iran had shown interest in acquiring nuclear technology long before the 1979 revolution. It is also clear from IAEA discoveries that Iran has pursued two tracks: uranium enrichment and production of plutonium.[14] Both of these methods can produce the materials that can be used for nuclear reactors and for nuclear weapons. The IAEA does not believe, however, that Iran has yet succeeded in achieving either goal. In a recent press article, Mohamed ElBaradei, the director general of the IAEA, was quoted as saying, "To develop a nuclear weapon, you need a significant quantity of highly enriched uranium or plutonium, and no one has seen that in Iran."[15]

Plutonium Production

Tehran has given enough importance to the production of plutonium to take two different tracks to achieve that capacity. First, it is building heavy water production plants, which U.S. officials claim serve only one purpose: to supply the heavy water that is optimal for producing weapons-grade plutonium. The Iranian government, on the other hand, has claimed that their purpose is isotope production for its civilian nuclear energy program.[16]

The second track being pursued is the production of light water power reactors. The main reactor is at Bushehr, which is designed to produce civilian nuclear technology. Bushehr is also the reactor that Russia agreed to supply the fuel for and recover the spent fuel from. The U.S. undersecretary for arms control and international security, John R. Bolton, claimed in 2004 that Bushehr would produce enough plutonium per year to manufacture nearly 30 nuclear weapons.[17]

The following chronology by the International Atomic Energy Agency shows the history of Iran's plutonium separation experiments:[18]

- **1987–1988:** The separation process was simulated using imported unirradiated uranium dioxide, or UO_2 (DU); dissolution and purification took place in the Shariaty building at the Tehran Nuclear Research Center (TNRC); pressed and sintered pellets were manufactured at the fuel fabrication laboratory (FFL) using imported UO_2 (DU); the UO_2 pellets were further manipulated into aluminum and stainless steel capsules at the FFL.

- **1988–1993:** The capsules (containing a total of 7 kilograms (kg) of UO_2 in the form of powder, pressed pellets and sintered pellets) were irradiated in the Tehran Research Reactor (TRR).

- **1991–1993:** Plutonium was separated from some of the irradiated UO_2 targets in the capsules (about 3 kilograms of the 7 kilograms of UO_2) and plutonium solutions produced; these activities were carried out at the Shariaty building and, after the activities were transferred in October/November 1992, at the Chamaran building at TNRC; the research and development-related irradiation and separation of plutonium were terminated in 1993.

- **1993–1994:** The unprocessed irradiated UO_2 was initially stored in capsules in the spent fuel pond of TRR and later transferred into four containers and buried behind the Chamaran building.

- **1995:** In July, purification of the plutonium solution from the 1988–1993 period was carried out in the Chamaran building; a planchet (disk) was prepared from the solution for analysis.

- **1998:** In August, additional purification of plutonium from the 1988–1993 period was carried out in the Chamaran building; another planchet was prepared from the solution for analysis.

- **2000:** The glove boxes from the Chamaran building were dismantled and sent to the Esfahan Nuclear Technology Center (ENTC) for storage; one glove box was moved to the molybdenum, iodine, and xenon (MIX) radioisotope production facility.

- **2003:** Due to construction work being carried out behind the Chamaran building, two containers holding the unprocessed irradiated UO_2 were dug up, moved, and reburied.

In September 2005, the IAEA analysis of Iran's plutonium separation experiments concluded that the solutions that were tested were 12 to 16 years old, which seemed to corroborate Iran's claims. In addition, the IAEA carried out verification tests for unprocessed irradiated UO_2 targets stored in four containers; those results also conformed to Iranian claims, although the IAEA argued that the number of targets provided by Iran was much lower than the actual number. The IAEA's analysis stated that "a final assessment of Iran's plutonium research activities must await the results of the destructive analysis of the disks and targets."[19]

Uranium Enrichment

Many weapons experts believe that Iran's uranium enrichment program is much more advanced than its plutonium production program. Moreover, it does not rely on Iran's nuclear reactors. Hans Blix, former chief UN weapons inspector in Iraq, has said that Tehran's plans to build a 40-megawatt (MW) research reactor at Bushehr, which is considered Iran's main plutonium production facility, should not be the main concern. He argued that the light water reactor was not ideal for plutonium production. "What is uncomfortable and dangerous," he added, "is that they have acquired the capacity to enrich their own uranium that they dig out of the ground . . . . If you can enrich to five percent you can enrich it to 85 percent."[20]

These concerns were further exacerbated following the announcement on April 11, 2006, by Mahmoud Ahmadinejad, Iran's president, that Iran had been successful at enriching uranium. "At this historic moment, with the blessings of God almighty and the efforts made by our scientists, I declare here that the laboratory-scale nuclear fuel cycle has been completed and young scientists produced enriched uranium needed to the degree for nuclear power plants [on April 9]." The head of the Atomic Energy Organization of Iran (AEOI) and Iran's vice president, Gholamreza Aghazadeh, stated that Iranian nuclear scientists

- Had started enriching uranium to a level—3.5 percent—needed for fuel on a research scale using 164 centrifuges, but not enriched enough to build a nuclear bomb;

- Had produced 110 tons of uranium hexafluoride (UF_6)— nearly double the amount that it claimed to have enriched in 2005;

- Aim to increase the enrichment percentage of U-235, the isotope needed for nuclear fission, which is much rarer than the more prevalent U-238 isotope; and

- Plan to expand its enrichment program to be able to use 3,000 centrifuges at the nuclear center at Natanz by the end of 2006.[21]

Mohammad Saeedi, deputy chief of the AEOI, reiterated that Iran aimed to expand uranium enrichment to industrial-scale at Natanz.

In addition to installing 3,000 centrifuges at Natanz by 2006, Saeedi claimed that Iran intends to expand the total number of centrifuges to 54,000, which would be used to fuel a 1,000-megawatt nuclear power plant.[22]

While some believe that Iran's claims are credible, others speculated that Iran made the announcement to send a message that military strikes or sanctions would not deter it from achieving a full nuclear cycle. Much also depended on what the announcement really meant. Iran had previously obtained at least 2 percent enrichment from the experimental use of centrifuges, and possibly significantly higher levels. The IAEA had previously made it clear that it lacked the data to determine how far Iran had actually progressed. Iran also had reached enrichment levels as high as 8 percent through experimental use of laser isotope separation, although it seemed far from being able to scale up such efforts beyond laboratory tests.[23]

The Iranian claims also said nothing about how efficient the claimed use of a small 164-centrifuge chain was, or about its life cycle and reliability, or about the ability to engineer a system that could approach weapons-grade material.[24] As the following chapters show, it is at best possible to speculate about how many P-1-type of centrifuge derivatives Iran would need to produce a nuclear device and then move on to develop a significant weapons production capability. The number, however, would probably be in the thousands in terms of continuously operating machine equivalents to slowly get the fissile material for a single device or "bomb in the basement," and tens of thousands to support a serious nuclear weapons delivery capability.

One thing was already clear long before the new Iranian claims. There was nothing the United Nations or the United States could do to deny Iran the technology to build a nuclear weapon. The IAEA's discoveries had revealed that Iran already had functioning centrifuge designs, reactor development capability, and plutonium separation capability. It had experimented with polonium in ways that showed it could make a neutron initiator, had the technology to produce high-explosive lenses and beryllium reflectors, could machine fissile material, and had long had a technology base capable of producing the same non-fissile actual weapon designs used by Pakistan in its nuclear weapons design efforts. It also seemed highly likely that it had acquired P-2 centrifuge designs and the same basic Chinese design data for a fissile weapon suitable for mounting on a ballistic missile that North Korea had sold to Libya.

As a result, both the claims of Iran's president about achieving a major breakthrough and President Bush's responding statement, that Iran would not be allowed to acquire the technology to build a nuclear weapon, seemed to be little more than vacuous political posturing. Ahmadinejad's statement seemed to be an effort to show the UN that it could not take meaningful action and exploit Iranian nationalism. The Bush statement was a combination of the basic technical ignorance of the president's speechwriters and an effort to push the UN toward action and convince Iran that it could face the threat of both serious sanctions and military action if diplomacy failed. It effectively ignored the fact that Iran not only already had the technology, but could disperse it to the point where it was extremely unlikely that any UN inspection effort could find it, even if Iran allowed inspections, or that any military option could seriously affect Iran's technology base—as distinguished from its ability to create survivable large-scale production facilities and openly deploy nuclear-armed delivery systems.

In reality, such developments were at most evolutionary and had been expected. Diplomats and officials from the IAEA were quick to point out that the announcement by Iran should not be a sign of concern and that Iran may face many technical hurdles before it can enrich enough quantities of uranium at high levels to produce a nuclear weapon. One European official said that while the 164-machine centrifuges were more industrial, "it's not like they haven't come close to achieving this in the past." This assessment has been reflected in reports by the IAEA, which argue that Iran has used centrifuges and laser to enrich uranium throughout the 1990s and even before.[25]

To put such rhetoric in context, most of Tehran's uranium conversion experiments took place between 1981 and 1993 at the Tehran Nuclear Research Center and the Esfahan Nuclear Technology Center. According to the IAEA, Iran's uranium enrichment activities also received some foreign help in 1991. However, it is clear that some activities continued throughout 2002.

The IAEA outlined its findings regarding Tehran's uranium enrichment as follows:

In 1991, Iran entered into discussions with a foreign supplier for the construction at Esfahan of an industrial scale conversion facility. Construction on the facility, UCF, was begun in the late 1990s. UCF consists of several conversion lines, principal among which is the line for the conversion of UOC to UF6 with an annual design production capacity of 200 t [metric ton] uranium as UF6. The UF6 is to be sent to the uranium enrichment facilities at Natanz, where it will be enriched up to 5 percent U-235 and the product and tails returned to UCF for conversion into low enriched UO2 and depleted uranium metal. The design information for UCF provided by Iran indicates that conversion lines are also foreseen for the production of natural and enriched (19.7 percent) uranium metal, and natural UO2. The natural and enriched (5 percent U-235) UO2 are to be sent to the Fuel Manufacturing Plant (FMP) at Esfahan, where Iran has said it will be processed into fuel for a research reactor and power reactors.

. . . In March 2004, Iran began testing the process lines involving the conversion of UOC into UO2 and UF4, and UF4 into UF6. As of June 2004, 40 to 45 kg of UF6 had been produced therefrom. A larger test, involving the conversion of 37 t of yellowcake into UF4, was initiated in August 2004. According to Iran's declaration of 14 October 2004, 22.5 t of the 37 t of yellowcake had been fed into the process and that approximately 2 t of UF4, and 17.5 t of uranium as intermediate products and waste, had been produced. There was no indication as of that date of UF6 having been produced during this later campaign.[26]

The IAEA inspections found traces of contamination from advanced enrichment activities at Natanz. Iran claimed that the contamination was from equipment it had purchased in the 1980s from aboard (presumably from Pakistan). Reports by the IAEA, however, showed that Iran may have started its enrichment program in the 1970s and that the Iranians were already partially successful at uranium conversion.

Iran has tried two different methods to enrich uranium ever since the time of the shah. First, Iran's nuclear research program has facilities that are dedicated to manufacturing and testing centrifuges; related to this is its ultimate goal of producing 50,000 centrifuges in

Natanz. Second, Iran also pursued enriching uranium through laser enrichment. According to Mohamed ElBaradei, the director general of the IAEA, Iran was able to enrich up to 1.2 percent using centrifuges and up to 15 percent using lasers.[27]

Some of Iran's gas centrifuge program depended on help from Pakistan. Although reports by the director general of the IAEA do not mention Pakistan by name, Iran's gas centrifuges can be traced back to the mid-1990s when the Pakistani nuclear scientist Abdul Qadeer Khan, known as A.Q. Khan, approached an Iranian company and offered P-1 documentations and components for 500 centrifuges. (P-1 and P-2 refer to two designs for centrifuges by Pakistan.) Iran claimed that it received only the P-1 and not the P-2 design. Both Iran and Pakistan would later admit to this transaction and provide the documents to support these allegations.[28]

According to the IAEA, Tehran received P-1 components and documentations in January 1994. Tehran, however, claimed that it did not receive any components until October 1994. Regardless of the month of delivery, one more important element remains unresolved. The IAEA refers to this transaction as the "1987 offer," which reportedly provided Iran with a sample machine, drawings, descriptions, and specifications for production, as well as materials for 2,000 centrifuge machines.[29]

In addition, Iran received the P-2 design in 1994/1995 from Pakistan, but claimed that all of its components were designed and manufactured in Iran. Furthermore, Iran claimed that it did not pursue any work on the P-2 design between 1995 and 2002 due to shortages in staff and resources at the Atomic Energy Organization of Iran (AEOI), and that it focused instead on resolving outstanding issues regarding the P-1 design. The IAEA, however, was not convinced that Iran had not pursued further development of the P-2 design and called on Iran in September 2005 to provide more information on the history of its P-2 developments.[30]

This helps explain why experts have argued that Iran's goal of producing 50,000 centrifuges in Natanz should be a matter of serious concern for the international community. For example, David Albright and Corey Hinderstein of the Institute for Science and International Security (ISIS) argued in January 2006 that Iran planned to install centrifuges in modules of 3,000 machines that were designed to produce low-enriched uranium (LEU) for civilian power reactors. If, however, half of those machines were used to create highly enriched uranium (HEU), they could produce enough HEU for one nuclear weapon a year. Furthermore, if Iran does achieve its goal of 50,000 centrifuges, Albright and Hinderstein argued, "at 15–20 kilograms per weapon, that would be enough for 25–30 nuclear weapons per year."[31]

A much smaller facility might, however, be adequate. A study by Frank Barnaby for the Oxford Research Group estimates that Iran's current centrifuges could produce about 2.5 separative work units (SWUs) a year, with a range of 1.9–2.7 SWUs. If Iran had the P-2, each centrifuge would produce roughly 5 SWU a year.[32] A fully operational 3,000-centrifuge facility could then produce some 7,500 SWU or about 40 kilograms of heavily enriched uranium a year, and it would probably take a total capacity of 5,000 machines to keep 3,000 online at all times.[33] As is discussed later, the 1,500-centrifuge pilot facility that Iran is now seeking to operate could conceivably produce a single weapon in two to three years.

As for the other enrichment route, Iran acknowledged it had started a laser enrichment program in the 1970s. It claimed that it used two different tracks in its program: (1) atomic vapor laser isotope separation (AVLIS) and (2) molecular isotope separation (MLIS). However, Iran depended on key contracts with four (unnamed) countries to build its laser enrichment program. The following chronology was presented by the IAEA:[34]

- **1975:** Iran contracted with one supplier for the establishment of a laboratory to study the spectroscopic behavior of uranium metal; the project had been abandoned in the 1980s because the laboratory had not functioned properly.

- **Late 1970s:** Iran contracted with a second supplier to study MLIS. Four carbon monoxide (CO) lasers and vacuum chambers were delivered, but the project was terminated due to the political situation before major development work had begun.

- **1991:** Iran contracted with a third supplier for the establishment of a laser spectroscopy laboratory (LSL) and a comprehensive separation laboratory (CSL), where uranium enrichment would be carried out on a milligram scale based on the AVLIS process. The contract also provided for the supply of 50 kg of natural uranium metal.

- **1998:** Iran contracted with a fourth supplier for information related to laser enrichment and the supply of relevant equipment. However, because the supplier was unable to secure export licenses, only some of the equipment was delivered (to Lashkar Ab'ad).

The IAEA seems to be more confident about its findings regarding Iran's laser enrichment developments than about its findings concerning Iran's gas centrifuges. This is due largely to Iranian cooperation, but also to the fact that Iran had nothing to hide, as its foreign contractors had failed to deliver on the four contracts. According to the IAEA, Iran claimed that the laser spectroscopy laboratory and the MLIS laboratory (the first two contracts) were never fully operational.

As for the third contract, the IAEA estimated the contract was completed in 1994, but that the CSL and LSL had technical problems and were unsuccessful between 1994 and 2000.

Iran responded to these findings by claiming that the two labs were dismantled in 2000. In addition, the IAEA concluded that, "as confirmed in an analysis, provided to the Agency, that had been carried out by the foreign laboratory involved in the project, the highest average enrichment achieved was 8 percent, but with a peak enrichment of 13 percent."

Finally, the fourth contract, signed in 1998, failed due to the supplier's inability to obtain export licenses. Tehran claimed that it had tried to procure the equipment and parts, but that it was unsuccessful.[35]

These failures almost certainly strained Tehran's ability to advance its uranium enrichment activities using the laser enrichment track. This may explain why Iran did less to try to conceal its laser enrichment program than the details of its centrifuge program. According to the IAEA, Tehran's declarations largely corresponded with the IAEA inspectors' findings. For example, Iran claimed that its enrichment level was 0.8 percent U-235, while the IAEA concluded that Iran reached an enrichment level of 0.99 percent ± 0.24 percent U-235.[36]

The IAEA findings regarding this aspect of Tehran's enrichment program are summarized in the following two paragraphs:

The Agency has completed its review of Iran's atomic vapor laser isotope separation (AVLIS) program and has concluded that Iran's descriptions of the levels of enrichment achieved using AVLIS at the Comprehensive Separation Laboratory (CSL) and Lashkar Ab'ad and the amounts of material used in its past activities are consistent with information available to the Agency to date. Iran has presented all known key equipment, which has been verified by the Agency. For the reasons described in the Annex to this report, however, detailed nuclear material accountancy is not possible.

It is the view of the Agency's AVLIS experts that, while the contract for the AVLIS facility at Lashkar Ab'ad was specifically written for the delivery of a system that could achieve 5 kg of product within the first year with enrichment levels of 3.5 percent to 7 percent, the facility as designed and reflected in the contract would, given some specific features of the equipment, have been capable of limited HEU production had the entire package of equipment been delivered. The Iranian AVLIS experts have stated that they were not aware of the significance of these features when they negotiated and contracted for the supply and delivery of the Lashkar Ab'ad AVLIS facility. They have also provided information demonstrating the very limited capabilities of the equipment delivered to Iran under this contract to produce HEU (i.e., only in gram quantities).[37]

The accuracy of such findings is critical because isotope separation is far more efficient than centrifuge separation, much less costly once mature, uses far less power, and is much harder to detect.[38]

Other aspects of Iranian activity were less reassuring. Following Iran's announcement that it had converted 37 tons of yellowcake into UF_4 in May 2005, experts estimated that this amount of uranium could "theoretically" produce more than 200 pounds of weapons-grade uranium, or enough to produce 5–6 crude nuclear weapons. The head of Iran's Supreme National Security Council, Hasan Rowhani, was quoted in 2005 as follows: "Last year, we could not produce UF_4 and UF_6. We didn't have materials to inject into centrifuges to carry out enrichment, meaning we didn't have UF_6 .... But within the past year, we completed the Isfahan facility and reached UF_4 and UF_6 stage. So we made great progress."[39]

In February 2006, in advance of the IAEA board meeting, it was reported in the press that a report was circulated to IAEA member states regarding what press reports called "the Green Salt Project." The information in the report came largely from the U.S. intelligence community. The project name was derived from "green salt," or uranium tetrafluoride, which is considered an intermediate material in converting uranium ore into uranium hexafluoride, UF_4, which is central to producing nuclear fuel.[40]

The project was reportedly started in spring 2001 by an Iranian firm, Kimeya Madon, under the auspices of the IRGC. U.S. officials believe that Kimyea Madon completed drawings and technical specifications for a small uranium conversion facility (UCF), and they argue that the drawings provide "pretty compelling evidence" for Iran's clandestine uranium conversion program. In addition, there was evidence that the Iranians envisioned a second UCF. It remains uncertain why the project stopped in 2003. Some speculated that the planned UCF was to replace Esfahan in case of a military strike against it. Another view is that Iran scratched the plan after it was revealed that the new UCF was not "as good as what they had" at Esfahan.[41]

Another important development in examining Iran's uranium enrichment activities was the IAEA's discovery of "a document related to the procedural requirements for the reduction of UF_6 to metal in small quantities, and on the casting and machining of enriched, natural and depleted uranium metal into hemispherical forms," as the IAEA's February 4, 2006, resolution emphasized.[42]

A description of the document first appeared in the IAEA's November 2005, report. The "one-page document" apparently was related to Pakistan's offer in 1987 concerning centrifuges, and the IAEA made the following assessment:

> As previously reported to the Board, in January 2005 Iran showed to the Agency a copy of a hand-written one-page document reflecting an offer said to have been made to Iran in 1987 by a foreign intermediary for certain components and equipment. Iran stated that only some components of one or two disassembled centrifuges, and supporting drawings and specifications, were delivered by the procurement network, and that a number of other items of

equipment referred to in the document were purchased directly from other suppliers. Most of these components and items were included in the October 2003 declaration by Iran to the Agency.

The documents recently made available to the Agency related mainly to the 1987 offer; many of them dated from the late 1970s and early- to mid-1980s. The documents included detailed drawings of the P-1 centrifuge components and assemblies; technical specifications supporting component manufacture and centrifuge assembly; and technical documents relating to centrifuge operational performance. In addition, they included cascade schematic drawings for various sizes of research and development (R&D) cascades, together with the equipment needed for cascade operation (e.g., cooling water circuit needs and special valve consoles). The documents also included a drawing showing a cascade layout for 6 cascades of 168 machines each and a small plant of 2000 centrifuges arranged in the same hall. Also among the documents was one related to the procedural requirements for the reduction of UF6 to metal in small quantities, and on the casting and machining of enriched, natural and depleted uranium metal into hemispherical forms, with respect to which Iran stated that it had been provided on the initiative of the procurement network, and not at the request of the Atomic Energy Organization of Iran (AEOI).[43]

As noted earlier, the foreign intermediary is believed to have been A.Q. Khan, the Pakistani nuclear scientist. The United Kingdom argued that the document on casting uranium into hemispheric form had no application other than for nuclear weapons. Experts agreed with this assessment.[44] IAEA officials, however, were more cautious. One senior IAEA official was quoted as saying that the document "is damaging," but he argued that the hand-written document was not a blueprint for making nuclear weapons because it dealt with only one aspect of the process.[45]

Many experts believe that to understand Iran's nuclear program, one must understand its gas centrifuge program—particularly whether the ability to establish a test run of 1,500 centrifuges at Natanz would give Iran enough capacity to produce highly enriched uranium (HEU). David Albright and Corey Hinderstein of the ISIS argued that Iran may well be on its way to achieving that capacity:

Each P-1 centrifuge has an output of about 3 separative work units (swu) per year according to senior IAEA officials. From the A.Q. Khan network, Iran acquired drawings of a modified variant of an early-generation Urenco centrifuge. Experts who saw these drawings assessed that, based on the design's materials, dimensions, and tolerances, the P-1 in Iran is based on an early version of the Dutch 4M centrifuge that was subsequently modified by Pakistan. The 4M was developed in the Netherlands in the mid-1970s and was more advanced than the earlier Dutch SNOR/CNOR machines. Its rotor assembly has four aluminum rotor tubes connected by three maraging steel bellows.

With 1,500 centrifuges and a capacity of 4,500 swu per year, this facility could produce as much as 28 kilograms of weapon-grade uranium per year, assuming a tails assay of 0.5 percent, where tails assay is the fraction of uranium 235 in the waste stream. This is a relatively high tails assay, but such a tails assay is common in initial nuclear weapons programs. As a program matures and grows, it typically reduces the tails assay to about 0.4 percent and later perhaps to 0.3 percent to conserve uranium supplies.

By spring 2004, Iran had already put together about 1,140 centrifuge rotor assemblies, a reasonable indicator of the number of complete centrifuges. However, only about 500 of these rotors were good enough to operate in cascades, according to knowledgeable senior IAEA officials. The November 2004 IAEA report stated that from spring to October 10, 2004, Iran had assembled an additional 135 rotors, bringing the total number of rotors assembled to 1,275. As mentioned above, a large number of these rotors are not usable in an operating cascade.

Iran is believed to have assembled more centrifuges prior to the suspension being re-imposed on November 22, 2004. Without more specific information, it is assumed that Iran continued to assemble centrifuges at a constant rate, adding another 70 centrifuges for a total of 1,345 centrifuges. However, the total number of good centrifuges is estimated at about 700.[46]

These developments led some observers to question whether Iran had received more help from Pakistan that it had admitted. Some experts argued that the A.Q. Khan network tended to hand over the

"whole package," as was the case with Libya, and they questioned whether Iran received only the few pages that it shared with the IAEA.[47] These
revelations show how little is known about how advanced Iran's uranium enrichment program might be.

As noted earlier, most experts believe that Iran's uranium enrichment program is far more dangerous and advanced than its plutonium production activities. They argue that the danger of the enrichment
program is that, regardless of the level of enrichment attained, if Iran
can enrich uranium at a low level, it will have the knowledge to enrich
it at higher levels and produce the weapons-grade uranium used for
nuclear weapons.[48]

In addition, experts are concerned that Iran may acquire uranium
from other nations. For example, during a visit by the Iranian parliament speaker, Gholam Ali Haddad-Adel, in early 2006, Iran and Venezuela signed an agreement that allowed Iran to explore Venezuela's
strategic minerals. Venezuelan opposition figures to President Hugo
Chavez claimed that the deal could involve the production and transfer of uranium from Venezuela to Iran. The United States, however,
downplayed such reports. A State Department official was quoted as
saying, "We are aware of reports of possible Iranian exploitation of Venezuelan uranium, but we see no commercial activities in Venezuela."[49]

The Uncertain Nature of Iran's Centrifuge Designs

The uncertainties relating to centrifuge design are a critical problem.
Centrifuges can differ radically in complexity of manufacture, dependence on imports, and research and development requirements. They
can differ sharply in theoretical capacity, reliability and life cycle, and
maintenance needs.

Operating a chain or cascade imposes major additional design and
operating constraints. Large numbers of systems may have to be
linked together with desired operating standards that require them to
be operating 24 hours a day nearly 365 days a year. Concealment into
scattered cascades of smaller numbers and the transfer of enriched
material between such complexes impose further problems. So does
"folding" a large number of centrifuges into cascades that can fit in
ordinary buildings. Power requirements present another problem
because large power feeds can be detected.

In Iran's case, further uncertainties exist because the real-world performance of Iran's adaptation of the P-1 centrifuge is not known, and the IAEA's questions about its acquisition of P-2 centrifuge data have never been answered.[50] Iran initially claimed that the IAEA's discoveries that it might have designs and magnets for the P-2 did not have to be reported to the IAEA. Hasan Rowhani, secretary of Iran's Supreme National Security Council, stated in February 2004 that Iran did not have to report because it did not have the centrifuge and was only conducting related research or designing a prototype: "The issue is in a research stage and the agency's criticism about P-2 is not acceptable."[51]

On June 17, 2004, State Department spokesman Richard Boucher described Iran's treatment of the IAEA's questions as follows:

> . . . it only points out more how hollow Iran's denials and statements have been because what the IEA said is, in their report, they said that Iran had not told them about the magnets, but they then found out later that they had heard about it in—I guess there was— Iran produced a tape recording of an Iranian private citizen telling an IAEA inspector orally in January that he did import P-2 magnets.
>
> . . . we would note that up until May, the official position of the Iranian Government was that it had not imported P-2 centrifuge parts and the Director General's report also indicates not until May that Iran acknowledged, for the first time, details about seeking to procure 4000 magnets with specifications suitable for P-2 use.
>
> So even though you had an Iranian telling the inspector in January that they had tried to buy magnets, that they had bought P-2 magnets, the official position of the Iranian Government, the denials of the Iranian Government continued all the way through May. So, once again, we're faced with a situation of finding that Iran has, in this case, not only denied what the inspectors knew, but denied what an Iranian had told the inspectors. We have, you know, repeated indications where in February that they also wrote to the IAEA that only P-2 drawings had been received in 1994, without any components of the P-2 centrifuge. Again, the Iranians, apparently, already prior to that date, told the IAEA that they had imported these magnets for the P-2s.

So we're, once again, left in the situation where we find that Iran has spent months and months and months denying things that were known, months and months trying to pretend that it was not doing things that finally became known and then it finally admitted it. We think it is important that scrutiny of the IAEA continue on Iran, and we are working with other governments at the IAEA to produce a resolution for the board that will say that, that will continue that process.[52]

Work by David Albright and Corey Hinderstein suggests that Iran may well have acquired at least the designs for the P-2 from the A.Q. Khan network, which was supplying centrifuges to Libya, plus more than $3 million of parts.[53]

It is clear that the A.Q. Khan network sold both P-1 and P-2 centrifuges, and that the P-1 centrifuge is a more simple design that uses an aluminum rotor, while the P-2 centrifuge uses a maraging steel rotor. The A.Q. Khan network is known to have sold some 500 P-1 centrifuges to Iran in the mid-1990s; these seem to have been used P-1s that Pakistan retired from its program as the P-2 was phased in and that members of the A.Q. Khan network supposedly removed and sold "in secret."

Albright and Hinderstein report that only small numbers of P-2s were ever sold, and that the first two demonstration models sold to Libya (out of a potential order of 10,000) were used machines, one of which could not be used for enrichment with uranium hexafluoride gas because, "it did not have the final surface coating necessary to prevent corrosion by uranium."

The early production for Libya's order was to come from a Malaysian firm called SCOPE, which was to provide the maraging steel components. The components were to be assembled in Turkey, with additional Turkish parts, plus parts from a range of suppliers like Switzerland, Britain, France, Italy, Spain, the United Arab Emirates (UAE), Germany, and South Africa. Libya, however, was to be given the complete manuals for production and was to purchase at least a small production facility.[54]

The Iranian resistance group NCRI (or MEK) has made the following claims:

[A] major portion of the above-mentioned centrifuges have been manufactured by secret companies affiliated with the Defense Ministry. The Defense industry has secret companies under similar names of Machine-Alat and Abzar Daghig (machinery and precise equipment) that are involved in manufacturing parts and assembling centrifuges. Some of the companies affiliated with the Defense Ministry are located in Isfahan.

One of these companies is Elka Felezkar Sanat Novin (Elka Metalworks New Industry). This company is involved in preparing metal parts including those used in centrifuges. The Iranian regime's Atomic Energy Organization or one of its front companies places the orders to this company. Using advanced laser equipment, "Elka Felezkar Sanat Novin" cuts steel plates according to the specifications and bends them accordingly.

Companies Fara Felezkaran and Electronic. These three companies (these two and Elka Felezkar Sanat Novin) are located in the suburbs of Tehran. The address is Abe-ali road, five kilometers past highway patrol station of the Jajrood—after Kamrad gas station, Sang Lashgari alley, next to Nasim Traghzieh Company.[55]

Some of the ambiguities surrounding Iran's efforts seem to have been resolved. Iran's president claimed in early April 2006 that Iran was conducting research and development on P-2 centrifuges that he said had four times the output of Iran's P-1s. This claim, however, may be more political than a statement of serious progress, as no information exists to validate the claim and R&D is not the same as having either a finished design or one with the required operating capability and reliability. As a result, there is no way to know how far Iran has progressed, how quickly it could move in the future, or how it could use its technology base to avoid new inspections or react to a military attack on its existing facilities.

A Continuing Process of Discovery

It is clear that there is still much more to learn. As noted earlier, in early 2006 the *New York Times* reported on new U.S. intelligence estimates that suggested that Iran's "peaceful" program included a "military-nuclear dimension." This assessment was reportedly based on information provided by the United States to the IAEA, and it referred to a secret program called "the Green Salt Project." The project was created to work on uranium enrichment, high explosives, and adapting nuclear warheads to Iranian missiles. The report suggested that there was evidence of "administrative interconnections" between weaponization and nuclear experts in Iran's nuclear program. Tehran argued that the claims were "baseless" and promised to provide further clarification.[56]

These claims of a link between Iran's civilian and military nuclear tracks seem to support the comments by Secretary of State Powell in November 2004. Yet it remains uncertain if the sources of intelligence were the same. Secretary Powell argued that the U.S. intelligence had information that Iran was trying to adapt its nuclear research to fit its Shahab-3 missile, and that it made no sense for Iran to work on advancing its delivery systems unless it was also working on the warheads for those systems. Other U.S. officials, however, argued that the information Powell used came from unconfirmed sources and should not be seen as a definitive proof.[57]

The source for the information in question seems to be a stolen laptop computer that contained designs by Kimeya Madon for a small-scale uranium gas production facility. The documents also contained modifications to Iran's Shahab-3 missile in a way, U.S. officials believe, to fit a nuclear warhead. Members of the U.S. intelligence community reportedly believed that the files on the computer were authentic, but said there was no way to prove that. They argued that while the documents possibly were forged by Iranian opposition groups or fabricated by a third country like Israel, it was unlikely. The authenticity of the documents also seemed to have been confirmed by British intelligence.[58]

What concerns U.S. officials is that while nowhere on the laptop was the word "nuclear" mentioned even though the documents mentioned the names of military officers who were linked to Mohsen Fakrizadeh. Fakrizadeh is believed to direct "Project 111," which U.S. intelligence officials think has been responsible for weaponizing Iran's nuclear research efforts and missile development. In addition, the United States believes that the project is the successor to Project 110, which used to be the military arm of Iran's nuclear research program.

These revelations are "cloaked" with uncertainty, however, and the United States believes that the only way to know the truth about "Project 111" is if Fakrizadeh cooperates with IAEA inspectors.[59]

These concerns about Iranian weaponization efforts were exacerbated by the IAEA's discovery of a document relating to reducing UF_6 to small quantities of metal as well as casting enriched and natural depleted uranium into hemispherical forms.[60] This is believed to be the first link the IAEA has shown between Iran's military and civilian nuclear program. Many argue that the discovery of this document was the turning point in the IAEA's negotiation efforts with Tehran, and that Iran's failure to disclose this document early in the inspections was a cause for concern for the agency.

Press reports have also claimed that there was further evidence of Iran's effort to weaponize its nuclear research. A U.S. intelligence assessment was leaked to the *Washington Post*, which reported that, according to U.S. officials, Iran's nuclear researchers have completed the drawings for "a deep subterranean shaft"— a 400-meter underground tunnel with remote-controlled sensors to measure pressures and temperatures. U.S. experts believed that the tunnel was being prepared for an underground nuclear test. One U.S. official was quoted as saying, "The diagram is consistent with a nuclear test-site schematic," because the drawings envisioned a test control team to be so far away—10 kilometers—from the test site. But the United States believes that the tunnel was still in the drawing stage and not yet under construction. The evidence for the tunnel and Iran's weaponization efforts were the closest thing to a "smoking gun" for proving that Iran was working on a nuclear weapons program.[61]

This lack of clarity illustrates the point that Iran can gain as much from concealing and obfuscating its weaponization activities as from hiding or obfuscating the nature of its nuclear program. As long as Iran does not actually test a full nuclear explosion, it can develop and can test potential weapons and warhead designs in a wide range of ways. It can also prepare for underground testing, and test simulated weapons underground to validate many aspects of the test system—including venting—without exploding a bomb until it is ready for the international community to know it has actually tested a weapon.

It can develop and deploy its missile program with conventional warheads, and create considerable confusion over the nature of its warhead and bomb tests, concealing whether it has carried out extensive research on CBRN weaponization as part of what it claims is the testing of conventional weapons. Telemetry can be encrypted, avoided, and made deliberately misleading. The same is true of static explosive testing or the use of air-delivered warheads and bombs. So far, the international community and outside experts have generally failed to explore the rationale for Iran's missile efforts and other weaponization activities. Meanwhile, the IAEA and CWC lack a clear mandate for inspection and analysis of such activities, and the BWC does not address the issue.

Notes

[1] Earlier unclassified CIA reports on problems like the ballistic missile threat often projected alternative levels of current and future capability. The qualifications and possible futures are far less well-defined in more recent reports. For example, see CIA, "Unclassified Summary of a National Intelligence Estimate, Foreign Missile Developments and the Ballistic Missile Threat Through 2015," National Intelligence Council, December 2001, available at http://www.cia.gov/nic/pubs/other_products/Unclassifiedballisticmissilefinal.htm.

[2] There is no way to determine just how much the Special Plans Office team set up within the Office of the Secretary of Defense to analyze the threat in Iraq was designed to produce a given conclusion or politicized intelligence. The Defense Department has denied this and stated that the team created within its policy office was not working on Iraq per se, but on global terrorist interconnections. It also stated that the Special Plans Office was never tied to the Intelligence Collection Program—a program to debrief Iraqi defectors—and relied on CIA inputs for its analysis. Rather, it states that the special team simply conducted a review, presented its findings in August 2002, and then team members returned to other duties. See Jim Garamone, "Policy Chief Seeks to Clear Intelligence Record," American Forces Information Service, June 3, 2003; and Douglas J. Feith, undersecretary of defense for policy, and William J. Luti, deputy undersecretary of defense for special plans and Near East and South Asian affairs (briefing, June 4, 2003, available at http://www.defenselink.mil/transcripts/2003/tr20030604-0248.html).

Some intelligence experts dispute this view, however, and claim that the team was used to put pressure on the intelligence community. Such "B-teams" also have a mixed history. They did help identify an intelligence community tendency to underestimate strategic nuclear efforts of the Soviets during the Cold War. However, the analysis by the "Rumsfeld Commission" of missile threats to the United States was a heavily one-sided assessment designed to justify national missile defense. Also see Greg Miller, "Pentagon Defends Role of Intelligence Unit on Iraq," *Los Angeles Times,* June 5, 2003; and David S. Cloud, "The Case for War Relied on Selective Intelligence," *Wall Street Journal,* June 5, 2003.

[3] Some press sources cite what they claim was a deliberate effort to ignore a September 2002 Defense Intelligence Agency (DIA) report on Iraqi chemical weapons capabilities entitled "Iraq—Key WMD Facilities: An Operational Support Study." See James Risen, "Word that U.S. Doubted Iraq Would Use Gas," *New York Times,* June 18, 2003; and Tony Capaccio, "Pentagon 2002 Study Reported No Reliable Data on Iraq Weapons," *USA Today,* June 6, 2003.

In fact, the unclassified excerpts from the DIA report show that DIA was not stating that Iraq did not have chemical weapons, but, rather, that the agency had "no reliable information on whether Iraq is producing and stockpiling chemical weapons, or where Iraq has—or will—establish its chemical weapons facilities." The report went on to say that "although we lack any direct information, Iraq probably possesses CW agent in chemical munitions, possibly including artillery rockets, artillery shells, aerial bombs, and ballistic missile warheads. Baghdad also probably possesses bulk chemical stockpiles, primarily containing precursors, but that also could consist of some mustard agent of stabilized VX."

If anything, the report is a classic example of what happens when intelligence reports do state uncertainty and the user misreads or misuses the result.

[4] "UN Atomic Agency Seeks to Visit Key Iranian Defense Site: Diplomats," Agence France-Presse, September 10, 2004.

[5] Alireza Jafarzadeh, "Iranian Regime's Plan and Attempts to Start Uranium Enrichment at Natanz Site" (statement at the National Press Club, Washington, D.C., January 10, 2006).

[6] "Iran Says It Will Resume Uranium Conversion Today," Global Security Newswire, August 11, 2005, available at http://www.nti.org/d_newswire/issues/2005/8/1/6860ebe5-d0a1-428e-829d-6005c7b26698.html.

[7] Dafna Linzer, "Powell Says Iran Is Pursuing Bomb," *Washington Post,* November 18, 2004, sec. A-1.

[8] Dafna Linzer, "Nuclear Disclosure on Iran Unverified," *Washington Post,* November 19, 2004, sec. A-1.

[9] Linzer, "Powell Says Iran Is Pursuing Bomb."

[10] Linzer, "Nuclear Disclosure on Iran Unverified."

[11] Sonni Efron, Tyler Marshall, and Bob Drogin, "Powell's Talk of Arms Has Fallout," *Los Angeles Times,* November 19, 2004.

[12] Carla Anne Robbins, "As Evidence Grows of Iran's Program, U.S. Hits Quandary," *Wall Street Journal*, March 18, 2005, p. 1.

[13] IAEA, *Implementation of the NPT Safeguards Agreement in the Islamic Republic of Iran: Report by the Director General*, November 15, 2004, p. 18, available at http://www.iaea.org/Publications/Documents/Board/2004/gov2004-83_derestrict.pdf.

[14] John R. Bolton, "Preventing Iran from Acquiring Nuclear Weapons" (remarks to the Hudson Institute, Washington, D.C., August 17, 2004).

[15] Dafna Linzer, "Strong Leads and Dead Ends in Nuclear Case against Iran," *Washington Post*, February 8, 2006, sec. A-1.

[16] Bolton, "Preventing Iran from Acquiring Nuclear Weapons."

[17] Ibid.

[18] IAEA, *Implementation of the NPT Safeguards Agreement in the Islamic Republic of Iran: Report by the Director General*, September 2, 2005, Annex 1, p. 14, available at http://www.iaea.org/Publications/Documents/Board/2005/gov2005-67.pdf.

[19] Ibid., p. 7.

[20] "Iran Far from Nuclear Bomb-Making Capacity: Ex-UN Weapons Chief Blix," Agence France-Presse, June 23, 2005.

[21] Ali Akbar Dareini, "Iran Hits Milestone in Nuclear Technology," Associated Press, April 11, 2006.

[22] Ali Akbar Dareini, "Iran to Move to Large Scale Enrichment," Associated Press, April 12, 2006.

[23] *Wikipedia* defines laser isotope separation as follows: "In this method a laser is tuned to a wavelength which excites only one isotope of the material and ionizes those atoms preferentially. The resonant absorption of light for an isotope is dependent upon its mass and certain hyperfine interactions between electrons and the nucleus, allowing finely tuned lasers to only interact with one isotope. After the atom is ionized it can be removed from the sample by applying an electric field. This method is often abbreviated as AVLIS (atomic vapor laser isotope separation). This method has only recently been developed as laser technology has improved, and is currently not used extensively. However, it is a major concern to those in the field of nuclear proliferation because it may be cheaper and more easily hidden than other methods of isotope separation.

A second method of laser separation is known as MLIS, Molecular Laser Isotope Separation. In this method, an infrared laser is directed at uranium hexafluoride gas, exciting molecules that contain a U-235 atom. A second laser frees a fluorine atom, leaving uranium pentafluoride which then precipitates out of the gas. Cascading the MLIS stages is more difficult than with other methods because the UF5 must be refluorinated (back to UF6) before being introduced into the next MLIS stage. Alternative MLIS schemes are currently being developed (using a first laser in the near-infrared or visible region) where an enrichment of over 95% can be obtained in a single stage, but the methods have not (yet) reached industrial feasibility. This method is called OP-IRMPD (Overtone Pre-excitation—IR Multiple Photon Dissociation)." [*Wikipedia*, available at http://en.wikipedia.org/wiki/Isotope_separation]

[24] *Wikipedia* provides the following technical background on cascades and centrifuges: "All large-scale isotope separation schemes employ a number of similar stages which produce successively higher concentrations of the desired isotope. Each stage enriches the product of the previous step further before being sent to the next stage. Similarly, the tailings from each stage are returned to the previous stage for further processing. This creates a sequential enriching system called a cascade.

The only alternative to isotope separation is to manufacture the required isotope in its pure form. This may be done by irradiation of a suitable target, but care is needed in target selection and other factors to ensure that only the required isotope of the element of interest is produced. Isotopes of other elements are not so great a problem as they can be removed by chemical means.

This is particularly relevant in the preparation of high-grade plutonium-239 for use in weapons and in military propulsion reactors. It is not in practice possible to separate Pu-239 from Pu-240 or Pu-241. Fissile Pu-239 is produced following neutron capture by uranium-238, but further neutron capture will produce non-fissile Pu-240 and worse, then Pu-241 which is a fairly strong neutron emitter. Therefore, the uranium targets used to produce military plutonium must be irradiated for only a short time, to minimise the production of these unwanted isotopes. Conversely salting plutonium with Pu-241 renders it unsuitable for nuclear weapons.

. . . the diffusion method relies on the fact that in thermal equilibrium, two isotopes with the same energy will have different average velocities. The lighter atoms (or the molecules containing them) will travel more quickly and be more likely to diffuse through a membrane. The difference in speeds is proportional to the square root of the mass ratio, so the amount of separation is small and many cascaded stages are needed to obtain high purity. This method is expensive due to the work needed to push gas through a membrane and the many stages necessary.

The first large-scale separation of uranium isotopes was achieved by the United States in large gaseous diffusion separation plants at Oak Ridge Laboratories, which were established as part of the Manhattan Project. These used uranium hexafluoride gas as the process fluid.

. . . Centripetal effect schemes rapidly rotate the material allowing the heavier isotopes to go closer to an outer radial wall. This too is often done in gaseous form using a Zippe-type centrifuge.

Gas centrifuges using uranium hexafluoride have largely replaced gaseous diffusion technology for uranium enrichment. As well as requiring less energy to achieve the same separation, far smaller scale plants are possible, making them an economic possibility for a small nation attempting to produce a nuclear weapon. Pakistan is believed to have used this method in developing its nuclear weapons.

Vortex tubes were used by South Africa in their Helikon vortex separation process. The gas is injected tangentially into a chamber with special geometry that further increases its rotation to a very high rate, causing the isotopes to separate. The method is simple because vortex tubes have no moving parts, but [are] energy intensive (about 50 times greater than gas centrifuges). A similar process, known as Jet Nozzle, was created in Germany, with a demonstration plant built in Brazil, and they [have] gone as far as developing a site to fuel the country's nuclear plants." [*Wikipedia*, available at http://en.wikipedia.org/wiki/Isotope_separation]

[25] Nazila Fathi and Christine Hauser, "Iran Marks Step in Nuclear Development," *New York Times*, April 11, 2006.

[26] IAEA, *Implementation of the NPT Safeguards Agreement: Report by the Director General*, November 15, 2004.

[27] Bolton, "Preventing Iran from Acquiring Nuclear Weapons."

[28] IAEA, *Implementation of the NPT Safeguards Agreement: Report by the Director General*, September 2, 2005.

[29] Ibid.

[30] Ibid.

[31] David Albright and Corey Hinderstein, "Iran's Next Steps: Final Tests and the Construction of a Uranium Enrichment Plant," Institute for Science and International Security (ISIS), Issue Brief, January 12, 2006, available at http://www.isis-online.org/publications/iran/irancascade.pdf.

[32] *Wikipedia* defines the SWU (separative work unit) as follows: "a complex unit which is a function of the amount of uranium processed and the degree to which it is enriched, i.e., the extent of increase in the concentration of the U-235 isotope relative to the remainder.

The unit is strictly: Kilogram Separative Work Unit, and it measures the quantity of separative work (indicative of energy used in enrichment) when feed and product quantities are expressed in kilograms. The effort expended in separating a mass F of feed of assay xf into a mass P of product assay xp and waste of mass W and assay xw is expressed in terms of the number of separative work units needed, given by the expression $SWU = WV(xw) + PV(xp) - FV(xf)$, where $V(x)$ is the "value function," defined as $V(x) = (1 - 2x) \ln((1 - x)/x)$.

... If, for example, you begin with 100 kilograms (220 pounds) of natural uranium, it takes about 60 SWU to produce 10 kilograms (22 pounds) of uranium enriched in U-235 content to 4.5%." [*Wikipedia*, available at http://en.wikipedia.org/wiki/Isotope_separation]

[33] Frank Barnaby, "Iran's Nuclear Activities," Oxford Research Group, February 2006, available at http://www.oxfordresearchgroup.org.uk/publications/briefings/IranNuclear.htm.

[34] IAEA, *Implementation of the NPT Safeguards Agreement in the Islamic Republic of Iran: Report by the Director General*, September 1, 2004, Annex, p. 7, available at http://www.iaea.org/Publications/Documents/Board/2004/gov2004-60.pdf.

[35] Ibid.

[36] Ibid.

[37] IAEA, *Implementation of the NPT Safeguards Agreement: Report by the Director General*, September 1, 2004, Annex, p. 7.

[38] Barnaby, "Iran's Nuclear Activities."

[39] Ali Akbar, "Iran Confirms Uranium-To-Gas Conversion," Associated Press, May 9, 2005.

[40] Elaine Sciolino and William J. Broad, "Atomic Agency Sees Possible Link of Military to Iran Nuclear Work," *New York Times*, February 1, 2006, sec. A-1.

[41] Linzer, "Strong Leads and Dead Ends in Nuclear Case against Iran."

[42] IAEA, *Implementation of the NPT Safeguards Agreement in the Islamic Republic of Iran: Resolution Adopted on 4 February 2006*, February 4, 2006, available at http://www.iaea.org/Publications/Documents/Board/2006/gov2006-14.pdf.

[43] IAEA, *Implementation of the NPT Safeguards Agreement in the Islamic Republic of Iran: Report by the Director General*, November 18, 2005, p. 11, available at http://www.iaea.org/Publications/Documents/Board/2005/gov2005-87.pdf.

[44] Ian Traynor, "Papers Found in Iran are Evidence of Plans for Nuclear Weapon Manufacture, Says UK," *Guardian* (Manchester), November 25, 2005, available at http://www.guardian.co.uk/iran/story/0,,1650423,00.html.

[45] "Iran Hands over Suspected Atom Bomb Blueprint: IAEA," Agence France-Presse, November 18, 2005.

[46] David Albright and Corey Hinderstein, "The Clock Is Ticking, but How Fast?" Institute for Science and International Security (ISIS), Issue Brief, March 27, 2006, available at http://www.isis-online.org/publications/iran/clockticking.pdf.

[47] Ibid.

[48] "Iran Far from Nuclear Bomb-Making Capacity: Ex-UN Weapons Chief Blix," Agence France-Presse, June 23, 2005.

[49] Kelly Hearn, "Iranian Pact with Venezuela Stokes Fears of Uranium Sales," *Washington Times*, March 13, 2006, sec. A-1.

[50] Some questions have been addressed. See IAEA, "Communication of 13 June 2004 from the Permanent Mission of the Islamic Republic of Iran concerning the Report of the Director General," Information Circular 630, GOV/2004/34, June 16, 2004, available at http://aolsearch.aol.com/aol/search?encquery=c2d8bdc 991a7abe41e0508cdc4c4c7e6&invocationType=keyword_rollover&ie=UTF-8.

[51] Statement by Hasan Rowhani, Supreme National Security Council of Iran, February 2004, available at http://english.people.com.cn/200402/26/eng2004 0226_135937.shtml; and http://www.mehrnews.com/en/NewsDetail.aspx?News ID=61933.

[52] Statement by Richard Boucher, U.S. State Department, June 17, 2004, available at Iran Watch, http://www.iranwatch.org/government/US/DOS/us-dos -boucher-061704.htm.

[53] David Albright and Corey Hinderstein, "Uncovering the Nuclear Black Market: Working Toward Closing Gaps in the International Nonproliferation Regime," Institute for Science and International Security (ISIS) (paper prepared for the Institute for Nuclear Materials Management [INMM] annual meeting, Orlando, Florida, July 2, 2004).

[54] Ibid.

[55] National Council of Resistance of Iran (NCRI), "Defense Ministry and the Revolutionary Guards Engaged in Production of Centrifuges," August 18, 2005, available at http://www.iranwatch.org/privateviews/ncri/perspex-ncri-centrifuges -081805.htm.

[56] Sciolino and Broad, "Atomic Agency Sees Possible Link of Military to Iran Nuclear Work."

[57] Linzer, "Powell Says Iran Is Pursuing Bomb."

[58] Linzer, "Strong Leads and Dead Ends in Nuclear Case against Iran."

[59] Ibid.

[60] IAEA, *Implementation of the NPT Safeguards Agreement: Resolution Adopted on 4 February 2006*.

[61] Linzer, "Strong Leads and Dead Ends in Nuclear Case against Iran."

CHAPTER SIX

THE HISTORY OF IRAN'S NUCLEAR PROGRAMS

There are reasons that it is Iran's "possible" nuclear weapons programs, and not its chemical and biological weapons programs, that have become the center of international concern and attention. Iran has openly admitted its ambition to acquire "nuclear technology," but Tehran has consistently insisted that all of its efforts are intended to serve peaceful purposes. The result has been a long international "duel" between Iran and the International Atomic Energy Agency, and between Iranian denials and charges made by other governments and outside experts.

Experts have long questioned why Iran needs nuclear power, given its vast gas and oil resources. There have been many analyses—even some Iranian analyses—showing that Iran's use of nuclear reactors will not be cost-effective for decades, if ever. But Iran has insisted since the late 1960s, that it will run out of fossil fuel and that nuclear power is cost-effective enough in the near term to allow it to profit by freeing up oil and gas for export. More recently, Tehran has insisted that its population has doubled over the last 30 years, that even gas is used more productively in exports than as a substitute for nuclear power, and that it is in Iran's national security interest to have a full nuclear fuel cycle that hostile states cannot interrupt.

This "duel" has now reached the point of an international crisis. Since 2002, Iran and the IAEA have been in on-and-off negotiations and inspection modes. The IAEA has discovered a number of disturbing details about Iran's uranium enrichment program that are similar to Libya's nuclear weapons program, including the possible ability to produce P-2 centrifuges. Iran has also conducted experiments with uranium hexafluoride (UF_6) that could fuel a weapons-oriented enrichment program, and it has worked on a heavy water plant that could be used in a reactor design that would produce fissile material far more efficiently than its Russian-supplied light water reactor.

IRAN'S NUCLEAR PROGRAM UNDER THE SHAH

To fully understand the debate over Iran's nuclear ambitions, one must understand the history of Iran's efforts. Iran has denied that it was developing nuclear weapons since reports first surfaced in the early 1970s, during the time of the shah. However, many believe that Iran's nuclear ambitions were the product of the Cold War and its close alliance with the United States. The United States' Atoms for Peace Program can be traced back to the Eisenhower administration and to President Dwight Eisenhower's speech to the United Nations in December 1953 in which he argued that nuclear technology should be used for peaceful purposes.[1]

Experts believe that Iran's close relationship with the United States during the Cold War allowed Iran to initiate its nuclear research. Its agreement with the United States under the Atoms for Peace program required that Iran make a commitment not to pursue nuclear weapons, but it allowed Iran to pursue "peaceful" nuclear research with only limited real-world controls. Iran and the United States also signed an agreement in 1957 that laid the groundwork for the delivery of a 5-megawatt light water research reactor. The reactor was commissioned in 1967 at the Tehran Nuclear Research Center.[2]

Somewhat ironically, U.S. experts encouraged Iran to diversify its energy resources and suggested that Tehran should acquire "several nuclear reactors." The proposal reportedly came from the Stanford Research Institute. The shah did not accept all of the proposals in such studies, but they did influence him to consider plans to build up to 23 nuclear reactors. In 1975 the Autonomic Energy Organization of Iran signed an agreement with the Massachusetts Institute of Technology to train Iranian nuclear scientists. Other countries also played a part in building Iran's nuclear research facilities. For example, France assisted Iran in building the nuclear technology center at Esfahan in the mid-1970s, and the Esfahan reactors were supplied by China.[3]

As a result, Iran's nuclear research capabilities and facilities expanded during the shah's reign—albeit under close U.S. scrutiny. The following chronology tracks key areas of nuclear developments in Iran under the shah:[4]

- **1957**: Under the U.S. Atoms for Peace program, the United States and Iran sign a civil nuclear cooperation agreement that provides for technical assistance, the lease of several kilograms of enriched uranium, and cooperation on research on the peaceful uses of nuclear energy.

  The Institute of Nuclear Science, under the auspices of the Central Treaty Organization (CENTO), moves from Baghdad to Tehran, prompting Shah Mohammed Reza Pahlavi to develop a personal interest in nuclear energy.

- **1959**: The shah orders the establishment of a nuclear research center at Tehran University.

- **1960**: Iran arranges to purchase a 5-megawatt research center at Tehran University.

- **February 11, 1961**: The U.S. Department of State disagrees with the Joint Chiefs of Staff's suggestion to place nuclear weapons in Iran.[5]

- **1967**: Iran builds the Tehran Nuclear Research Center (TNRC) at Tehran University. It has a 5-megawatt pool-type thermal research reactor supplied by the United States and is to be operated by the Atomic Energy Organization of Iran.[6] The United States supplies Iran with "hot cells" capable of separating only grams of uranium (hot cells are defined as "heavily shielded rooms with remotely operated arms used to chemically separate material irradiated in the research reactor, possibly including plutonium-laden "targets").[7]

- **November 1967**: The reactor at the Tehran Nuclear Research Center goes critical, using 93 percent enriched uranium supplied by the United States.[8]

- **July 1, 1968**: Iran signs the Nuclear Non-Proliferation Treaty (NPT).

- **March 1969**: The Commissariat à l'Energie Atomique (CEA) of France and Iran agree for the CEA to repair the research reactor in Tehran.[9]

- **March 13, 1969:** The White House extends the Agreement for Cooperation concerning Civil Uses of Atomic Energy of 1957 for another 10 years.[10]

- **March 5, 1970:** After being ratified by the Majlis (the Iranian parliament), the NPT comes into effect.[11]

- **1970s:** The United States encourages Iran to expand its non-oil energy base. A study by the Stanford Research Institute concludes that Iran will need an electrical capacity of 20,000 megawatts by 1990; the U.S. government suggests that Iran should use nuclear energy and work with American companies to develop this capacity.[12]

- **December 1972:** The Iranian government announces that it intends to obtain nuclear power plants within 10 years, and Iran's Ministry of Water and Power begins to study the possibility of constructing a nuclear power plant in southern Iran.[13]

- **March 1974:** Iran establishes the Atomic Energy Organization of Iran (AEOI), to be headed by the Swiss-trained nuclear physicist Dr. Akbar Etemad. The organization's budget for 1975 is set at $30.8 million.[14]

- **May 1974:** Iran signs a nuclear cooperation agreement with India, and the communiqué states that contracts will be made "between the atomic energy organizations in the two countries in order to establish a basis for cooperation in this field."[15] Iran's safeguards agreement with the IAEA enters into force (May 15).[16]

- **June 1974:** The shah says that Iran will have nuclear weapons "without a doubt and sooner than one would think." The statement is denied by Iran's embassy in Paris, and the shah later declares that "not only Iran, but also other nations in the region should refrain from planning to gain atomic arsenals." The United States and Iran reach a provisional agreement for the United States to supply two nuclear reactors and enriched uranium fuel.[17]

- **November 1974:** The Iranian government awards a contract to Kraftwerk Union (KWU) of West Germany (a subsidiary of Siemens) to construct two Siemens 1,200-megawatt nuclear reactors at Bushehr.[18] It also signs a contract with Framatome of France for two 900-megawatt reactors at Bandar-e Abbas. The agreements stipulate that France and Germany will provide enriched uranium for the initial loading and 10 years' worth of supplies. Plans are provided on a "super turnkey" basis with the French and German companies supplying nuclear facilities and the supporting infrastructure. Iran also agrees to form a U.S.-Iran Joint Commission to strengthen ties between the two countries, including in the areas of nuclear energy and power generation.

- **Mid-1970s:** Denmark supplies Iran with 10 kilograms (kg) of highly enriched uranium (HEU) and 25 kg of natural uranium for research reactor fuel. Note: After Iraq's bombing attacks on Iran's Bushehr reactors in November 1987, the International Atomic Energy Agency (IAEA) confirms that Iran had moved a small amount of research reactor fuel to the site in hopes of heading off an attack. One source indicates the fuel was supplied by Denmark.[19]

- **1975:** U.S. specialist George Quester suggests that Iran's Atomic Energy Commission has a staff of approximately 150 people trained in nuclear physics, with more than half of the commission's foreign staff coming from Argentina. In addition, Iran has advisors from Britain, the United States, and India and is also sending students abroad for training in nuclear science.[20]

The AEOI and the Massachusetts Institute of Technology reach agreement for MIT to begin training Iranian nuclear engineers. Iran also founds the Esfahan Nuclear Technology Center (ENTC), which will operate with French assistance and train personnel who will work at the Bushehr reactors that will be constructed.[21]

The shah claims that it would be "ridiculous" for Iran to have nuclear weapons, considering the arsenals held by the United States and Soviet Union. He also says his country has "no intention of acquiring nuclear weapons but if small states began building them, then Iran might have to reconsider its policy."

The United States and Iran sign an agreement for eight reactors valued at $6.4 billion. The U.S. Atomic Energy Commission will supply Iran with fuel for two 1,200-megawatt light water reactors and signs a provisional agreement to offer fuel for as many as six additional reactors with a total power capacity of 8,000 mega-watts electric (MWe). (The agreements are subject to U.S. governmental approval).[22]

- **February 1975:** Iran and India sign a nuclear cooperation agreement. A U.S. State Department memorandum says Iran is interested in at least four dual-purpose nuclear power and desalination plants, worth about $1 billion each.[23] In March, Iran says it will award contracts to U.S. firms for nuclear power and desalination plants of up to 8,000 MWe. Iran says it is prepared to invest $2.75 billion in a private enrichment plan in the United States.

- **March 1975:** Iran pushes for reprocessing facilities to be located within its borders. The United States and Iran continue discussions on the issue. Officials at the U.S. Energy Research and Development Administration rank countries in descending order of their likelihood to seek nuclear weapons development: India, Taiwan, South Korea, Pakistan, Indonesia, and Iran [least likely].

- **May 9, 1975:** A U.S. State Department briefing memorandum to Secretary of State Henry Kissinger says that the outstanding issue in the U.S.-Iranian nuclear accord is whether to allow Iran to reprocess U.S.-supplied plutonium.

- **August 1975:** A German team from Kraftwerk Union begins work on the Bushehr reactors on the basis of a letter of intent.

- **October 1975–September 1976:** The budget for the AEOI is more than $1 billion for fiscal year 1976.

- **1976:** Iran agrees to buy $700 million of yellowcake from South Africa in exchange for help in financing an enrichment plant in South Africa. "According to the U.S. State Department, an official with the Atomic Energy Organization of Iran confirms, despite public denial, that a secret agreement was reached for Iran to purchase uranium, which may have originated in Namibia. Independent sources are unable to verify the delivery of the material."[24]

Kraftwerk Union wins a contract to construct nuclear plants in Iran.

- **May 1976:** "The United States supplies 226 kg of depleted uranium to Iran for aircraft wing ballast."[25]

- **July 1, 1976:** The AEOI signs an agreement with Kraftwerk Union for the construction of the Bushehr nuclear power plant at a cost of 7.8 billion DM, 5.8 billion of which Iran has already paid. The agreement stipulates that KWU will construct two pressurized light water units 18 kilometers (km) southwest of Bushehr. Both units will have outputs of 1,296 megawatts (MW). The AEOI signs additional agreements with KWU for the supply of 200,000 cubic meters of pure water and the required fuel for the Bushehr plant.

- **August 1976:** Talks between Iran and the United States on nuclear cooperation are suspended after disagreement on safeguards.

- **October 1976:** French president Valery Giscard d'Estaing signs an agreement for Iran to purchase two French reactors immediately and six more in the future.

- **1977:** Iran agrees to pay 943 million French francs (approximately $180 million) for future uranium enrichment services from the Eurodif consortium's Tricastin plant.

- **May 13, 1977:** France agrees to build two 900 MW nuclear power generators in Iran worth $2 billion. The plants will be built in the town of Darkhovin on the Karun River, near Ahvaz. France says it is ready to build eight additional nuclear plants for $16 billion if the United States withdraws from an agreement to build eight plants. The nuclear reactors under construction in Germany for Bushehr are 30 percent complete.

- **August 9, 1977:** Iran states that it has no intention of constructing a reprocessing facility.

- **September 13, 1977:** France agrees to sell Iran two nuclear reactors and to train 350 Iranian technicians.

- **October 1977:** France and Iran finalize a deal for two French reactors to be built at Darkhovin.

- **October 3, 1977:** The Iranian news agency reports that Iran and Austria will cooperate in nuclear waste storing.

- **November 11, 1977:** Iran and Kraftwerk Union sign a letter of intent to build four additional 1,200 MWe pressurized water reactors in Iran worth $5 billion, two near the Indus area of Esfahan and the other two between Esfahan and Lake Rezaiyyah (modern-day Lake Urmiyyah) on the Iranian-Turkish border.

- **October 1978:** Facing internal criticism about Iran's nuclear power program and financial difficulties, the shah postpones the purchase of four additional reactors from Kraftwerk Union. Akbar Etemad, director of the Atomic Energy Organization of Iran, resigns amid allegations of mismanagement and embezzlement.

- **October 17, 1978:** A secret U.S. Department of State telegram from the U.S. embassy in Iran to the secretary of state says now is not a good time to conclude a bilateral nuclear agreement between the United States and Iran because the unstable political situation in Iran and a reorganization of Iranian bureaucracy has halted all proceedings.

- **Late 1970s:** The United States obtains intelligence data indicating that the shah has set up a clandestine nuclear weapons development program. Also, according to Akbar Etemad, director of the Atomic Energy Organization of Iran until October 1978, researchers at the Tehran Nuclear Research Center are involved in laboratory experiments that could have applications for reprocessing spent fuel.

- **1979:** The United States stops supplying highly enriched uranium to Iran. Iran cancels a deal with the French for the Karun River nuclear power plant at Darkhovin near Ahvaz. Approximately one-tenth of the tonnage of plant equipment for the reactor at Bushehr is shipped from West Germany before the project is halted in 1979. The *Middle East Economic Review* reports that Iran is seeking to purchase a 30 MW research reactor.

While this chronology may seem detailed, there are long periods for which very little data are available on any aspect of Iran's nuclear efforts, leaving serious gaps in the historical flow of the evidence. U.S. experts also confirm that Iran was detected attempting to buy controlled technologies like laser isotope separation during this period, that it made some illegal purchases, and that it collected literature on nuclear weapons design and production. Iran has also always claimed to comply with arms control agreements, and, for each new discovery, has always found an explanation claiming its actions were peaceful and either research programs or efforts to create a national nuclear power program.

POST-REVOLUTION UNCERTAINTIES:
THE 1980s AND 1990s

There are strong indications that Ayatollah Khomeini revived Iran's nuclear weapons program after Iraq started to use chemical weapons against Iran during the Iran-Iraq War. While Iran continued to state that it is not developing nuclear weapons, and some of its clerics stated that such weapons were against Islamic principles, senior Iranian officials and clerics have asserted Iran's right to have nuclear weapons and the kind of nuclear fuel cycle that Iran could use to produce weapons grade materials.

Evidence has surfaced again and again that Iran might be lying, and that many of Iran's "peaceful" nuclear activities were actually under the direct or indirect control of the Islamic Revolutionary Guards Corps. However, there was no conclusive evidence Iran was developing a weapon.

The history of every aspect of Iran's nuclear programs during the 1980s and 1990s is more uncertain than events during the time of the shah. The following chronology, however, shows that Tehran's intention to rebuild its nuclear research facilities did not stop at the start of the revolution in 1979:[26]

- **1979:** Following the Iranian revolution, construction at the Bushehr plant is suspended, with Bushehr 1 90 percent complete and Bushehr 2 50 percent complete.[27]

- **April 11, 1979:** Fereydun Sahabi, Iran's deputy minister of energy and supervisor of the Atomic Energy Organization of Iran, states that the AEOI is significantly cutting back its activities.

- **May 1979:** A Khomeini adviser tells energy specialist Dr. Fereydun Fesharaki, "It is your duty to build the atomic bomb for the Islamic Republican Party."

- **1980s:** Iran looks for companies to finish the Bushehr reactor but with no success. U.S. pressure prevents Kraftwerk Union from working in Iran. A variety of companies from Argentina, Spain, Germany, Italy, and Czechoslovakia express their intent to work with Iran but to no avail.[28]

- **1984:** Iran opens a nuclear research center at Esfahan with the assistance of China.

- **March 1984:** Iraq bombs both Bushehr plants.[29]

- **April 1984:** *Jane's Defence Weekly* reports that West German intelligence estimates that Iran may have a nuclear bomb within two years. According to a French report, "very enriched uranium" from Pakistan can contribute to this effort.

- **February 1985:** Iraq bombs Bushehr for the second time.[30]

- **March 1985:** Iraq bombs Bushehr for the third time.[31]

- **November 1985:** Iran signs an agreement with an unnamed foreign contractor for a water desalination plant to provide fresh water for use in nuclear plants.

- **December 1985:** Argentina and Iran sign a nuclear cooperation agreement in which Argentina agrees to supply Iran with 20 percent enriched uranium (HEU).

- **February 1986:** Abdul Qadir Khan, Pakistan's leading nuclear scientist, makes a secret visit to Bushehr. Pakistan and Iran sign a secret nuclear cooperation agreement later in the year.

- **July 1986:** Iraq bombs Bushehr for the fourth time.[32]

- **1987:** Iran says it plans to build a yellowcake plant in Yazd Province.

- **January 1987:** At a secret meeting, Iranian officials decide to allocate additional funds toward developing nuclear weapons.[33]

- **January 1987:** Fereydun Fesharaki, who headed the shah's secret nuclear weapons program, returns to Iran after a seven-year exile; all of his expenses are paid by the government.[34]

- **November 1987:** Iraq bombs Bushehr for the fifth and sixth times; at this point, the core areas of both facilities are completely destroyed.[35]

- **1988:** Iran approaches Pakistan for help in enriching uranium. The head of Pakistan's uranium enrichment program begins to hold talks with officials of the Atomic Energy Organization of Iran. Rumors persist that Pakistan is helping Iran to develop nuclear weapons.

Iran receives a delivery of large quantities of uranium concrete from South Africa. A book reports that Iran owns 15 percent of the Rossig uranium mine in Namibia.[36]

- **Early 1990s:** The Iranian government makes a decision that 10 nuclear units will provide 20 percent of energy in Iran by 2005.[37]

- **February 7, 1990:** Iran's speaker of the parliament, Mehdi Karrubi, inaugurates the Jabir bin al-Hayyan laboratory. Operated by the Atomic Energy Organization of Iran, it will be geared to teaching nuclear technology.[38]

- **March 1990:** Iran possibly opens a uranium ore processing plant near the Saghand uranium mine in Yazd province.[39]

- **March 6, 1990:** The Soviet Union and Iran sign a protocol for the USSR to build two VVER 440 reactors in Iran. In turn, Iran will provide 3 billion cubic meters of natural gas. The countries also agree to cooperate on nuclear research for peaceful purposes. The agreement also provides for the Soviet Union to complete the two 1,293 MW pressurized water reactors at Bushehr.[40]

- **March 14, 1990:** The Esfahan Nuclear Technology Center opens. The center includes subcritical mass reactors and neutron production laboratories designed and built by the AEOI for the purpose of gaining the technology to design nuclear reactors. The reactors use natural uranium.

- **March 15, 1990:** *Nuclear Developments* reports that according to a *Jane's* publication, Chile, Iran, South Korea, and Libya can produce nuclear weapons.[41]

- **Third quarter 1990:** According to the *PPNN Newsbrief,* delays in production at the Pilcanyeu enrichment plant mean that Argentina may have to revise its contracts for delivery of 20 percent enriched uranium for the research reactors it has supplied to Algeria, Iran, and Peru.[42]

- **1991:** Iran purchases a cyclotron accelerator from Ion Beam Applications, a Belgian company. The cyclotron is meant to be used in Iran's Nuclear Medical Research Center in Karaj. The center is purportedly civilian, but Chinese and Russian technicians have been seen at the site.[43]

China provides Iran with 1,000 kg of natural uranium hexafluoride, a gas that can be used to enrich uranium.[44]

- **September 1991:** U.S. satellite photos show construction on a plutonium production plant and a large number of Chinese technicians at Esfahan.[45] Construction also begins at Esfahan on a 27-kilowatt (kW) research reactor provided by China.

- **November 1991:** Hans Blix, director general of the International Atomic Energy Agency, says he has "no cause for concern" about Iran's attempts to acquire nuclear technology. At the same time, he says the IAEA may begin implementing special inspections with Iran as a possible test case.

A statement by China's foreign ministry (November 4) announces the details of China's cooperation with Iran; it says that China signed deals to provide Iran with an electromagnetic separator for isotope production in 1989 and a small reaction in 1991. The statement reads: "These facilities are used for nuclear medical diagnosis and nuclear physics research, isotope production, education and personnel training. . . . Guided by the internationally observed regulations, China had requested the International Atomic Energy Agency to enforce safeguards before these facilities were shipped." Joseph Snyder, a U.S. State Department press officer, commented that "we are concerned that any dual-use equipment sold to Iran for commercial purposes could be diverted to other applications."[46]

- **December 1991:** Nuclear warheads from Kazakhstan are reportedly transferred to Iran through Turkmenistan.[47]

- **1992:** The International Atomic Energy Agency twice inspects nuclear facilities identified in news media and intelligence reports as sites where Iran is developing nuclear weapons. The IAEA finds no evidence of illegal activity either time. In another visit to a nuclear facility cited as having a fissile material production pilot program, inspectors find no evidence of undeclared activities.

The United States says that the IAEA was unable to detect the alleged activities because it did not have access to the same detailed, highly classified intelligence information that the United States had. Diplomatic sources, however, suggest that the United States offer the IAEA limited intelligence information on Iran's alleged covert nuclear activities. The validity of U.S. data, however, is not shared unanimously by governmental officials. For the first time, Iran declares its Esfahan site to the IAEA.[48]

- **January 1992:** Hamian Vahdati, the presumed head of Iran's nuclear program, says no country can be taken seriously without a nuclear research program, and that Iran wants to have the technology and knowledge to make nuclear weapons in case it needs them. Mahmud Vaezi, deputy foreign minister, says that Iran opposes nuclear weapons buildup.[49]

  Syria and Iran sign a "nuclear pact," according to which Iran will offer Syria a "nuclear umbrella" in case of an Israeli attack.

- **February 26, 1992:** Reza Amrollahi, president of the Iran Atomic Energy Organization, tells the International Atomic Energy Agency Board of Governors that Iran will complete the reactors of Bushehr.[50]

- **March 1992:** India resumes its agreement to sell a 10 MW nuclear research reactor to Iran.[51]

- **March 1992:** Paul Muenstermann, vice president of Germany's Federal Intelligence Service (BND), says that Iran received two of three nuclear warheads and medium-range nuclear delivery systems that are missing from Kazakhstan.[52]

- **June 1992:** Kazakh deputy Ozhas Suleymanov says the three missing nuclear weapons said to have been transferred to Iran have been found at Semipalatinsk.[53]

- **October 1992:** Ayatollah Mohajerani, deputy president of Iran, says that, "because the enemy [Israel] has nuclear facilities, the Muslim states too should be equipped with the same capacity."[54]

- **October 1, 1992:** *Nucleonics Week* reports that Liu Xuehong, deputy director general of the Ministry of Energy and Bureau of

International Cooperation at the China National Nuclear Corporation, says China cannot supply a 20 MW reactor to Iran due to "technical reasons." Iran was seeking a 25-to-30 MW heavy water–moderated natural uranium-fueled reactor.[55]

- **November 14, 1992:** According to Mayak Radio Network (Moscow), buyers from Azerbaijan bought an undisclosed portion of the uranium stolen from the Chepetsk plant; they apparently intend to sell it to Iran.[56]

- **December 1992:** Iran offers $3.5 billion to Pakistan to share its nuclear technology.[57]

- **1993:** China provides Iran with an HT-6B Tokamak fusion reactor that is installed at the Plasma Physics Research Center of Azad University.[58]

- **January 23, 1993:** Gad Yaacobi, Israel's ambassador to the United Nations, says Iran devotes $800 million per year to the development of nuclear weapons; he also says that Iran has become "the main threat now" to peace in the Middle East.[59]

- **February 1993:** The IAEA confirms that Argentina will export a shipment of 20 percent enriched uranium to Iran in 1993.[60]

- **February 21, 1993:** Iran and China sign a deal to construct two 300 MW nuclear power plants in Ahvaz.[61]

- **March 5, 1993:** According to *Proliferation Issues*, the Russian Federation Foreign Intelligence Service (FIS) has issued a report that says Iran does not possess nuclear weapons, and even with outside help, it will take Iran more than 10 years to develop nuclear weapons.[62]

- **April 13, 1993:** The Iranian parliament ratifies nuclear cooperation agreements with Russia and China. Iran will buy two VVER-440s—440 MW reactors—from Russia and two 300 MWe pressurized water reactors similar to those at Qinshan from China.[63]

- **June 18, 1993:** According to the voice of the Islamic Republic of Iran, Amir Kabir Technological University and the Atomic Energy Organization of Iran have produced an X-ray tube using cobalt-57, designed to detect uranium.[64]

- **October–November 1993:** A team from the IAEA visits three nuclear research centers, at Tehran, Esfahan, and Karaj, but is not given full access to all activities or to soil and particle samples at the sites. IAEA spokesman David Kyd reports that the team "found no evidence which was inconsistent with Iran's declaration that all its nuclear activities are peaceful."[65]

- **November 11, 1993:** Italian customs officials seize eight steam condensers for nuclear reactors, manufactured by Ansaldo, and prevent them from being exported to Iran.[66]

- **January 1994:** Italian inspectors seize ultrasound equipment at the port of Bari. The equipment can be used for reactor testing and was bound for Iran.[67]

- **March 1994:** A Chinese-supplied 27 kilowatt thermal (kWt) miniature neutron source reactor (MNSR) goes critical in March 1994.[68]

- **March 21, 1994:** Russia begins work on the first unit of Iran's 1,000 MW plant, according to a source at the plant. The plan is for the Bushehr nuclear power plant to be finished in four years. The report also suggests that 85 percent of the construction and 65 percent of the mechanical and electrical work at Bushehr is complete.[69]

- **September 1994:** A senior Iranian diplomatic official tells *Nucleonics Week* that Iran is reconsidering its membership in the NPT because the West is stifling Iran's access to nuclear power technology even though Iran is meeting its NPT obligations.[70]

- **September 11, 1994:** The head of the AEOI announces that the Bonab nuclear research center in West Azerbaijan province will conduct nuclear research for "agricultural purposes."[71]

- **September 19, 1994:** Uri Saguy, head of Israel's Army intelligence, says that Iran is likely to have developed a nuclear weapon within about eight years.[72]

- **December 5, 1995:** The *Iran Brief* reports that, according to intelligence sources in Washington, "China recently delivered a consignment of uranium hexafluoride to Iran, also known as UF_6, or more simply, as 'hex.' Hex is the gaseous form of uranium used in the enrichment process to obtain weapons-grade uranium."[73]

- **January 1995:** Following a visit, the IAEA reports that the Moallem Kalayeh facility near the city of Qazvin, allegedly housing uranium enrichment gas centrifuges, is a recreation facility for nuclear industry staff.[74]

President Akbar Hashemi Rafsanjani inaugurates the Bonab nuclear research center; it remains unclear, however, whether construction is beginning or ending.[75]

- **January 8, 1995:** Russia's minister of atomic energy, Viktor Mikhailov, and Reza Amrollahi, head of the Atomic Energy Organization of Iran, sign an $800 million contract for Russia to build a VVER-1,000 MWe reactor at Bushehr within four years.[76]

- **January 19, 1995:** President Rafsanjani inaugurates a nuclear medical research and production unit at Karaj. The facility will be used to produce radioactive materials for medical scans. It contains a cyclotron accelerator with a 30 million electron-volt power.[77]

- **February 25, 1995:** According to the Associated Press, a nuclear power plant will soon be connected to Iran's electricity grid, indicating that the plant may be near completion.[78]

- **April 21, 1995:** *Deutsche Presse-Agentur* reports Iran will sign an indefinite extension to the NPT only if the five nuclear powers agree to first reduce and then eliminate their nuclear arsenals.[79]

- **May 11, 1995:** At a joint press conference with U.S. president Bill Clinton, Russian president Boris Yeltsin announces that Russia will eliminate all "military" aspects of its nuclear deal with Iran, meaning "the creation of nuclear weapons-grade fuel and a centrifuge and the construction of silos."[80]

- **May 24, 1995:** Rainer Funke, parliamentary secretary of the German Ministry of Justice and member of the Bundestag, says that "plants placed at the disposal of Iran are not capable of producing atomic weapons."[81]

- **May 30, 1995:** Sergey Tretyakov, Russian ambassador to Iran, says "'we are convinced that Iran has no ambitions in the nuclear field. . . . when someone wants to develop a nuclear bomb, they must have the political will and the technological base. The Iranians don't have such aspirations—but even if they had, I think it would take them 50 years."[82]

- **June 1, 1995:** Reza Amrollahi, head of the Atomic Energy Organization of Iran, reportedly says that Iran will open three more yellowcake-milling facilities in Bandar-e Abbas and Bandar-e Langeh in addition to the one at Saghand.

- **June 26, 1995:** President Rafsanjani announces the completion of the first phase of a nuclear research center in Bonab.[83]

- **July 3, 1995** IAEA director general Hans Blix says that inspections have not detected any evidence of nuclear-military programs in Iran.[84]

- **August 12, 1995:** Russia signs a contract with Iran to supply Russian nuclear fuel to Iran for 10 years.

- **September 5, 1995:** Russia and Iran sign a contract for Russia to construct two additional light water VVER-440—440 MW—nuclear reactors at Bushehr.[85]

- **September 12, 1995:** Mehdi Safari, Iran's ambassador to Russia, tells Russian journalists that Iran has no desire to make nuclear weapons and that the Bushehr nuclear power station will be Iran's "first and last."[86]

- **September 27, 1995:** Chinese foreign minister Qian Qichen reportedly tells U.S. secretary of state Warren Christopher that China will not sell two 300 MW nuclear reactors to Iran. Two days later, he tells the United Nations that the site in Iran is unsuitable and that the deal has been "suspended for the time being."[87]

- **October 19, 1995:** China signs a deal with Iran to provide it with uranium processing technology. According to the *Sunday Times*, "The plant converts raw uranium into metal or gas that can then be enriched to make either fuel for nuclear weapons or for power reactors. Iran is likely to argue that the plant will be used for the latter. But nuclear experts doubt that, saying Iran does not have the facilities to manufacture reactor fuel. The plant's capacity of 100–120 tons per year also means it is much too big to be a pilot plant for research."[88]

- **December 6, 1995:** Dust-Mohammadi, technical affairs deputy of the Atomic Energy Organization of Iran, says that the location for the two nuclear reactors to be built by China has been moved from Darkhovin to Bushehr because Bushehr has "potential and plentiful water resources."[89]

- **January 2, 1996:** President Rafsanjani inaugurates a new research in Tehran. He also says Bushehr will be operational by 1999 and that, "making use of nuclear technology for peaceful purposes is something without which a country could not find its real standing in the world."[90]

- **January 7, 1996:** Brigadier General Yaaqov Amidror, the deputy head of the Israeli Defense Forces (IDF) Intelligence Branch, says that Iran will be able to produce unconventional weapons within five years.[91]

- **January 25, 1996:** Intelnews of Kiev reports that the Turboatom plant in Kharkov will sign a contract with ZagranAtomEnergoStroy for producing two turbines for the Bushehr nuclear power plant.[92]

- **February 6, 1996:** Reza Amrollahi, head of the AEOI, says that Iran has developed laser technology and produced zero-power and miniature reactors.

- **February 7, 1996:** Yevgeniy Mikerin of the Russian Ministry of Nuclear Power Engineering says that the Bushehr nuclear power plant will receive fuel from a Russian chemical plant that makes fuel cassettes for Chernobyl-type VVER-1,000 reactors.[93]

- **March 1996:** Spain and Iran negotiate a $1.5 billion agreement that includes nuclear cooperation: "Nuclear cooperation between the two countries is aimed at concluding a contract on technical monitoring of the implementation of the Iranian nuclear reactor project in Bushehr and the introduction of Western technologies into its implementation. It was agreed that the Iranian government would allocate 100m dollars for the requisite monitoring of the implementation of the Bushehr reactor project."[94]

- **March 4, 1996:** Russian minister of atomic energy Viktor Mikhailov says that the project at Bushehr should be completed in 2.5 years.[95]

- **March 1996:** According to sources at the Kurchatov Energy Institute in Moscow, Russia, Iran, India, and China sign a protocol to establish the Asian Fusion Research Foundation to further research in nuclear fusion energy.

- **March 28, 1996:** Western diplomatic sources say that Iran has bought enriched uranium from Russian diplomats in Mazar-e-Sharif in northern Afghanistan.[96]

- **April 14, 1996:** Albert Chernishev, the Russian deputy foreign minister, says that Russia's agreement with Iran is based on reactors that cannot produce plutonium to be used for nuclear weapons.[97]

- **May 1996:** According to a source at the AEOI, a Chinese-Iranian team will look for uranium deposits in eastern Iran.[98]

- **May 11, 1996:** China makes a pledge to the United States not to assist with nuclear facilities that are not internationally safeguarded.[99]

- **June 1, 1996:** Iranian president Rafsanjani tells an open session of the parliament that Iran has "endless" gas reserves and 93 billion barrels of oil reserves, which could, with improved technology, last for 150 years.[100]

- **June 7, 1996:** Sergey Tetrayakov, the Russian ambassador to Iran, says that the Bushehr project can be completed in 48 months.[101]

- **July 5, 1996:** Reza Amrollahi, head of the Atomic Energy Organization of Iran, announces Iran's intent to sell its share in a French uranium-enrichment plant.[102]

- **July 7, 1996:** According to a report by the Islamic Republic News Agency, the first reactor unit at Bushehr will be operational by 1999 and will expand the country's electricity capacity to 2,400 MW.[103]

- **August 20, 1996:** According to Reza Amrollahi, head of Atomic Energy Organization of Iran, two 300 MW nuclear power plants will be constructed by China and will be ready in nine years.[104]

- **September 25, 1996:** Iran signs the Comprehensive Test Ban Treaty, while also stating reservations that the treaty "fails to be within a framework of [a] comprehensive nuclear disarmament treaty,

[...] that in the field of control and supervision, national technical equipment only plays a complementary and temporary role [...]" and that Israel should not be in "the Middle East and eastern Asia group."[105]

- **October 16, 1996:** According to *Yadernyy Kontrol* (Moscow), Iran has "a 5 MW TRR light water reactor supplied by the United States, which uses 20 percent enriched uranium that Iran gets from Argentina; a zero-capacity heavy water reactor; a neutron source using 90 percent enriched uranium; a light water training reactor of subcritical capacity; and a graphite training reactor of subcritical capacity. All but the 5 MW reactor were supplied by China."[106]

- **December 12, 1996:** U.S. officials tell *Nucleonics Week* that China is short on meeting the conditions that the United States wants before activating a 1984 Sino-U.S. nuclear cooperation agreement between the two countries. The Chinese expression of interest in exporting a uranium hexafluoride conversion plant to Iran is of particular concern to the U.S. administration.[107]

- **March 6, 1997:** According to Iranian president Rafsanjani, the Bushehr nuclear power plant will be able to produce 2,000 MW of power.[108]

- **March 21, 1997:** Yevgeny Reshetnikov, deputy minister at the Russian Ministry of Atomic Energy (Minatom), says that the assembly of the light water reactor at Bushehr will begin in early 1998 and that its scheduled commission is 2001.[109]

- **June 2, 1997:** Iran announces that the first phase of its $33 million electron accelerator is now in operation. The center, which is in Yazd, will be used for industrial purposes and is believed to have a 3MeV (megaelectronvolt) Van de Graaff accelerator.[110]

- **June 24, 1997:** Mohammad Sadeq Ayatollahi, Iran's permanent representative to the International Atomic Energy Agency, says that the Bushehr plant will be operational in three years and that nuclear power is part of the government's plan to reduce dependence on oil; he says Iran plans to get 20 percent of its energy from nuclear power.[111]

- **June 28, 1997:** A joint estimate by European intelligence services, addressed to European Union leaders, concludes that Iran will have nuclear weapons in five or at most seven years, and that it will also possess long-range ballistic missiles capable of delivering them 3,000 km.[112]

- **February 1998:** China decides not to sell Iran hundreds of tons of anhydrous hydrogen fluoride, a chemical that can be used to enrich uranium. The sale, intended for the Esfahan Nuclear Research Center, was suspended for almost two years after China pledged to the United States that it would not make such sales to Iran.[113]

- **February 2, 1998:** Iranian subcontractors are falling behind schedule in building the reactor hall at Bushehr, producing 5 months worth of work in 25 months. Iran converts many of the contracts to Russian subcontractors on a "turn key" basis, giving the Russian team greater control over the entire project effort and systems integration.[114]

- **March 6, 1998:** Ukrainian foreign minister Hennadiy Udovenko and U.S. secretary of state Madeleine Albright sign an agreement for new export controls on weapons technology and a deal under which Ukraine will cancel its proposed nuclear cooperation with Iran.[115]

- **April 10, 1998:** The *Jerusalem Post* reports that according to top-secret Iranian documents, Iran paid $25 million for two tactical atomic weapons smuggled from the former Soviet Union.[116] The report is denied by the spokesperson for the Russian nuclear energy ministry and by the foreign minister of Kazakhstan.

- **July 29, 1998:** President Clinton signs an executive order barring U.S. aid to seven Russian firms found to have passed sensitive weapons technology to, among others, Iran.[117]

- **November 24, 1998:** Yevgeny Adamov, Russian atomic energy minister, signs an agreement with Mohammed Aghazadeh, head of the Iran's Atomic Energy Organization, to complete the Bushehr power plant and to study the possibility of building a second plant in Iran.[118]

■ **Late November 1998:** Projections on the completion of the Bushehr plant differ. According to the head of the Atomic Energy Organization of Iran, the plant will be ready in 52 months; the deputy minister of the Russia's Atomic Energy Ministry claims the plant will not be completed for 10 years; and the Russian foreign ministry says the first phase of the reactor will be completed in May 2003.[119]

■ **February 1999:** Iran agrees to buy turbines from a Russian factory in St. Petersburg, increasing significantly, but by an unspecified amount, its $850 million deal with Russia for building the Bushehr reactor.[120] The Izhorskiye Zavody machine-building company "will produce equipment for the first circuit of the reactor: the reactor vessel, the steam generator casing, the lid for the No 1 unit, as well as inner appliances. Such production takes three years, which means the equipment will be delivered late in 2001."[121]

■ **September 1999:** Four men are arrested in Georgia while trying to sell 1 kg of uranium-235. Shukri Abramidze, leader of the Georgia Academy of Sciences Physics Institute's Atomic Center, believes the U-235 was destined for Iran.[122]

■ **November 15, 1999:** The head of the AEOI says that 26 percent of the nuclear power plant in Bushehr is completed and that 25 percent of the station's power engineering equipment has been installed to date.[123]

This timeline highlights the uncertainty surrounding Iran's nuclear efforts during the 1980s and 1990s. The two milestones that many experts believe are central to understanding developments in Iran's nuclear program, however, are the 1987 and the mid-1990s offers by the A.Q. Khan network. The nature of those offers, however, remains a mystery. Iran claims that it received the drawings of centrifuges but not the designs. After initial denials, Pakistan admitted that the A.Q. Khan network offered help to Iran. It has been reported that people who were involved in the A.Q. Khan network have offered contradictory explanations about what was delivered.[124]

THE "LOST YEARS": 2000–2002

The details of Iran's nuclear programs from late 2000 to 2002 are even less clear than usual. Nevertheless, there were some interesting developments:[125]

- **January 15, 2000:** Japanese authorities arrest two former executives of Sunbeam, a Japanese optical equipment manufacturer, on suspicion that in 1995 they exported sensitive equipment to Iran; the authorities believe Iran may then have sold the equipment to North Korea in exchange for missile technology.[126]

- **February 1, 2000:** According to Yevgeny Reshetnikov, Russian deputy minister of atomic energy, the installation of the reactor at Bushehr in Iran is running 18 months behind schedule and is now expected to be completed in March 2002. According to the minister, "large-scale physical works at the site have only just begun," while it is unclear how many of the German items at the site will need to be replaced.[127]

- **March 14, 2000:** President Clinton signs the Iran Nonproliferation Act of 2000, which, among other things, bans "extraordinary payments" to Russia for financing the International Space Station in the event that Russian firms are found to be supporting Iran's nuclear weapons program.

- **April 4, 2000:** According to the Russian daily *Izvestiya*, Russian atomic energy minister Yevgeny Adamov said that Russia and Iran have reached an agreement for $3.3 billion to build three more nuclear reactors, one in Bushehr and two in a place as yet undetermined.[128]

- **April 22, 2000:** The Georgian Institute of Physics concludes that the 920 grams of the uranium that was seized in September 1999 is up to 30 percent enriched uranium-235, suggesting that it came from abroad as the substance is no longer used in Georgia.[129]

- **May 11, 2000:** Russian president Vladimir Putin signs a decree allowing Russian companies to export nuclear material to countries that have not agreed to accept full international safeguards, although the move may be directed at Russian trade with India rather than Iran.[130]

- **May 22, 2000:** According to Mehdi Safar, Iran's ambassador to Moscow, the Bushehr nuclear power plant is about 40 percent complete.[131]

- **June 1, 2000:** Iranian officials say that their country will not sign the "additional protocol" for more intrusive IAEA safeguards unless the United States ends its antagonism toward Iran's nuclear development program.[132]

- **September 21, 2000:** Russia agrees to freeze a deal for supplying Iran with laser technology that U.S. officials believe could be used to split isotopes. Yuri Bespalko, chief of the Atomic Energy Ministry's press service, states, "We think that the equipment meant for Iran does not fall under the limits of the international exports regime. . . . Nevertheless, the topic is sensitive, especially for the United States, and a decision has been made to give the issue more consideration." Boris Yatsenko, director of the Microtechnology Center at the Yefremov Institute, says that "neither the Soviet Union nor Russia has ever developed laser technology to split uranium isotopes . . . . It is senseless to speak about the possibility of exporting such a laser technology, since nobody in the world has it."[133]

- **December 27, 2000:** *Al-Sharq Al-Awsat* reports that the United States is investigating a ring smuggling uranium and plutonium from Ukraine to Iran and Iraq. The investigations are centering around a Kurd named Hanafi Yukazan, who was arrested in May in Bulgaria carrying highly enriched uranium.[134]

- **January 16, 2001:** Vitaly Nasono, spokesman for the Russian nuclear energy minister, says that the Bushehr reactor will be completed as planned in 2003, and that Russia is conducting a feasibility study for building a sector reactor in Iran.[135]

- **March 8, 2001:** According to the deputy head of the Atomic Energy Organization of Iran, the Bushehr plant is 50 percent complete. He adds that "the Russian experts' level of management and planning did not equal their level of technical qualifications."[136]

- **March 12, 2001:** The public relations service of Izhorskiye Zavody (St. Petersburg) says that the reactor equipment for the Bushehr nuclear power plant is 90 percent complete.[137]

- **March 16, 2001:** Vladimir Slivyak, cochairman of Ekozashchita, says in an interview that when it signed the contract to build the Bushehr nuclear power plant, "Russia assumed obligations that cannot be realized. The reactor was 40 percent completed by the German division of Siemens, and we received the contract on the condition that we finish all construction by the end of 2001. According to associates of Atomstroyeksport, the authors of the contract were aware that the deadline was unrealistic. Specialists are also certain that the deadline that has now been announced, the end of 2002 is also unrealistic—six years are needed."[138]

- **March 22, 2001:** Four 82-ton water tanks are about to be delivered, via St. Petersburg, to the Bushehr nuclear power plant.[139]

- **April 15, 2001:** Workers begin laying the foundations for a steam power generator at Bushehr.[140]

- **May 28, 2001:** According to Khusro Abedi, an official with the Atomic Energy Organization of Iran, the Bushehr nuclear power plant is 52 percent complete and will be finished in the next three years.[141]

- **June 27, 2001:** According to Vladimir Vinogradov, Russia's deputy atomic energy minister, the first unit at Bushehr is 80 percent complete.[142]

- **July 9, 2001:** Binyamin Ben-Eliezer, Israel's minister of defense, says that Iran could have nuclear weapons by 2005; "as far as we know, by the year 2005 they will, they might, be ready."[143]

- **September 7, 2001:** A CIA report reads: "The expertise and technology gained, along with the commercial channels and contacts established—particularly through the Bushehr nuclear power plant project—could be used to advance Iran's nuclear weapons research and development program."[144]

- **September 19, 2001:** Yevgeny Adamov, the Russian minister of atomic energy, says that Russia has started building another nuclear reactor in Iran.[145]

- **October 2, 2001:** The Russian Atomic Energy Ministry announces that it plans to deliver the first of two nuclear VVER-type reactors to Bushehr by November 2001. The reactor will weigh 317 tons and will be assembled upon arrival in Bushehr.[146]

- **February 11, 2002:** The Kolomensky Zavod holding company starts building 3,100 kW diesel plants to be used for emergency cooling and emergency power in a nuclear plant. Iran is supposed to get four DGU6200 diesel generator plants, each with two 15-9DG diesel generators, plus one DGU-3100 plant, including one 15-9DG diesel generator.[147]

- **February 14, 2002:** Deputy nuclear energy minister Valery Lebedev says Russia will complete the Bushehr plant by late 2004 or early 2005. He also pledges that the spent nuclear fuel will be returned to Russia.[148]

- **March 21, 2002:** Bushehr plant director Majid Teymouri says that operation of the Bushehr-1 pressurized water reactor (PWR) is "about four months behind schedule."[149]

- **April 27, 2002:** Construction is complete on the main component of the 1,000 MW nuclear power plant in Bushehr.[150]

- **May 10, 2002:** A U.S. spy satellite shows that Iran has moved U.S.-made Improved Hawk air defense missiles to Bushehr.[151]

- **July 12, 2002:** Russia's atomic energy minister, Alexander Rumyantsev, says of Bushehr that "construction of the first power unit is nearing completion . . . . Heavy equipment is being supplied, along with the reactor's body, pipes and pumping equipment. In August, a turbine will be delivered."[152]

- **July 26, 2002:** The Russian government announces a 10-year plan to build six nuclear reactors in Iran, four in Bushehr and two in a future plant in Akhvaz.[153]

The result of these developments was to reveal a long list of nuclear programs and facilities—that are at best ambiguous in character. Iran's efforts since the 1980s did not provoke controversy with the international community, however, and did not lead to active scrutiny of its nuclear program.

NUCLEAR REVELATIONS: 2002–2003

This situation changed following the attacks of 911, the U.S. scrutiny of Iraq's WMD program, and the United States labeling Iran a member of the club of the "Axis of Evil." Iran's nuclear program became the subject of more concern. This change in the scrutiny of Iran's nuclear program can partially be traced back to August 14, 2002, when the National Council of Resistance of Iran (NCRI) identified a "secret" Iranian nuclear program.[154]

The revelation focused on a heavy water production facility at Arak and a nuclear fuel production plant at Natanz. The groups also outlined five different "active" nuclear projects, including power plants in Bushehr, Arak, and Esfahan. In addition, the NCRI identified four research centers at Karaj, Bonab, Saghand, and Amirabad.[155]

On September 16, 2002, Reza Aghazadeh, the president of the Atomic Energy Agency of Iran, declared—at the 46th General Conference of the International Atomic Energy Agency in Vienna—that

> Iran is embarking on a long-term plan, based on the merits of energy mix, to construct nuclear power plants with a total capacity of 6,000 MW within two decades. Naturally, such a sizeable project entails with it an all out planning, well in advance, in various fields of nuclear technology such as fuel cycle, safety and waste management. I take this opportunity to invite all the technologically advanced member States to participate in my country's ambitious plan for the construction of nuclear power plants and the associated technologies such as fuel cycle, safety and waste management techniques.[156]

During the general conference, the director general of the IAEA and Aghazadeh, who was also the vice president of Iran, met to discuss Iran's declaration. According to a later report by the IAEA's director general, Iran expressed its intention of developing "its nuclear fuel cycle, and agreed on a visit to the two sites [Natanz and Arak] later in 2002 by the Director General, accompanied by safeguards experts, and to a discussion with Iranian authorities during that meeting on Iran's nuclear development plans."[157]

In September 2002, commercial satellite photos confirmed the existence of major new Iranian nuclear sites in Natanz and near Arak, whose existence and nature Iran had made major efforts to conceal and whose underground facilities had been completed in ways deliberately designed to conceal their scale and importance. The IAEA confirmed that it was seeking access to inspect these sites, and U.S. officials were quoted as saying that the large facility in Natanz appeared to be a uranium enrichment plant.

In December of the same year, the United States accused Iran of pursuing nuclear weapons and demanded that it cooperate with the IAEA inspection. Iranian officials denied the existence of nuclear weapons. Hamid Reza Assefi, Iran's ambassador to the United Nations, said in an interview that "I can categorically tell you that Iran does not have a nuclear weapons program . . . . Any facility we have . . . if it is dealing with nuclear technology, it is within the purview of our peaceful nuclear program."[158]

Tehran Invites the IAEA

These exchanges started a process of IAEA inspection efforts and Iranian failures to fully respond that still continues. On February 9, 2003, Iran's president, Mohammad Khatami, invited the IAEA to visit Iranian nuclear facilities, including Natanz. In response to this call, the head of the IAEA, Dr. Mohamed ElBaradei, traveled to Tehran during February 22–23, 2003, to discuss the scope of Iranian cooperation with IAEA inspections.

IAEA experts and inspectors visited Iran on several occasions. The agency was not satisfied with Iran's cooperation and, on June 6, 2003, a preliminary report was published that concluded that "Iran has failed to meet its obligations under its Safeguards Agreement with respect to the reporting of nuclear material, the subsequent processing and use of that material and the declaration of facilities where the material was stored and processed."[159]

The IAEA's June 2003 report added that the quantities of the materials under question included roughly 1.8 tons of uranium—a small amount for conducting nuclear research—and that the uranium would require processing to make it suitable for nuclear explosive devices. The IAEA did, however, call these failures "a matter of concern." It also raised the following challenges to the Islamic Republic:

(a) The completion of a more thorough expert analysis of the research and development carried out by Iran in the establishment of its enrichment capabilities. This will require the submission by Iran of a complete chronology of its centrifuge and laser enrichment efforts, including, in particular, a description of all research and development activities carried out prior to the construction of the Natanz facilities. As agreed to by Iran, this process will also involve discussions in Iran between Iranian authorities and Agency enrichment experts on Iran's enrichment program, and visits by the Agency experts to the facilities under construction at Natanz and other relevant locations.

(b) Further follow-up on information regarding allegations about undeclared enrichment of nuclear material, including, in particular, at the Kalaye Electric Company. This will require permission for the Agency to carry out environmental sampling at the workshop located there.

(c) Further enquiries about the role of uranium metal in Iran's nuclear fuel cycle.

(d) Further enquiries about Iran's program related to the use of heavy water, including heavy water production and heavy water reactor design and construction.[160]

Following these challenges, the director general of the IAEA, Mohamed ElBaradei, traveled to Tehran and met with Iranian officials on July 9, 2003. The two sides agreed that IAEA experts (headed by the IAEA's deputy director for safeguards, Pierre Goldschmidt) and Iranian officials would discuss further the technical issues regarding Iran's nuclear program and its implementation of the safeguards. Those meetings took place in July and August of 2003.

In September 2003, Dr. ElBaradei declared that "it is now clear that, beginning in the mid-1980s, Iran embarked on an extensive fuel cycle research and development. . . ." On September 12, 2003, the IAEA board moved on a resolution calling for Iran to fully cooperate with the inspection. The resolution stated that the IAEA board was "expressing grave concern that, more than one year after initial IAEA inquiries to Iran about undeclared activities, Iran has still not enabled the IAEA to provide the assurances required by Member States that all nuclear material in Iran is declared and submitted to Agency safe-guards and that there are no undeclared nuclear activities in Iran."[161]

The October 2003 Ultimatum

That exchange marked the lowest point thus far in the IAEA-Tehran negotiations. The resolution noted that the IAEA was concerned about four key developments in Iran's nuclear research program:

- First, it stated that sampling at Natanz revealed the contamination of the site by "two types of highly enriched uranium."

- Second, the inspection efforts "found considerable modifications had been made to the premises at the Kalaye Electric Company."

- Third, it asked Iran to update its statements concerning changes in nuclear materials since Tehran last reported to the IAEA.

- Fourth, the IAEA stated that "despite the Board's statement in June 2003 encouraging Iran, as a confidence-building measure, not to introduce nuclear material into its pilot centrifuge enrichment cascade at Natanz, Iran has introduced such material."[162]

The resolution also issued an ultimatum to Iran to reveal all the details of its nuclear activities by October 31, 2003.

Iran objected to the ultimatum, rejected the language of the resolution, and claimed that Tehran has fully cooperated with the IAEA. Iran's vice president said that Iran had "serious problems with this resolution. From its inconsistency with the NPT to its deadline for cooperation and its venomous language are all problematic. These are our preliminary views on this resolution. We are studying the resolution carefully and will officially respond to it in a few days."[163]

September 2003 also marked the start of close involvement by the EU3 (Britain, France, and Germany) in the negotiations. This involvement started in June 2003 following what the EU3 foreign ministers saw as Iran's failure to disclose its nuclear program and cooperate with the IAEA. It also came on the heels of the failure to prevent a war in Iraq. The initial opposition of the European countries to the invasion of Iraq in March 2003, and the subsequent lack of WMDs in Iraq, forced the EU3 to try to think of ways to stop Iran from following in the footsteps of Iraq. The situation was also exacerbated by U.S. pressure to push the Iranian file to the United Nations Security Council and call for imposing economic sanctions.

Tehran initially objected to the EU3's efforts. But in September and October 2003 the foreign ministers of the EU3 traveled to Iran, and on October 21, 2003, they reached an agreement to enhance Iranian cooperation with the IAEA-EU3. The IAEA and Iran's Ministry of Foreign Affairs released a joint statement saying "the Iranian authorities and the ministers, following extensive consultations, agreed on measures aimed at the settlement of all outstanding IAEA [International Atomic Energy Agency] issues with regards to the Iranian nuclear [program] and at enhancing confidence for peaceful cooperation in the nuclear field." The statement declared that Iran agreed "voluntarily to suspend all uranium enrichment and reprocessing activities as defined by the IAEA." The two sides also agreed that Iran would sign the IAEA Additional Protocols. The Iranian government reiterated its willingness to work within the NPT framework, and both sides agreed on "the right of Iran to enjoy peaceful use of nuclear energy in accordance with NPT."[164]

This promise of cooperation did not lead to Iran's fully meeting the demands of the IAEA board that were set in the September 2003 resolution. On the deadline of the ultimatum, October 31, 2003, the head of the IAEA, Mohamed ElBaradei, released a statement on Iran's declaration:

> Last week we received what I was assured was a complete and accurate declaration of Iran's past nuclear activities. We immediately started an intensive verification process and are making good progress. Our inspectors are currently in Iran visiting sites, interviewing key personnel and taking samples with a view to verifying the accuracy and completeness of this declaration. Sometime towards the end of the second week of November, I will be issuing a report to the Board of Governors with the results at that time of this verification process. Further, I have been told to expect by next week a letter from the Iranian government accepting the terms of the Additional Protocol. When this happens, it will be a very positive step forward, particularly in terms of enabling us to effectively regulate all future nuclear activities in Iran.[165]

The letter from Tehran to the IAEA board of governors arrived on Monday November 10, 2003. In it, Iran announced that it was ready to suspend its uranium enrichment programs, stop all reprocessing activities in Natanz, and not import any enrichment materials. These reassurances drove the head of the IAEA to declare on November 26, 2003, "This is a good day for peace, multilateralism and non-proliferation." ElBaradei added that the international community came together to address the Iranian nuclear program, and that it sent a message that the "nuclear non-proliferation regime must be respected and upheld."[166]

This led to Iran and IAEA signing the protocols on December 18, 2003. The IAEA expressed its satisfaction in a statement by Dr. ElBaradei: "Iran has committed itself to a policy of full disclosure and has decided, as a confidence building measure, not only to sign the Additional Protocol, making way for more robust and comprehensive inspections, but also to take the important step of suspending all enrichment related and reprocessing activities and to accept IAEA verification of this suspension. These are positive and welcome steps which I very much hope will be sustained."[167]

IRAN'S CONCEALMENT EFFORTS IN 2004

Iran did sign the protocols in December 2003, but did not ratify them, and, as it has since then, it restricted the IAEA's inspections to known and declared nuclear facilities or limited inspections only by prior agreement. It also became clear during 2004 that Iran was not prepared to cooperate fully with all of the IAEA's efforts and that many new issues remained unresolved, among them the definition of "suspending" all uranium enrichment activities and what is meant by "transparent" actions.

The IAEA issued another report in February 2004. While it praised Iran's signing of the additional protocols, it reiterated its concern about Iran's lack of transparency, particularly regarding Tehran's lack of disclosure of whether it has P-2 centrifuge designs. This was a worrisome sign, but diplomats were quoted as saying that the IAEA was "nowhere close to saying Iran has a nuclear weapon."[168]

The IAEA carried out a few inspections during the early months of 2004, including one between January 10 and 28 during which it inspected and took samples from Natanz, Karaj, the Esfahan Nuclear Technology Center, the Tehran Nuclear Research Center, the Kalaye Electric Company, and Jabr Ibn Hayan Laboratories. In addition, the IAEA conducted a follow-up safeguards inspection on February 15–19, 2004.[169]

Revelations of Foreign Assistance

The year 2004 marked a turning point in the IAEA's reports regarding Iran's low-enriched uranium (LEU), highly enriched uranium (HEU), and P-1 and P-2 centrifuge designs. Some of these concerns were expressed in a resolution by the IAEA on March 13, 2004, which outlined three key areas of "serious concern" for the inspection team and Iran:[170]

> ...(f) *Noting with serious concern* that the declarations made by Iran in October 2003 did not amount to the complete and final picture of Iran's past and present nuclear program considered essential by the Board's November 2003 resolution, in that the Agency has since uncovered a number of omissions—e.g., a more advanced centrifuge design than previously declared, including associated research, manufacturing and testing activities; two mass spectrometers used in the laser enrichment program; and designs for the construction of hot cells at the Arak heavy water research reactor—which require further investigation, not least as they may point to nuclear activities not so far acknowledged by Iran,
>
> (g) *Noting with equal concern* that Iran has not resolved all questions regarding the development of its enrichment technology to its current extent, and that a number of other questions remain unresolved, including the sources of all HEU contamination in Iran; the location, extent, and nature of work undertaken on the basis of the advanced centrifuge design; the nature, extent and purpose of activities involving the planned heavy water reactor; and evidence to support claims regarding the purpose of polonium-210 experiments, and
>
> (h) *Noting with concern* . . . . although the timelines are different, Iran's and Libya's conversion and centrifuge program share several common elements, including technology largely obtained from the same foreign sources.

The last point referred to evidence that had surfaced that Pakistan had helped Iran in its enrichment program. The revelation came after it was discovered that the A.Q. Khan network might have sold P-2 nuclear designs to several countries, including Libya, and possibly Iran. The IAEA report indicated that Pakistan had helped Iran since 1995, and may have delivered the P-2 design to the Iranians. The IAEA warned that Iran intended to "turn 37 tons of nearly raw uranium called yellowcake, into uranium hexafluoride." Experts contend that this could be enough to create 5–6 atomic weapons.[171]

This revelation further concerned the IAEA because the October 31, 2003, declaration by Iran, which was supposed to have been complete, failed to disclose the P-2 design:[172]

> The omission from Iran's letter of 21 October 2003 of any reference to its possession of the P-2 centrifuge design drawings and associated research, manufacturing and mechanical testing activities is a matter of serious concern, particularly in view of the importance and sensitivity of those activities. It runs counter to Iran's declaration, a document characterized by Iran as providing "the full scope of Iranian nuclear activities" and a "complete centrifuge R&D chronology." The Director General has continued to emphasize to Iran the importance of declaring all the details of Iran's nuclear program.

Tehran attempted to answer these charges in a report of its own on March 5, 2004, to the IAEA board. Iran explained the omissions and answered the IAEA's concerns on two key issues. It argued that both the P-2 centrifuge design and the polonium-210 (Po-210) experiments were reported to the IAEA, and that the agency was aware of Iran's research and development (R&D) activities:

- On the P-2 centrifuge design, Iran argued that its enrichment program at Natanz was based on the P-1 design, which was the reason for omitting the centrifuges from its declaration in October 2003. It also stated that the IAEA was informed of the R&D on the P-1 design during the inspectors' visits to Natanz. Concerning the allegation that Iran received the design from abroad, the report stated that while it was true that the "general engineering design" of the P-2 was obtained from a third party, the components of the P-2 design were not. The report declared that some of those components were produced domestically.[173]

■ On the issue of polonium-210 experiments, Iran claimed that although it was not required to declare them, "the project was aborted more than 13 years ago." However, the report argued that "Po-210 has various applications for peaceful purposes including [radioisotope thermoelectric generators] RTGs. Even in a purely hypothetical scenario of the intention to use Po-210 for production of [a] neutron source, the neutron source had several theoretically sound peaceful applications, including reactors, neutron logging in oil and gas explorations and other neutron activation analyses."[174]

The IAEA rebutted these counterclaims and reiterated that the issue at hand was the lack of credible declaration by the Iranian government. Even though Iran claimed that it had received the design only for the centrifuge and not for its components, the IAEA argued, "in none of the discussions with Iran in 2003 did Iranian officials make any reference to the acquisition of drawings from a foreign source, or to any mechanical tests for P-2 type centrifuges." [175]

Following these claims, counterclaims, and rebuttals, the IAEA board met on March 15, 2004, and reiterated its dissatisfaction with Iran's cooperation and declaration with regard to its Po-210 and P-2 projects. The U.S. ambassador to the IAEA, Kenneth C. Brill, outlined the United States' view of Iran's actions with regard to the IAEA, comparing Iran's declaration to that of Libya:[176]

Iran, in contrast, is continuing to pursue a policy of denial, deception, and delay. Time after time, when IAEA inspectors have confronted the Iranian government with verified facts it could no longer contest, Iran has revised its story and blamed others for its duplicity. But from the beginning the responsibility for prolonging this investigation has lain solely with Iran itself.

Despite Iran's earlier commitment to stop all enrichment and centrifuge projects, Iran declared on June 27, 2004, that it would continue to manufacture centrifuges and to experiment with uranium hexafluoride, two of the activities of most concern to the IAEA. Iran

saw this as a means of retaliation against the EU3 agreement to censure Iran in an IAEA resolution in early June. The Iranians claimed
that because the EU3 did not keep their commitments, Iran did not
have to keep its promises. ElBaradei argued that this move by Iran
would increase the "confidence deficit." The move also prompted the
Bush administration to once again threaten to turn Iran's case over to
the United Nations Security Council.[177]

The United States did not seek to refer Iran's nuclear file to the
Security Council, but reports by the director general of the IAEA,
dated September 1, 2004, and October 15, 2004, provided detailed
descriptions of unresolved issues, such as LEU and HEU contamination at Iranian nuclear sites. The IAEA also provided significant indications that Iran was continuing its nuclear development program,
and it reported that Iran had already sought to create centrifuge
enrichment facilities, had experimented with laser isotope separation,
and may have had a design for more advanced P-2 centrifuges than had
been reported. The director general's reports did not confirm that Iran
was actively pursuing nuclear weapons per se, and Iran once again presented a number of other explanations for its activities. The IAEA did,
however, cite case after case where major questions remained and indicated that Iran did seem committed to a nuclear program.

The Paris Agreement: November 15, 2004

Once again, EU3 involvement produced another agreement with Tehran. The agreement was reached on November 15, 2004, and emphasized the need for suspending Iran's enrichment activities. It became
known as the Paris Agreement, and it read in part:

> To build further confidence, Iran has decided, on a voluntary basis,
> to continue and extend its suspension to include all enrichment re-
> lated and reprocessing activities, and specifically: the manufacture
> and import of gas centrifuges and their components; the assembly,
> installation, testing or operation of gas centrifuges; work to under-
> take any plutonium separation, or to construct or operate any plu-
> tonium separation installation; and all tests or production at any
> uranium conversion installation. The IAEA will be notified of this

suspension and invited to verify and monitor it. The suspension will be implemented in time for the IAEA to confirm before the November Board that it has been put into effect. The suspension will be sustained while negotiations proceed on a mutually acceptable agreement on long-term arrangements.

Sustaining the suspension, while negotiations on a long-term agreement are under way, will be essential for the continuation of the overall process. In the context of this suspension, the E3/EU and Iran have agreed to begin negotiations, with a view to reaching a mutually acceptable agreement on long term arrangements. The agreement will provide objective guarantees that Iran's nuclear program is exclusively for peaceful purposes. It will equally provide firm guarantees on nuclear, technological and economic cooperation and firm commitments on security issues.

A steering committee will meet to launch these negotiations in the first half of December 2004 and will set up working groups on political and security issues, technology and cooperation, and nuclear issues. The steering committee shall meet again within three months to receive progress reports from the working groups and to move ahead with projects and/or measures that can be implemented in advance of an overall agreement.

In the context of the present agreement and noting the progress that has been made in resolving outstanding issues, the E3/EU will henceforth support the Director General reporting to the IAEA Board as he considers appropriate in the framework of the implementation of Iran's Safeguards Agreement and Additional Protocol.

The E3/EU will support the IAEA Director General inviting Iran to join the Expert Group on Multilateral Approaches to the Nuclear Fuel Cycle.

Once suspension has been verified, the negotiations with the EU on a Trade and Cooperation Agreement will resume. The E3/EU will actively support the opening of Iranian accession negotiations at the WTO.

Irrespective of progress on the nuclear issue, the E3/EU and Iran confirm their determination to combat terrorism, including the activities of Al Qaeda and other terrorist groups such as the MeK.

They also confirm their continued support for the political process in Iraq aimed at establishing a constitutionally elected Government. [178]

This change in the Iranian position seems to have been motivated in part by Tehran's fear that its actions could lead to a political challenge or some form of sanctions by the UN Security Council. That fear triggered Iran's agreement to suspend its nuclear program three days before the IAEA's November 25 meeting in Vienna. On November 22, 2004, the Iranians announced that "to build confidence and in line with implementing the Paris Agreement, Iran suspended uranium enrichment (and related activities) as of today." Iran's foreign ministry spokesman, Hamid Reza Asefi, was quoted as saying that "Iran's acceptance of suspension is a political decision, not an obligation, [which is] the best decision under the current circumstances.[179] Mohamed ElBaradei was quoted as saying that due to the Paris Agreement, "I think pretty much everything has come to a halt."[180]

The United States, however, expressed mistrust about Iran's promise and cited Iran's history of concealment. On November 17, 2004, the U.S. secretary of state, Colin Powell, reiterated that Iran had not given up its determination to acquire a nuclear weapon or a delivery system that was capable of carrying such weapon. "I have seen some information that would suggest that they have been actively working on delivery systems . . . . You don't have a weapon until you put it in something that can deliver a weapon . . . . I am not talking about uranium or fissile material or the warhead; I'm talking about what one does with a warhead," Secretary Powell stated.[181]

In early December 2004, U.S. intelligence experts gave a background briefing that followed up on Secretary Powell's statements. They indicated that they were convinced that Iran was aggressively seeking to develop a nuclear warhead for its Shahab series of missile, and that it was actively working on the physics package for such a warhead design.[182] The U.S. officials stated that this information did not come from Iranian opposition sources like the Mujahedin-e Khalq.

THE PIVOTAL ROLE OF THE EU3 IN 2005

The United States continued its pressure on Iran during 2005, working with the IAEA and relying on the EU3 framework. Some in the

United States, however, felt that Mohamed ElBaradei was being soft on Iran's nuclear program. He was to run for a third term as the head of the IAEA in March 2005 (he won), and it was no secret that some U.S. officials did not want him to win. They wanted the IAEA to be more aggressive against Iran's concealment and cheating activities.

ElBaradei answered these criticisms by saying that "the results in Iran are something I am quite proud of. Eighteen months ago, Iran was a black box—we didn't know much about what was happening. Now, we have a fairly good picture of what is happening. Through our tenacity, Iran's facilities that could produce fissile material are frozen."[183]

The head of the IAEA went on to add that although "Iran has clearly cheated in the past—that is something we reported," and he noted that the hard work by the EU3 was pivotal to the success of the IAEA's efforts to stop Iran from acquiring a nuclear program. Dr. ElBaradei also argued that the discussion of military solutions in the United States was not helping European diplomatic efforts with Tehran, and he added that the international community must understand the motivation behind any country's efforts to acquire nuclear weapons. He was quoted as saying, "You need to address [Iran's] sense of isolation and its need for technology and economic [benefits]. They have been under sanctions for 20 years."[184]

This argument went to the heart of Iran's public rationale for its programs to acquire nuclear power and its "need" for a full nuclear fuel cycle to support its power reactors. The Iranians argued that past U.S. sanctions and other efforts to isolate Iran had showed them that their national security required them to be self-sufficient in meeting their energy needs. As noted earlier, they argued that, despite having the second-largest oil and gas reserves in the world, the growth of their population and the lack of foreign investments in their oil and gas infrastructures meant they needed to diversify their energy sources. The IAEA counterargument had been that access to peaceful nuclear technology might help solve Iran's energy problems, but that Tehran had to be transparent about the history of its nuclear program, declare all of its foreign sources, and suspend its low-enriched uranium and high-enriched uranium activities.

Pierre Goldschmidt, the head of the IAEA safeguards, briefed the IAEA board on the inspectors' findings in early March 2005. He said he was expecting progress in getting answers for the source of the LEU and HEU contamination of the centrifuge components. His report was based on IAEA visits to suspected sites in early 2005, including sites outside Iran where it was believed that centrifuge components were stored before their shipment to Iran.

Goldschmidt also revealed to the board that Iran had received an offer in 1987 by a foreign source to deliver a disassembled sample machine; drawings, specifications, and calculations for a "complete plant"; and materials for 2,000 centrifuge machines. The board was told that Iran admitted it had received some, but not all, of the components, which Iran also claimed to have declared to the IAEA. The foreign intermediary, however, was not named in the briefing.[185]

The early months of 2005, also saw a change in U.S. policies toward the EU3 negotiations and more U.S. support for the efforts of the IAEA. President George W. Bush, Vice President Richard Cheney, and Secretary of State Condoleezza Rice all voiced support for the EU3's diplomatic efforts to stop Iran's nuclear program. Vice President Cheney was quoted as saying that "I can't think of anybody who is eager to see the Iranians develop that kind of capability. Now, we are moving to support efforts to resolve it diplomatically."[186]

The diplomatic efforts by the EU3 coincided with the approaching Iranian elections in June 2005. The EU3 faced the dilemma of waiting for the elections to take place and dealing with a new leadership, or moving ahead with the current negotiations. Iran was still under the leadership of Mohammad Khatami and offered the EU3 a phased framework of negotiations in March 2005.[187]

The proposed General Framework for Objective Guarantees, reproduced in table 6.1, was a four-phase plan. In the first phase, Iran offered to ratify the Additional Protocols, resume the work of the UCF, adhere to the IAEA surveillance of UF_6 (uranium hexafluoride) storage, and permanently ban the production of nuclear weapons. In exchange, Iran wanted the EU3 to guarantee Iran's access to EU markets, recognize Iran as a major source of energy for Europe, and commission a study for assisting Iran in building nuclear power plants (to be built under phase 4). The first phase was to run from April to July 2005. The EU3 expressed its willingness to accept the proposal, but not as the basis for negotiations, as they felt that Iran had refused to stop work on its heavy water reactor.

In essence, the proposal would have insured Iran's access to nuclear power plants under the supervision of the EU3 in exchange for a guarantee from Tehran to ratify the Additional Protocols. Britain, France, and Germany, however, felt that giving Iran access to nuclear technology in exchange for political guarantees would keep Iran from using such technologies to build nuclear weapons.[188]

The EU3 also convinced the Bush administration that Iran must be offered some economic incentives to abandon its nuclear ambitions. In March 2005, the United States dropped its objections to Iran's application to the World Trade Organization (WTO) and agreed to "consider" the EU3 proposal to provide Iran with the license to purchase spare parts for civilian aircraft. Some believed that the United States agreed to this knowing that Iran would not agree, which would allow the United States to use Iran's refusal to gather international support for punitive actions against Iran. Others, however, saw this proposal as an inducement that Iran could accept for at least suspending its research temporarily, but not enough for it to end its nuclear ambitions.[189]

Iran's view of the EU3 proposal was very different. Tehran insisted that the Europeans were asking Iran to completely drop its uranium enrichment program, which was unacceptable because it was Iran's national right to have access to civilian nuclear fuel. President Mohammad Khatami was quoted as saying, "If the Europeans insist on a cessation, that is obviously a break of the agreement we reached with them . . . . If they break the agreement, whatever happens after, the responsibility lies with the Europeans."[190]

In May 2005, Iran announced that it was resuming enrichment activities in its uranium enrichment conversion facilities in Esfahan. The Iranian foreign minister, Kamal Kharrazi, said that resuming experiments on uranium conversion in pursuit of peaceful nuclear energy is Iran's "natural right." He added, however, that he foresaw an Iran-EU3 agreement.[191] Iran also confirmed on May 9, 2005, that it converted 37 tons of raw uranium into gas. Mohammad Saeedi, the deputy head of the Atomic Energy Organization of Iran, said, "We converted

Table 6.1
General Framework for Objective Guarantees between Iran and the EU3, May 3, 2005

Phase	Action by Iran	Action by EU3/EU
1	■ Approval of the Additional Protocol in the Cabinet ■ Policy Declaration on Iran's Open Fuel Cycle (No Reprocessing) ■ Presentation of Legislation on Peaceful Use of Nuclear Technology, including Permanent Ban on Production, Stockpiling and Use of Nuclear Weapons to the Majlis ■ Resumption of the Work of the UCF ■ Storage of UF6 Under Agency Surveillance	■ Declaration of EU Policy to Guarantee Iran's Access to EU Markets and Financial and Public and Private Investment Resources ■ Declaration of EU Recognition of Iran as a Major Source of Energy Supply for Europe ■ Launching of Feasibility Studies for Building of New Nuclear Power Plants in Iran by E3/EU Members
	■ **Establishment of a Joint Counter-Terrorism Task Force**	
	■ **Establishment of a Joint Export Control Task Force**	
2	■ Presentation of the Additional Protocol to the Majlis for Ratification ■ Strengthening of Legal Export Control Mechanisms ■ Policy Declaration on the Ceiling of Enrichment at LEU Level ■ Policy Declaration on Conversion of All Enriched Uranium to Fuel Rods ■ Assembly, Installation and Testing of 3,000 Centrifuges in Natanz	■ Declaration of EU Policy to Guarantee Iran's Access to Advanced and Nuclear Technology ■ Declaration of EU Readiness to participate in Building New Nuclear Power Plants in Iran ■ Signing of Contracts for Construction of Nuclear power Plants in Iran by E3/EU Members
	■ **Joint Commitment to Principles Governing Relations**	
	■ **Cooperation on Security in the Persian Gulf**	

(continued)

Table 6.1 *(continued)*

Phase	Action by Iran	Action by EU3/EU
3	■ Employing All Appropriate Measures for Adoption of the Legislation on Peaceful Use of Nuclear Technology, including Permanent Ban on Production, Stockpiling and Use of Nuclear Weapons by the Majlis ■ Allowing Continuous On-Site Presence of IAEA Inspectors, which Can Include E3/EU Nationals at the UCF and Natanz ■ Commissioning of the Above Centrifuges in Natanz ■ Immediate Conversion of the Total Product of the Above to Fuel Rods ■ Incremental Manufacturing, Assembly and Installation of Centrifuge Components up to the Numbers Envisaged for Natanz	■ Normalizing Iran's Status Under G8 Export Control Regulations ■ Firm Guarantees on the Supply of Fuel Necessary for Iranian Nuclear Power Reactors to complement Iran's Domestic Production ■ Presentation and Active Follow Up of an EU Initiative to Establish a Zone Free From Weapons of Mass Destruction in the Middle East
	■ **Establishment of a Task Force on Strategic Cooperation** ■ **Establishment of a Task Force on Defense Requirements**	
4	■ Employing All Appropriate Measures for Ratification of the Additional Protocol by the Majlis ■ Commencement of Phased Commissioning of Natanz ■ Immediate Conversion of the Total Product of the Above to Fuel Rods	■ Conclusion of Contracts for Defense Items ■ Beginning of Construction of New Nuclear Power Plants in Iran by E3/EU Members
	■ **Joint Commitment to Principles Governing Relations** ■ **Cooperation on Security in the Persian Gulf**	

Source: Available from NuclearFiles.org, at http://www.nuclearfiles.org/menu/key-issues/nuclear-weapons/issues/proliferation/iran/index.htm.

all the 37 tons of uranium concentrate known as yellowcake into UF_4 at the Isfahan (Esfahan) Uranium Conversion Facility before we suspended work there [in November 2004]."[192]

The EU3 and the United States felt that Iran was not living up to its commitments, including those promises offered by Iran in its March 2005 "Objective Guarantees." Iran, on the other hand, argued that the EU3 refused to accept such a framework as the basis of negotiations and reiterated its right to get access to civilian nuclear technology.

As a result, Iran's resumption of its uranium enrichment activities prompted the EU3 to threaten Iran with referral to the Security Council and thus the risk of UN sanctions. British prime minister Tony Blair said at a news conference that "we certainly will support referral to the U.N. Security Council if Iran breeches its undertakings and obligations." This sentiment was also expressed by U.S. secretary of state Condoleezza Rice: "The Security Council always remains an option should the Iranians not live up to their obligations, but we are still hopeful that they will recognize where they are."[193]

Changing of the Guard: Iran's Presidential Elections

It was clear that the coming election for the presidency might influence the way in which Iran proceeded. Many in the EU3 hoped for a Rafsanjani victory in the June 2005 presidential election. This was especially true after Rafsanjani said—as he announced his candidacy for president—that "the sound strategy is that we should continue talks with the Europeans; and Europeans and we should be patient to build a sort of confidence which can enable us to carry out the enrichment."[194]

At the same time, others believed that the election would not change Iran's nuclear policy because the decision was largely that of the Supreme Leader and his key supporters. The Ministry of Foreign Affairs spokesman, Hamid Reza Asefi, said that "whoever is the next president, a permanent suspension is not in the cards." Asefi added that the president of the republic has "a certain influence," but that it was Tehran's policy to continue its pursuit of nuclear energy.[195] This was confirmed by the secretary of the Foreign Policy Committee of Iran's Supreme National Security Council, Hoseyn Mussavian, who claimed that the elections would only confirm Iran's nuclear policy because, he said, 95 percent of Iranians supported a civilian nuclear program.[196]

Both outsiders and Iranians were surprised by the election results. Rafsanjani did not win. Instead, Mahmoud Ahmadinejad, who was seen as a hardliner on the nuclear issue, was elected. Ahmadinejad immediately signaled his support for moving forward with Tehran's nuclear program. On June 27, 2005, he was quoted as saying, "It is the right of the Iranian nation to move forward in all fields and acquire modern technology. Nuclear technology is the outcome of scientific progress of Iranian youth."[197]

Less than two months after the elections, on August 1, 2005, Iran decided to remove the IAEA seals on the process lines and the UF_4 at the uranium conversion facility in Esfahan. Iran's Foreign Ministry spokesman announced on August 10, 2005, that "some minutes ago we received a letter from the IAEA, authorizing Iran to remove the seals at the Esfahan plant."[198]

The IAEA responded by unanimously adopting a resolution on August 11, 2005, that called on Iran to stop its uranium enrichment activities and expressed its concern with Tehran's decision to restart nuclear research at the uranium conversion facility in Esfahan:[199]

> Expresses serious concern at the 1 August 2005 notification to the IAEA that Iran had decided to resume the uranium conversion activities at the Uranium Conversion Facility in Esfahan, at the Director General's report that on 8 August Iran started to feed uranium ore concentrate into the first part of the process line at this facility and at the Director General's report that on 10 August Iran removed the seals on the process lines and the UF4 at this facility.

According to diplomats in Vienna, the IAEA's August 11, 2005, resolution gave Tehran an implicit deadline of September 3, 2005, before being referred to the UN Security Council —the same deadline that the IAEA board had given its director general to issue another report on the implementation of the safeguards.[200]

In a sign of its frustration, the EU3 decided to call off talks with Iran that had been scheduled for August 31, 2005. Germany, France, and the United Kingdom felt Iran breached the Paris Agreement with its resumption of its enrichment program at Esfahan. A French Foreign Ministry spokesman was quoted as saying, "So by common accord between the three Europeans it is clear that there will be no negotiations meeting . . . as long as the Iranians remain outside the Paris Agreement."[201]

A Turning Point in the EU3-Iran Negotiations

The Iranian government's strategy was to try to stop Iran's referral to the UN Security Council through ongoing negotiations with the EU3, especially given the European objection to the United States' action on Iraq. This worked for the first several months of the negotiations. The tough rhetoric coming from the EU3 ministers at the end of August 2005, however, marked a turning point in the EU3-Iranian negotiations. The EU3 felt that no matter what was offered to the Iranians, Tehran reneged on its promises: Iran had broken its commitments to the Paris Agreement, restarted a uranium enrichment program, and removed the seals on its nuclear facilities.

The IAEA September 2, 2005, report stated that Iran produced approximately 7 tons of the gas used in uranium enrichment in the span of one month, which is believed to be enough to produce a nuclear bomb. In addition, the IAEA document reportedly said that Iran produced 15,000 pounds of uranium hexafluoride. Experts argued that, depending on the level of enrichment, this gaseous feedstock could be used to produce a nuclear weapon.[202]

The IAEA September 2005 report argued that two major issues needed further clarification: the origin of LEU and HEU contamination and the extent of Iran's efforts to import, manufacture, and use centrifuges of both the P-1 and P-2 designs. The IAEA asserted:

> With respect to the first issue—contamination—as indicated above, based on the information currently available to the Agency, the results of the environmental sample analysis tend, on balance, to support Iran's statement about the foreign origin of most of the observed HEU contamination. It is still not possible at this time, however, to establish a definitive conclusion with respect to all of the contamination, particularly the LEU contamination. This un-

derscores the importance of additional work on the scope and chronology of Iran's P-1 and P-2 centrifuge programmes, which could greatly contribute to the resolution of the remaining contamination issues.

With respect to the second issue—the P-1 and P-2 centrifuge programmes—although, as indicated above, some progress has been made since November 2004 in the verification of statements by Iran regarding the chronology of its centrifuge enrichment programme, the Agency has not yet been able to verify the correctness and completeness of Iran's statements concerning those programmes.

While Iran has provided further clarifications, and access to additional documentation, concerning the 1987 and mid-1990s offers related to the P-1 design, the Agency's investigation of the supply network indicates that Iran should have additional supporting information that could be useful in this regard. Iran has agreed to endeavor to provide further supporting information and documentation. Iran has also been asked to provide additional details on the process that led to Iran's decision in 1985 to pursue gas centrifuge enrichment and on the steps leading to its acquisition of centrifuge enrichment technology in 1987.[203]

A European official was quoted as saying, "The Iranians are up to their old games again . . . . They think they can ignore the past two years and start again. It is just another delaying tactic."[204] The European Union foreign policy chief, Javier Solana, expressed his frustration with the negotiations. On September 2, 2005, he said that Iran may be referred to the UN Security Council if Tehran does not meet the September 3 deadline. Iran's Majlis Committee for National Security and Foreign Policy responded with a bill that threatened withdrawing from the Additional Protocol that was signed in December 2003 and even getting out of the framework of the NPT.

These developments led the United States to pressure its allies to refer Iran to the Security Council. Before the UN General Assembly meeting in New York in September 2005, the Bush administration briefed diplomats about Iran's nuclear weapons program. The briefing was titled "A History of Concealment and Deception" and covered what the United States believed were Iran's efforts to conceal its nuclear weapons program. Diplomats, including U.S. officials, argued that the problem with the U.S. briefing was that the facts were not definitive and that the briefing did not acknowledge other views and possibilities about Iran's nuclear capabilities. Many saw it as a disturbing reminder of the U.S. presentation to the Security Council that had provided a totally misleading picture of Iraq's efforts to develop CBRN weapons and delivery systems.[205]

Despite the disagreement over the U.S. presentation, the EU3 and the IAEA moved the process forward by pressuring Iran to give the IAEA's inspection team access to nuclear facilities and to be transparent about its past activities. These frustrations were echoed by the IAEA deputy director general, Pierre Goldschmidt. He argued that he was powerless to force Tehran to cooperate and that the UN Security Council must give the inspection team more powers to carry out its work of determining the status of Iran's nuclear program. He added:

> It is reaching the point where it is beyond critical . . . . The IAEA can only work on the basis of the facts that are presented to it, and there have been many serious omissions by the Iranians. The Iranians are exploiting all the loopholes in the international agreements. As to why they are doing this you can draw your own conclusions. As it stands, the investigating authority of the agency is too limited with regard to Iran. To do its job properly it needs to have more authority than is currently available to it. [206]

Throughout September 2005, nothing meaningful came out of Tehran except repeated assertions of its "inalienable right" to acquire peaceful nuclear technology. As noted earlier, Iran tried to isolate the United States from the EU3 through negotiations, but the EU3's frustration seemed to have reached the point of no return, and the same was true, albeit to a lesser extent, for the IAEA.

Mohamed ElBaradei claimed that "the ball is very much in Iran's court on this issue." In addition, France, Germany, and the United Kingdom circulated a draft resolution to the IAEA that would have required the Iranian nuclear file to be moved to the Security Council with the threat of economic sanctions. However, the U.S. envoy to the

IAEA, Greg Schulte, reiterated that the diplomatic option was still on the table, "but this would require Iran to change its course and to cooperate fully with the IAEA to cease its conversion activities and to go back to the negotiating table."[207]

Iran objected to these threats on November 17, 2005, arguing that the resolution weakened the IAEA's role as an independent organization. Tehran argued that the proposed resolution ordering Iran to stop its enrichment program had no "circumstantial basis" because its uranium conversion facilities were under the surveillance of IAEA inspections. In addition, the Iranian statement argued that Iran "voluntarily" suspended its enrichment activities and heavy water reactors as part of the Paris Agreement, but that those agreements were "not legally binding" and that resuming such activities did not violate the NPT framework.

Nevertheless, the IAEA reported on November 18, 2005, that there still were outstanding issues that Iran had not met. The report focused on the so-called 1987 offer, which referred to the offer Iran received in 1987 from a foreign source for some components, drawings, and equipment that could be used for production of centrifuges. Most importantly, the document included "detailed drawings of the P-1 centrifuge components and assemblies." As noted earlier, the third party is believed to be the A.Q. Khan network.[208]

EU3 PATIENCE RUNS OUT: EARLY 2006

The concerns of the EU3, the IAEA, and the United States were further exacerbated in early January 2006 when Iran decided once again to resume its nuclear research. Iranian officials reiterated that their nuclear research was "nonnegotiable." Ali Larijani, the secretary of the High Council of National Security, said, "Research has its own definition. It is not related to industrial production. Hence, it was never part of the negotiations."[209]

This announcement pushed the IAEA, EU3, and United States to criticize Tehran's decision. The French Foreign Ministry called the decision "very worrying." Germany announced that it was "concerned" by Iran's announcement and called on Iran to suspend all of its nuclear research.[210]

The EU3 Declaration of January 12, 2006

The EU3 met on January 12, 2006, and announced that although they would continue to work for a diplomatic solution, their negotiations with Tehran had reached a dead end. Their joint statement explained their position in detail:

E3/EU ministers met today to consider the situation following Iran's resumption on 9 January of enrichment related activity. Iran's nuclear activities have been of great concern to the international community since 2003, when Iran was forced to admit to the International Atomic Agency Authority that it was building a secret installation to enrich uranium, which could be used to produce material for nuclear weapons. The IAEA Director General at the time found Iran's policy of concealment had resulted in many breaches of its obligation to comply with the provisions of its Safeguards Agreement. Under the IAEA's rules, this should have been reported to the Security Council then.

We launched our diplomatic initiative because we wanted to offer an opportunity to Iran to address international concerns. Our objective was to give Iran a means to build international confidence that its nuclear programme was for exclusively peaceful purposes, and to develop a sound relationship between Europe and Iran.

Given Iran's documented record of concealment and deception, the need for Iran to build confidence has been and continues to be the heart of the matter. It was Iran's agreement to suspend all enrichment-related and reprocessing activities while negotiations were underway that gave us the confidence to handle the issue within the IAEA framework, rather than refer it to the Security Council. We had strong support from the IAEA Board, which repeatedly urged Iran to suspend these activities and stressed that the maintenance of full suspension was essential.

Last August, Iran resumed uranium conversion at Isfahan, in breach of IAEA Board Resolutions and the commitments she had given us in the Paris Agreement of November 2004. The IAEA Board reacted by passing a Resolution in September formally finding that Iran was in non-compliance with its Safeguards Agreement, and declaring that the history of concealment of Iran's programme and the nature of its activities gave rise to questions that were within the competence of the Security Council. Since then the IAEA has raised more disturbing questions about Iran's links with the A.Q. Khan network, which helped build Libya and North Korea's clandestine military nuclear programmes.

Nonetheless, in response to requests from many of our international partners and despite the major setbacks through unilateral Iranian actions, we agreed to delay a report to the Security Council and go the extra mile in search of a negotiated solution. We held a round of exploratory talks in Vienna on 21 December 2005 to see if we could agree [on] a basis for resuming negotiations. We made crystal clear that a resumption of negotiations would only be possible if Iran refrained from any further erosion of the suspension.

Iran's decision to restart enrichment activity is a clear rejection of the process the E3/EU and Iran have been engaged in for over two years with the support of the international community. In addition it constitutes a further challenge to the authority of the IAEA and international community. We have, therefore, decided to inform the IAEA Board of Governors that our discussions with Iran have reached an impasse.

The Europeans have negotiated in good faith. Last August we presented the most far reaching proposals for co-operation with Europe in the political, security and economic fields that Iran has received since the Revolution. These reaffirmed Iran's rights under the NPT and included European support for a strictly civilian nuclear programme in Iran, as well as proposals that would have given Iran internationally guaranteed supplies of fuel for its nuclear power programme.

But Iran was to refrain from the most sensitive activities until international confidence was restored. Such a step would not affect Iran's ability to develop a civil and nuclear power industry. We proposed that the agreement be reviewed every ten years. The Iranian government summarily rejected our proposal, and all the benefits that would have flowed from it, nor have they taken up proposals by others. The Iranian government now seems intent on turning its back on better relations with the international community, thereby dismissing the prospect for expanded economic, technological and political cooperation with the international community which would bring tremendous benefits for Iran's young, talented and growing population.

This is not a dispute between Iran and Europe, but between Iran and the whole international community. Nor is it a dispute about Iran's rights under the NPT. It is about Iran's failure to build the necessary confidence in the exclusively peaceful nature of its nuclear programme. Iran continues to challenge the authority of the IAEA Board by ignoring its repeated requests and providing only partial co-operation to the IAEA. It is important for the credibility of the NPT and the international non-proliferation system generally, as well as the stability of the region, that the international community responds firmly to this challenge.

We continue to be committed to resolving the issue diplomatically. We shall be consulting closely with our international partners in the coming days and weeks. We believe the time has now come for the Security Council to become involved to reinforce the authority of IAEA Resolutions. We will, therefore, be calling for an Extraordinary IAEA Board meeting with a view for it to take the necessary action to that end. [211]

Referral to the UN Security Council

In its February 2, 2006, meeting, the IAEA reiterated the agency's demand for further clarification from Iran on the source of contamination, the nature of the Pakistani 1987 and mid-1990s offers, the characteristics of its P-1 centrifuges, and its P-2 centrifuge capabilities. The IAEA demanded more transparency from Tehran, and by the end of their February meeting member states largely agreed on referring Iran to the UN Security Council.[212]

On February 4, 2006, the IAEA board adopted a resolution referring Iran to the Security Council. The resolution highlighted several important points:

- The IAEA was not in a position to resolve important issues regarding Iran's nuclear program or to conclude that there were no undeclared nuclear materials or activities in Iran.

- It emphasized Iran's failures and breaches of the safeguards that it had agreed to under the IAEA and NPT, and demanded transparency.

- It asked Iran to prove that its nuclear program "is exclusively for peaceful purposes resulting from the history of concealment of Iran's nuclear activities, the nature of those activities and other issues arising from the Agency's verification of declarations made by Iran since September 2002."

- It demanded that Iran "re-establish full and sustained suspension of all enrichment-related and reprocessing activities, including research and development, to be verified by the Agency."

- It demanded that Iran "(1) reconsider the construction of a research reactor moderated by heavy water; (2) ratify promptly and implement in full the Additional Protocol; (3) pending ratification, continue to act in accordance with the provisions of the Additional Protocol which Iran signed on 18 December 2003; (4) implement transparency measures,…which extend beyond the formal requirements of the Safeguards Agreement and Additional Protocol, and include such access to individuals, documentation relating to procurement, dual use equipment, certain military-owned workshops and research and development as the Agency may request in support of its ongoing investigations."

- It expressed "serious concern that the Agency is not yet in a position to clarify some important issues relating to Iran's nuclear programme, including the fact that Iran has in its possession a document on the production of uranium metal hemispheres, since, as reported by the Secretariat, this process is related to the fabrication of nuclear weapon components; and, noting that the decision to put this document under Agency seal is a positive step, requests Iran to maintain this document under Agency seal and to provide a full copy to the Agency." [213]

Iran responded to the resolution with the threat to stop all of its "cooperation" with the IAEA, and reiterated its position that its nuclear activities were intended for peaceful purposes. In a statement to the IAEA director general, the secretary of the Supreme Security Council, Ali Larijani, asserted that if the IAEA board refers Iran to the UN Security Council "it would be the final blow to the confidence of the

Islamic Republic of Iran and will totally destroy it." Dr. Larijani went on to argue that Iran would have no choice but to "suspend all voluntary measures and extra cooperation with the Agency."[214]

The United Nations Security Council first took action by issuing a statement on March 29, 2006, that expressed "serious concerns" regarding Iranian compliance with the IAEA, and urged Iran to fully cooperate. In addition, it gave the director general of the IAEA 30 days to report to the UNSC and the board of the IAEA on Iranian compliance. The following is the UNSC statement in full:

> The Security Council reaffirms its commitment to the Treaty on the Non Proliferation of Nuclear Weapons and recalls the right of States Party, in conformity with articles I and II of that Treaty, to develop research, production and use of nuclear energy for peaceful purposes without discrimination.
>
> The Security Council notes with serious concern the many IAEA reports and resolutions related to Iran's nuclear programme, reported to it by the IAEA Director General, including the February IAEA Board resolution (GOV/2006/14).
>
> The Security Council also notes with serious concern that the Director General's report of 27 February 2006 (GOV/2006/15) lists a number of outstanding issues and concerns, including topics which could have a military nuclear dimension, and that the IAEA is unable to conclude that there are no undeclared nuclear materials or activities in Iran.
>
> The Security Council notes with serious concern Iran's decision to resume enrichment-related activities, including research and development, and to suspend cooperation with the IAEA under the Additional Protocol.
>
> The Security Council calls upon Iran to take the steps required by the IAEA Board of Governors, notably in the first operative paragraph of its resolution GOV/2006/14, which are essential to build confidence in the exclusively peaceful purpose of its nuclear programme and to resolve outstanding questions, and underlines, in this regard, the particular importance of re-establishing full and sustained suspension of all enrichment-related and reprocessing activities, including research and development, to be verified by the IAEA.

The Security Council expresses the conviction that such suspension and full, verified Iranian compliance with the requirements set out by the IAEA Board of Governors would contribute to a diplomatic, negotiated solution that guarantees Iran's nuclear programme is for exclusively peaceful purposes, and underlines the willingness of the international community to work positively for such a solution, which will also benefit nuclear non-proliferation elsewhere.

The Security Council strongly supports the role of the IAEA Board of Governors and commends and encourages the Director General of the IAEA and its secretariat for their ongoing professional and impartial efforts to resolve outstanding issues in Iran, and underlines the necessity of the IAEA continuing its work to clarify all outstanding issues relating to Iran's nuclear programme.

The Security Council requests in 30 days a report from the Director General of the IAEA on the process of Iranian compliance with the steps required by the IAEA Board, to the IAEA Board of Governors and in parallel to the Security Council for its consideration.[215]

The Iranian strategy for dealing with the United Nations Security Council has shifted from dismissing the council's power to confronting it. Ayatollah Ali Khamenei, the Iranian Supreme Leader, characterized the UNSC as "a paper factory for issuing worthless and ineffective orders." He added that Iran would "resist any pressure and threat . . . . [because] if Iran quits now, the case will not be over." Other Iranian officials have also argued that one of the positive results from their negotiations with the EU3 was that Iran is "in fact much more prepared to go the U.N. Security Council."[216]

WHAT THE IAEA INSPECTIONS DID AND DID NOT PROVE

The IAEA inspection efforts provide many insights into Iran's efforts, but do not resolve the outstanding issues. The patterns of Iranian declarations and IAEA findings revealed Iran's concealment efforts and nuclear research efforts, but they do not prove the existence of an Iranian "military" nuclear program. The reports by the IAEA raised many questions about the unknowns in Iran's efforts and revealed some major uncertainties about Iran's nuclear import patterns but uncovered no unambiguous nuclear weaponization effects.

The reports did, however, reveal many undeclared Iranian nuclear research efforts. These included uranium enrichment activities and plutonium separation experiments. On the uranium conversion side, the IAEA revealed Iran's centrifuge activities, and the work on atomic vapor laser isotope separation and molecular laser isotope separation techniques. In addition, the reports revealed undeclared imported fissile materials, contaminated equipments, and possible centrifuge designs. There were also discrepancies in Iran's declarations to the IAEA about the history of its nuclear activities, the nature of A.Q. Khan's 1987 offer, and the source of contamination of Natanz.[217]

No "Smoking Gun"

Tehran was neither indicted nor exonerated by the IAEA inspectors. The IAEA inspections did not find the "smoking gun" that proves Iranian nuclear weapons capabilities. In February 2005, the IAEA director general had argued that the role of the IAEA was not to judge Iran's intentions, but to analyze facts about Iran's nuclear issues. "We at the IAEA lack conclusive evidence. We have yet to see a smoking gun that would convict Tehran. I can make assumptions about intentions, but I cannot verify intentions, just facts," ElBaradei was quoted as saying.[218]

When asked about possible economic sanctions against Iran for its enrichment activities, Mohammed ElBaradei was quoted as saying, "Sanctions are a bad idea. We are not facing an imminent threat. We need to lower the pitch . . . . Nobody has the right to punish Iran for enrichment . . . . We have not seen nuclear materials diverted to a nuclear weapon but we are not saying that the programme is used exclusively for peaceful purposes because we still have work to do."[219]

There are two views about what the IAEA said and did not say. Some believe that concluding that Iran's nuclear capabilities are not yet far advanced is premature, because the IAEA inspectors do not know everything about Tehran's nuclear program. Many, including the former deputy director general of the IAEA, Pierre Goldschmidt, have argued that the IAEA and the enforcement mechanisms of the NPT must be granted more authority by the UN Security Council, and that the IAEA must have the authority to look beyond traces of nuclear materials, including any signs that Iran is taking steps that may lead to a nuclear program.[220]

Others, however, argue that the IAEA's inspections have reached a dead end. They ask why Iran concealed activities or lied on its declarations to the IAEA if it had nothing to hide. They argue that Iran's history of concealing, reneging on its promises, and failing to report key areas of its nuclear research program make it impossible for the IAEA inspections to succeed. In addition, such experts do not believe there is a difference between Iran's civilian program and its covert military program, and they argue that once the Iranians get the nuclear know-how, they will weaponize the technology and adapt their nuclear warheads to their ballistic missiles.

While the success of the IAEA inspections was publicly in question by the West, senior Western intelligence officials argued that Iran was in fact worried about the "effectiveness of the IAEA inspections." It was reported that Iran had formed a team of nuclear specialists to "infiltrate" the IAEA inspection teams. According to press reports, the team was being headed by the former head of the Iranian parliament's energy committee, Hosein Afarideh. Reportedly, the team was based at the AEOI and its mission was to prevent further leaks and findings by the IAEA regarding Tehran's nuclear program.[221] These claims, however, remain unverifiable.

An Expert Summary of the Impact of the IAEA's Inspections and Reports

They key issue thus becomes the weight of the evidence. It is not so much what any one report revealed, or the lack of smoking guns, but the cumulative results of the IAEA's work over time. Geoff Odlum of the U.S. State Department has developed the following summary of the overall impact of the IAEA's work in recent years:

> Since late 2002, the IAEA has been undertaking a rigorous investigation into concerns about undeclared nuclear activities and facilities in Iran. From June 2003 to November 2005, the IAEA issued nine written reports on Iran's nuclear program, publicly available on the IAEA's website. Beginning with his third report, issued in

November 2003, IAEA Director General ElBaradei confirmed that for almost 20 years, Iran had been pursuing undeclared work in some of the most sensitive aspects of the nuclear fuel cycle, and had systematically hidden that work from the IAEA. Those activities constituted "numerous breaches and failures" of Iran's obligation to comply with its safeguards agreement. Specifically, Dr. ElBaradei has reported:

- Six failures to report the import, transfer, processing, and use of nuclear material, including the use of uranium hexafluoride gas in centrifuge enrichment experiments and production of depleted and enriched uranium from 1999 to 2002, the use of uranium metal in laser enrichment experiments and production of enriched uranium between 1993 and 2000, the production of uranium compounds between 1981 and 1993, and the production and irradiation of uranium targets, and the processing and separation of plutonium from those targets, between 1988 and 1998.

- Two failures to declare facilities where nuclear material was stored or processed, including a pilot centrifuge enrichment facility and two laser enrichment laboratories.

- Six failures to provide design information or updated design information for numerous facilities where nuclear material was stored or processed.

- "Failure on many occasions to cooperate to facilitate the implementation of safeguards, as evidenced by extensive concealment activities."

In addition to these confirmed safeguards breaches and failures, IAEA DG ElBaradei's September and November 2005 reports confirm, that "In view of the fact that the Agency is not yet in a position to clarify some important outstanding issues after two and a half years of intensive inspections and investigation, Iran's full transparency is indispensable and overdue."

Dr. ElBaradei has requested extended access and cooperation from Iran in a number of important areas, including "access to individuals, documentation related to procurement, dual use equipment, certain military owned workshops and research and development locations." While the IAEA has found no evidence of diversion of *declared* nuclear materials, Iran's lack of cooperation leaves the IAEA unable to conclude that there are no *undeclared* nuclear materials or activities in Iran.

The latest report from the IAEA is the update provided by Deputy Director General (DDG) Heinonen on January 31, 2006. That report came one day before a special session of the IAEA Board convened following Iran's early January decision to break IAEA seals and resume enrichment-related activities. DDG Heinonen's update makes clear not only that Iran is still not fully cooperating with the IAEA to resolve serious doubts about the correctness and completeness of Iran's declarations, but also reports for the first time additional information that appears to contradict Iran's claim that its program is peaceful.[222]

This summary does not prove Iran is acquiring nuclear weapons, but it does show just how much the cumulative result of the IAEA's work raises serious doubts about Iran's actions. It also shows how Iran can pursue many different strategies in the future. Iran is not under the pressure of war. It can afford to pause and "cheat and retreat." It can posture and bluster, then appear to comply, wait, and move forward. The very ambiguity of its past actions shows how many different ways it can avoid providing a "smoking gun" or overt effort in the future.

Iran's strategy in dealing with the IAEA was summarized by Hassan Rowhani, the head of Iran's Supreme National Security Council. According to press reports, Rowhani briefed policymakers in Tehran in September 2005 about the Iranian-IAEA negotiations. He was quoted as saying, "While we were talking with the Europeans in Tehran, we were installing equipment in parts of the facility in Isfahan, but we still had a long way to go to complete the project . . . . In fact, by creating a calm environment, we were able to complete the work on Isfahan."[223]

As the following chapters show, Iran probably has the technology base to create a series of small centrifuge facilities it could disperse widely in throughout the country, harden and/or conceal, and use to gradually develop weapons-grade facilities. Such an effort would be slower and less efficient in some ways than Iran's current enrichment plans, but much would depend on Iran's ability to improve the efficiency of its P-2 centrifuge designs—an activity it could probably carry out with little risk of detection and inspection and which in any case would be ambiguous under the terms of the NPT.

One key issue is just how far Iran could go in improving its centrifuge capabilities and in making laser isotope separation practical. The P-2 is often assumed to have roughly twice the separative work unit (SWU) output of the P-1, an important but not radical change. If so, Iran's plans for a 50,000 P-1 centrifuge plant would still require a large facility with some 25,000–30,000 centrifuges, and the P-2 design is considerably more demanding to keep in constant operation than the P-1 and to bring up to speed once activity is halted.

At least one open source report has claimed, however, that truly advanced centrifuge designs like the URENCO T21 have the theoretical capacity to produce 50 times the output of the P-1. This claim seems exaggerated and the T21 bearing, which circulates oil between it and its support cup, and its other design features are extremely demanding. So is operation and preservation of rotor integrity. Nevertheless, if such reports are approximately correct, several years of centrifuge operation and research using even Iran's existing small 164 P-1 centrifuge cascade would make it far easier to create "folded," dispersed, or more compact facilities. A train of some 1,500–3,000 centrifuges would be more than adequate to produce at least one weapon's worth of enriched material per year.[224]

If Iran separated its facility construction, centrifuge research, and centrifuge production activities until it was ready to deploy at a major level, this would be difficult for even the best inspection effort to detect, confirm, and characterize. The same would be true if it simply brought all of its suspect activities on-line, including its large centrifuge facilities and new reactors, for purely peaceful purposes under full IAEA inspection. In both cases Iran could make major progress toward a rapid deployment or breakout capability without violating the NPT.

The same is true of virtually every aspect of nuclear warhead design and testing other than the actual testing of a full nuclear device. A great deal of nuclear warhead and bomb research and design is almost impossible to detect and verify. Testing of simulated nuclear weapons is at best ambiguous and hard to detect and characterize even with advanced intelligence collection systems. Iran is well aware of the various efforts Iraq made to conceal its activities from UN inspection and U.S. and other intelligence collection, and of Iraq's failures and successes.

Iran has decades of experience in dealing with IAEA inspectors, and it is learning a great deal more about Western intelligence capabilities from the efforts of the EU3 and the United States to pressure it to comply with the NPT. Similarly, charges by Israel and the Iranian opposition sometimes also help Iran learn what can and cannot be collected by outside sources. The unfortunate fact is that it is almost impossible for anyone to try to enforce a nonproliferation regime without teaching a proliferator a great deal about how to conceal its activities.

If Iran is proliferating, it had long engaged in what is now an ongoing duel in which it can pursue many different strategies in the future. There is no one moment in time when Iran has to comply or not comply. It has time, flexibility, and many future options.

Notes

[1] Dwight D. Eisenhower, "Atoms for Peace" (speech to the United Nations General Assembly, New York, December 8, 1953, available at http://www.eisenhowerinstitute.org/programs/globalpartnerships/safeguarding/atomsspeech.htm).

[2] International Institute for Strategic Studies (IISS), *Iran's Strategic Weapons Programmes: A Net Assessment,* IISS Strategic Dossier (London: IISS, September 2005), p. 10.

[3] Mohammad Sahimi, "Iran's Nuclear Program. Part I: Its History," *Payvand's Iran News,* October 10, 2003, available at http://www.payvand.com/news/03/oct/1015.html.

[4] This chronology relies heavily on the Nuclear Threat Initiative (NTI) chronology, news stories, and International Atomic Energy Agency (IAEA) reports.

[5] NTI, "Iran Profile: Nuclear Chronology, 1957–1985," available at http://www.nti.org/e_research/profiles/Iran/1825.html.

[6] Sahimi, "Iran's Nuclear Program. Part I: Its History."

[7] David Albright, "An Iranian Bomb?" *Bulletin of the Atomic Scientists* (January 1995), available at http://www.bullatomsci.org.

[8] NTI, "Iran Profile: Nuclear Chronology, 1957–1985."

[9] Ibid.

[10] Ibid.

[11] Sahimi, "Iran's Nuclear Program. Part I: Its History."

[12] Ibid.

[13] NTI, "Iran Profile: Nuclear Chronology, 1957–1985."

[14] Ibid.

[15] Ibid.

[16] Ibid.

[17] Ibid.

[18] Sahimi, "Iran's Nuclear Program. Part I: Its History."

[19] NTI, "Iran Profile: Nuclear Chronology, 1957–1985."

[20] Ibid.

[21] Ibid.

[22] Ibid.

[23] Ibid.

[24] Ibid.

[25] Ibid.

[26] This chronology relies heavily on the chronology created by the Nuclear Threat Initiative (NTI), news stories, and IAEA reports.

[27] Sahimi, "Iran's Nuclear Program. Part I: Its History."

[28] Ibid.

[29] Ibid.

[30] Ibid.

[31] Ibid.

[32] Ibid.

[33] NTI, "Iran Profile: Nuclear Chronology, 1987," available at http://www.nti.org/e_research /profiles/Iran/1825_1857.html.

[34] Ibid.

[35] Sahimi, "Iran's Nuclear Program. Part I: Its History."

[36] Ibid.

[37] Ibid.

[38] Ibid.

[39] Ibid.

[40] Ibid.

[41] NTI, "Iran Profile: Nuclear Chronology, 1990," available at http://www.nti.org/e_research /profiles/Iran/1825_1860.html.

[42] Ibid.

[43] NTI, "Iran Profile: Nuclear Chronology, 1991," available at http://www.nti.org/e_research /profiles/Iran/1825_1864.html.

[44] Sahimi, "Iran's Nuclear Program. Part I: Its History."

[45] Ibid.

[46] "China Releases Details of Nuclear Program with Iran," Associated Press, November 4, 1991.

[47] NTI, "Iran Profile: Nuclear Chronology, 1991."

[48] NTI, "Iran Profile: Nuclear Chronology, 1992," available at http://www.nti.org/e_research /profiles/Iran/1825_1869.html.

[49] Ibid.

[50] Ibid.

[51] Ibid.

[52] Ibid.

[53] Ibid.

[54] Ibid.

[55] Ibid.

[56] Ibid.

[57] Ibid.

[58] NTI, "Iran Profile: Nuclear Chronology, 1993," available at http://www.nti.org/e_research /profiles/Iran/1825_1870.html.

[59] Ibid.

[60] Ibid.

[61] Ibid.

[62] Ibid.

[63] Ibid.

[64] Ibid.

[65] Ibid.

[66] Ibid.

[67] Anthony H. Cordesman, *Iran and Nuclear Weapons: A Working Draft*, CSIS, February 21, 2000, available at http://www.csis.org/media/csis/pubs / irannuclear.pdf.

[68] Andrew Koch and Jeanette Wolf, *Iran's Nuclear Facilities: A Profile,* Center for Nonproliferation Studies, 1998, available at http://cns.miis.edu/pubs/reports/pdfs/iranrpt.pdf.

[69] NTI, "Iran Profile: Nuclear Chronology, 1994," available at http://www.nti.org/e_research/profiles/Iran/1825_1871.html.

[70] Mark Hibbs, "Iran May Withdraw from NPT over Western Trade Barriers," *Nucleonics Week* 35, no. 38 (September 22, 1994).

[71] "Blix Visits Iranian Nuclear Sites," *Iran Brief,* August 1, 1997.

[72] NTI, "Iran Profile: Nuclear Chronology, 1994."

[73] "Chinese Uranium Sale," *Iran Brief,* December 5, 1994.

[74] Michael Rubin, "Iran's Burgeoning WMD Program," *Middle East Intelligence Bulletin* 4, no. 3 (March/April 2002), available at http://www.meib.org/articles/0203_irn1.htm.

[75] "Blix Visits Iranian Nuclear Sites," *Iran Brief.*

[76] NTI, "Iran Profile: Nuclear Chronology, 1995," available at http://www.nti.org/e_research /profiles/Iran/1825_1872.html.

[77] Ibid.

[78] Ibid.

[79] Ibid.

[80] Ibid.

[81] Ibid.

[82] Robert Fisk, "Russian Envoy Downplays Iran's Nuclear Ambitions," *Independent* (London), May 30, 1995.

[83] NTI, "Iran Profile: Nuclear Chronology, 1995."

[84] Ibid.

[85] Ibid.

[86] Ibid.

[87] Ibid.

[88] Nick Rufford, "China Defies U.S. with Iran Nuclear Deal," *Sunday Times* (London), October 15, 1995.

[89] NTI, "Iran Profile: Nuclear Chronology, 1995."

[90] NTI, "Iran Profile: Nuclear Chronology, 1996," available at http://www.nti.org/e_research /profiles/Iran/1825_1873.html.

[91] Ibid.

[92] Ibid.

[93] Ibid.

[94] "Spain Providing Credits for Deal Involving Energy and Nuclear Projects," BBC News, March 5, 1996.

[95] "Russia to Ship Nuclear Equipment to Iran," Xinhua News Agency, March 4, 1996.

[96] Tim McGirk, "Iranians 'Buying Ex-Soviet Uranium,'" *Independent* (London), March 28, 1996.

[97] NTI, "Iran Profile: Nuclear Chronology, 1996."

[98] "Uranium Exploration with China," *Iran Brief*, May 6, 1996.

[99] Cordesman, *Iran and Nuclear Weapons: A Working Draft*.

[100] "Iran President: We Have Large Oil Reserves, Endless Gas," Associated Press, June 1, 1996.

[101] NTI, "Iran Profile: Nuclear Chronology, 1996."

[102] Ibid.

[103] Ibid.

[104] Ibid.

[105] Ibid.

[106] Ibid.

[107] Mark Hibbs, "China Has Far to Go Before U.S. Will Certify, Agencies Now Say," *Nucleonics Week* (December 12, 1996).

[108] NTI, "Iran Profile: Nuclear Chronology, 1997," available at http://www.nti.org/e_research /profiles/Iran/1825_1874.html.

[109] Ibid.

[110] Ibid.

[111] "Iranian Parliament to Investigate Inefficiency at Nuclear Power Plant," Agence France-Presse, June 25, 1997.

[112] "EU Leaks Report on Nuclear Program," *Iran Brief*, July 3, 1997.

[113] Cordesman, *Iran and Nuclear Weapons: A Working Draft*.

[114] Ibid.

[115] "Ukraine Cancels Nuclear Deal with Iran, Pleases U.S.," Associated Press, March 6, 1998.

[116] Steve Rodan, "Iran Paid $25m. for Nuclear Weapons, Documents Show," *Jerusalem Post*, April 10, 1998.

[117] "Clinton Signs Order Hitting Russian Groups on Technology Transfers," Associated Press, July 29, 1998.

[118] "Russia Signs Agreement for Completion of Iranian Nuclear Plant," Associated Press, November 24, 1998.

[119] NTI, "Iran Profile: Nuclear Chronology, 1998," available at http://www.nti.org/e_research /profiles/Iran/1825_1875.html.

[120] Cordesman, *Iran and Nuclear Weapons: A Working Draft.*

[121] "Russian Company Starts Building Nuclear Power Equipment for Iran," BBC Worldwide Monitoring, February 12, 1999.

[122] NTI, "Iran Profile: Nuclear Chronology, 1999," available at http://www.nti.org/e_research /profiles/Iran/1825_1876.html.

[123] Ibid.

[124] Dafna Linzer, "Strong Leads and Dead Ends in Nuclear Case against Iran," *Washington Post,* February 8, 2006, sec. A-1.

[125] This chronology relies heavily on the chronology created by the Nuclear Threat Initiative (NTI), news stories, and IAEA reports.

[126] NTI, "Iran Profile: Nuclear Chronology, 2000," available at http://www.nti.org/e_research/profiles/Iran/1825_1877.html.

[127] "Bushehr Reactor Installation Running behind Schedule," *Nuclear News* 43, no. 2 (February 1, 2000).

[128] NTI, "Iran Profile: Nuclear Chronology, 2000."

[129] Ibid.

[130] David Hoffman, "Russia to Allow Nuclear Exports; Despite '92 Pact, Putin Moves to Advance Power-Plant Deals," *Washington Post*, May 12, 2000.

[131] NTI, "Iran Profile: Nuclear Chronology, 2000."

[132] Mark Hibbs, "Iran Won't Accept More Inspections Unless U.S. Stops Nuclear Blockade," *Nucleonics Week* 41, no. 22 (June 1, 2000).

[133] "Russia Freezes Laser Deal with Iran," Associated Press, September 21, 2000.

[134] NTI, "Iran Profile: Nuclear Chronology, 2000."

[135] "Russia Expands Nuke Project in Iran," Associated Press, January 16, 2001.

[136] NTI, "Iran Profile: Nuclear Chronology, 2001," available at http://www.nti.org/e_research/profiles/Iran/1825_1878.html.

[137] Ibid.

[138] Ibid.

[139] Ibid.

[140] Ibid.

[141] Ibid.

[142] Ibid.

[143] "Israeli Defense Minister: Iran Could Have Nuclear Weapons by 2005," Associated Press, July 9, 2001.

[144] "Iran Maintains Active Program to Get Nuclear, Biological and Chemical Weapons, CIA Says," Associated Press, September 7, 2001.

[145] NTI, "Iran Profile: Nuclear Chronology, 2001."

[146] Michael Wines, "Russia and Iran Sign Arms Deal; Nuclear Reactors on the Way," *New York Times*, October 3, 2001.

[147] NTI, "Iran Profile: Nuclear Chronology, 2002," available at http://www.nti.org/e_research/profiles/Iran/1825_1879.html.

[148] "Official: Russia Committed to Completing Nuclear Reactor in Iran," Associated Press, February 14, 2002.

[149] "Bushehr 1 Plant Changes to Fit VVER Mean Startup in Early 2004," *Nucleonics Week* 43, no. 12 (March 21, 2002).

[150] NTI, "Iran Profile: Nuclear Chronology, 2002."

[151] Bill Gertz and Rowan Scarborough, "Inside the Ring," *Washington Times*, May 10, 2002.

[152] "Russia Pledges to Accept Spent Nuclear Fuel from Iranian Power Plant," Associated Press, July 12, 2002.

[153] Angela Charlton, "Russia Plans New Nuclear, Oil Cooperation with Iran despite U.S. Opposition," Associated Press, July 26, 2002.

[154] The National Council of Resistance of Iran (NCRI) is the political arm of Mujahedin-e Khalq (MEK), a Marxist-Islamist organization that operated from Iraq until the invasion of 2003. MEK is a militant group that is also on the list of U.S. State Department terrorist organizations. MEK is estimated to have several thousand members.

[155] Alireza Jafarzadeh, "New Information on Top Secret Projects of the Iranian Regime's Nuclear Program" (remarks by Washington representative of the National Council of Resistance of Iran [NCRI], August 14, 2002, available at http://www.iranwatch.org/privateviews/NCRI/perspex-ncri-topsecretprojects-081402.htm).

[156] Statement by Reza Aghazadeh at the 46th General Conference of the IAEA in Vienna, September 16, 2002, available at http://www.iaea.org/About/Policy/GC/GC46/iran.pdf.

[157] International Atomic Energy Agency (IAEA), *Implementation of the NPT Safeguards Agreement in the Islamic Republic of Iran: Report by the Director*

General, June 6, 2003, p. 2, available at http://www.iaea.org/Publications/Documents/Board/2003/gov2003-40.pdf.

158 David Ensor, "U.S. Has Photos of Secret Iran Nuclear Sites," CNN, December 13, 2002, available at http://archives.cnn.com/2002/WORLD/meast/12/12/iran.nuclear/.

159 IAEA, *Implementation of the NPT Safeguards Agreement: Report by the Director General,* June 6, 2003, p. 7.

160 Ibid., pp. 7–8.

161 IAEA, *Implementation of the NPT Safeguards Agreement in the Islamic Republic of Iran: Resolution Adopted by the Board on 12 September 2003,* September 12, 2003, p.2, available at http://www.iaea.org/Publications/Documents/Board/2003/gov2003-69.pdf.

162 Ibid.

163 Statement by Reza Aghazadeh at the 47th General Conference of the IAEA in Vienna, September 15, 2003, available at http://www.iaea.org/About/Policy/GC/GC47/Statements/iran.pdf.

164 The statement is available at http://www.iaea.org/NewsCenter/Focus/IaeaIran/statement_iran21102003.shtml.

165 IAEA, "Update on IAEA Verification in Iran" (media advisory, October 31, 2003, available at http://www.iaea.org/NewsCenter/MediaAdvisory/Iran/ma_iran_3110.html).

166 Mohamed ElBaradei, "Opening Remarks at the Press Conference on the Outcome of the Board of Directors' Consideration of the Implementation of Safeguards in the Islamic Republic of Iran" (statement by the IAEA director general, November 26, 2003; the full statement is available at http://www.iaea.org/NewsCenter/Statements/2003/ebsp2003n026.html).

167 IAEA, "Iran Signs Additional Protocols on Nuclear Safeguards: Signing Ceremony Takes Place at IAEA" (staff report, December 18, 2003, available at http://www.iaea.org/NewsCenter/News/2003/iranap20031218.html).

168 Christiane Amanpour, "Iran Made Radioactive Element," CNN, February 24, 2004, available at http://edition.cnn.com/2004/WORLD/meast/02/24/iran.nuclear/index.html.

169 IAEA, *Implementation of the NPT Safeguards Agreement in the Islamic Republic of Iran: Report by the Director General,* February 24, 2004, p. 3, available at http://www.nuclearfiles.org/menu/key-issues/nuclear-weapons/issues/proliferation/iran/iaeareport2_24_04.pdf.

170 IAEA, *Implementation of the NPT Safeguards Agreement in the Islamic Republic of Iran: Resolution Adopted by the Board on 13 March 2004,* March 13,

2004, pp. 1-2, available at http://www.iaea.org/Publications/Documents/Board/ 2004/gov2004-21.pdf.

[171] David Sanger, "Pakistan Found to Aid Iran Nuclear Efforts," *New York Times,* September 2, 2004.

[172] IAEA, *Implementation of the NPT Safeguards Agreement: Report by the Director General,* February 24, 2004, p. 12.

[173] IAEA Secretariat, *Communication of 5 March 2004 from the Permanent Mission of the Islamic Republic of Iran concerning the Report of the Director General contained in GOV/2004/11,* March 5, 2004, pp. 5-6, available at http:// www.iaea.org/Publications/Documents/Infcircs/2004/infcirc628.pdf.

[174] Ibid.

[175] IAEA Secretariat, *Secretariat Response to Comments and Explanatory Notes Provided by Iran in INFCIRC/628 on the Director General's Report on "Implementation of the NPT Safeguards Agreement in the Islamic Republic of Iran," GOV/ 2004/11,* March 30, 2004, p. 4, available at http://www.iaea.org/NewsCenter/ Focus/IaeaIran/iaea_note172004.pdf.

[176] Kenneth C. Brill, "Statement on the Implementation of Safeguards in the Islamic Republic of Iran" (statement to IAEA Board of Governors on March 13, 2004, available at http://www.iaea.org/NewsCenter/Statements/Misc/2004/ brill13032004.html).

[177] Ian Traynor, "Iran to Resume Nuclear Program," *Guardian* (Manchester), June 28, 2004, available at http://www.guardian.co.uk/iran/story/0,12858 ,1248785,00.html.

[178] Mohamed ElBaradei, *Communication Dated 26 November 2004 Received from the Permanent Representatives of France, Germany, the Islamic Republic of Iran and the United Kingdom Concerning the Agreement Signed in Paris on 15 November 2004,* November 15, 2004, available at http://www.iaea.org/Publications/ Documents/Infcircs/2004/infcirc637.pdf.

[179] George Jahn, "Iran Satisfies IAEA Regarding Enrichment," Associated Press, November 15, 2004.

[180] Ali Akbar Dareini, "Iran Suspends Uranium Enrichment," Associated Press, November 22, 2004.

[181] Robin Wright and Keith Richburg, "Powell Says Iran Is Pursuing Bomb," *Washington Post,* November 18, 2004, sec. A-1.

[182] Bill Gertz, "U.S. Told of Iranian Effort to Create Nuclear Warhead," *Washington Times,* December 2, 2004, p. 3.

[183] Lally Weymouth, "Q&A: ElBaradei, Feeling the Nuclear Heat," *Washington Post,* January 30, 2005, sec. B-1.

[184] Ibid.

[185] IAEA, "IAEA Board Briefed on IAEA Safeguards in Iran" (staff report, March 1, 2005, available at http://www.iaea.org/NewsCenter/News/2005/board_briefing.html).

[186] Alec Russell, "Iran Challenges US over Nuclear Programme," *Daily Telegraph* (London), February 7, 2005, p. 10.

[187] International Institute for Strategic Studies, *Iran's Strategic Weapons Programmes: A Net Assessment*, September 2005, pp. 27–28.

[188] Ibid.

[189] Robin Wright and Peter Baker, "U.S. Backs Europeans on Incentives for Iran," *Washington Post*, March 11, 2005, sec. A-14.

[190] Jad Mouawad, "Iran Offers Europe 'Guarantees' on Its Nuclear Program," *New York Times*, March 17, 2005.

[191] "Iran to Soon Resume Sensitive Nuclear Activities," Radio Free Europe/Radio Liberty (RFE/RL), May 10, 2005, available at http://www.rferl.org/featuresarticle/2005/05/629730F8-36AE-4752-B4B3-E1B2CC8E9509.html.

[192] Ali Akbar, "Iran Confirms Uranium-to-Gas Conversion," Associated Press, May 9, 2005.

[193] Paula Wolfson, "Bush Backs Europeans' Tough Line on Iran," Voice of America, May 12, 2005, available at http://www.voanews.com/english/archive/2005-05/2005-05-12-voa79.cfm?CFID=23764315&CFTOKEN=15317551.

[194] "Rafsanjani: Continuation of Iran-EU3 Dialogue Best Option," Islamic Republic News Agency (IRNA), May 11, 2005.

[195] "Iran Says It Will Resume Uranium Enrichment Regardless of Election Outcome," Associated Press, June 24, 2005.

[196] "Iran Determined to Continue Civilian Nuclear Program," BBC Monitoring International Reports, June 24, 2005, available through LexisNexis.

[197] "Ahmadinejad: Iran Will Continue Nuclear Program, Says Does Not Need U.S. Help," Islamic Republic News Agency (IRNA), June 26, 2005.

[198] "IAEA Allows Iran to Remove Nuclear Seals—Official," Reuters, August 10, 2005.

[199] IAEA, *Implementation of the NPT Safeguards Agreement in the Islamic Republic of Iran and Related Board Resolutions: Resolution Adopted by the Board on 11 August 2005*, August 11, 2005, p.2, available at http://www.iaea.org/Publications/Documents/Board/2005/gov2005-64.pdf.

[200] William J. Kole, "UN Agency's Restrained Response to Iran Signals Preference for Talks over Sanctions," Associated Press, August 12, 2005.

[201] "Europeans Call off Nuclear Talks with Iran—France," Reuters, August 23, 2005.

[202] George Jahn, "U.N. Report Says Iran Has Produced Tons of Gas Needed for Uranium Enrichment," Associated Press, September 2, 2005.

[203] IAEA, *Implementation of the NPT Safeguards Agreement in the Islamic Republic of Iran: Report by the Director General*, September 2, 2005, p. 11, available at http://www.iaea.org/Publications/Documents/Board/2005/gov2005-67.pdf.

[204] Con Coughlin, "UN Inspectors 'Powerless to Stop Atom Bomb Plans in Iran,'" *Daily Telegraph* (London), September 11, 2005, available at http://www.telegraph.co.uk/news/main.jhtml?xml=/news/2005/09/11/wiran11.xml&sSheet=/portal/2005/09/11/ixportal.html.

[205] Dafna Linzer, "U.S. Deploys Slide Show to Press Case Against Iran," *Washington Post*, September 14, 2005, sec. A-7.

[206] Coughlin, "UN Inspectors 'Powerless to Stop Atom Bomb Plans in Iran.'"

[207] "IAEA Urged to Refer Tehran to UN," BBC News, September 19, 2005.

[208] IAEA, *Implementation of the NPT Safeguards Agreement in the Islamic Republic of Iran: Report by the Director General*, November 18, 2005, p. 11, available at http://www.iaea.org/Publications/Documents/Board/2005/gov2005-87.pdf.

[209] Elaine Sciolino, "Iran Declares Its Nuclear Plan Nonnegotiable," *New York Times*, January 5, 2006.

[210] Ibid.

[211] Germany, United Kingdom, France, and EU High Representative, "Statement by Germany, United Kingdom, France and EU High Representative on Iranian Nuclear Issue," Europa, January 12, 2006, available at http://europa-eu-un.org/articles/en/article_5554_en.htm.

[212] IAEA, "Developments in the Implementation of the NPT Safeguards Agreement in the Islamic Republic of Iran and Agency Verification of Iran's Suspension of Enrichment-related and Reprocessing Activities: Update Brief by the Deputy Director General for Safeguards," January 31, 2006, available at http://www.iaea.org/NewsCenter/Statements/DDGs/2006/heinonen31012006.pdf.

[213] IAEA, *Implementation of the NPT Safeguards Agreement in the Islamic Republic of Iran: Resolution Adopted on 4 February 2006*, February 4, 2006, available at http://www.iaea.org/Publications/Documents/Board/2006/gov2006-14.pdf.

[214] IAEA Secretariat, *Communication Dated 2 February 2006 Received from the Permanent Mission of the Islamic Republic of Iran to the Agency*, February 3, 2006, available at http://www.iaea.org/Publications/Documents/Infcircs/2006/infcirc666.pdf.

215 United Nations Security Council, "Calls on Iran to Take Steps Required by IAEA Board of Governors; Requests Report from IAEA Director General in 30 Days," March 29, 2006, available at http://www.un.org/News/Press/docs/2006/sc8679.doc.htm.

216 Elaine Sciolino, "Showdown At U.N.? Iran Seems Calm," *New York Times*, March 14, 2006.

217 Sharon Squassoni, "Iran's Nuclear Program: Recent Developments," Congressional Research Service (CRS), November 23, 2005, p. 2.

218 Interview with *Der Spiegel*, February 21, 2005, available at http://www.iaea.org/NewsCenter/Transcripts/2005/derspiegel21022005.html.

219 "IAEA's ElBaradei Says Iran Sanctions 'Bad Idea,'" Reuters, March 30, 2006.

220 Pierre Goldschmidt, "The Urgent Need to Strengthen the Nuclear Non-Proliferation Regime," Carnegie Endowment for International Peace, *Policy Outlook*, no. 25 (January 2005).

221 Con Coughlin, "Iran Sets Up Secret Team to Infiltrate UN Nuclear Watchdog, Say Officials," *Daily Telegraph* (London), January 30, 2006, available at http://www.telegraph.co.uk/news/main.jhtml?xml=/news/2006/01/30/wiran30.xml&sSheet=/news/2006/01/30/ixworld.html.

222 Geoff Odlum, "Iran's Nuclear Program: Indicators of Intent?" (U.S. State Department draft briefing for the University of California Institute on Global Conflict and Cooperation [IGCC], February 2006).

223 Sciolino, "Showdown at U.N.? Iran Seems Calm."

224 Sir John Thompson and Geoffrey Forden, "Multinational Facilities May Solve Iranian Nuclear Stalemate," *Jane's Intelligence Review*, April 1, 2006.

CHAPTER SEVEN

THE UNCERTAIN CHARACTER OF IRAN'S NUCLEAR FACILITIES

As the previous chapters have shown, Iran's uranium enrichment and plutonium production activities are taking place in a long list of known and suspect nuclear facilities, many of which have raised serious questions regarding their character and the nature of Iran's nuclear research, development, and production activities. Iran has a large and well-dispersed mix of state industries and military facilities it can use to hide its activities or to shelter and disperse them. There are no accurate unclassified lists of such facilities. Map 7.1 shows key nuclear sites that have been the focus of IAEA inspections. The map also shows how dispersed and diverse these facilities are.

Claims have been made in various press reports and by opposition sources over the years that Iran is carrying out parts of a nuclear weapons program in a wide range of sites—only some of which have turned out to be real or probable. As the previous chapter has shown, however, suspect activities have been found in many of the facilities that have been declared or discovered.

Table 7.1 shows the IAEA's designation of key nuclear facilities. This list, and subsequent analysis of the nature of developments at these sites, shows again how difficult it is to understand the overall structure and scale of Iran's activities, to know whether they are weapons-related, and to know enough to target them. It is possible, however, to provide a broad description of the known activities at 18 major or potentially important sites.

Enough is also known about these sites to reveal a further pattern of concealment and uncertainty, as well as many of the difficulties in

Map 7.1 Key Known Iranian Nuclear Sites

Source: International Institute of Strategic Studies (IISS), *Iran's Strategic Weapons Programmes: A Net Assessment,* IISS Strategic Dossier (London: IISS, September 2005). Reproduced by permission of Taylor & Francis Books UK.

both inspecting and targeting such sites. It should be stressed, however, that the following site descriptions are unclassified, that the IAEA has a far more detailed picture of their nature and capability, and that any military targeting of a given site would be based on years of intelligence collection and analysis whose character and accuracy are impossible to estimate.

ANARAK

Iran has stated that small amounts of imported UO_2 were prepared for targets at Jabr Ibn Hayan Multipurpose Laboratories (JHL), irradiated at the Tehran Research Reactor (TRR), and sent to a laboratory belonging to the MIX Facility in Tehran for separation of I-131 in a lead-shielded cell.

Iran informed the IAEA that the remaining nuclear waste was solidified and eventually transferred to a waste disposal site at Anarak. There reportedly is uranium ore near Anarak, not far from Yazd. The

Talmesi Mine near Anarak has produced seelite, which occurs with uranospinite. The IAEA accused Iran of failing to report design information for Anarak. The agency argued that uranium was imported in 1991.[1]

ARAK

Arak was identified by the Iranian opposition group, the NCRI, in 2002 as the site where it believes Tehran has been building a heavy water reactor. This discovery seems to have surprised inspectors because it was believed that Iran's nuclear research used light water reactors, as is the case in Bushehr. Experts have expressed concern because heavy water reactors produce a significant amount of plutonium that can be used for nuclear weapons. Following the revelations in 2002, Tehran announced its plans for building a heavy water reactor in Arak.[2]

The IAEA estimated in 2004 that Iran was at least five years away from completing the Arak reactor:

> Iran is in the process of constructing the IR-40 reactor at Arak (although originally planned to be built at Esfahan, a decision is said to have been taken in 2002 to build the reactor at Arak instead). The basic design of the IR-40 was completed in 2002, and provides for the use of natural uranium oxide as fuel. It is planned to go into operation in 2014 . . . . The IR-40 is said to have been based on indigenous design. The purpose of the reactor was declared to be research and development and the production of radioisotopes for medical and industrial use.
>
> Iran is also building a heavy water production plant (HWPP) at Arak, and has said that it intends to start producing heavy water there in 2004 . . . . In its letter of 21 October 2003, Iran acknowledged that two hot cells had been foreseen for the reactor project. In that letter, Iran also made reference to its plans for nine hot cells for the production of radioisotopes (molybdenum, iodine, xenon, cobalt-60 and iridium-192); specifically, "four for the production of radioisotopes, two for the production of cobalt and iridium and three for waste management processing" (along with ten back-up manipulators). According to the information provided in that letter, however, neither the design nor detailed information about the

Table 7.1
Relevant Nuclear Locations in Iran Designated by the IAEA
(as of November 2004)

Location	Facility/Reactor	Status (November 2004)
Tehran Nuclear Research Center (TNRC)	Tehran Research Reactor (TRR)	Operating
	Molybdenum, iodine, and xenon radioisotope production facility (MIX facility)	Constructed, but not operating
	*Jabr Ibn Hayan Multipurpose Laboratories (JHL)	Operating
	*Waste handling facility (WHF)	Operating
Tehran	*Kalaye Electric Company	Dismantled pilot enrichment facility; being converted to centrifuge enrichment R&D
Bushehr	Bushehr Nuclear Power Plant (BNPP)	Under construction
Esfahan Nuclear Technology Center (ENTC)	Miniaturized neutron source reactor (MNSR)	Operating
	Light water subcritical reactor (LWSCR)	Operating
	Heavy water zero power reactor (HWZPR)	Operating
	Fuel fabrication laboratory (FFL)	Operating
	Uranium chemistry laboratory (UCL)	Closed down
	Uranium conversion facility (UCF)	Hot testing/ commissioning stage
	Graphite subcritical reactor (GSCR)	Decommissioned
	*Fuel manufacturing plant (FMP)	In detailed design stage, construction to have begun in 2004
	*Zirconium production plant (ZPP)	Under construction
Natanz	*Pilot fuel enrichment plant (PFEP)	Operational; currently suspended
	*Fuel enrichment plant (FEP)	Under construction; currently suspended

(continued)

Table 7.1 *(continued)*

Karaj	*Radioactive waste storage	Partially operating
Lashkar Ab'ad	*Pilot uranium laser enrichment plant	Dismantled
Arak	*Iran Nuclear Research Reactor (IR-40)	In detailed design phase
	*Hot cell facility for production of radioisotopes	Declared as no longer being under consideration
	*Heavy water production plant (HWPP)	Under construction
Anarak	*Waste storage site	Waste to be transferred to JHL

Source: Adapted from IAEA, *Implementation of the NPT Safeguards Agreement in the Islamic Republic of Iran: Report by the Director General*, November 15, 2004, Annex 1.

*Declared in 2003.

dimensions or the actual layout of the hot cells were available yet, since the Iranian authorities did not know the characteristics of the manipulators and lead glass shielding windows which they could procure.

In the IR-40 design information provided by Iran in November 2003, Iran confirmed that it had tentative plans for a building, in the proximity of the IR-40 facilities, with hot cells for the production of "long lived radioisotopes." Iran agreed to submit the relevant preliminary design information with respect to that building in due course. In May 2004, Iran provided updated design information for the reactor, in which it noted that the planning of hot cells for "long lived radioisotopes" was no longer under consideration in light of difficulties with the procurement of equipment.

In August 2004, Iran presented to the Agency detailed drawings that Iran had received from a foreign company in 1977 for hot cells that were to have been constructed at Esfahan. Iran stated that it had not yet made more detailed plans for hot cells for the IR-40 complex at Arak, but that it had used information from those drawings as the basis for specifications in its efforts to procure manipulators for hot cells intended for the production of cobalt and iridium isotopes.

In a letter dated 19 August 2004 Iran reconfirmed the nine hot-cell project at Arak. During its October 2004 visit to Iran, the Agency showed Iran evidence of Iran's enquiries about the purchase of hot cell manipulators and lead glass windows, and requested clarification of how such precise and detailed specifications could have been provided on a procurement request if no preliminary hot cell designs existed. In response, Iran gave the Agency documents relevant to other enquiries about lead glass windows. Iran reiterated, however, that the specifications it had used for its enquiries had been based on designs provided by a foreign supplier in the 1970s, as well as on its own experience with the hot cells at the MIX Facility (a laboratory for the production of radioisotopes of molybdenum, iodine and xenon from natural uranium oxide) at TNRC. Iran provided a sketch of the hot cells with a calculated capability of handling activity levels from 100 to 10 000 curies (3.7 to 370 TBq). However, Iran stated that the design would be completed only upon successful procurement by Iran of manipulators and lead glass windows. The Agency has received some of the requested information from Iran, which it is assessing, but is still awaiting other information.[3]

Iran informed the IAEA that it had carried out laboratory-scale experiments to produce heavy water at the Esfahan Nuclear Technology Center.It also said that two hot cells had been foreseen for its project at Arak, and that yet another building with hot cells is planned for the production of radioisotopes. However, Iran still appears to be at least five years away from completing the heavy water reactor at Arak. According to reports published in Russia, apparently based on information developed by the Russian Federal Security Service, the facilities at Arak are collocated with those involved in R&D of unguided missiles and modifications of the Scud-C missile.

The head of Iran's Supreme National Security Council, Hasan Rowhani, said in May 2005 that Iran made steady process in building a 40-megawatt heavy water nuclear reactor at Arak: "In technical terms, we didn't have suspension in the Arak heavy water plant even for one day. . . . That means we've constantly made progress. It's possible that production of heavy water will be completed in upcoming months."[4] It remains uncertain how credible this projection was.

But the fact Iran has tried to get hot cells for the Arak site that are suitable for plutonium separation work—and has refused IAEA requests for further information related to its hot cell procurement effort—is an issue. So is the building of a reactor that is supposed to duplicate the function of Iran's underutilized 10-megawatt light water research reactor for producing medical and industrial isotopes.

ARDAKAN

Ardakan was first revealed in November 2003 by the NCRI and was reportedly scheduled to be completed in mid-2005. Some reports indicate that a uranium mill with an annual capacity of 120,000 metric tons of ore and an annual output of 50 metric tons of uranium was being built 35 kilometers north of Ardakan city.[5]

The IAEA investigated the sites and reported the following on November 15, 2004:

> The ore is to be processed into uranium ore concentrate (UOC/yellowcake) at the associated mill at Ardakan, the Yellowcake Production Plant. The design capacity of the mill corresponds to that of the mine (50 t of uranium per year). The mill startup is forecast to coincide with the start of mining at Saghand. The mill site is currently at an early stage of development; the installation of the infrastructure and processing buildings has been started. In the south of Iran, near Bandar Abbas, Iran has constructed the Gchine uranium mine and its co-located mill. The low but variable grade uranium ore found in near-surface deposits will be open-pit mined and processed at the associated mill. The estimated production design capacity is 21 t of uranium per year. Iran has stated that, as of July 2004, mining operations had started and the mill had been hot tested, during which testing a quantity of about 40 to 50 kg of yellowcake was produced.[6]

BUSHEHR

Bushehr is located at the site of a German-built reactor project the shah commissioned in the 1970s and was bombed during the Iran-Iraq war. and The new reactor is being built to Russian designs and will use some 90 tons of Russian-supplied enriched uranium. There are two reactor sites at Bushehr, but no work is taking place on the second site.

The reactor's design is not suited to produce high levels of plutonium, as long as it operates as designed. High levels would present problems because of the amount of Pu-240 produced relative to Pu-239, and developments at Bushehr have been uncertain. The following chronology tracks developments in Bushehr and shows its high dependence on foreign assistance, particularly from the Germans and the Russians:

- **November 1974:** Iran signed an agreement to buy two 1,200-megawatt (MW) pressurized water reactors (PWRs) from a German firm, Kraftwerk Union (KWU), to be installed at Bushehr. Germany was to provide enriched uranium for the initial loading and ten years' worth of reloads.[7]

- **August 1975:** A team from KWU starts working on Bushehr "on the basis of a letter of intent."[8]

- **July 1976:** The AEOI officially signs the contract with KWU to install the two PWRs at Bushehr at the cost of 7.8 billion DM.[9]

- **May 1977:** The two PWRs were 33 percent complete.[10]

- **April 1979:** The two PWRs were 50 percent complete.[11]

- **May 1979:** The two PWRs were 77 percent complete.[12]

- **June 1979:** KWU halted its work at Bushehr because of Iran's failure to pay $450 million. KWU handed over the control of the two PWRs to the Iranians because Tehran refused to extend the work permits of the German workers working at Bushehr. The project was worth $5.0 billion, and one of the reactors reportedly was 85 percent complete.[13]

- **August 1979:** KWU formally terminated the construction of the PWRs at Bushehr. Most reports say that the first reactor was 75–85 percent complete, the second reactor was 45–70 percent complete, and 90 percent of the parts had been shipped.[14]

- **1980:** Iran asked KWU to return the initial payments it had received or else complete the project. They litigated their disagreement in Geneva and Iran won.[15]

- **March 1982:** An agreement was reached on the resumption of work on one of the two PWRs.[16]

- **October 1982:** India announced that it was sending engineers to inspect Bushehr. The results of the inspections were unclear.[17]

- **March 1984:** Iraq attacked the Bushehr reactor. It attacked again in February 1985, March 1985, July 1986, November 1987, and July 1988.[18] The damage to the reactor was unclear, especially given that the reactor was aging and had lacked maintenance for many years, since the suspension of work in 1979.

- **October 1985:** A team from KWU visited Bushehr to conduct a feasibility study on completing at least one of the PWRs.[19]

- **February 1986:** A.Q. Khan secretly visited Bushehr. Pakistan and Iran signed a secret nuclear cooperation agreement later in the year. Khan revisited Bushehr in January 1987.[20]

- **October 1986:** Iran approached Argentina to discuss the possible involvement of Argentina and Spain in the construction of the Bushehr reactors. In addition, there was discussion about a German-Argentinean-Spanish consortium to finish the Bushehr reactor.[21]

- **August 1992:** KWU formally told Tehran that its PWR deal was canceled indefinitely.[22]

Iran signed two agreements with Russia on constructing a nuclear power plant. Moscow agreed to construct nuclear power plants, cycle nuclear fuel, supply reactors, reprocess nuclear fuel, train Iranian nuclear scientists, and provide isotopes for academic and civilian research.[23]

- **January 1995:** The Atomic Energy Organization of Iran (AEOI) and the Russian company Zarubezhatomenergostroi completed negotiations on constructing the Bushehr nuclear plants.[24] They signed an $800 million contract by which Moscow was to complete one of two nuclear reactors within four years.

- **January 1996:** The Russian-Iranian contract on the Bushehr reactors went into effect. Russia was obligated to deliver the plants within 55 months.[25]

- **March 1996:** More than 600 Russian engineers were working at the Bushehr nuclear power plant.[26]

- **January 1997:** Russian atomic energy minister Viktor Mikhailov said that 1,000 Russian engineers will work at the Bushehr nuclear power plant in Iran.[27]

- **March 1997:** President Rafsanjani said Bushehr will be capable of producing 2,000 MW of power.[28]

- **July 1997:** A Ukrainian company agreed to develop a slow-rotation turbine for Iran's nuclear power plant in Bushehr. The turbine operates at 1,500 rotations per minute and is considered safer and less expensive than a fast-rotating turbine.[29]

- **September 2002:** Russian technicians began construction of Iran's first nuclear reactor at Bushehr despite strong objections from the United States.[30]

- **January 2005:** Iran and Russian disagreed about the payment of spent nuclear fuel.

- **February 2005:** Russia and Iran signed an agreement by which Russia would supply the nuclear fuel for the Bushehr facility and recover all spent fuel.

According to IAEA estimates in November 2004, Bushehr is scheduled to reach initial criticality in 2006. Some 600–1,000 Russians are estimated to be working on the project. Some 750 Iranian technicians, trained in Russia, will take over the plant once it becomes operational. As noted earlier, Russia agreed in 1995 to provide Iran with plutonium to fuel the nuclear reactor and collect its spent fuel and reiterated its commitment in the February 2005 agreement.

In May 2005, Russia announced that it planned to send the first delivery of nuclear fuel to Iran by the end of 2005. The agreement called for sending 100 tons of nuclear fuel. Alexander Rumyantsev, the head of the Russian Atomic Ministry, said, "They [the Iranians] have to start to fire it up mid-2006. The fuel has to be at the plant six months before that."[31]

The commitment by Tehran to repatriate spent fuel to Russia is seen with suspicion by the United States. Under the agreement with Moscow, Iran was not required to return the waste nuclear fuel for several years after the delivery of the fuel. Given Tehran's history in Bushehr and its dealing with the IAEA, the Bush administration expressed its concerns that Iran may reprocess the spent fuel to isolate the plutonium before it is repatriated to Russia. In addition, the Iranians announced that for the remaining 20–40 years of the Bushehr reactor's life, Tehran would supply its own enriched fuel to operate the reactor.[32]

The United States officially supported Russia's plan, but the United States was concerned with possible misuse of the reactor. Some U.S. officials claimed that the cost of building Bushehr went beyond what was required for civilian nuclear power plants. They also estimated that Bushehr might ultimately be used to produce plutonium at a rate high enough to produce nearly 30 nuclear weapons.[33] These claims remain unverifiable, but Iran is considering the construction of three to five more power reactor facilities, which may or may not be located at Bushehr.

Other experts feel such concerns are exaggerated. For example, Hans Blix, former chief UN weapons inspector, said that the plant was initially built by the Germans and that the Russians tried to install only low-grade nuclear technology. He added that the problem with the Bushehr reactor was that it was not ideal for producing plutonium: "It is possible, but very difficult." He added that the international community should be more concerned with Iran's uranium enrichment program than with its plutonium separation experiments.[34]

Others, however, argue that Bushehr can be used to produce more weapons-grade materials by changing the fuel loading cycle of the reactor. They believe it also can be used to develop the skills and technology necessary to design other reactors that are better suited to producing weapons-grade plutonium.[35] Bushehr is central to Iran's ability to produce plutonium, and this largely depends on Russia's help. In addition, it has been reported that, because of the site's importance, several batteries of U.S.-made Hawk (improved) surface-to-air missiles have been placed around Bushehr for fear of military strikes against the reactor.

ESFAHAN (ISFAHAN)

The University of Isfahan operates Iran's largest nuclear research center, which is said to employ as many as 3,000 scientists. Facilities are said to include a fuel fabrication laboratory (FFL); uranium chemistry laboratory (UCL); uranium conversion facility (UCF); and fuel manufacturing plant (FMP). In addition, two reactors subject to IAEA inspections are located at Esfahan:

- The miniaturized neutron source reactor (MNSR), a 30-kilowatt light water reactor in operation since the mid-1990s that uses U/Al fuel enriched to 90.2 percent U-235; and the heavy water zero power reactor (HWZPR).

- A 100-watt heavy water reactor has been in operation since the mid-1990s. It uses natural uranium metal fuel. Iran also has a light water subcritical reactor (LWSCR) using uranium metal fuel, which operates a few days during the year, and a decommissioned graphite subcritical reactor (GSCR) that used uranium metal fuel.

According to some sources, this is a primary location for the Iranian nuclear weapons program, with the main buildings located at Roshandasht, 15 kilometers southeast of Esfahan. At one point, Iran sought to build a uranium hexafluoride (UF_6) conversion plant at the center with Chinese assistance. The IAEA did find that Iran performed at least some unreported plutonium separation experiments at the facility and has made Esfahan a key focus of its investigations. Its November 2004 report noted:

> Iran carried out most of its experiments in uranium conversion between 1981 and 1993 at TNRC and at the Esfahan Nuclear Technology Centre (ENTC), with some experiments (e.g., those involving pulse columns) being carried out through early 2002.
>
> In 1991, Iran entered into discussions with a foreign supplier for the construction at Esfahan of an industrial scale conversion facility. Construction on the facility, UCF, was begun in the late 1990s. UCF consists of several conversion lines, principal among which is the line for the conversion of UOC to UF6 with an annual design production capacity of 200 tons of uranium as UF6. The UF6 is to be sent to the uranium enrichment facilities at Natanz, where it will be enriched up to 5 percent U-235 and the product and tails returned to UCF for conversion into low enriched UO2 and depleted

uranium metal. The design information for UCF provided by Iran indicates that conversion lines are also foreseen for the production of natural and enriched (19.7 percent) uranium metal, and natural UO2. The natural and enriched (5 percent U-235) UO2 are to be sent to the Fuel Manufacturing Plant (FMP) at Esfahan, where Iran has said it will be processed into fuel for a research reactor and power reactors.

In March 2004, Iran began testing the process lines involving the conversion of UOC into UO2 and UF4, and UF4 into UF6. As of June 2004, 40 to 45 kg of UF6 had been produced therefrom. A larger test, involving the conversion of 37 t of yellowcake into UF4, was initiated in August 2004. According to Iran's declaration of 14 October 2004, 22.5 tons of the 37 tons of yellowcake had been fed into the process and that approximately 2 tons of UF4, and 17.5 tons of uranium as intermediate products and waste, had been produced. There was no indication as of that date of UF6 having been produced during this later campaign.

Iran has stated that UCF was to have been constructed under a turn-key contract with a foreign supplier, but that when the contract was cancelled in 1997, Iran retained the engineering designs and used them as the basis to construct UCF with Iranian resources. Iran provided preliminary design information to the Agency in July 2000. The Agency has been carrying out continuous design information verification (DIV) since that time. The Agency's enquiry into the chronology and scope of Iran's uranium conversion activities has focused on two central issues:

- Assessment of Iran's statements concerning the basis for its design of UCF (including conversion experiments), with a view to ascertaining whether Iran has declared all of its activities involving nuclear material; and

- Assessment of the declared intended uses for the products of the various UCF process lines.

. . . In 1985, Iran brought into operation a Fuel Fabrication Laboratory (FFL) at Esfahan, about which it informed the Agency in 1993 and for which design information was provided to the Agency in 1998. It is still in operation, and is suitable for producing, on a small scale, fuel pellets. The fuel manufacturing plant to be constructed at Esfahan (FMP) is scheduled to be commissioned in 2007. According to the preliminary design information that has been provided by Iran, the facility is planned to produce 40 tons per year of UO2 fuel (with a maximum enrichment of 5 percent) for research and power reactors. Iran is also building a Zirconium Production Plant (ZPP) at Esfahan which, when complete, will have a capacity to produce 10 tons of zirconium tubing per year . . . . In a letter dated 5 May 2003, Iran informed the Agency of its plan to commence in 2003 the construction of FMP. On 1 November 2003, Iran submitted preliminary design information for FMP stating that the plant capacity would be 30 t UO2 per year. On 31 August 2004, Iran submitted updated design information which reflected an increase in plant capacity to 40 t UO2 per year, declared to have been to accommodate the fuel needs for the Bushehr Nuclear Power Plant (BNPP) (about 25 t UO2 per year) and the 40 MW pressurized heavy water research reactor (IR-40) (about 10 t UO2 per year).[36]

The Esfahan uranium conversion facility restarted its operations in August 2005, when Iran ended the suspension imposed by the IAEA. According to a study by the Institute for Science and International Security (ISIS), between August 2005 and late February 2006 Iran was able to produce 85 tons of uranium hexafluoride (UF_6). Observers worry about this development, as approximately 5 tons of UF_6 are needed to make enough HEU for a nuclear bomb. This means that 85 tons of UF_6 would be enough for 15 nuclear weapons. According to the ISIS, despite impurities in the UF_6, it will not interfere with the operation of the centrifuges at Esfahan.[37]

The importance of Esfahan, however, goes beyond its enrichment activities and possible heavy water research. It reportedly is an important production site for Iranian missiles, including the Shahab-1, Shahab-2, and Shahab-3. (Other rumored locations are Damghan, Parchin, and Qazvin.) Many conventional military facilities are also in the area, including facilities for munitions production, tank overhaul, and helicopter and fixed-wing aircraft maintenance. The main operational facilities for the army's aviation units are located at Esfahan, presumably at Khatamin Air Base northeast of the city. Esfahan is also considered one of the Islamic Republic's chemical weapons facilities.[38]

KALAYE POWER PLANT

Kalaye is considered one of the most uncertain nuclear sites in Iran, partly because it is a civilian electric company and partly because Iran did not declare it. The IAEA has investigated the Kalaye plant since 2003, and there are links between this power plant and other sites of interests such as Natanz.

The IAEA investigation of the Kalaye Electric Company has included environmental samples and interviews with Iranian specialists:

Between February and October 2003, Iran took a number of steps intended to conceal the origin, source and extent of Iran's enrichment programme, including: denying access to the Kalaye Electric Company workshop in February 2003 and refusing to permit the Agency to take environmental samples there in March 2003; dismantling equipment used at the workshop and moving it to Pars Trash (another subsidiary company of the AEOI located in Tehran); renovating part of the Kalaye Electric Company workshop in order to prevent detection of the use of nuclear material; and submitting incorrect and incomplete declarations. A detailed description of these efforts is reflected in the previous reports of the Director General to the Board.

... Iran also acknowledged that the Kalaye Electric Company workshop in Tehran had been used for the production of centrifuge components, but stated that there had been no testing of centrifuges assembled from these components involving the use of nuclear material, either at that workshop or at any other location in Iran.

... In August 2003, Iran amended these statements, informing the Agency that the decision to launch a centrifuge enrichment programme had actually been taken in 1985, and that Iran had in fact received drawings of the P-1 centrifuge through a foreign intermediary around 1987. Iran stated that the centrifuge R&D programme had been situated at TNRC between 1988 and 1995, and had been moved to the Kalaye Electric Company workshop in 1995. According to Iran, the centrifuge R&D activities were carried out at the Kalaye Electric Company workshop between 1995 and 2003, and were moved to Natanz in 2003.

During its August 2003 visit to Iran, the Agency was shown electronic copies of the centrifuge engineering drawings (including the general arrangement, sub-assembly and component drawings). Agency inspectors were also able to visit and take environmental samples at the Kalaye Electric Company workshop, where they noted that, since their first visit to the workshop in March 2003, considerable renovation had been made to one of the buildings on the site. As was anticipated by the Agency at the time, the renovation, which was carried out in connection with Iran's attempt to conceal the activities carried out there, has interfered with the Agency's ability to resolve issues associated with Iran's centrifuge enrichment programme, since the Agency was unable to see the equipment in situ and could not take environmental samples while the equipment was there.

In its letter of 21 October 2003, Iran finally acknowledged that "a limited number of tests, using small amounts of UF6," had been conducted in 1999 and 2002 at the Kalaye Electric Company workshop.

. . . In addition to its enquiries into Iran's acquisition of enrichment technology, the Agency has conducted extensive environmental sampling (approximately 300 samples) at locations where Iran has declared that centrifuge components were manufactured, processed and/or stored (including Natanz, the Kalaye Electric Company workshop, TNRC, Farayand Technique, Pars Trash and centrifuge component manufacturing workshops in Iran), as necessary, with a view to assessing the correctness and completeness of Iran's declarations concerning its enrichment activities.

. . . Numerous particles of ~54% U-235 (in the range of 50%–60%) were found on imported components and on tested rotors assembled using the imported components; some ~54% U-235 contamination was also found at the Kalaye Electric Company workshop.[39]

As the IAEA report showed, Iran eventually admitted to using the Kalaye power plant to produce centrifuges, and the environmental samples actually showed U-235 enriched to roughly 54 percent. Some argued that Tehran's use of this civilian power plant to enrich U-235 at such a high level should be a matter of concern, particularly regarding future Iranian developments in civilian nuclear technology.

KARAJ

The Karaj facility is located some 160 kilometers northwest of Tehran and includes a building with a dosimetry laboratory and an agricultural radiochemistry laboratory. Other buildings will house a calutron electromagnetic isotope separation system, purchased from China, for obtaining target materials to be radiated with neutron streams in a 30-million-electronvolt cyclotron. These research systems are not easily adaptable to nuclear weapons design efforts. There may also be a facility nearby for rocket R&D and production.[40]

The IAEA has made the following assessment of the history of activities and developments at Karaj:

In its letter dated 21 October 2003, Iran finally acknowledged that, between 1975 and 1998, it had concluded contracts related to laser enrichment using both AVLIS [atomic vapor laser isotope separation] and MLIS [molecular isotope separation] techniques with four foreign entities. In the letter, Iran provided detailed information on the various contracts, and acknowledged that it had carried out laser enrichment experiments using previously undeclared imported uranium metal at TNRC between 1993 and 2000, and that it had established a pilot plant for laser enrichment at Lashkar Ab'ad, where it had also carried out experiments using imported uranium metal. According to information provided subsequently by the Iranian authorities, the equipment used there had been dismantled in May 2003, and transferred to Karaj for storage together with the uranium metal used in the experiments, before the Agency was permitted to visit Lashkar Ab'ad in August 2003. The equipment and material were presented to Agency inspectors at Karaj on 28 October 2003.

During the Agency's complementary access to the mass spectrometry laboratories at Karaj in December 2003, the Agency examined two mass spectrometers that had not been included in Iran's declaration of 21 October 2003. Iran acknowledged that the mass spectrometers had been used at Karaj in the past to provide analytical services (isotope enrichment measurements) to the AVLIS programme, and gave the Agency a list of samples that had been analyzed. The Agency collected environmental samples from the mass spectrometers; no uranium particles were found in these samples. As requested by the Agency following complementary access at Karaj, Iran submitted additional information to the Agency on 5 January 2004 to clarify the role of the mass spectrometers in relation to Iran's uranium enrichment programme. The laboratory containing the equipment is now part of the safeguarded facility at Karaj.[41]

LAVISAN-SHIAN

Lavisan-Shian, located in northeastern Tehran, was identified in May 2003 by the NCRI as a suspected site for centrifuge development, laser enrichment, and the development of chemical and biological weapons. Some analysts claimed in December 2004 that Iran was testing conventional explosives at the site in ways that indicated the tests might be to simulate nuclear explosions and test high-explosive lenses and warheads. The NCRI claimed that the site was producing beryllium and polonium-210; both are important to developing the neutron initiator to trigger a nuclear chain reaction for an atomic bomb.[42]

Iran has admitted that "defense-related nuclear work" was carried out at Lavisan by the Physics Research Center (PHRC) between 1989 and 2004, but has denied any work on nuclear material. The IAEA confirmed that the PHRC tried to acquire "dual use materials and equipment which have applications...in the nuclear military area." The IAEA has also obtained satellite photos that seem to support the possibility of weapons-related high explosive test but cannot confirm it.

The IAEA first inspected this site in June 2004, but experts argued that by then, Iran had razed its buildings and removed all equipment. Experts argued that if the IAEA inspections found nothing, why did Iran bar the IAEA from visiting the site earlier?[43]

The IAEA assessment of Lavisan-Shian and of Iran's decision to raze the site was ambiguous and focused on two whole body counters that were located at Lavisan.[44] In its November 2004 report, the IAEA outlined its assessment as follows:

Iran has stated that the site had been razed in response to a decision ordering the return of the site to the Municipality of Tehran in connection with a dispute between the Municipality and the Ministry of Defence. In response to a request by the Agency, Iran provided additional documentation in support of this explanation, which is currently being assessed. Between 28 and 30 June 2004, the Agency visited the Lavisan-Shian site, where it took environmental samples. The Agency also took environmental samples from two whole body counters (one formerly located at Lavisan-Shian, the other located at Esfahan), and a trailer said to have contained one of the counters while it was located at Lavisan-Shian. Though Iran's description of events concerning the whole body counters, as related to this site, appears to be plausible, the trailer said to have contained the other counter still remains to be presented for sampling.

Iran provided a description and chronology of three organizations that had been located at Lavisan-Shian between 1989 and 2004. As described by Iran, the Physics Research Centre (PHRC) had been established at that site in 1989, the purpose of which had been "preparedness to combat and neutralization of casualties due to nuclear attacks and accidents (nuclear defence) and also support and provide scientific advice and services to the Ministry of Defence." Iran provided a list of eleven activities conducted at the PHRC, but, referring to security concerns, declined to provide a list of the equipment used at the Centre. In a letter to the Agency dated 19 August 2004, Iran stated further that "no nuclear material declarable in accordance with the Agency's safeguard[s] was present" and reiterated its earlier statement that "no nuclear material and nuclear activities related to fuel cycle were carried out at Lavisan-Shian."

Iran explained that the activities of the PHRC at Lavisan had been stopped in 1998, and that the Centre had been changed to the Biological Study Centre, which was involved in biological R&D and "radioprotection" activities. According to Iran, in 2002 the Applied Physics Institute was also located at that site, and although some of the biological activities continued there, the main objective was to use the capabilities of universities in the country (in particular, at the Malek Ashtar University near Esfahan) for the education and R&D needs of the Ministry of Defence.

The vegetation and soil samples collected from the Lavisan-Shian site have been analyzed, and reveal no evidence of nuclear material. It should be borne in mind, however, that detection of nuclear material in soil samples would be very difficult in light of the razing of the site. In addition, given the removal of the buildings, the Agency is not in a position to verify the nature of activities that have taken place there.[45]

IAEA inspectors revisited the Lavisan-Shian site in August 2005 and seem to have concluded that Iran's claims about the whole body counters were plausible. Iran also attempted to clarify the reason for razing the site, which it argued was done by the Municipality of Tehran as a result of a dispute with the Ministry of Defense.

In its September 2005 report, the IAEA concluded that the information provided by Tehran appeared credible and consistent with what their inspections found. However, it demanded further clarification from the Iranians regarding the work of the Physics Research Center that used to be located at Lavisan, which was suspected of having equipment that could be used for uranium conversion activities.[46] Iran told the IAEA in January 2006 that, despite documentation indicating the equipment was for the PHRC, it was actually destined for a university laboratory. The head of the PHRC also worked at the laboratory. Iran, however, declined to make the "professor" available for an interview. Iran has also refused IAEA requests for access to interview other officials associated with the PHRC and Lavisan.

NATANZ

Iran's goals for Natanz are uncertain. Press reports, claims by NCRI, Iranian statements, IAEA inspections, and estimates by outside experts conflict in key areas. The nature of the research at Natanz definitely includes uranium enrichment, but the number of centrifuges, the level of enrichment, and the source of contamination are unclear.

The Iranian government has claimed that the Natanz plant is part of its civilian nuclear program. It is believed to have been Tehran's main site for gas centrifuge activity, and subsequent IAEA inspections found traces of uranium contamination. Iran claimed that the contamination came from equipment that it purchased in the 1980s (believed to be from Pakistan) and not from its own uranium enrichment program. Press reports, however, claimed that Natanz was the site of 100–200 gas centrifuges.[47]

There is a fuel enrichment plant (FEP) of some 100,000 square meters. The MEK claims that the plant has two 25,000-meter halls built 8 meters deep in the ground and protected by a concrete wall 2.5 meters thick. According to some estimates, the plant could house as many as 50,000 centrifuges, producing enough weapons-grade uranium for 20 weapons a year.

Other estimates suggest a total of 5,000 centrifuges capable of producing enough enriched uranium for several nuclear weapons a year. The MEK claims that some parts for centrifuges were imported and others were built at a plant in Esfahan . They were then tested at the Kalaye plant in Ab-Ali and sent to Natanz for final assembly. It claims two villages near Natanz—Lashgarabad and Ramandeh—have uranium enrichment plants hidden behind trees in orchards and were surrounded by security guards; according to the MEK, they function as a backup to the Natanz site in case that facility comes under military attack. The labs are reported to be in the Hasthgerd region near Karaj, about 40 kilometers (25 miles) west of Tehran. There are also reports that laser isotope separation (LIS) experiments took place at Natanz, as well as at Ramandeh (part of the Karaj Agricultural and Medical Centre) and at a laser laboratory at Lashkar Ab'ad.

The IAEA described a far more modest effort:

> In 2001, Iran began the construction of two facilities at Natanz: the smaller scale PFEP, planned to have some 1000 centrifuges for enrichment up to 5 percent U-235; and the large scale commercial FEP, which is planned to contain over 50 000 P-1 centrifuges for enrichment up to 5 percent U-235.
>
> On 25 June 2003, Iran introduced UF_6 into the first centrifuge at PFEP. As of October 2003, the installation of a 164-machine cascade was being finalized. In November 2003, the cascade was shut down. As of the Agency's latest inspection on 11 October 2004, the cascade had not been operated and no further UF_6 gas had been fed into centrifuges at PFEP. FEP has been scheduled to start receiving

centrifuges in early 2005, after the design is confirmed by the tests to be conducted in PFEP.

According to Iran, the only work that has been done on the P-2 design was carried out between 2002 and 2003, largely at the workshop of a private company under contract with the AEOI, and the work was limited to the manufacture and mechanical testing of a small number of modified P-2 composite rotors. Iran has stated that "no other institution (including universities), company or organization in Iran has been involved in P-2 R&D" and that "no P-2 R&D has been undertaken by or at the request of the Ministry of Defense." Iran has also said that all R&D on P-2 centrifuges had been terminated and that no other work on that, or on any other centrifuge design, was done prior to 2002 or has been done since 2003. However, in its Additional Protocol declarations, Iran has foreseen P-2 R&D activities for the future.[48]

The National Council of Resistance in Iran asserted on January 10, 2006, that Iranian nuclear research at Natanz was still moving ahead toward a weapons capability. Alireza Jafarzadeh, then president of NCRI, claimed that Tehran was planning to "begin injecting uranium hexafluoride gas into centrifuge machines in Natanz and officially start the enrichment process," and that Tehran had built 5,000 centrifuges at Natanz. The NCRI also claimed that Tehran was constructing centrifuge cascade installation platforms at Natanz and that the construction was being handled by the Kala Electric Company. The NCRI also maintained that the experts working at Natanz were agents of the Islamic Revolutionary Guards Corps and Iran's Ministry of Defense.[49]

Independent experts have cited different statistics for how many centrifuge cascades were being built. For example, the founding president of the Nuclear Control Institute, Paul Leventhal, said that Tehran was planning to restart a 164-centrifuge cascade, which is considered "too small to produce enough highly enriched uranium for a bomb." He added, however, that the amount was large enough for a large commercial-scale enrichment program, and that if the information to construct 5,000 centrifuges was correct, "then we have a major crisis on our hands."[50]

It has been reported separately that Tehran had 1,000 centrifuges in 2006, far fewer than what was reported to be Iran's ultimate goal of building 50,000 centrifuges to enrich uranium. Iran, however, claimed that its enrichment activities at Natanz were for fueling the Bushehr rector that was being built by Russia and for its civilian nuclear energy.[51] These claims, counterclaims, and different estimates highlight the uncertainly surrounding the true nature of some of the most important suspected nuclear facilities in Iran.

In addition, nuclear experts believe that Natanz with its 1,000 centrifuges and 50,000 machines does not pose an urgent threat of producing weapons-grade uranium. Some have argued that for Natanz to enrich uranium at an industrial scale, the 1,000 centrifuges would have to work around the clock for two to three years.[52]

Other experts, however, have argued that Tehran can dramatically decrease the required time for producing weapons-grade uranium—to as few as 180 days, according to some experts—if it could acquire natural uranium that has already been enriched. Experts argue that even if the uranium was enriched as low as 4 percent, it would speed up the Natanz enrichment timetable significantly. This, they say, is largely because it is much harder to enrich natural uranium from 0 percent to 4 percent than from 4 percent to 90 percent.[53]

Some of these experts, including David Albright and Corey Hinderstein of the Institute for Science and International Security (ISIS), have argued that if Iran uses only half of the centrifuges at Natanz (500) and feeds them low-enriched uranium, it could produce weapons-grade fuel for a nuclear bomb in just six months.[54] Albright and Hinderstein caution, however, that those were their "worst case" estimates and could be affected by possible technical difficulties, political uncertainties, and the impact of either IAEA inspections or military strikes.[55]

One key additional problem with such estimates is that they assume either a P-1 or P-2 level of efficiency and that Iran cannot produce far more advanced designs. As has been touched on earlier, however, at least one open source report has claimed that truly advanced centrifuge designs like the URENCO T21 have the theoretical capacity to produce 50 times the output of the P-1.[56]

In February 2006, Iran restarted its pilot fuel enrichment Plant (PFEP) at Natanz, which it first constructed in 2001. The PFEP was designed to hold thousands of centrifuges, including six 164-machine cascades and many smaller test cascades. The installation of the first cascade was finished in fall 2003, but the cascade has not operated since enrichment was stopped in October 2003. However, according to the ISIS, Iran resumed enriching uranium at the PFEP by early March 2006. In addition, Iran has also started to move on introducing uranium hexafluoride (UF_6) or "yellowcake":

> Iran has also moved process tanks and an autoclave, used to heat uranium hexafluoride into a gas prior to insertion into a centrifuge cascade, into the underground Fuel Enrichment Plant (FEP) at Natanz. The FEP is the main production facility and is designed to hold eventually 50,000–60,000 centrifuges. Iran also told the IAEA that it intends to start the installation of the first 3,000 P1 centrifuges in the underground cascade halls at the FEP in the fourth quarter of 2006.[57]

Iran's enrichment activities at Natanz are not without problems. According to the IAEA, nearly 30 percent of the centrifuges were not operational due to technical difficulties. In addition because of the suspension of enrichment in late 2003, key components of the centrifuges such as the pipes connecting the machines have been damaged. To introduce uranium hexafluoride, therefore, Iran must first prepare the cascade at Natanz. These problems may, however, not be "significant enough" to stop Iran from feeding UF_6 into its cascade machines. If Iran can avoid major technical difficulties, it can repeat the process to create larger cascades that can be used to enrich uranium.[58]

PARCHIN

Parchin is located 30 kilometers southwest of Tehran. It is owned and run by Iran's military industry and is designed for developing and producing munitions, rockets, and high explosives, including chemical explosives. In September 2004, U.S. officials expressed concern about the work done with beryllium, which has civilian applications but can also be used with plutonium to process a neutron initiator that can trigger a nuclear bomb. In addition, U.S. officials claimed that testing of "high-explosive shaped charges with an inert core of depleted uranium" was taking place.[59]

Experts believe that Parchin was the site that Secretary of State Colin Powell referred to in November 2004 when he argued that evi-

dence suggested that Iran was working on reducing the size of its nuclear warheads to fit the Shahab-3 missiles. It is also the site that U.S.
officials argued proves the claim that Iran was working on obtaining
equipment "in the nuclear military area," as the site reportedly has
"hundreds of bunkers."[60]

Soon after these allegations appeared in press reports, the IAEA
director general, Mohamed ElBaradei, said that the IAEA inspection
teams were aware of Parchin. He asserted that the agency did not believe there was evidence to suggest that Iran was carrying on nuclear
activities at the site. The IAEA reportedly asked to visit the site, but
Iran refused to grant the agency permission. Tehran, on the other
hand, denied that it was asked by the IAEA about Parchin.[61]

The Institute for Science and International Security (ISIS) conducted a study about Parchin following these revelations. Based on
overhead images, the ISIS study concluded that although evidence
that the site was conducing nuclear-related research was ambiguous,
Parchin was a "logical" site for nuclear weapons research and production. ISIS pointed out that some of the buildings and bunkers that
appeared on the images were suited for testing high explosives. In addition, there appeared to be excavation around Parchin, which the
ISIS study argued could involve tunneling, which might indicate that
the site was being prepared for armament testing.[62]

Iran allowed the IAEA to visit Parchin in January 2005, and the inspectors took environmental samples from the site. However, the inspectors were allowed to visit and inspect only one of the four sections
of Parchin that they had asked to visit.[63] The IAEA director general
stated that the IAEA was not able to conclude that nuclear activities
were not taking place at Parchin.

The IAEA did conclude that it found no evidence suggesting traces
of nuclear contamination. But many believe that the IAEA inspections
were not adequate. Mohamed ElBaradei qualified the IAEA's position
on Parchin in his September 15, 2005, report to the board of governors:

> The Agency has discussed with the Iranian authorities open source
> information relating to dual use equipment and materials which
> have applications in the conventional military area and in the civil-
> ian sphere as well as in the nuclear military area. As described by the
> DDG-SG in his 1 March 2005 statement to the Board, in January

2005, Iran agreed, as a transparency measure, to permit the Agency to visit a site located at Parchin in order to provide assurance regarding the absence of undeclared nuclear material and activities at that site. Out of the four areas identified by the Agency to be of potential interest, the Agency was permitted to select any one area. The Agency was requested to minimize the number of buildings to be visited in that area, and selected five buildings. The Agency was given free access to those buildings and their surroundings and was allowed to take environmental samples, the results of which did not indicate the presence of nuclear material, nor did the Agency see any relevant dual use equipment or materials in the locations visited. In the course of the visit, the Agency requested to visit another area of the Parchin site. The Agency has been pursuing this matter with Iran since then with a view to being able to access the locations of interest at Parchin.

. . . The Agency has, however, continued to seek Iran's cooperation in following up on reports relating to equipment, materials and activities which have applications in the conventional military area and in the civilian sphere as well as in the nuclear military area. Iran has permitted the Agency, as a measure of transparency, to visit defence related sites at Kolahdouz, Lavisan and Parchin. While the Agency found no nuclear related activities at Kolahdouz, it is still assessing information (and awaiting some additional information) in relation to the Lavisan site. The Agency is also still waiting to be able to re-visit the Parchin site.[64]

The IAEA's request to revisit Parchin also came after revelations in the press that the United States had been spying on Iran and that U.S. Special Forces were conducing operations inside Iran. Iran was concerned about the IAEA inspections being used for intelligence gathering by the United States, and warned the IAEA that Parchin was a conventional defense site and that spying would not be tolerated.[65] Some experts believe that the difficulty in accessing Parchin is because it might well be a conventional missile production plant that is unrelated to nuclear research.

The NCRI, however, has argued that the IAEA was not allowed to visit all the sites. According to the NCRI, Parchin has 12 different sections, but the Iranians led the IAEA inspectors to section 10, which was used for air defense weapons manufacturing. The NCRI claims to have identified a secret tunnel in section 1 of Parchin as the area where "nuclear and laser research" was being carried out. Experts such as David Albright have argued that the NCRI must provide evidence to back up these claims.[66]

The NCRI has not provided such evidence. Parchin, however, remains one of the sites that are not fully inspected. The director general of the IAEA said that his agency could not confirm or disprove the existence of nuclear activities at Parchin—"the jury is still out."[67]

TEHRAN NUCLEAR RESEARCH CENTER

The Tehran Nuclear Research Center (TNRC) is another important site. As noted earlier, the IAEA discovered polonium-210 (Po-210) at TNRC. The chronology assembled by the IAEA on Iran's plutonium processing history showed that the TNRC was one of the sites that Tehran used to produce plutonium as early as 1987.

The main research arm is the Jabr Ibn Hayan Research Department, or JIHRD. According to the Atomic Energy Organization of Iran, Iran's main atomic energy agency, the JIHRD is central to the TNRC and Iran's overall nuclear research. The AEOI describes its civilian research activities as follows:

> JIHRD acts as a back up complex in the field of Research and Development in the Nuclear Fuel Cycle, production of 99Mo, 131I and 133Xe radioisotope , in addition to providing a wide range of laboratory services for Nuclear Fuel Production Division at AEOI. This complex provides the best and the most up to date equipments and capabilities not only in AEOI but also in all Research Centers of Iran. The main facilities in this research laboratories are as follows: Nuclear Spectrometry Laboratories which consist of Gamma-Ray Spectrometry System, Alpha-Particle Spectrometry, Liquid Scintillation Counting Spectrometer, Neutron Activation Analysis facilities, and Radiocarbon Dating Laboratory. Instrumental Analysis Laboratories, which consist of UV, IR, XRF, ICP, Atomic Absorption, Thermal Analyses, GC and GLC.[68]

The Federation of American Scientists (FAS) describes the TNRC as one of the most sophisticated research centers in Iran. The FAS analysis also argues that the TNRC has the capability to produce yellowcake:

> Since 1968 the Tehran Nuclear Research Center (located in subur-ban Amirabad at 35°33'00"N 51°20'00"E) has included a research reactor with a nominal capacity of 5 megawatts provided by the United States under IAEA safeguards. The reactor core was due to be upgraded and replaced with Argentine assistance in the late 1980s. Construction of an installation for producing radioisotopes is complete, and there are unconfirmed reports that this facility can produce plutonium from spent nuclear fuel. The Center also in-cludes an installation for producing "yellow cake," which has not operated recently due to unsatisfactory technical condition. The Ebn-e Qasem laser technology research laboratory entered service in October 1992, although the laboratory has no lasers suitable for separating uranium isotopes.
>
> The research program of the Tehran-based Center for Theoreti-cal Physics and Mathematics of the Atomic Energy Organization of Iran (AEOI) includes theoretical physics, and other R&D related to high energy physics, including particle physics, mathematical physics, astrophysics, theoretical nuclear physics, statistical me-chanics, theoretical plasma physics, and mathematics.[69]

The IAEA has expressed dissatisfaction with Iran's declaration re-garding the function of the TNRC. The IAEA's reports have focused on the history of the TNRC and on Iranian concealment activities that have raised many questions. In November 2004, the IAEA summa-rized its efforts to understand the full scope of nuclear research at the TNRC as follows:

> Iran has explored two other potential uranium production routes. One was the extraction of uranium from phosphoric acid. Using research scale equipment, small quantities of yellowcake were suc-cessfully produced at the Tehran Nuclear Research Centre (TNRC) laboratories. Iran has stated that there are no facilities in Iran for separating uranium from phosphoric acid other than the research facilities at TNRC. The second route explored by Iran was the pro-duction of yellowcake using percolation leaching. Using this tech-

nique, Iran produced an estimated several hundred kilograms of yellowcake using temporary facilities, now dismantled, located at the Gchine mining site.

. . . Iran carried out most of its experiments in uranium conversion between 1981 and 1993 at TNRC and at the Esfahan Nuclear Technology Centre (ENTC), with some experiments (e.g., those involving pulse columns) being carried out through early 2002.

. . . Following the discovery by the Agency of indications of depleted UF4 in samples of waste taken at the Jabr Ibn Hayan Multipurpose Laboratories (JHL) at TNRC, Iran acknowledged, in a letter dated 19 August 2003, that it had carried out UF4 conversion experiments on a laboratory scale during the 1990s at the Radiochemistry Laboratories of TNRC using depleted uranium which had been imported in 1977 and exempted from safeguards upon receipt, and which Iran had declared in 1998 (when the material was de-exempted) as having been lost during processing.

In October 2003, Iran further acknowledged that, contrary to its previous statements, practically all of the materials important to uranium conversion had been produced in laboratory and bench scale experiments (in kilogram quantities) carried out at TNRC and at ENTC between 1981 and 1993 without having been reported to the Agency. The information provided in Iran's letter of 21 October 2003 stated that, in conducting these experiments, Iran had also used yellowcake imported by Iran in 1982 but only confirmed in 1990 as having been received. Iran subsequently explained that it had decided to stop domestic R&D on UF4 and UF6 in 1993 in anticipation of its receipt of assistance from a foreign supplier in the design and construction of UCF.

. . . In its letter of 21 October 2003, Iran acknowledged that the uranium metal had been intended not only for the production of shielding material, as previously stated, but also for use in its laser enrichment programme (the existence of which, as discussed below, Iran had previously not acknowledged, and which was only declared to the Agency in that same letter of 21 October 2003). Iran stated that the uranium metal process line at UCF had been developed by Iranian scientists at the TNRC laboratories, and that a small quantity of the metal produced at TNRC during the development tests (about 2 kg) had been given to the laser group for its evaluation.

... According to Iran, gas centrifuge R&D testing began at TNRC in 1988 and continued there until 1995, when those activities were moved to a workshop of the Kalaye Electric Company, a company in Tehran belonging to the Atomic Energy Organization of Iran (AEOI). Between 1994 and 1996, Iran received another—apparently duplicate—set of drawings for the P-1 centrifuge design, along with components for 500 centrifuges. According to Iran, it was at this time as well when Iran received design drawings for a P-2 centrifuge through the same network. Between 1997 and 2002, Iran assembled and tested P-1 centrifuges at the Kalaye Electric Company workshop where Iran says it fed UF6 gas into a centrifuge for the first time in 1999 and, in 2002, fed nuclear material into a number of centrifuges (up to 19 machines).

... As with respect to its centrifuge enrichment activities, Iran's responses between February 2003 and October 2003 to the Agency's enquiry into the possible existence in Iran of a laser enrichment programme were characterized by concealment, including the dismantling of the laser enrichment laboratories at TNRC and the pilot laser enrichment plant at Lashkar Ab'ad and the transfer of the equipment and material involved to Karaj, and by failures to declare nuclear material, facilities and activities.

... In early October 2003, the Iranian authorities acknowledged that Iran had imported, and installed at TNRC, laser related equipment imported from two States in 1992 and 2000 in connection with those studies.

... In the letter, Iran provided detailed information on the various contracts, and acknowledged that it had carried out laser enrichment experiments using previously undeclared imported uranium metal at TNRC between 1993 and 2000, and that it had established a pilot plant for laser enrichment at Lashkar Ab'ad, where it had also carried out experiments using imported uranium metal. According to information provided subsequently by the Iranian authorities, the equipment used there had been dismantled in May 2003, and transferred to Karaj for storage together with the uranium metal used in the experiments, before the Agency was permitted to visit Lashkar Ab'ad in August 2003. The equipment and material were presented to Agency inspectors at Karaj on 28 October 2003.[70]

U.S. officials have expressed their concerns about research activities at the TNRC. John Bolton, the former undersecretary for arms control and international security, said that the fact that Po-210 was found at the TNRC was of serious concern to the United States. Bolton argued that Po-210 can be used either in neutron initiators in certain designs of nuclear weapons or for batteries of space satellites. He concluded, however, that because Tehran did not have a space program, "the nuclear weapons application is obviously of concern."[71]

URANIUM MINES AND FACILITIES

In addition to understanding Iranian nuclear research facilities, it is important to assess Iran's uranium and plutonium resources. Estimates are as uncertain as the nature of its nuclear sites. Most estimates, however, show that Iran's uranium resources are limited. It has proven reserves of approximately 3,000 tons of uranium, and it may have as much as 20,000–30,000 tons of U3O8. It was reported that Iran has opened as many as 10 uranium mines since 1988. Iran reportedly enjoyed the help of experts from Germany, Argentina, Czechoslovakia, Hungary, Russia, and China in exploring its uranium reserves.[72]

Iran has two key uranium mines: Talmesi and Meskani Uranium Mines and Saghand. They are seen as the two sites with the most uranium reserves.[73] Saghand is located in the northeastern part of Yazd province, and, according to the Atomic Energy Organization of Iran, the Saghand uranium deposit has 1,550,000 tons of ore reserves at a density of 553 ppm average grade. At one time, it was estimated that the mine would be operational by the end of 2004. The AEOI claimed that it would have a lifetime of 17 years with a capacity of 1.2 million tons of ore per year.[74] In November 2003, it was estimated that 100 specialists, engineers, and workers were working on its development stage, and it was projected to have 233 workers by the time it was operational.[75]

Saghand's status remained uncertain in early 2006, but the IAEA reported the following in November 2004:

> At the Saghand Mine, located in Yazd in central Iran, low grade hard rock ore bodies will be exploited through conventional underground mining techniques. The annual estimated production design capacity is forecast as 50 t of uranium. The infrastructure and shaft sinking are essentially complete, and tunneling towards the ore bodies has started. Ore production is forecast to start by the end of 2006. The ore is to be processed into uranium ore concentrate (UOC/yellowcake) at the associated mill at Ardakan, the Yellowcake Production Plant. The design capacity of the mill corresponds to that of the mine (50 t of uranium per year). The mill startup is forecast to coincide with the start of mining at Saghand. The mill site is currently at an early stage of development; the installation of the infrastructure and processing buildings has been started.[76]

Other important mining sites are Talmesi and Meskani Uranium Mines. Located in Anarak district in the central part of Iran, they have roughly 200 tons of category EAR-II uranium ore. Reportedly, the two mines have been "systematically exploited" since 1935, but uranium was not discovered until the 1990s.[77]

The IAEA also reported on a third mine located in the southern part of the country called Gchine. In November 2004, the IAEA published the following assessment:

> In the south of Iran, near Bandar Abbas, Iran has constructed the Gchine uranium mine and its co-located mill. The low but variable grade uranium ore found in near-surface deposits will be open-pit mined and processed at the associated mill. The estimated production design capacity is 21 t of uranium per year. Iran has stated that, as of July 2004, mining operations had started and the mill had been hot tested, during which testing a quantity of about 40 to 50 kg of yellowcake was produced.[78]

The "final" IAEA assessments of Iran's uranium mines remain unpublished. But according to the U.S. State Department, the IAEA continues to investigate the "complex arrangements governing the past and current administration of the mine," including how a newly founded company with little experience in ore processing could have carried out so quickly—between 2000 and mid-2001—the designing, procurement, construction, and testing of the plant.

OTHER SUSPECTED SITES

Other sites have been suspected of being nuclear facilities. This additional list reinforces how difficult it is to understand the overall structure and scale of Iran's activities, to know whether they are weapons-related, and to know enough to target them:[79]

- **Bonab:** This was reportedly the site of the Bonab Energy Research Center. It was inspected in 1997 by the IAEA, which declared that there were no clandestine nuclear activities there.[80]

- **Chalus:** It has been reported that an underground nuclear weapons development facility might potentially be located inside a mountain south of this coastal town. The facility has been variously reported as being staffed by experts from Russia, China, and North Korea.

- **Darkhovin** (also referred to as Ahvaz, Darkhouin, Esteghlal, and Karun): Darkhovin is a suspected underground nuclear weapons facility of an unspecified nature located on the Karun River south of the city of Ahvaz. It is reported to be under the control of the Islamic Revolution Guards Corps.

- **Kolahdouz** (also referred to as Kolahdooz, or Kolahdoz): The Kolahdouz complex, located 14 kilometers west of Tehran, is the site of some of Iran's armored weapons production facilities. It is a large complex that the MEK claims has a concealed nuclear weapons plant, including uranium enrichment, and operates as a supplement to the uranium enrichment site in Natanz. A technical team of the IAEA visited the industrial complex in Kolahdouz and took environmental samples, but no work was seen at those locations that could be linked to uranium enrichment.

- **Meysami Research Center:** The principal activity at this center is to hold chemical agent detectors, and the center *may* have a role in chemical and nuclear weapons efforts.

ASSESSING IRAN'S NUCLEAR SITES

Chapter 6 has already summarized the issues Iran's facilities have raised for IAEA inspection. Moreover, it is clear from the histories provided in the previous chapters that there are almost certainly more discoveries to come. It is also clear from the facility-by-facility descriptions in this chapter that Iran has great experience in concealing or changing the activities of any given facility while still claiming that such activity was for peaceful and/or defensive purposes.

This raises obvious points for inspection, executing military options, and the enforcement of sanctions or other actions by the UN. Iran has shown it can hide the existence of facilities for some time and create hardened underground facilities with little surface signature. It has repeatedly demonstrated the ability to conceal as well as to obfuscate when a facility is discovered. It has at best complied with the IAEA "defensively." It has never made a convincing effort at transparency, and it has shown that it can rapidly dismantle or change the character of a facility. Whatever its motives, Iran has been and *is* actively conducting the equivalent of a nuclear shell game.

Even so, the way Iran has treated its nuclear facilities does not constitute definitive evidence that it is moving toward production of a nuclear weapon. As is the case with the other indicators discovered to date, there is always another explanation. Moreover, Iran can claim with some justification that it must conceal, disperse, or harden even peaceful facilities if it does not want them to be attacked. There have been too many attacks and wars in the region, and too many outside threats, for any one to reject Iran's concerns.

What is clear is that Iran, like Iraq under Saddam Hussein, has at a minimum created a mix of facilities whose character is so uncertain that it is unclear that even intrusive ongoing inspection could absolutely guarantee that Iran is not moving forward to acquire a nuclear weapon. The dilemma this creates for both Iran and the international community is that this history makes verification of any future compliance by Iran extremely difficult, and it means that Iran's facilities and activities will be suspect indefinitely into the future.

Further, it creates a military dilemma for both Iran and any potential attacker. To be effective, a military strike against Iran's nuclear efforts would virtually have to attack all probable and possible Iranian facilities to have maximum impact in denying Iran the capability to acquire a nuclear weapon or ensuring that its efforts would be delayed for some years.

Iran's lack of transparency, and its "edifice complex," may deter limited strikes simply because the results would be so uncertain. On the other hand, they could just as easily lead to much larger-scale and more lethal strikes than would otherwise be the case. There is the risk from a military viewpoint that the more difficult Iran makes it to target its facilities and the more it hardens or invests in a given facility, the more it would be struck. The problem for anyone who starts a shell game is that some players either will insist that all shells be made transparent or else will proceed to smash all the shells.

Notes

[1] International Atomic Energy Agency (IAEA), *Implementation of the NPT Safeguards Agreement in the Islamic Republic of Iran: Report by the Director General*, September 15, 2005, available at http://www.iaea.org/Publications/Documents/Board/2005/gov2005-67.pdf.

[2] Robin Gedye, "Iran's Nuclear History," *Daily Telegraph* (London), October 9, 2003, available at http://www.telegraph.co.uk/news/main.jhtml?xml=/news/2003/09/10/wiran210.xml&sSheet=/news/2003/09/10/ixnewstop.html.

[3] IAEA, *Implementation of the NPT Safeguards Agreement in the Islamic Republic of Iran: Report by the Director General*, November 15, 2004, available at http://www.iaea.org/Publications/Documents/Board/2004/gov2004-83_derestrict.pdf.

[4] Ali Akbar, "Iran Confirms Uranium-to-Gas Conversion," Associated Press, May 9, 2005.

[5] GlobalSecurity.org, "Ardekan [Ardakan] Nuclear Fuel Site," available at http://www.globalsecurity.org/wmd/world/iran/ardekan.htm.

[6] IAEA, *Implementation of the NPT Safeguards Agreement: Report by the Director General*, November 15, 2004.

[7] Nuclear Threat Initiative (NTI), "Iran Profile: Nuclear Chronology, 1957–1985," available at http://www.nti.org/e_research/profiles/Iran/1825.html.

[8] Ibid.

[9] Ibid.

[10] Ibid.

[11] Ibid.

[12] Ibid.

[13] Ibid.

[14] Ibid.

[15] Ibid.

[16] Ibid.

[17] Ibid.

[18] Ibid.

[19] Ibid.

[20] Ibid.

[21] Ibid.

[22] Ibid.

[23] Vladimir A. Orlov and Alexander Vinnikov, "The Great Guessing Games: Russia and the Iranian Nuclear Issue," *Washington Quarterly* 28, no. 2 (Spring 2005): 49–66.

[24] Ibid.

[25] Ibid.

[26] Ibid.

[27] Ibid.

[28] Ibid.

[29] Ibid.

[30] "Timeline: Iran," BBC News, available at http://news.bbc.co.uk/1/hi/world/middle_east/country_profiles/806268.stm.

[31] "Russia to Send First Fuel to Iranian Nuke Plant at the Year's End: Official," Agence France-Presse, May 12, 2005.

[32] "Beyond Bushehr: Iran's Nukes," *Jane's Intelligence Digest*, March 11, 2005.

[33] John R. Bolton, "Preventing Iran from Acquiring Nuclear Weapons" (remarks to the Hudson Institute, Washington, D.C., August 17, 2004).

[34] "Iran Far from Nuclear Bomb-Making Capacity: Ex-UN Weapons Chief Blix," Agence France-Presse, June 23, 2005.

[35] GlobalSecurity.org, "Weapons of Mass Destruction: Nuclear Weapons Potential": "According to Paul Leventhal of the Nuclear Control Institute, if Iran were to withdraw from the Nonproliferation Treaty and renounce the agreement with Russia, the Bushehr reactor could produce a quarter ton of plutonium per year, which Leventhal says is enough for at least 30 atomic bombs.

Normally for electrical power production the uranium fuel remains in the reactor for three to four years, which produces a plutonium of 60 percent or less Pu-239, 25 percent or more Pu-240, 10 percent or more Pu-241, and a few percent Pu-242. The Pu-240 has a high spontaneous rate of fission, and the amount of Pu-240 in weapons-grade plutonium generally does not exceed 6 percent, with the remaining 93 percent Pu-239. Higher concentrations of Pu-240 can result in pre-detonation of the weapon, significantly reducing yield and reliability. For the production of weapons-grade plutonium with lower Pu-240 concentrations, the fuel rods in a reactor have to be changed frequently, about every four months or less." Extract available at http://www.globalsecurity.org/wmd/world/iran/bushehr.htm.

[36] IAEA, *Implementation of the NPT Safeguards Agreement: Report by the Director General*, November 15, 2004.

[37] David Albright and Corey Hinderstein, "The Clock Is Ticking, but How Fast?" Institute for Science and International Security, Issue Brief, March 27, 2006, available at http://www.isis-online.org/publications/iran/clockticking.pdf

[38] Federation of American Scientists, "Esfahan," September 30, 2000, available at http://www.fas.org/nuke/guide/iran/facility/esfahan.htm.

[39] IAEA, *Implementation of the NPT Safeguards Agreement: Report by the Director General*, November 15, 2004.

[40] GlobalSecurity.org, "Karaj," available at http://www.globalsecurity.org/wmd/world/iran/karaj.htm.

[41] IAEA, *Implementation of the NPT Safeguards Agreement: Report by the Director General*, November 15, 2004.

[42] Paul Leventhal (statement at the National Press Club, Washington, D.C., January 31, 2006, available at http://www.nci.org/06nci/01-31/PL-statement.htm).

[43] Ibid.

[44] A whole-body counter is a device used to measure the total radiation in the body; it usually contains a number of sensitive detectors and shielding to block out ambient radiation.

[45] IAEA, *Implementation of the NPT Safeguards Agreement: Report by the Director General*, November 15, 2004.

[46] IAEA, *Implementation of the NPT Safeguards Agreement: Report by the Director General*, September 15, 2005.

[47] Gedye, "Iran's Nuclear History."

[48] IAEA, *Implementation of the NPT Safeguards Agreement: Report by the Director General*, November 15, 2004.

[49] Alireza Jafarzadeh, "Iranian Regime's Plan and Attempts to Start Uranium Enrichment at Natanz Site" (statement at the National Press Club, Washington, D.C., January 10, 2006).

[50] Paul Leventhal (statement at the National Press Club, January 10, 2005, available at http://www.nci.org/06nci/01/Leventhal_press_conference_statement_011006.htm).

[51] George Jahn, "For Iran, It's When, Not If," Associated Press, January 27, 2006.

[52] William J. Broad, "Small-Scale Atomic Research by Iran Is Risky, Experts Say," New York Times, March 8, 2006, p. 14.

[53] Ibid.

[54] Ibid.

[55] Albright and Hinderstein, "The Clock Is Ticking, but How Fast?"

[56] Sir John Thompson and Geoffrey Forden, "Multinational Facilities May Solve Iranian Nuclear Stalemate," Jane's Intelligence Review, April 1, 2006.

[57] Albright and Hinderstein, "The Clock Is Ticking, but How Fast?"

[58] Ibid.

[59] "UN Atomic Agency Seeks to Visit Key Iranian Defense Site: Diplomats," Agence France-Presse, September 10, 2004.

[60] David Sanger, "Iran Agrees to Inspection of Military Base," New York Times, January 6, 2006, p. 12.

[61] "IAEA Says No Sign of Nuclear Activity at Suspected Iranian Site," Agence France-Presse, September 17, 2004.

[62] David Albright and Corey Hinderstein, "Parchin: Possible Nuclear Weapons–Related Site in Iran," Institute for Science and International Security (ISIS), Issue Brief , September 15, 2004, available at http://www.isis-online.org/publications/iran/parchin.html.

[63] Richard Bernstein, "Nuclear Agency Says Iran Has Blocked Investigations," New York Times, March 2, 2005, p. 7.

[64] IAEA, Implementation of the NPT Safeguards Agreement: Report by the Director General, September 15, 2005.

[65] "UN Nuclear Inspectors Want Second Crack at Parchin Military Site in Iran," Agence France-Presse, January 18, 2005.

[66] "Iranian Resistance Claims UN Missed Nuclear Sites in Iran," Agence France-Presse, November 23, 2005.

[67] "UN Nuclear Inspectors Want Second Crack at Parchin Military Site in Iran."

[68] Atomic Energy Organization of Iran (AEOI), "Jabr Ibn Hayan Research Department," available at http://www.aeoi.org.ir/NewWeb/Recenter.asp?id=28.

[69] Federation of American Scientists, "Tehran," available at http://www.fas.org/nuke/guide/iran/facility/tehran.htm.

[70] IAEA , *Implementation of the NPT Safeguards Agreement: Report by the Director General,* November 15, 2004.

[71] Bolton, "Preventing Iran from Acquiring Nuclear Weapons."

[72] NTI, "Iran Profile: Nuclear Facilities, Saghand," available at http://www.nti.org/e_research/profiles/Iran/3119_3182.html.

[73] GlobalSecurity.org, "Uranium Mines: Iran," available at http://www.globalsecurity.org/wmd/world/iran/mines.htm.

[74] AEOI, "Saghand Mining Department," 2002, available at http://www.aeoi.org.ir/NewWeb/Fuel/Saghand/Saghand.htm.

[75] NTI, "Iran Profile: Nuclear Facilities, Saghand."

[76] IAEA, *Implementation of the NPT Safeguards Agreement: Report by the Director General,* November 15, 2004.

[77] NTI, "Iran Profile: Nuclear Facilities, Saghand."

[78] IAEA, *Implementation of the NPT Safeguards Agreement: Report by the Director General,* November 15, 2004.

[79] The following list summarizes the far more comprehensive descriptions of Iranian nuclear facilities developed by GlobalSecurity.org, headed by John Pike. The full analysis for Iranian facilities can be found at the GlobalSecurity.org Web site; see "Iran Nuclear Facilities" at http://www.globalsecurity.org/wmd/world/iran/nuke-fac.htm.

[80] Michael Rubin, "Iran's Burgeoning WMD Programs," *Middle East Intelligence Bulletin* 4, no. 3 (March/April 2002), available at http://www.meib.org/article/0203_irn1.htm.

CHAPTER EIGHT

POSSIBLE DATES FOR IRAN'S ACQUISITION OF NUCLEAR WEAPONS

There is no way to be certain that Iran will push its nuclear programs forward to the point that it has actual weapons. In fact, there is a long history of estimates of possible dates that does little more than warn that such estimates are either extremely uncertain or of limited value.

Past estimates by the United States, Israel, and independent organizations have been highly contradictory and unreliable, and such estimates are inherently uncertain. In addition, past assessments of possible dates often were based on the unrealistic assumption that Iran's nuclear program would evolve without interruptions, technical difficulties, or voluntary suspensions. For example, the majority of estimates during the 1990s predicted that Iran would acquire nuclear weapons by 2000. This did not happen.

A PAST HISTORY OF UNCERTAIN AND WRONG JUDGMENTS

The following timeline shows different U.S. assessments and highlights the uncertainty of intelligence estimates since the early 1990s:[1]

- **Late 1991:** In congressional reports and CIA assessments, the United States estimates that there is a "high degree of certainty that the government of Iran has acquired all or virtually all of the components required for the construction of two to three nuclear weapons." A February 1992 report by the U.S. House of Representatives suggests that these two or three nuclear weapons will be operational between February and April 1992.[2]

- **Late October 1991:** A U.S. National Intelligence Estimate report says that Iran's nuclear program appears disorganized and in its early stages. Richard H. Solomon, U.S. assistant secretary of state for East Asian and Pacific affairs, says that China has sold nuclear-related technologies to Iran despite its earlier assurances that it would not.[3]

- **November 1991:** Israeli officials contend that, using Pakistani assistance, Iran could make a nuclear bomb by the end of the decade. U.S. officials estimate that it would take 10 to 15 years. According to a November 1 *New York Times* report, U.S. analysts insist that Iran has neither the money nor the professional personnel to produce a nuclear weapon in a short time. One expert said that although China may assist Iran in nuclear weapons development, the assistance "will certainly not be on the scale of Western help to Iraq." [4]

- **February 24, 1993:** CIA director James Woolsey says that Iran is still 8 to 10 years away from being able to produce its own nuclear weapon, but with assistance from abroad it could become a nuclear power earlier.[5]

- **December 13, 1993:** According to *Defense News*, the CIA "believes that Iran could have nuclear weapons within eight to 10 years, even without critical assistance form abroad." [6]

- **February 16, 1994:** According to the latest CIA estimates, Iran could develop a nuclear bomb in six to eight years, although its nuclear weapons program is still in an early stage and relies on foreign technology and expertise.[7]

- **September 23, 1994:** CIA director James Woolsey says that "Iran is eight to ten years away from building [nuclear] weapons, and that help from the outside will be critical in reaching that timetable. Iran has been particularly active in trying to purchase nuclear materials or technology clandestinely from Russian sources. Iran is also looking to purchase fully-fabricated nuclear weapons in order to accelerate sharply its timetable."[8]

- **January 1995:** The director of the U.S. Arms Control and Disarmament Agency, John Holum, testifies that Iran could have the bomb by 2003.[9]

- **January 5, 1995:** U.S. defense secretary William Perry says that Iran may be less than five years from building an atomic bomb, although "how soon . . . depends how they go about getting it." Perry said buying or stealing a bomb from one of the Soviet states could happen in "a week, a month, five years." Alternatively, if Tehran could obtain a large amount of highly enriched uranium, then "five years is on the high end."[10]

- **January 19, 1995:** Special U.S. Representative for Nonproliferation Thomas Graham says that Iran has "no current program'" for producing weapons-grade fissile materials. "They are not that far along," he added.[11]

- **February 29, 1996:** Lynn Davis, U.S. undersecretary of state, says that Iran is "many years away" from possessing a nuclear weapons capability, but stealing nuclear technology or material "can reduce the time dramatically in terms of developing a weapon."[12]

- **April 29, 1996:** Israeli prime minister Shimon Peres says "he believes that in four years, they [Iran] may reach nuclear weapons."[13]

- **March 1997:** John Holum, director of the U.S. Arms Control and Disarmament Agency, testifies to a House panel that Iran could develop a nuclear bomb sometime between 2005 and 2007.[14]

- **June 26, 1997:** General Binford Peay, U.S. military commander in the Persian Gulf, says that Iran may have nuclear weapons "some time at the turn of the century, the near-end of the turn of the century" if it gets access to fissionable material.[15]

- **October 21, 1998:** General Anthony Zinni, head of U.S. Central Command, says Iran could have the capacity to deliver nuclear weapons within five years. "If I were a betting man," he said, "I would say they are on track within five years, they would have the capability."[16]

- **November 21, 1999:** According to a senior Israeli official, Iran will have a nuclear capability within five years, unless Russian military aid to Iran stops.[17]

- **January 17, 2000:** A new CIA assessment on Iran's nuclear capabilities says that the CIA cannot rule out the possibility that Iran may possess nuclear weapons. The assessment is based on the CIA's admission that it cannot monitor Iran's nuclear activities with any precision and hence cannot exclude the prospect that Iran may have nuclear weapons.[18]

- **September 20, 2000:** According to the CIA, Iran is "attempting to develop the capability to produce both plutonium and highly enriched uranium, and it is actively pursuing the acquisition of fissile material and the expertise and technology necessary to form the material into nuclear weapons." A CIA official also claimed that Iran could be in a position to test fire an intercontinental ballistic missile (ICBM) within five years.[19]

- **February 6, 2002:** CIA director George Tenet tells the U.S. Senate that Iran is seeking long-range ballistic missiles and weapons of mass destruction and will probably succeed in having them by 2015.[20] He also said that Iran "may be able to indigenously produce enough fissile material for a nuclear weapon by the end of this decade. . . . Obtaining material from outside could cut years from this estimate."[21]

It is important to note that the IAEA inspections of 2003–2006 produced no evidence that Iran was making nuclear weapons. However, they also did not prove that Tehran had no nuclear weapons program. It may well be that Iran is using its "civilian research program" to advance its nuclear military capabilities, but this scarcely is a basis for predicting whether Iran has the capabilities to weaponize its nuclear technology. That capability depends not only on how advanced Tehran's nuclear program is, but also on how advanced Iran's delivery systems are and the options Iran chooses to deliver such weapons.

THE DIFFICULTY OF ESTIMATING POSSIBLE DATES

Setting a timetable for Iran's nuclear capability depends on knowing Iran's ability to enrich large amounts of uranium. Some experts believe that the IAEA inspectors delayed Iran's acquiring the capability to produce highly enriched uranium at an "industrial" level. For example, when Iran resumed its uranium enrichment program on January 10, 2006, and the EU3 threatened Iran with UN Security

Council sanctions, Tehran threatened that it would "begin industrial enrichment." This prompted experts to speculate that if Iran moved to enrich large quantities of uranium at an advanced level, Tehran's nuclear capabilities might be only a few years away.[22]

Iran's chief delegate to the IAEA, Sirus Nasseri, stated in August 2005 that Iran would be a "nuclear fuel producer and supplier within a decade."[23] If true, this means it might take Iran 10 years to reach industrial production of fissile material.

The former CIA deputy director for intelligence, John McLaughlin, made the following broad comments about the uncertainties in estimating efforts to proliferate in an interview in January 2000:

> I would say the problem of proliferation of weapons of mass destruction is becoming more complex and difficult . . . . We're starting to see more evidence of what I might call kind of secondary proliferation. That is more evidence of sharing of information and data among countries that are striving to obtain weapons . . . . As the systems mature in the obvious countries like North Korea and Iran, they themselves have the potential to start becoming sources of proliferation as distinct from aspirants. And that begins to complicate the whole picture . . . . In the intelligence business (denial and deception) is an art form unto itself, it is how do you deny information to the other side and how do you deceive the other side? . . . Countries that are building such weapons are learning more and more about how to do that, making our job harder, . . . So if there is an issue that is to me personally worrying, it's the increasing complexity of the proliferation challenge . . . . To some degree we're dealing with problems that are fueled by hundreds of years of history. At the same time this past is colliding with the future, because you have these same people now using laptop computers and commercial encryption . . . . You're not going to find that information on their Web sites. You're going to have to go out and get it somewhere clandestinely, either through human collection or through technical means. [24]

There are experts who believe that Iran is working so actively on the design of missile warheads and bombs that it may well be significantly closer to having a bomb than the data on its nuclear efforts alone would indicate. Some experts also believe that Iran has a covert nuclear weapons design and enrichment effort that it developed in parallel with its more overt "civilian" nuclear research activities, and that the elements of this program are well dispersed and designed to have "denial covers" so that Iran can claim they are peaceful research or else work conducted in the past. These experts state that the information they rely on has not been provided by opposition sources.[25]

Much hinges on Iran's level of centrifuge development, including its covert ability to acquire and/or manufacture centrifuges and to assemble them into chains that can be hidden and deployed in large underground/sheltered facilities or in buildings that appear to have other uses.

Experts disagree about the level of technology Iran has, which can make the difference between chains of hundreds of centrifuges and chains of thousands. There is also no agreement about whether Iran has moved beyond the limited levels of efficiency found in the P-2 centrifuges being manufactured for Libya. Rotor design and overall efficiency are critical in determining the size of the facilities needed to spin uranium hexafluoride into enriched uranium, and how quickly Iran could acquire a weapon. There are significant time gaps and uncertainties in the data Iran has provided to the IAEA, and it may have advanced beyond the designs of the 20 centrifuges it has declared to the IAEA. This, however, is a major "wild card" in estimating Iran's progress.[26]

Another "wild card" is that the timeline for producing a nuclear weapon would change radically if Iran could buy fissile material from another nation or source—such as the 500 kilograms of fissile material the United States airlifted out of Kazakhstan in 1994. That was enough material to make up to 25 nuclear weapons, and the United States acted primarily because Iran was actively seeking to buy such material.[27] If Iran could obtain weapons-grade material, a number of experts believe that it could probably develop a gun or simple implosion nuclear weapon in 9 to 36 months, and that it might be able to deploy an implosion weapon suited for a missile warhead or bomb delivery in the same period.

The risk of transfers of fissile material is significant. U.S. experts believe that all of the weapons and fissile material remaining in the former Soviet Union are now stored in Russian facilities. The security of those facilities is still erratic, however, and there is a black market in nuclear material. Although the radioactive material sold to date on the black market by the Commonwealth of Independent States (CIS) and central European citizens has consisted largely of plutonium 240, low-grade enriched uranium, or isotopes of material of little value in a nuclear weapons program, that is no guarantee for the future. There are also no guarantees that Iran will not be able to purchase major transfers of nuclear weapon components and nuclear ballistic missile warhead technology.

INDEPENDENT ESTIMATES

There are many sources of independent estimates. Outside observers have tried for years to predict possible timelines for Iran's nuclear weapons. As has been noted, some have set short timelines. For example, Dany Shoham, a senior researcher at Bar-Ilan University's Begin-Sadat Center for Strategic Studies, estimated on February 26, 2001, that Iran was only few years away from a nuclear bomb:

> Iran has and is implementing the very same concept as Iraq—the total acquisition of all types of non-conventional weapons and, in conjunction, the development of delivery systems, primarily in the form of ballistic missiles . . . . Iran, which is the most technologically advanced country in the Middle East with the exception of Israel, has been in a more advantageous position than Iraq. It has not been under the international microscope as much as its neighbor and has been pursuing its aims in these various fields in a far more sophisticated and elegant manner.[28]

On January 30, 2005, when asked for a timeline for Iran's ability to acquire nuclear weapons, ElBaradei said, "It depends on whether they have been doing weaponization. We haven't seen signs of that. But they have the know-how. If they resume the fuel cycle, they should be able to get the fissile material within a year or two. If they have that, they are a year away from a weapon. It's a matter of time, because they have the know-how and the industrial infrastructure."[29]

Former chief UN weapons inspector Hans Blix, however, has argued that Iran is a long way from acquiring nuclear weapons. "They have many years to go before they will be able to produce highly enriched uranium for a bomb and I believe there is plenty of room for negotiations," Blix was quoted as saying. He argued that Iran's plans to build a 40-megawatt heavy water reactor in Bushehr "are very much in their infancy and the West is not particularly worried and maybe [can] count on being able to talk the Iranians out of it."[30]

Gary Samore of the International Institute for Strategic Studies (IISS) has said that given the technical obstacles of producing a nuclear warhead, it may take Iran five years to produce an atomic bomb: "They're trying to avoid international reaction and I think it's perhaps more likely that they try to develop their nuclear capabilities over a much longer period of time, a decade or 15 years."[31]

Still others have provided mid-term estimates for Iranian capability. David Albright of the Institute for Science and International Security (ISIS) estimated that even if Iran did not achieve its goal of 50,000 centrifuges at Natanz, it had bought enough components of the centrifuges on the black market to produce 1,500 "operating centrifuges." This is enough to produce 45 pounds of highly enriched uranium, which is estimated to produce one crude nuclear weapon. Albright estimated that Iran could reach this capability within three years (2009).[32]

Albright and Corey Hinderstein qualified their prediction that Iran may acquire nuclear weapons by 2009 as a "worst-case assessment." They argued on January 12, 2006, "Given another year to make enough HEU for a nuclear weapon and a few more months to convert the uranium into weapon components, Iran could have its first nuclear weapon in 2009. By this time, Iran is assessed to have had sufficient time to prepare the other components of a nuclear weapon, although the weapon may not be deliverable by a ballistic missile." They added that such an estimate is "highly uncertain" and that U.S. intelligence thought the assessment was overly optimistic because it did not take into account possible technical and scientific difficulties.[33]

In March 2006, a briefing by IAEA experts in Vienna revealed that Iran might be closer than was known to testing its 164-machine cascades, which spin uranium hexafluoride gas into enriched uranium. This revelation prompted U.S. officials to speculate that Iran might be closer to acquiring nuclear weapons. U.S. officials admitted that time estimates are necessarily uncertain, as they depend largely on assumptions about Iran's technical capabilities that could change in the near future. Still, one U.S. official was quoted as follows: "Iran could be as little as two to three years away from having nuclear weapons, with all the necessary caveats and assumptions and extrapolations about them overcoming technical hurdles."[34]

There are several ways in which Iran can achieve this. According to Albright and Hinderstein of the ISIS, however, there are two "worst-case" scenarios regarding when Iran can acquire nuclear weapons, and each of these scenarios estimates that Iran may not able to acquire weapons before 2009:

- In their "clandestine option" scenario, the authors argue that Iran could try to avoid detection and build clandestine enrichment plants at a location that has not been identified by the international community, the IAEA, or the United States. In this case, they say, if Iran decided in early 2006 to secretly build a centrifuge enrichment plant, it could assemble 1,500 centrifuges by 2007. This move could delay Iran's ability to produce enough HEU—highly enriched uranium—to build its first nuclear weapons, as it would mean moving large components from Natanz to the new "secret" facility, which could not go unnoticed. Iran would also need to integrate the components into the new systems, build emergency and safety mechanisms, and test the new centrifuges.[35]

  According to the ISIS study, "Iran could start immediately to accomplish these steps, even before the final testing of the 164-machine cascades at Natanz, but final completion of the clandestine plant is highly unlikely before the end of 2007." Even if Iran achieves that, however, it would need one year to produce HEU for a nuclear weapon. Taking into account technical difficulties, Tehran could use this clandestine facility to produce its first nuclear weapon in 2009.[36]

- The second scenario—what the ISIS study calls the "breakout using FEP" scenario—would be if Iran continues its enrichment activities at Natanz. Iran has expressed its goal of installing the first module of 3,000 centrifuges at Natanz's fuel enrichment plant (FEP) by the end of 2006. At its current assembly rate of 70–100 centrifuges per month, Iran can achieve that goal in 2008. Although these centrifuges are built to produce low-enriched uranium, Iran can use the modules to produce highly enriched uranium by 2009 or 2010, according to the ISIS estimate.[37]

As noted earlier, although these estimates are "worst case," one can expect technical difficulties and installation inefficiencies to delay the timetable even further. Also, any weapon produced may not be small enough to be delivered with Iran's missile capabilities.[38]

It is equally important to note, however, that whether it chooses the "breakout" or the "clandestine" path, Iran is unlikely to produce enough HEU, the material needed to produce nuclear weapons, before the year 2009. In each estimate, the authors contend that "Iran appears to need at least three years before it could have enough HEU to make a nuclear weapon. Given the technical difficultly of the task, it could take Iran much longer."[39]

The ISIS study outlined key questions that are fundamental to developing meaningful estimates about how soon Iran can acquire nuclear weapons. These include technical difficulties in producing fissile materials, political uncertainties regarding the nature of the Iranian regime, possible military strikes against Iranian nuclear sites, and the resources Iran employs to enrich uranium.[40]

These questions make the uncertainty in "guesstimating" a timetable all the more uncertain. In addition, it is clear that judging a timetable for Iran's acquisition of its first nuclear weapons largely depends on Tehran's capability to master its gas centrifuge program without interruption by IAEA inspections, technical difficulties, or possible military strikes.

ISRAELI ESTIMATES

Israeli estimates have also varied. On May 13, 2003, Israeli foreign minister Silvan Shalom stated that there was no question that Iran intended to acquire nuclear weapons, and added that "the important question is not whether they will have a bomb in 2009, 2010 or 2011, but when they will have the know-how to produce a bomb. According to our estimates, we are talking about six to nine months."[41]

On January 24, 2005, the head of the Mossad, Meir Dagan, told the Israeli parliament that Iran's nuclear program was almost "at the point of no return." He added that if Iran enriches uranium in 2005, it would take Tehran two to three more years to acquire nuclear weapons. "The moment you have the technology for enrichment, you are home free," Dagan said.[42]

Israeli estimates, however, are extremely volatile. General Aharon Zeevi Farkash, the head of Israel's Directorate of Military Intelligence (AMAN), stated in August 2004 that "once they have the ability to produce enough enriched uranium, we estimate that the first bomb will be constructed within two years—i.e., the end of 2006 or the beginning of 2007."[43]

General Farkash revised this estimate in January 2005 to predict that Iran would be able to acquire nuclear weapons between 2007 and 2009. He also predicted that Iran was six months away from enriching uranium (by June 2005)—which he described as the "point of no return." The date passed and there were no evidence that Iran actually enriched uranium.[44]

Estimates were further revised in 2005. According to press reports, Israeli intelligence changed their views in August 2005 about Iran's military and civilian nuclear program. The estimate that was leaked to the *Jerusalem Post* held that Iran would have a nuclear bomb "probably" by 2010; this revision was based on the assessment that Iran did not have a "secret military track." An IDF official was quoted as follows:

> We no longer think that a secret military track runs independent of the civilian one . . . . If it were then they could acquire weapons in 2007 . . . . We have changed our estimation. Now we think the military track is dependent on the civilian one. However, from a certain point it will be able to run independently. But not earlier than 2008.[45]

Following the revelation that the U.S. National Intelligence Estimate (NIE) predicted that Iran could be 10 years away from becoming a nuclear power, General Farkash said that "barring an unexpected delay, Iran is going to become nuclear capable in 2008 and not in 10 years as was recently reported in the American press."[46]

U.S. ESTIMATES

U.S. estimates vary from year to year, from one agency to another, and from one administration to another. The lessons of the Iraq WMD intelligence failure loom large over all estimates concerning Iran's nuclear capabilities, intentions, or timetables for nuclear weapons. They also tend to encourage the United States to be cautious. At the same time, the reorganization of the U.S. intelligence community is still under way, and it is too early to tell how such reforms will influence estimates of Iran's WMD programs.

The deputy director of national intelligence, General Michael V. Hayden, summarized these "reforms" as follows:

> We've made our products—whether they be the morning briefing for the president or the national intelligence estimate—more communal, although I must admit that the Central Intelligence Agency's DI [Directorate of Intelligence] is the core of our community's analysis. That said, we've gotten other people participating earlier in the process in a more realistic way. In our products, there has been a higher tolerance for ambiguity in terms of "we're more certain about this and less certain about that." [47]

The Silberman-Robb commission, which President George W. Bush ordered to assess the quality of U.S. intelligence on proliferation, concluded that the U.S. intelligence on Iran was "inadequate." Other officials described the U.S. data as "scandalous." Although the full findings of the reports on Iran and North Korea were classified, U.S. officials who were briefed on the reports said that the panel criticized the lack of human spying in Iran by the United States. Other intelligence officials argued that the setback of U.S. intelligence capabilities against Iran started in the 1980s when the Iranian security services successfully penetrated the Central Intelligence Agency's spy network in Iran. [48]

U.S. experts make it clear that there is a diversity of views about Iran's intentions as well as its actual capabilities. As noted earlier, some estimates dating back to the early 1990s stated that Iran would acquire nuclear weapons by the turn of the century (i.e., by 2000). More recent analyses, while seeming to confirm Iran's intention to pursue "nuclear technology," differ in scope and conclusions about actual WMD capabilities and timetables for when such capabilities may be acquired by Tehran.

There seems to be less disagreement about Iran's intentions to acquire nuclear weapons. On November 18, 2005, the U.S. secretary of state, Colin Powell said, "There is no doubt in my mind—and it's fairly straightforward from what we've been saying for years—that they have been interested in a nuclear weapon that has utility, meaning that it is something they would be able to deliver, not just something that sits there."[49]

The 2006 Annual Threat Assessment by the director of national intelligence (DNI) reiterated the U.S. position about Iran's clandestine nuclear program, but gave no estimate of when Iran might acquire nuclear weapons. On February 2, 2006, John D. Negroponte said that Iran is a "hard target" to penetrate, but offered the following unclassified assessment of Iran's nuclear activities:

> Our concerns about Iran are shared by many nations, by the IAEA, and of course, Iran's neighbors.
>
> Iran conducted a clandestine uranium enrichment program for nearly two decades in violation of its IAEA safeguards agreement, and despite its claims to the contrary, we assess that Iran seeks nuclear weapons. We judge that Tehran probably does not yet have a nuclear weapon and probably has not yet produced or acquired the necessary fissile material. Nevertheless, the danger that it will acquire a nuclear weapon and the ability to integrate it with the ballistic missiles Iran already possesses is a reason for immediate concern. Iran already has the largest inventory of ballistic missiles in the Middle East, and Tehran views its ballistic missiles as an integral part of its strategy to deter—and if necessary retaliate against—forces in the region, including U.S. forces.[50]

There have been many different U.S. intelligence estimates, particularly about how advanced Iran's nuclear program is and how long it may take Tehran to acquire the capabilities to produce a nuclear weapon.

For example, Robert Gates, then director of Central Intelligence, testified to Congress in February 1992 that Iran was "building up its special weapons capability as part of a massive . . . effort to develop its military and defense capability."[51] In 1992, reports in the press about the CIA's National Intelligence Estimates indicated that the CIA estimated that Iran could have a nuclear weapon by the year 2000. Reports coming out of Israel in January 1995 also claimed that the United States and Israel estimated Iran could have a nuclear weapon in five years.[52]

Lt. General Binford Peay, the commander of USCENTCOM, stated in June 1997, "I would predict to you that it would be some time at the turn of the next century . . . I wouldn't want to put a date on it. I don't know if its 2010, 2007, 2003. I am just saying its coming closer. Your instincts tell you that that's the kind of speed they are moving at."[53]

During this same period, U.S. intelligence sources denied the reports coming out of Israel and estimated that it might take 7 to 15 years for Iran to acquire a nuclear weapon.[54] As mentioned earlier, John Holum testified to Congress in 1995 that Iran could have the bomb by 2003. In 1997, he testified that Iran could have the bomb by 2005–2007.[55] Although two years had passed in which Iran might have made substantial progress, the U.S. estimate of the earliest date at which Iran could make its own bomb slipped by two to four years.

U.S. Secretary of Defense William Perry stated on January 9, 1995, "We believe that Iran is trying to develop a nuclear program. We believe it will be many, many years until they achieve such a capability. There are some things they might be able to do to short-cut that time."[56] In referring to "short cuts," Secretary Perry was concerned with the risk that Iran could obtain fissile material and weapons technology from the former Soviet Union or some other nation capable of producing fissile material.

In 1996, John M. Deutch, then the director of central intelligence, testified to Congress that "we judge that Iran is actively pursuing an indigenous nuclear weapons capability. . . . Specifically, Iran is attempting to develop the capability to produce both plutonium and highly enriched uranium. In an attempt to shorten the timeline to a weapon, Iran has launched a parallel effort to purchase fissile material, mainly from sources in the former Soviet Union." He indicated that Iran's indigenous uranium-enrichment program seemed to be focused on the development of gas centrifuges, and that Iran's nuclear weapons program was still at least 8 to 10 years away from producing nuclear arms, although that time could be shortened significantly with foreign assistance.[57]

A detailed Department of Defense report on proliferation issued in 1997 did not comment on the timing of Iran's nuclear efforts. It did, however, draw broad conclusions about the scale of the Iranian nuclear program and how it fit into Iran's overall efforts to acquire weapons of mass destruction. What is striking about this report is that some eight years later, its conclusions still seem to broadly reflect the Department's views regarding Iran's efforts to acquire both weapons of mass destruction and long-range missiles:

Iran's national objectives and strategies are shaped by its regional political aspirations, threat perceptions, and the need to preserve its Islamic government. Tehran strives to be a leader in the Islamic world and seeks to be the dominant power in the Gulf. The latter goal brings it into conflict with the United States. Tehran would like to diminish Washington's political and military influence in the region. Iran also remains hostile to the ongoing Middle East peace process and supports the use of terrorism as an element of policy. Within the framework of its national goals, Iran continues to give high priority to expanding its NBC [nuclear, biological, and chemical] weapons and missile programs. In addition, Iran's emphasis on pursuing independent production capabilities for NBC weapons and missiles is driven by its experience during the 1980–1988 war with Iraq, during which it was unable to respond adequately to Iraqi chemical and missile attacks and suffered the effects of an international arms embargo.

Iran perceives that it is located in a volatile and dangerous region, virtually surrounded by potential military threats or unstable neighbors. These include the Iraqi government of Saddam Hussein, Israel, U.S. security agreements with the Gulf Cooperation Council (GCC) states and accompanying U.S. military presence in the Gulf, and instability in Afghanistan and the Central Asian states of the former Soviet Union.

Iran still views Baghdad as the primary regional threat to the Islamic Republic, even though Iraq suffered extensive damage during the Gulf War. Further, Iran is not convinced that Iraq's NBC programs will be adequately restrained or eliminated through continued UN sanctions or monitoring. Instead, the Iranians believe that they will face yet another challenge from their historical rival.

Tehran is concerned about strong U.S. ties with the GCC states because these states have received substantial amounts of modern Western conventional arms, which Tehran seeks but cannot acquire, and because U.S. security guarantees make these states less susceptible to Iranian pressure. While Tehran probably does not believe GCC nations have offensive designs against the Islamic Republic, it may be concerned that the United States will increase mistrust between Iran and the Arab states. It also likely fears that the sizable U.S. military presence in the region could lead to an attack against Iran. Iran may also be concerned by Israel's strategic projection capabilities and its potential to strike Iran in a variety of ways. For all these reasons, Tehran probably views NBC weapons and the ability to deliver them with missiles as decisive weapons for battlefield use, as deterrents, and as effective means for political intimidation of less powerful neighboring states.

In recent years, Iran's weak economy has limited the development of its NBC weapons and missile programs, although oil price increases in 1996 may have relieved the pressure at least temporarily. Tehran's international debt exceeds $30 billion, although Iran is meeting its debt repayment obligations. Iran also is facing a rapidly growing population that will exact greater future demands from its limited economy. Despite these internal problems, Iran assigns a high priority to attaining production self-sufficiency for NBC weapons and missiles. Therefore, funding for these efforts is likely to be a high priority for the next several years.

Tehran has attempted to portray U.S. containment efforts as unjust, in an attempt to convince European or Asian suppliers to relax export restrictions on key technologies. At the same time, foreign suppliers must consider the risk of sanctions or political embarrassment because of U.S.-led containment efforts.

Iran's nuclear program, focusing on electric power production, began during the 1970s under the shah. Research and development efforts also were conducted on fissile material production, although these efforts were halted during the Iranian revolution and the Iran-Iraq war. However, the program has been restarted, possibly in reaction to the revelations about the scope of Iraq's nuclear weapons program.

Iran is trying to acquire fissile material to support development of nuclear weapons and has set up an elaborate system of military and civilian organizations to support its effort. Barring outright acquisition of a nuclear weapon from a foreign source, Iran could pursue several other avenues for weapon development. The shortest route, depending on weapon design, could be to purchase or steal fissile material. Also, Iran could attempt to produce highly enriched uranium if it acquired the appropriate facilities for the front-end of the nuclear fuel cycle. Finally, Iran could pursue development of an entire fuel cycle, which would allow for long-term production of plutonium, similar to the route North Korea followed.

Iran does not yet have the necessary infrastructure to support a nuclear weapons program, although [it] is actively negotiating for purchase of technologies and whole facilities to support all of the above strategies. Iran claims it is trying to establish a complete nuclear fuel cycle to support a civilian energy program, but this same fuel cycle would be applicable to a nuclear weapons development program. Iran is seeking foreign sources for many elements of the nuclear fuel cycle. Chinese and Russian supply policies are key to whether Iran will successfully acquire the needed technology, expertise, and infrastructure to manufacture the fissile material for a weapon and the ability to fashion a usable device. Russian or Chinese supply of nuclear power reactors, allowed by the NPT, could enhance Iran's limited nuclear infrastructure and advance its nuclear weapons program.

Iran has had a chemical weapons production program since early in the Iran-Iraq war. It used chemical agents to respond to Iraqi chemical attacks on several occasions during that war. Since the early 1990s, it has put a high priority on its chemical weapons program because of its inability to respond in kind to Iraq's chemical attacks and the discovery of substantial Iraqi efforts with advanced agents, such as the highly persistent nerve agent VX. Iran ratified the CWC, under which it will be obligated to eliminate its chemical program over a period of years. Nevertheless, it continues to upgrade and expand its chemical warfare production infrastructure and munitions arsenal.

Iran manufactures weapons for blister, blood, and choking agents; it is also believed to be conducting research on nerve agents. Iran has a stockpile of these weapons, including artillery shells and bombs, which could be used in another conflict in the region.

Although Iran is making a concerted effort to attain an independent production capability for all aspects of its chemical weapons program, it remains dependent on foreign sources for chemical warfare-related technologies. China is an important supplier of technologies and equipment for Iran's chemical warfare program. Therefore, Chinese supply policies will be key to whether Tehran attains its long-term goal of independent production for these weapons.

Iran's biological warfare program began during the Iran-Iraq war. The pace of the program probably has increased because of the 1995 revelations about the scale of Iraqi efforts prior to the Gulf War. The relative low cost of developing these weapons may be another motivating factor. Although this program is in the research and development stage, the Iranians have considerable expertise with pharmaceuticals, as well as the commercial and military infrastructure needed to produce basic biological warfare agents. Iran also can make some of the hardware needed to manufacture agents. Therefore, while only small quantities of usable agent may exist now, within 10 years, Iran's military forces may be able to deliver biological agents effectively. Iran has ratified the BWC.

Iran has an ambitious missile program, with SCUD B, SCUD C, and CSS-8 (a Chinese surface-to-surface missile derived from a surface-to-air missile) missiles in its inventory. Having first acquired SCUD missiles from Libya and North Korea for use during the Iran-Iraq war, the Iranians are now able to produce the missile themselves. This has been accomplished with considerable equipment and technical help from North Korea. Iran has made significant progress in the last few years toward its goal of becoming self-sufficient in ballistic missile production.

Iran produces the solid-propellant 150 kilometer range Nazeat 10 and 200 kilometer range Zelzal unguided rockets. Iran also is trying to produce a relatively short-range solid-propellant missile. For the longer term, Iran's goal is to establish the capability to produce medium range ballistic missiles to expand its regional influence. It is attempting to acquire production infrastructure to enable it to produce the missiles itself. Like many of Iran's other efforts, success with future missile capabilities will depend on key equipment and technologies from China, North Korea, and Russia.

Iran's missiles allow it to strike a wide variety of key economic and military targets in several neighboring countries, including Turkey, Saudi Arabia, and the other Gulf states. Possible targets include oil installations, airfields, and ports, as well as U.S. military deployment areas in the region. All of Iran's missiles are on mobile launchers, which enhance their survivability. Should Iran succeed in acquiring or developing a longer-range missile like the North Korean No Dong, it could threaten an even broader area, including much of Israel.

Iran has purchased land-, sea-, and air-launched short range cruise missiles from China; it also has a variety of foreign-made air-launched short range tactical missiles. Many of these systems are deployed as anti-ship weapons in or near the Gulf. Iran also has a variety of Western and Soviet-made fighter aircraft, artillery, and rockets available as potential means of delivery for NBC weapons.

In the future, as Iran becomes more self-sufficient at producing chemical or biological agents and ballistic missiles, there is a potential that it will become a supplier. For example, Iran might supply related equipment and technologies to other states trying to develop capabilities, such as Libya or Syria. There is precedent for such action; Iran supplied Libya with chemical agents in 1987. [58]

Martin Indyck, then the assistant secretary of state for Near East affairs, testified to the Senate Foreign Relations Committee on July 28, 1998, that Iran's Shahab-3 and Shahab-4 missile programs were clearly linked to its efforts to acquire nuclear weapons. He made it clear that the missiles would give Iran the range to hit targets in Israel, Turkey, and Saudi Arabia. In regard to Iran's nuclear program, Indyck stated that Iran had a "clandestine nuclear weapons program. People tend to say that a nuclear weapons capability is many years off. Our assessments vary. I would want to be a bit cautious about that because I believe there are large gaps in our knowledge of what is going on there because it's a clandestine program."[59]

The director of the CIA did not address this subject in his testimony to Congress on the "World Wide Threat" on February 2, 2000. U.S. intelligence did, however, continue to flag the Iranian nuclear threat as part of its broader assessments of Iran's efforts to proliferate. Since 1997, the Non-Proliferation Center of the office of the director of Central Intelligence has issued a series of unclassified reports on Iran's efforts to acquire nuclear weapons technology. The most recent version of the report was issued in February 2000 and focused on developments in Iran since 1998:

> Iran remains one of the most active countries seeking to acquire WMD and ACW [advanced conventional weapons] technology from abroad. In doing so, Tehran is attempting to develop an indigenous capability to produce various types of weapons—nuclear, chemical, and biological—and their delivery systems. During the reporting period, Iran focused its efforts to acquire WMD- and ACW- related equipment, materials, and technology primarily on entities in Russia, China, North Korea and Western Europe.
>
> For the first half of 1999, entities in Russia and China continued to supply a considerable amount and a wide variety of ballistic missile-related goods and technology to Iran. Tehran is using these goods and technologies to support current production programs and to achieve its goal of becoming self-sufficient in the production of ballistic missiles. Iran already is producing Scud short-range ballistic missiles (SRBMs) and has built and publicly displayed prototypes for the Shahab-3 medium-range ballistic missile (MRBM), which had its initial flight test in July 1998 and probably has achieved "emergency operational capability"—i.e., Tehran could deploy a limited number of the Shahab-3 prototype missiles in an operational mode during a perceived crisis situation. In addition, Iran's Defense Minister last year publicly acknowledged the development of the Shahab-4, originally calling it a more capable

ballistic missile than the Shahab-3, but later categorizing it as sole-ly a space launch vehicle with no military applications. Iran's Defense Minister also has publicly mentioned plans for a "Shahab 5."

For the reporting period, Tehran continued to seek considerable dual-use biotechnical equipment from entities in Russia and Western Europe, ostensibly for civilian uses. Iran began a biological warfare (BW) program during the Iran-Iraq war, and it may have some limited capability for BW deployment. Outside assistance is both important and difficult to prevent, given the dual-use nature of the materials, the equipment being sought, and the many legitimate end uses for these items.

Iran, a Chemical Weapons Convention (CWC) party, already has manufactured and stockpiled chemical weapons, including blister, blood, and choking agents and the bombs and artillery shells for delivering them. During the first half of 1999, Tehran continued to seek production technology, expertise, and chemicals that could be used as precursor agents in its chemical warfare (CW) program from entities in Russia and China. It also acquired or attempted to acquire indirectly through intermediaries in other countries equipment and material that could be used to create a more advanced and self-sufficient CW infrastructure.

Iran sought nuclear-related equipment, material, and technical expertise from a variety of sources, especially in Russia, during the first half of 1999. Work continues on the construction of a 1,000-megawatt nuclear power reactor in Bushehr, Iran, that will be subject to International Atomic Energy Agency (IAEA) safeguards. In addition, Russian entities continued to interact with Iranian research centers on various activities. These projects will help Iran augment its nuclear technology infrastructure, which in turn would be useful in supporting nuclear weapons research and development. The expertise and technology gained, along with the commercial channels and contacts established—even from cooperation that appears strictly civilian in nature—could be used to advance Iran's nuclear weapons research and developmental program.

Russia has committed to observe certain limits on its nuclear cooperation with Iran. For example, President Yel'tsin has stated publicly that Russia will not provide militarily useful nuclear technology to Iran. Beginning in January 1998, the Russian Government took a number of steps to increase its oversight of entities involved in dealings with Iran and other states of proliferation concern. In 1999, it pushed a new export control law through the Duma. Russian firms, however, faced economic pressures to circumvent these controls and did so in some cases. The Russian Government, moreover, failed in some cases regarding Iran to enforce its export controls. Following repeated warnings, the U.S. Government in January 1999 imposed administrative measures against Russian entities that had engaged in nuclear- and missile-related cooperation with Iran. The measures imposed on these and other Russian entities (which were identified in 1998) remain in effect.

China pledged in October 1997 not to engage in any new nuclear cooperation with Iran but said it would complete cooperation on two ongoing nuclear projects, a small research reactor and a zirconium production facility at Esfahan that Iran will use to produce cladding for reactor fuel. The pledge appears to be holding. As a party to the Nuclear Nonproliferation Treaty (NPT), Iran is required to apply IAEA safeguards to nuclear fuel, but safeguards are not required for the zirconium plant or its products.

Iran is attempting to establish a complete nuclear fuel cycle for its civilian energy program. In that guise, it seeks to obtain whole facilities, such as a uranium conversion facility, that, in fact, could be used in any number of ways in support of efforts to produce fissile material needed for a nuclear weapon. Despite international efforts to curtail the flow of critical technologies and equipment, Tehran continues to seek fissile material and technology for weapons development and has set up an elaborate system of military and civilian organizations to support its effort.[60]

Unofficial or leaked U.S. estimates appeared to grow more pessimistic during this period. The New York Times and the Washington Post published reports in January 2000 that the CIA estimated that it could not characterize the timing of the Iranian nuclear weapons program and that Iran might already have a bomb. Those reports, however, seem to have been based on an intelligence report that focused on the inherent uncertainties in estimating Iranian capabilities, and were not the result of any radical change in an estimate of how rapidly Iran could produce a weapon.[61]

Further leaks following the *New York Times* report indicated that the CIA had concluded that Iran was capable of completing the design and manufacture of all aspects of a nuclear weapon except the acquisition of fissile material—an accomplishment that Iraq had also mastered by 1990. Although the details of the report were never leaked, it seems likely that it concluded that Iran could now design medium-sized plutonium and uranium weapons and manufacture the high-explosive lens, neutron initiators, high-speed capacitors, and other components of the weapon. It could conduct fissile simulations of the explosive behavior of such designs using modern test equipment in ways similar to the Iraqi and Pakistani nuclear programs, and could rapidly assemble a weapon from these components if it could obtain illegal fissile material.

It seems likely that the report concluded that Iran had the technology for processing highly enriched plutonium simply because no country that had seriously attempted such processing had failed. But Iran would need fissile or borderline fissile uranium to make a bomb. As a result, the key uncertainty was whether the United States could monitor all potential sources of fissile material with enough accuracy to ensure that Iran did not have a weapon. The answer was no.

Although any such conclusions are speculative, it also seems likely that the U.S. intelligence community concluded that it was not possible to perfectly identify the level of Iran's nuclear weapons efforts, the specific organizations involved, the location and nature of all facilities, the foreign purchasing offices, and the technical success achieved.

U.S. intelligence certainly knows far more than it makes public. But Iran has been carrying out a covert program since the shah without one known case of a major defector or public example of a reliable breakthrough in human intelligence (HUMINT). Iran also learned during the Iran-Iraq War that it needed to ensure its facilities were not centralized and vulnerable, and that it had to conceal its activities as much as possible from any kind of intelligence surveillance. The strengthening of the NPT inspection regime has almost certainly rein-forced Iran's efforts to conceal its programs.[62]

An unclassified CIA report on Iran's efforts issued in the spring of 2004 covered developments through the end of 2003. It made the fol-lowing judgments about Iran's nuclear weapons efforts and other programs, and although these do not take account of the develop-ments in 2004, 2005, and 2006 that have been discussed earlier, they still seem to broadly reflect current U.S. intelligence assessments:

> Iran continued to vigorously pursue indigenous programs to produce nuclear, chemical, and biological weapons. Iran is also working to improve delivery systems as well as ACW. To this end, Iran continued to seek foreign materials, training, equipment, and know-how. During the reporting period, Iran still focused particu-larly on entities in Russia, China, North Korea, and Europe. Iran's nuclear program received significant assistance in the past from the proliferation network headed by Pakistani scientist A.Q. Khan.

> The United States remains convinced that Tehran has been pur-suing a clandestine nuclear weapons program, in contradiction to its obligations as a party to the Nuclear Non-proliferation Treaty (NPT). During 2003, Iran continued to pursue an indigenous nu-clear fuel cycle ostensibly for civilian purposes but with clear weap-ons potential. International scrutiny and International Atomic Energy Agency (IAEA) inspections and safeguards will most likely prevent Tehran from using facilities declared to the IAEA directly for its weapons program as long as Tehran remains a party to the NPT. However, Iran could use the same technology at other, covert locations for military applications.

> Iran continues to use its civilian nuclear energy program to jus-tify its efforts to establish domestically or otherwise acquire the entire nuclear fuel cycle. Iran claims that this fuel cycle would be used to produce fuel for nuclear power reactors, such as the 1,000-megawatt light-water reactor that Russia is continuing to build at the southern port city of Bushehr. However, Iran does not need to produce its own fuel for this reactor because Russia has pledged to provide the fuel throughout the operating lifetime of the reactor and is negotiating with Iran to take back the irradiated spent fuel.

An Iranian opposition group, beginning in August of 2002, revealed several previously undisclosed Iranian nuclear facilities, sparking numerous IAEA inspections since February 2003. Subsequent reports by the IAEA Director General revealed numerous failures by Iran to disclose facilities and activities, which run contrary to its IAEA safeguards obligations. Before the reporting period, the A.Q. Khan network provided Iran with designs for Pakistan's older centrifuges, as well as designs for more advanced and efficient models, and components.

The November 2003 report of the IAEA Director General (DG) to the Board of Governors describes a pattern of Iranian safeguards breaches, including the failure to: report the import and chemical conversion of uranium compounds, report the separation of plutonium from irradiated uranium targets, report the enrichment of uranium using both centrifuges and lasers, and provide design information for numerous fuel cycle facilities. In October 2003, Iran sent a report to the DG providing additional detail on its nuclear program and signed an agreement with the United Kingdom, France, and Germany that included an Iranian promise to suspend all enrichment and reprocessing efforts. On 18 December 2003, Iran signed the Additional Protocol (AP) to its IAEA Safeguards Agreement but took no steps to ratify the Protocol during this reporting period. [63]

In 2004, John R. Bolton, the State Department's undersecretary of arms control and international security, presented what might be considered the view of the "hardliners" in the Bush administration in testimony to the House International Relations Committee. Bolton outlined the U.S. assessment of Iran's nuclear program as follows:

The United States strongly believes that Iran has a clandestine program to produce nuclear weapons, and has been warning publicly about Tehran's weapons ambitions for over a decade.

We know Iran is developing uranium mines, a uranium conversion facility (UCF), a massive uranium enrichment facility designed to house tens of thousands of centrifuges, numerous centrifuge productions workshops, a heavy water production plant, and a laser enrichment facility. We know that Iran has violated its NPT and IAEA commitments by covertly enriching uranium, by covertly producing and separating plutonium, by secretly converting yellowcake into uranium hexafluoride (UF_6), and by secretly producing uranium metal and by failing to declare any of these activities to the IAEA. Iran secretly procured P-1 centrifuge components from the A.Q. Khan nuclear proliferation network, as well as P-2 components, developed the means to manufacture centrifuge components domestically (including in military workshops), and—contrary to its commitments to the IAEA and to three European governments—continues to produce components today. Iran has announced plans to "hot test" its UCF at Esfahan, which will produce UF_6, in clear violation of its promises to suspend all enrichment-related activity. Moreover, Iran continues with plans to build additional unnecessary nuclear capabilities, such as a heavy-water reactor—a facility ideally suited to produce large quantities of plutonium usable in a nuclear weapon, which also explains Iran's secret experiments with reprocessing plutonium behind the back of the International Atomic Energy Agency (IAEA). The designs for that facility underscore the weapons intent, as do Iran's experiments to produce polonium-210, a weapons initiator.

The costly infrastructure to perform all of these activities goes well beyond any conceivable peaceful nuclear program. No comparable oil-rich nation has ever engaged, or would be engaged, in this set of activities—or would pursue them for nearly two decades behind a continuing cloud of secrecy and lies to IAEA inspectors and the international community—unless it was dead set on building nuclear weapons.[64]

The director of the Defense Intelligence Agency, Vice Admiral Lowell E. Jacoby, outlined the DIA estimates of Iran's WMD program in testimony to the U.S. Senate in March 2005. He summarized the U.S. assessment of Iran's motivations and estimated a five-year window for Iran to be able to produce nuclear weapons:

Iran is likely continuing nuclear weapon-related endeavors in an effort to become the dominant regional power and deter what it perceives as the potential for U.S. or Israeli attacks. We judge Iran is devoting significant resources to its weapons of mass destruction and ballistic missile programs. Unless constrained by a nuclear non-proliferation agreement, Tehran probably will have the ability to produce nuclear weapons early in the next decade.[65]

In August 2005, however, it was reported that U.S. intelligence had revised those estimates. According to the *Washington Post,* the new National Intelligence Estimate had "credible information" about Iran's clandestine military work but stated that there was no information linking such work to nuclear weapons. The article did, however, cite important qualifications to the U.S. intelligence community estimates:[66]

- First, it stated that the United States remained uncertain about whether Iran's clerics made the final decision on acquiring nuclear weapons. According to one intelligence official quoted in the article, "It is the judgment of the intelligence community that, left to its own devices, Iran is determined to build nuclear weapons."

- Second, the new NIE reportedly revised the timeline to reflect possible technical obstacles in Iran's nuclear program. It stated that the March 2005 estimates (by the DIA) that Iran might be able to acquire a nuclear weapon in five years assumed that Iran would be moving ahead at full speed without technical difficulties and without delay from the inspections. If such complexities were taken into account, Iran would be "unlikely to produce a sufficient quantity of highly enriched uranium, the key ingredient for an atomic weapon, before 'early to mid-next decade.'"

- Third, the updated NIE took into account "a fading of suspicions that Iran's military has been running its own separate and covert enrichment effort." The *Post* article did state, however, that Iranian military have been working on missiles and centrifuge activities, which it argued "could be linked to a nuclear program."

- Fourth, the *Post* article quoted U.S. Undersecretary of State Robert G. Joseph as saying "we don't have perfect information or perfect understanding. But the Iranian record, plus what the

Iranians' leaders have said . . . lead us to conclude that we have to be highly skeptical." This also reflects the cautiousness and the lessons learned from asserting WMD capabilities with certainty.

At present, most U.S. experts believe that Iran has all the basic technology to build a bomb, but lacks any rapid route to getting fissile uranium and plutonium unless it can steal or buy it from another country. They also believe that Iran is increasingly worried about pre-emptive strikes by Israel or the United States. As a result, some feel that Iran has deliberately lowered the profile of its activities and is conducting its weapons design and development effort at only a low-to-moderate level.[67] As a result, many feel that Iran is at least five to seven years away from acquiring a nuclear device using its own en-riched material and might be six to nine years away from being able to design a nuclear weapon that can be fitted in the warhead of a long-range missile system.

ASSESSING IRAN'S NUCLEAR WEAPONS

All of these various estimates indicate that that Iran "probably" does not have nuclear weapons yet. This is the assessment of the IAEA, the United States, the Israelis, and virtually all intelligence agencies. There is no agreement, however, about when Iran might get nuclear weapons.

More generally, none of these estimates provide a meaningful basis for knowing either the kind of nuclear weapons Iran might develop and produce or the level of production it could achieve over time. This is not a critical set of issues as long as the only issue is preventing Iran from having a nuclear weapon. It is an absolutely critical set of issues the moment any consideration is given to dealing with Iran's nuclear program punitively.

It is clear that Iran already has the technical base to make fission weapons, and it has received substantial Chinese weapons design data for a moderately advanced fission weapon from North Korea. That information does not indicate, however, what designs Iran would ac-tually choose or be able to execute.

This makes it impossible to estimate Iran's production capabilities even if some estimate could be made about its facilities. The arms control literature often uses nominal weights of U-235 and Pu-239 for nuclear weapons. It also assumes that a given level of enrichment is needed for the "weapons grade" material used in such a bomb. These nominal estimates can be more misleading than useful.

The open literature has made it clear for decades that much lower levels of enrichment can produce a substantial explosion, and that there are many different weapons designs that use very different levels of weapons-grade material. For example, French designs are known to have tolerated two to three times higher percentages of Pu-240 than U.S. designs normally accept. Similarly, weapons have been tested with more than 20 percent Pu-240, and uranium weapons with levels of enrichment at or below 93.5 percent HEU (U-235) are known to be practical.[68]

Some of the techniques necessary to reduce the nominal amount of plutonium needed in a basic, unsophisticated implosion device ranging from roughly 10.5 to 13 kilograms to well below 6.5 kilograms are available on the Internet. Similar data are available for uranium weapons far smaller than the nominal 16.5 kilograms used for early implosion devices or the 29.3 kilograms for a basic gun device. Key hydrodynamic and instability data and some aspects of high-explosive lens design and advances are also readily available.[69] In addition, technical leaks from various weapons laboratories have compromised weapons design data relating to the amount of fissile material needed in a weapon, although Iran's ability to collect such data is uncertain.[70]

Much also depends on the desired size, shape, and weight of the weapon; the ability to predict a precise yield; the level of risk of accidental explosion a proliferator will accept; and the level of surety needed that a weapon will actually go off and not produce a "fizzle" or limited fissile event. Proliferators are not obliged to use U.S. designs with "point one" safety (less than a 1-in-1 million chance of the weapon delivering more than 2 kilograms of nuclear yield if the high explosives are detonated at the single most critical possible point).[71] They can also use very large and crude weapons designs if they are willing to use covert delivery means like trucks, ships, or large passenger aircraft.

At the same time, a truly sophisticated proliferator might need only about one-third to one-fifth of the nominal amount of weapons-grade material per bomb generally referred to in the open literature. "Sophisticated" is also a relative term. Most of the breakthroughs in miniaturizing nuclear weapons date back to the early and mid-1950s, and some basic advances are described in the open literature.[72] One source notes that powerful weapons have been manufactured for decades with total weights as low as 16 kilograms, including the casing:

> Using an advanced flying plate design it is possible to compress a 1-kg plutonium mass sufficiently to produce a yield in the 100-ton range. This design has an important implication on the type of fissile material that can be used. The high compression implies fast insertion times, while the low mass implies a low Pu-240 content. Taken together this means that a much higher Pu-240 content than normal weapon grade plutonium could be used in this type of design without affecting performance. In fact ordinary reactor grade plutonium would be as effective as weapon grade material for this use. Fusion boosting could produce yields exceeding 1-kt with this system.[73]

Some boosted nuclear weapons designs offer far higher yields than simple fission designs but only need a core of 3.5–4.5 kilograms of plutonium. Some uranium weapons designs benefit significantly from using a U-238 tamper.[74]

Most experts argue that advanced miniaturized designs would generally require at least underground testing. But some believe that sufficient weapons design and test data are now available to allow such designs to be made workable using conventional explosives and a noncritical mass of U-238, non-fissile plutonium, or depleted material. The technical details of such options are not a matter for the open literature, but Iran has to know that the possibility exists.

The other side of this story is Iran's willingness to risk deploying or using a nuclear weapon it has not tested, as well as the kind of weapon it can actually achieve. India and Pakistan have shown that other nuclear powers have conducted tests whose actual yield fell far short of the yield they initially claimed. There are still serious risks in not testing, or even in one-of-a-kind tests.

Those risks tend to be compounded with a missile warhead or small-to-medium-size bomb. The weapon must fit a given size, sustain

Table 8.1
Thermal and Blast Effects of Nuclear Weapons
(radius of effect in kilometers)

Yield in kilotons	Metals vaporize	Metals melt	Wood burns	Third-degree burns	5psi/ 160 mph winds	3 psi/ 116 mph winds
					Effects	
10	0.337	0.675	1.3	1.9	1.3	1.6
20	0.477	0.954	1.9	2.7	2.0	2.5
50	0.754	1.6	3.0	4.3	2.7	3.3
100	1.0	2.0	4.3	5.7	3.5	4.3
200	1.5	2.8	5.7	8.0	4.5	5.4

Source: Adapted from the Royal United Services Institute, *Nuclear Attack: Civil Defense* (London: RUSI/Brassey's, 1982), pp. 30–36.
Note: 1 kiloton = 1,000 tons of TNT; psi = pounds per square inch; mph = miles per hour.

considerable shock, and have highly reliable fuzing. For most purposes, the ability to select a given height of burst is critical to getting the best weapons effect.

As table 8.1 makes clear, nuclear weapons vary radically in yield and effect. Horrifying as any kind of nuclear explosion may be, smaller-yield weapons are much less lethal than high-yield weapons. The effects shown in table 8.1 do not cover thermonuclear or enhanced radiation weapons, as it is assumed that such designs will be beyond Iran's capabilities for at least a half a decade.[75] It is also not clear why Iran would design high-yield fusion weapons as opposed to "boosted" fission weapons that have yields substantially above the 25-kiloton range.[76] Furthermore, such data effectively assume that Iran would not deliberately seek weapons with yields below 10 kilotons unless these were needed for covert use.

Even so, the range of effects in table 8.1 is wide enough that weapons in the 10–20 kiloton range—the kind Iran is most likely to have initially—require accurate delivery against many military targets, and could be largely ineffective even against area targets if used with a missile with a high CEP (circular error probable). Such factors could lead to exchanges where Iranian leaders badly miscalculated what they could or could not do with nuclear weapons, felt forced to strike population or major civilian area targets, or used multiple weapons rather than one. The nature of the bomb does not matter if proliferation never goes beyond threat and deterrence. It is critical the moment war-fighting becomes a serious consideration.

Notes

[1] This chronology relies heavily on the chronology created by the Nuclear Threat Initiative (NTI), news stories, and International Atomic Energy Agency (IAEA) reports.

[2] Alon Pinhas, "Thinking the Unthinkable about Iran," *Jerusalem Post*, April 23, 1992.

[3] NTI, "Iran Profile: Nuclear Chronology, 1991," available at http://www.nti.org/e_research/profiles/Iran/1825_1864.html.

[4] Ibid.

[5] Douglas Jehl, "U.S. Outlines Concern over North Korean A-Arms," *New York Times*, February 25, 1993.

[6] NTI, "Iran Profile: Nuclear Chronology, 1993," available at http://www.nti.org/e_research/profiles/Iran/1825_1870.html.

[7] NTI, "Iran Profile: Nuclear Chronology, 1994," available at http://www.nti.org/e_research/profiles/Iran/1825_1871.html.

[8] James Woolsey, "Challenges to Peace" (speech to the Washington Institute for Near East Policy, September 23, 1994 [mimeo.]).

[9] Anthony H. Cordesman, *Iran and Nuclear Weapons: A Working Draft*, CSIS, February 21, 2000, available at http://www.csis.org/.

[10] Susanne M. Schafer, "Perry: Iran Closer to Nuclear Weapon," Associated Press, January 5, 1995.

[11] Mark Hibbs and Neal Sandler, "Iran Has 'No Program to Produce Fissile Materials,' U.S. Envoy Says," *Nucleonics Week*, February 2, 1995.

[12] NTI, "Iran Profile: Nuclear Chronology, 1996," available at http://www.nti.org/e_research/profiles/Iran/1825_1873.html.

[13] "Iran Could Have Nuclear Weapons in Four Years: Peres," Agence France-Presse, April 30, 1996.

[14] "Iran Running into Difficulties in Push for Nuclear Capability," Associated Press, May 5, 1997.

[15] "Iran Likely to Have Nuclear Weapons Capability Soon: U.S. Military," Agence France-Presse, June 26, 1997.

[16] "General Expects Iranian Nuclear Weapons in Five Years," Associated Press, October 21, 1998.

[17] "Israeli Official: U.S. Must Pressure Russia to End Military Cooperation with Iran," Associated Press, November 21, 1999.

[18] James Risen and Judith Miller, "CIA Tells Clinton an Iranian A-Bomb Can't Be Ruled Out," *New York Times*, January 17, 2000.

[19] Michael Smith, "Iran Gains Ground in Nuclear Arms," *Calgary (AB) Herald*, September 27, 2000.

[20] "CIA Chief Outlines Threats the World Over," Associated Press, February 6, 2002.

[21] John Diamond, "Israel: Iran Could Have Nuclear Arms in 5 Years, Defense Minister Calls Nation 'Twin' of Hussein's Iraq," *Chicago Tribune*, February 8, 2002.

[22] George Jahn, "For Iran, It's When, Not If," Associated Press, January 27, 2006.

[23] William J. Kole, "UN Agency's Restrained Response to Iran Signals Preference for Talks over Sanctions," Associated Press, August 12, 2005.

[24] Reuters, January 24, 2000, 18:32.

[25] Bill Gertz, "U.S. Told of Iranian Effort to Create Nuclear Warhead," *Washington Times*, December 2, 2004, p. 3; Douglas Jehl, "Iran Is Said to Work on New Missile," *International Herald Tribune*, December 2, 2004, p. 7; Douglas Jehl, "Iran Reportedly Hides Work on a Long-Range Missile, *New York Times*, December 2, 2004.

[26] Most experts feel Iran has not made significant progress in laser isotope separation or in any covert reactor program large enough to produce weapons materials.

[27] *New York Times*, May 14, 1995; *Washington Post*, November 5, 1997, sec. A-1.

[28] David Rudge, "Iran, Iraq in Non-Conventional Arms Race," *Jerusalem Post*, February 26, 2001.

[29] Lally Weymouth, "Q&A: ElBaradei, Feeling the Nuclear Heat," *Washington Post*, January 30, 2005, sec. B-1.

[30] "Blix: Iran Years Away from Nuke Weapons," Associated Press, June 23, 2005.

[31] "Iran Nuclear Weapons 'Years Away,'" BBC News, September 6, 2005.

[32] Jahn, "For Iran, It's When, Not If."

[33] David Albright and Corey Hinderstein, "Iran's Next Steps: Final Tests and the Construction of a Uranium Enrichment Plant," Institute for Science and International Security (ISIS), Issue Brief, January 12, 2006, available at http://www.isis-online.org/publications/iran/irancascade.pdf.

[34] Jonathan S. Landay and Warren P. Strobel, "Iran Closer to Producing Nuclear Weapons Fuel, U.S. Officials Worry," Knight Ridder Newspapers, March 23, 2006, available at http://www.realcities.com/mld/krwashington/news/columnists/jonathan_s_landay/14171206.htm.

[35] David Albright and Corey Hinderstein, "The Clock Is Ticking, but How Fast?" Institute for Science and International Security (ISIS), Issue Brief, March 27, 2006, available at http://www.isis-online.org/publications/iran/clockticking.pdf.

[36] Ibid.

[37] Ibid.

[38] Ibid.

[39] Ibid.

[40] Ibid.

[41] "Israel Says Iran Will Have Nuclear Bomb Knowledge," Reuters, May 13, 2005.

[42] "Mossad Warning over Nuclear Iran," BBC News, January 24, 2005, available at http://news.bbc.co.uk/2/hi/middle_east/4203411.stm.

[43] Jane's Intelligence Review, August 19, 2004; International Crisis Group, "Iran: Where Next on the Nuclear Standoff," Middle East Briefing, no. 15 (November 24, 2004), p. 15.

[44] Orly Halpern, "New Estimates on Iranian Nukes," Jerusalem Post, August 1, 2005.

[45] Ibid.

[46] "Israel Disputes U.S. Intelligence on Iran, Predicts Nuclear Capability within Three Years," Global Security Newswire, August 17, 2005, available at http://www.nti.org/d_newswire/issues/2005_8_17.html.

[47] Kevin Whitelaw, "Spookspeak, Decoded," U.S. News and World Report, December 19, 2005, available at http://www.usnews.com/usnews/news/articles/051219/19qa.htm.

[48] Douglas Jehl and Eric Schmitt, "Data Lacking on Iran's Arms, U.S. Panel Says," New York Times, March 9, 2005, p. 1.

[49] Robin Wright and Keith B. Richburg, "Powell Says Iran Is Pursuing Bomb," Washington Post, November 18, 2004, sec. A-1.

[50] John D. Negroponte, "Annual Threat Assessment of the Director of National Intelligence" (testimony by the director of national intelligence to the Senate Select Committee on Intelligence, February 2, 2006).

[51] *Los Angeles Times*, March 17, 1992, p. 1.

[52] *New York Times*, November 30, 1992, sec. A-1 and A-6, and January 5, 1995, sec. A-10; *Washington Times*, January 6, 1995, sec. A-15.

[53] Speech at the annual United States Central Command (USCENTCOM) conference, June 26, 1997.

[54] *New York Times*, January 10, 1995, sec. A-3; "Iran's Weapons of Mass Destruction," *Jane's Intelligence Review*, Special Report no. 6 (May 1995), pp. 4–14; Gerald White, *Risk Report* 1, no. 7 (September 1995); *Jane's Intelligence Review*, October 1995, p. 452.

[55] Associated Press, May 5, 1997.

[56] *Chalk Times*, January 10, 1995, p. 31; *Washington Times*, January 19, 1995, sec. A-18.

[57] Rodney W. Jones and Mark G. McDonough with Toby Dalton and Gregory Koblentz, *Tracking Nuclear Proliferation: A Guide in Maps and Charts, 1998* (Washington, D.C.: Carnegie Endowment for International Peace, 1999).

[58] Office of the Secretary of Defense, *Proliferation: Threat and Response*, U.S. Department of Defense, 1997 edition, available at http://www.defenselink.mil/pubs/prolif97/graphics.html.

[59] *Washington Times*, July 29, 1998, sec. A-12.

[60] Director of Central Intelligence, *Unclassified Report to Congress on the Acquisition of Technology Relating to Weapons of Mass Destruction and Advanced Conventional Munitions: 1 January through 30 June 1999*, CIA, available at http://www.cia.gov/cia/reports/721_reports/jan_jun1999.html. The report is issued every six months in response to a congressionally directed action in Section 721 of the FY 1997 Intelligence Authorization Act, which requires:

> (a) Not later than 6 months after the date of the enactment of this Act, and every 6 months thereafter, the Director of Central Intelligence shall submit to Congress a report on (1) the acquisition by foreign countries during the preceding 6 months of dual-use and other technology useful for the development or production of weapons of mass destruction (including nuclear weapons, chemical weapons, and biological weapons) and advanced conventional munitions; and (2) trends in the acquisition of such technology by such countries.
> At the DCI's request, the DCI Nonproliferation Center (NPC) drafts this report and coordinates it throughout the Intelligence Community. As directed by Section 721, subsection (b) of the Act, it is unclassified. As such, the report does not present the details of the Intelligence Community's assess-

ments of weapons of mass destruction and advanced conventional munitions programs that are available in other classified reports and briefings for the Congress.

[61] *New York Times,* January 17, 2000, sec. A-1 and A-8; Bloomberg News, January 17, 2000, 08:28; Reuters, January 17, 2000, 13:53; Associated Press, January 18, 2000, 02:11.

[62] Reuters, January 24, 2000, 18:55; January 26, 2000, 11:21.

[63] Director of Central Intelligence, *Unclassified Report to Congress on the Acquisition of Technology Relating to Weapons of Mass Destruction and Advanced Conventional Munitions: 1 July through 31 December 2003,* CIA, available at http://www.cia.gov/cia/reports/721_reports/july_dec2003.htm.

[64] John R. Bolton, "Iran's Continuing Pursuit of Weapons of Mass Destruction" (testimony before the U.S. House International Relations Subcommittee on the Middle East and Central Asia, June 24, 2004, available at http://www.state.gov/t/us/rm/33909.htm).

[65] Lowell E. Jacoby, "Current and Projected National Security Threats to the United States" (statement for the record by the director of the Defense Intelligence Agency [DIA] to the Senate Armed Services Committee, March 17, 2005).

[66] Dafna Linzer, "Iran Is Judged 10 Years from Nuclear Bomb," *Washington Post,* August 2, 2005, sec. A-1.

[67] Washington Times, May 17, 1995, sec. A-15; Office of the Secretary of Defense, Proliferation: Threat and Response, U.S. Department of Defense, April 1996, pp. 12–16.

[68] Nuclear Weapons Archive, http://nuclearweaponarchive.org/Nwfaq/Nfaq4-2.html#Nfaq4.2.

[69] These weights are deliberately chosen to be outdated and ambiguous. In addition, we have deliberately obfuscated about CBRN weapons design throughout this book and do not reference any aspect of CBRN weapons design that might aid a proliferator.

[70] For a summary of such factors that does not provide potential aid to a proliferator, see http://nuclearweaponarchive.org/Nwfaq/Nfaq4-2.html#Nfaq4.2.

[71] For a technical summary of nuclear weapons safing, arming, fuzing, and firing (SAFF), see Global Security.org, http://www.globalsecurity.org/wmd/intro/safe.htm.

[72] For a nonsensitive and well-written description of some aspects of this issue, see http://www.globalsecurity.org/wmd/intro/booster.htm.

[73] See Nuclear Weapons Archive, http://nuclearweaponarchive.org/Nwfaq/Nfaq4-2.html#Nfaq4.2.

[74] Ibid.

[75] A fusion weapon uses a fission nuclear weapon to fuse the heavy isotopes of hydrogen, deuterium, and tritium to release quantities of neutrons when the fusile material is compressed by the energy released by the nuclear fission device, or primary. The assumption that Iran may not be able to make such weapons may be wrong. The key features of advanced designs have been described in some detail in the open literature. The mathematics and practical engineering of such designs still are extremely demanding, however, and India and Pakistan have shown they have had major difficulties in actually making such weapons work with any efficiency.

[76] Boosted weapons have existed since the late 1940s. A small amount of deuterium and tritium (D-T) gas is placed inside the core of a fission device. Once the fission chain reaction begins, the D-T gas undergoes fusion, releasing an intense burst of high-energy neutrons (along with a small amount of fusion energy) that fissions the surrounding material more completely. See http://www.globalsecurity.org/wmd/intro/booster.htm.

CHAPTER NINE

DELIVERY SYSTEMS

It is one thing to have nuclear weapons; it is another to deliver them. Delivery depends on being able to build weapons small enough to fit current missile warheads or to build new missile technology to carry such weapons. In the case of Iran, its ability to acquire a delivery system also depends on knowing the extent of its nuclear technology. For example, if Iran's P-1 or P-2 designs were provided by A.Q. Khan—the same warhead designs that were sold to Libya—then it is the Chinese design with 500 kilograms of weight and one meter in diameter, which can fit Iran's current Shahab-3 missile.[1]

Although there is more information about Iran's missile program than there is about actual CBRN capabilities, several aspects of Iran's missile systems remain uncertain. Many experts, however, believe that (1) Iran's missile technology is more advanced than its nuclear capabilities, (2) Iran's missiles are too inaccurate to be used for conventional attacks, and (3) Iran's missile technology is getting more advanced by the day.

Iran continues to work actively on its missile warhead designs, and U.S. officials have expressed their concerns about this. Former secretary of state Colin Powell offered a warning on November 17, 2004—"You don't have a weapon until you put it in something that can deliver a weapon."[2] Other officials have expressed similar sentiments. The former director of the Nonproliferation Center at the Central Intelligence Agency, Gordon Oehler, said, "If someone has a good idea for a missile program, and he has really good connections, he'll get that program through."[3]

Some of these fears about Iran's active missile program were exacerbated by claims and threats by Iranian officials. For example, Yadollah Javani, head of the Islamic Revolutionary Guards' political bureau, stated in August 2004 that any Israeli attack on Iran would have "terrifying consequences," and that Israel would have to "permanently forget" about its nuclear research center and reactor at Dimona. He also warned that "the entire Zionist territory, including its nuclear facilities and atomic arsenal, are currently within range of Iran's advanced missiles."[4]

U.S. ASSESSMENT OF IRANIAN MISSILE CAPABILITIES

A 2003 unclassified CIA report made the following judgments about Iran's ballistic missile program. Although these comments do not take into account the developments in 2004, 2005, or 2006, they still seem to broadly reflect current U.S. intelligence assessments:

> Ballistic missile-related cooperation from entities in the former Soviet Union, North Korea, and China over the years has helped Iran move toward its goal of becoming self-sufficient in the production of ballistic missiles. Such assistance during 2003 continued to include equipment, technology, and expertise. Iran's ballistic missile inventory is among the largest in the Middle East and includes some 1,300-km-range Shahab-3 medium-range ballistic missiles (MRBMs) and a few hundred short-range ballistic missiles (SRBMs)—including the Shahab-1 (Scud-B), Shahab-2 (Scud C), and Tondar-69 (CSS-8)—as well as a variety of large unguided rockets. Already producing Scud SRBMs, Iran announced that it had begun production of the Shahab-3 MRBM and a new solid-propellant SRBM, the Fateh-110. In addition, Iran publicly acknowledged the development of follow-on versions of the Shahab-3. It originally said that another version, the Shahab-4, was a more capable ballistic missile than its predecessor but later characterized it as solely a space launch vehicle with no military applications. Iran is also pursuing longer-range ballistic missiles.[5]

John R. Bolton presented a similar assessment in testimony to the House International Relations Committee in June 2004:

Iran continues its extensive efforts to develop the means to deliver weapons of mass destruction. Thanks to assistance from entities—including government-owned entities—in North Korea, Russia, and China, Iran is developing a variety of liquid-propellant and solid-propellant ballistic missiles. Iran's ballistic missile inventory is among the largest in the Middle East and includes some 1,300-km-range Shahab-3 medium-range ballistic missiles (MRBMs) and a few hundred short-range ballistic missiles (SRBMs)—including the Shahab-1 (Scud-B), Shahab-2 (Scud-C), and Tondar-69 (CSS-8)—as well as a new solid-propellant SRBM, the Fateh-110. The 1,300-km-range Shahab-3 missile is a direct threat to Israel, Turkey, U.S. forces in the region, and U.S. friends and allies.

In addition, we believe Iran has programs to develop longer-range missiles that will be able to strike additional targets throughout the region or that will allow Iran to launch missiles against Israel from locations further within Iranian territory. Finally, Iran is likely to develop IRBMs (intermediate-range ballistic missiles) or ICBMs (intercontinental ballistic missiles) capable of delivering payloads to Western Europe or the United States. I want to emphasize this point: Iran is acquiring the means to produce ever more sophisticated and longer-range missiles. If they are successful in this endeavor, our attempts to slow the missile trade will have little effect on Iran's already-developing indigenous missile capability.

North Korea is one of the main suppliers of ballistic missiles, missile equipment, and production technology to Iran. North Korea provided Iran with the technology to produce the Scud-B (300 km range) and Scud-C (500 km range) missiles. In addition, the Shahab-3 medium-range ballistic missile is based on the North Korean [Nodong] missile.

Foreign assistance has been key to the development of Iran's ballistic missile programs. Such assistance during the first half of 2003 included equipment, technology, and expertise and has helped Iran move toward its goal of becoming self-sufficient in the production of ballistic missiles. Although Iran is not a member of the Missile Technology Control Regime (MTCR), a multilateral arrangement aimed at stemming the proliferation of ballistic missiles, or the International Code of Conduct Against Ballistic Missile Proliferation

Map 9.1   Estimated Ranges of Iran's Current and Potential Missiles

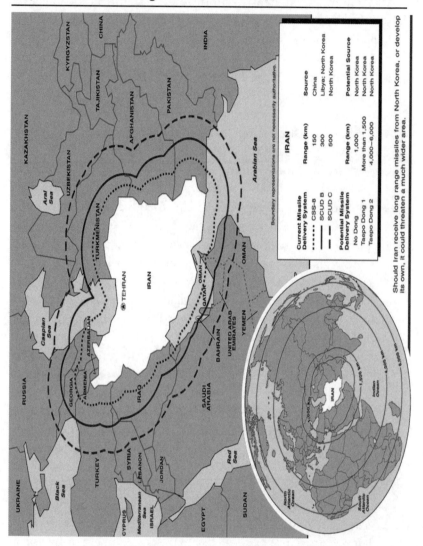

Source: Office of the Secretary of Defense, *Proliferation: Threat and Response,*
U.S. Department of Defense, 1997, available at http://www.defenselink.mil/
pubs/prolif97/meafrica.html#iran.

(ICOC), Iran has engaged in substantial trade in missile technology with countries that ought to know better.[6]

A more recent appraisal of Iran's missile program was offered by the director of the Defense Intelligence Agency, Vice Admiral Lowell E. Jacoby, on March 17, 2005:

> We judge Iran will have the technical capability to develop an ICBM by 2015. It is not clear whether Iran has decided to field such a missile. Iran continues to field 1300-km-range Shahab III MRBMs capable of reaching Tel Aviv. Iranian officials have publicly claimed they are developing a new 2000-km-range variant of the Shahab III. Iranian engineers are also likely working to improve the accuracy of the country's SRBMs.[7]

Much has been said about the threat from Iran's missiles. Map 9.1 shows estimated ranges of Iran's current and potential missiles. The map shows that the Chinese CSS-8 has the smallest range of 150 kilometers. Iran's Scud-C, on the other hand, has a range of 500 kilometers, which can reach southern Iraq, the Gulf States, the eastern province of Saudi Arabia, parts of Syria, and parts of Turkey. In addition, the map shows the potential ranges of the North Korean missiles: Nodong (1,000 kilometers, which can reach almost all of the Middle East), Taep'o-dong-1 (1,500 kilometers, which can reach all of the Middle East and parts of southern Europe), and the Taep'o-dong-2 (4,000–6,000 kilometers, which can reach almost all of Europe and theoretically beyond).

IRAN'S MISSILE ARSENAL

Iran continues to deploy surface-to-surface missiles and has its own systems in development. The number assigned to the army versus the Islamic Revolutionary Guards Corps is unclear, but the IRGC seems to hold and operate the majority of the long-range missiles. Iran seems to have some 12–18 Scud-B/C launchers with 250–350 missiles and 30 land-based CSS-8 launchers with 175 missiles. Iran refers to the Scud-B as the Shahab-1 and the Scud C as the Shahab-2. Although estimates of Iran's missiles differ, table 9.1 provides an assessment of Iran's current missile profiles.

Table 9.1
Estimated Iranian Missile Profiles, 2006

Designation	Stages	Progenitor missiles	Propellant	Range (kilometers)	Payload (kilograms)	IOC (year)	Inventory
Mushak-120	1	CSS-8, SA-2	Solid	130	500	2001	200
Mushak-160	1	CSS-8, SA-2	Liquid	160	500	2002	?
Mushak-200	1	SA-2	Liquid	200	500	n.a.	0
Shahab-1	1	Soviet SSN-4, No. Korea Scud-B	Liquid	300	987–1,000	1995	250–300
Shahab-2	1	Soviet SSN-4, No. Korea Scud-C	Liquid	500	750–989	?	200–450
Shahab-3	1	No. Korea Nodong-1	Liquid	1,300	760–1,158	2002	25–100
Shahab-4	2	No. Korea Taep'o-dong-1	Liquid	3,000	1,040–1,500	n.a.	0
Ghadr 101	multi	Pakistan Shaheen-1	Solid	2,500	n.a.	n.a.	0
Ghadr 110	multi	Pakistan Shaheen-2	Solid	3,000	n.a.	n.a.	0
IRIS	1	China M-18	Solid	3,000	760–1,158	2005	n.a.
Kh-55	1	Soviet AS-15 Kent, Ukraine	Jet engine	2,900–3,000	200 kilotons nuclear	2001	12
Shahab-5	3	No. Korea Taep'o-dong-2	Liquid	5,500	390–1,000	n.a.	0
Shahab-6	3	No. Korea Taep'o-dong-2	Liquid	10,000	270–1,220	n.a.	0

Source: Adapted from GlobalSecurity.org, available at: http://www.globalsecurity.org/wmd/world/iran/missile.htm; and the Federation of American Scientists, available at: http://www.fas.org/nuke/guide/iran/missile.

Note: n.a. = not available

The Iranian government stated as early as 1999 that it was developing such a large missile body or launch vehicle for satellite launches, and it has repeatedly denied that it is upgrading the Shahab series (especially the Shahab-3) for military purposes. Iran also has continued to claim that the "Shahab-4" program is aimed at developing a booster rocket for launching satellites. In January 2004, Iran's defense minister said that Iran would launch a domestically built satellite within 18 months. This had still not taken place in May 2006.[8]

In December 2005, the U.S. government announced its belief that Iran had built underground missile factories that were capable of producing Shahab-1, Shahab-2, and Shahab-3 missiles as well as testing new missile designs. It was also believed that Karimi Industries—one of the industrial groups reportedly associated with Iran's missile program—was housed at one of the secret bases working on perfecting Iran's nuclear warheads.[9]

U.S. officials insisted that this information did not come from Iranian opposition sources like the MEK and that it was reliable. They feel Iran has made significant strides in recent years using North Korean, Chinese, and Russian technology. If it begins work on the Shahab-5 and the Shahab-6 series, Iran may acquire delivery systems with the range to make it a global nuclear power instead of merely a regional one.

Shahab-1/Scud-B

The Soviet-designed Scud-B (17E) guided missile currently forms the core of Iran's ballistic missile forces. The missile was used heavily in the later years of the Iran-Iraq war. In 2006, it was estimated that Iran had between 50 and 300 Shahab-1's in its inventory.[10]

The Scud-B missile is a tactical missile. It has an approximate range of 290–300 kilometers (180–186 miles) with its normal conventional payload, and carries a 987–1,000-kilogram warhead. It has a diameter of 0.885 meter, a height of 11 meters, a launch weight of 5,860 kilograms, a stage mass of 4,873 kilograms, a dry mass of 1,100 kilograms, and a propellant mass of 3,760–3,671 kilograms.[11] It has a nominal CEP of 1,000 meters.

Iran acquired its Scuds in 1985 in response to Iraq's invasion. It obtained a limited number from Libya and then larger numbers from North Korea. It deployed these units with a special Khatam ol-Anbya force attached to the air element of the Pasdaran. Iran fired its first Scuds in March 1985. It fired as many as 14 Scuds in 1985, 8 in 1986, 18 in 1987, and 77 in 1988 during a 52-day period that came to be known as the "war of the cities": 61 were fired at Baghdad, 9 at Mosul, 5 at Kirkuk, 1 at Tikrit, and 1 at Kuwait. Iran fired as many as five missiles on a single day, and once fired three missiles within 30 minutes. This still worked out to an average of only about one missile a day, and Iran was down to only 10–20 Scuds when the war of the cities ended.

Iran's missile attacks were initially more effective than Iraq's attacks. This was largely a matter of geography. Many of Iraq's major cities were comparatively close to its border with Iran, but Tehran and most of Iran's major cities that had not already been targets in the war were outside the range of Iraqi Scud attacks. Iran's missiles, in contrast, could hit key Iraqi cities like Baghdad. This advantage ended when Iraq deployed extended-range Scuds.

The Scud-B is a relatively old Soviet design that first became operational in 1967, designated as the R-17E or R-300E. Its thrust is 13,160 kilograms-force (kgf); its burn time is between 62 and 64 seconds; and it has an Isp 62-Sl due to vanes steering drag loss of 4–5 seconds. The Scud-B possesses one thrust chamber and is a one-stage rocket (it does not break into smaller pieces). Its fuel is TM-185, and its oxidizer is the AK-27I.[12]

The Russian versions of the Scud-B can be equipped with conventional high-explosive, fuel air-explosive, runway-penetrating submunitions and chemical and nuclear warheads. Its basic design comes from the old German V-2 rocket design of World War II. It has moveable fins and is guided only during powered flight.

The Scud-B was introduced on the JS-3 tracked chassis in 1961 and appeared on the MAZ-543 wheeled chassis in 1965. The "Scud-B" missile later appeared on the transporter-erector-launcher (TEL) based on the MAZ-543 (8x8) truck. The introduction of this new cross-country wheeled vehicle gave the missile system greater road mobility and reduced the number of support vehicles required.

The export version of the Scud-B comes with a conventional high-explosive warhead weighing about 1,000 kilograms, of which 800 kilograms are the high explosive payload and 200 are the warhead structure and fusing system. It has a single-stage storable liquid rocket engine and is usually deployed on the MAZ-543—an eight-wheel transporter-erector-launcher. It has a strap-down inertial guidance, using three gyros to correct its ballistic trajectory, and uses internal graphite jet vane steering. The warhead hits at a velocity above Mach 1.5.

The following timeline tracks the history of the Scud-B after it was first introduced in Iran in 1985 and renamed the Shahab-1:

- **1985:** Iran began acquiring Scud-B (Shahab-1) missiles from Libya for use in the Iraq War.[13]

- **1986:** Iran turned to Libya as a supplier of Scud-Bs.[14]

- **1987:** A watershed year. Iran attempted to produce its own Scud-B missiles, but failed. Over the next five years, it purchased 200–300 Scud-B missiles from North Korea.[15]

- **1988:** Iran began producing its own Scud-Bs, though not in large quantities.[16]

- **1991:** It is estimated that Iran stopped producing its own Scud-Bs at approximately the time of the Gulf War and began purchasing the more advanced Scud-Cs (Shahab-2).[17]

- **1993:** Iran sent 21 missile specialists, led by Brigadier General Manteghi, to North Korea for training.[18]

Experts estimate Iran bought 200–300 Scud-Bs from North Korea between 1987 and 1992 and may have continued to buy more after that time. Israeli experts estimated that Iran had at least 250–300 Scud-B missiles and at least 8–15 launchers on hand in 1997. Most current estimates indicate that Iran now has 6–12 Scud launchers and up to 200 Scud-B (R-17E) missiles with a range of 230–310 kilometers (143–193 miles). Some estimates give higher figures. The IISS estimated in 2005–2006 that Tehran had 18 launchers, and 300 Scud missiles,[19] although it is uncertain how many of those are Scud-Bs and how many are Scud-Cs.

U.S. experts also believe that Iran can now manufacture virtually all parts of the Scud-B, with the possible exception of the most sophisticated components of its guidance system and rocket motors. This makes it difficult to estimate how many missiles Iran has in inventory and can acquire over time, and difficult as well to estimate the precise performance characteristics of its missiles, as it can alter the weight of the warhead and adjust the burn time and improve the efficiency of the rocket motors.

Shahab-2/Scud-C

The Scud-C is an improved version of the Scud-B. With a superior range and payload, it is a tactical missile first acquired by Iran in 1990. It has an approximate range of 805–1,126 kilometers (500–700 miles), a CEP of 50 meters, and it carries a 700–989-kilogram warhead. It has a diameter of 0.885 meter, a height of 11–12 meters, a launch weight of 6,370–6,500 kilograms, an unknown stage mass, an unknown dry mass, and an unknown propellant mass. In terms of propelling ability, its thrust is unknown, its burn time is unknown, and it has an effective Isp of 231. The Scud-C possesses one thrust chamber and is a one-stage rocket (it does not break into smaller pieces). Its fuel is Tonka-250, and its oxidizer is the AK 20P.[20]

The Scud-C missile was successfully completed and ready for production by 1987 (mainly by North Korea) and distributed to Iran several years later. According to some reports, Iran has created shelters and tunnels in its coastal areas that can be used to store Scuds and other missiles in hardened sites to reduce their vulnerability to air attack.

The Scud-C missile is more advanced than the Scud-B, although many aspects of its performance are unclear. North Korea seems to have completed development of the missile in 1987 after obtaining technical support from China. Although it is often called a "Scud-C," it seems to differ substantially in detail from the original Soviet Scud-B, and seems to be based more on the Chinese-made DF-61 than on a direct copy of the Soviet weapon.

Experts estimate that the North Korean missiles have a range of around 500 kilometers (310 miles), a conventional warhead with a high-explosive payload of 700 kilograms, and relatively good accuracy and reliability. Although some experts feel the payload of its conventional warhead may not be suitable for the effective delivery of chemical agents, Iran might modify the warhead to increase payload at the expense of range and restrict the using of chemical munitions to the most lethal agents such as persistent nerve gas. It might also concentrate its development efforts on arming its Scud-C forces with more lethal biological agents.

It is currently estimated that Iran has 50–150 Scud-Cs in its inventory.[21] The following timeline tracks the development of Iranian Scud-C missiles since the Gulf War:

- **1990:** It is estimated that Iran stopped producing large quantities of Scud-Bs at approximately the time of the Gulf War, and began purchasing the more advanced Scud-Cs (Shahab-2).[22]

- **1993:** Iran sent 21 missile specialists, led by Brigadier General Manteghi, to North Korea for training in missile technology.[23]

- **1994:** By this year, Iran had purchased 150–200 Scud-Cs from North Korea.[24]

- **1997:** Iran began production of its own Scud-C missiles. This is generally considered a technological leap for Iran, and it is believed that a large portion of the production capability and technology came from North Korea.[25]

Despite revelations during the 1990s about North Korean missile technology transfers to Tehran, Iran formally denied that it had such systems long after the transfer of the missiles became a fact. Hassan Taherian, an Iranian Foreign Ministry official, stated in February 1995, "There is no missile cooperation between Iran and North Korea whatsoever. We deny this."[26]

A senior North Korean delegation, however, had traveled to Tehran to close the deal on November 29, 1990, and met with Mohsen Rezaei, the former commander of the IRGC. Iran either bought the missile then or placed its order shortly thereafter. North Korea then exported the missile through its Lyongaksan Import Corporation. Iran imported some of the North Korean missile assemblies using its B-747s and seems to have used ships to import others.

Iran probably had more than 60 of the longer-range North Korean missiles by 1998, although other sources report 100 and one source reports 170. Iran may have 5–10 Scud-C launchers, each with several missiles. This total seems likely to include four North Korean TELs received in 1995.

Iran is seeking to deploy enough missiles and launchers to make its missile force highly dispersed and difficult to attack. Iran began to test its new North Korean missiles. There are reports it fired them from mobile launchers at a test site near Qom about 500 kilometers (310 miles) to a target area south of Shahroud. There are also reports that units equipped with such missiles have been deployed as part of Iranian exercises, like the Saeqer-3 (Thunderbolt 3) exercise in late October 1993.

In any case, such missiles are likely to have enough range and payload to enable Iran to strike all targets on the southern coast of the Gulf and all of the populated areas in Iraq except for the western region. Iran could also reach targets in part of eastern Syria, the eastern third of Turkey, and targets in the border area of the former Soviet Union, western Afghanistan, and western Pakistan.

Accuracy and reliability remain major uncertainties, as does the missile's operational CEP. Much would depend on the precise level of technology Iran deployed in the warhead. Neither Russia nor the People's Republic of China seems to have transferred the warhead technology for biological and chemical weapons to Iran or Iraq when they sold them the Scud-B missile and CSS-8. However, North Korea may have sold Iran such technology as part of the Scud-C sale. If it did, such a technology transfer would save Iran years of development and testing in obtaining highly lethal biological and chemical warheads. In fact, Iran would probably be able to deploy far more effective biological and chemical warheads than Iraq had at the time of the Gulf War.

Iran can now assemble Scud-C missiles using foreign-made components. It may soon be able to make the entire missile system and warhead packages in Iran. It also may be working with Syria in such development efforts, although Middle Eastern nations rarely cooperate in such sensitive areas.

Shahab-3

Iran appears to have entered into a technological partnership with North Korea after trading with the North Koreans for Scud-Cs throughout the 1990s. The visit to North Korea in 1993 by General Manteghi and his 21 specialists marks a possible turning point when Iran shifted from procurement to development.

Iran did not have the strike capability to attack Israel with its limited-range Scuds. As a result, the Iranians seem to have begun using some of the designs for the North Korean Nodong MRBM in an attempt to manufacture their own version of the missile, the Shahab-3. Between 1997 and 1998, Iran began testing the Shahab-3. While Iran claimed the Shahab-3's purpose was to carry payloads of submunitions, it is more likely that it would use the Shahab-3's superior range to carry a chemical, nuclear, or biological weapon.

Missile Description

Iran's new Shahab-3 series is a larger missile that seems to be based on the design of the North Korean Nodong-1/A, and Nodong-B missiles, which some analysts claim were developed with Iranian financial support. Although it is based on North Korean designs and technology, it is being developed and produced in Iran. This development effort is controlled and operated by the IRGC, and Iranian officials have claimed that the production of the Shahab-3 missiles was entirely domestic. The Iranian defense minister, Ali Shamkhani, stated in May 2005 that the production was made up of locally made parts, and that the production was continuing.[27]

As the following timeline shows, the Shahab-3 is a relatively young and constantly evolving system, but it has been tested several times:

- **October 1997:** Russia began training Iranian engineers on missile production for the Shahab-3.[28]

- **1998:** Iran began testing its own Shahab-3s. Problems with finding or making an advanced guidance system hindered many of the tests, however. Meanwhile, Iran began experimenting with the Shahab-4.[29]

- **July 23, 1998:** Iran launched its first test flight of the Shahab-3. The missile flew for approximately 100 seconds and then was detonated. It is not known if it malfunctioned or was deliberately detonated because the Iranians did not want to risk discovery.[30]

- **July 15, 2000:** Iran had its first successful test of a Shahab-3.[31]

- **Summer, 2001:** Iran began production of the Shahab-3.[32]

- **July 7, 2003:** Iran completed final tests of the Shahab-3. Allegations emerged that Chinese companies like Tai'an Foreign Trade General Corporation and China North industries Corporation had been helping Iran to overcome the missile's final technical glitches.[33] The missile was seen in Iranian military parades and displayed openly.

- **August 11, 2004:** Iran decreased the size of the Shahab-3 warhead, making a move toward being able to mount a nuclear warhead on a Shahab-3. At this point, the modified Shahab-3 was often referred to as the Shahab-3M.[34] The missile had a new, smaller, and "bottleneck" warhead. This kind of design has a slower reentry than a cone-shaped warhead and has advantages when using warheads containing chemical and biological agents.

- **September 19, 2004:** Another test took place and the missile was paraded on September 21 covered in banners saying "We will crush America under our feet" and "Wipe Israel off the map."[35]

- **May 31, 2005:** Iranian defense minister Ali Shamkhani claimed that Iran successfully tested a new missile motor using solid-fuel technology with a range of 2,000 kilometers (1,243 miles). Shamkhani was quoted as saying, "Using solid fuel would be more durable and increase the range of the missile."[36] It remains uncertain whether the reference was to the Shahab-3 or the modified Shahab-3, the IRIS missile.

As of early 2006, there had been some 10 launches at a rate of only one to two per year. Roughly 30 percent had fully malfunctioned, and six launches had had some malfunction. Iran had also tested two major payload configurations.[37]

Uncertain Performance

Discussions about the Shahab-3's range-payload, accuracy, and reliability will remain speculative until the system is far more mature. A long-range ballistic missile requires at least 10–30 tests in its final configuration to establish its true payload and warhead type, actual range-payload, and accuracy. Although highly detailed estimates of the Shahab-3's performance are available, at best they are rough engineering estimates and sometimes speculative to the point of being sheer guesswork using rounded numbers.[38]

The Shahab-3's real-world range will depend on both the final configuration of the missile and the weight of its warhead. Various sources now guess that the Shahab-3 has a range between 1,300 and 2,000 kilometers, but the longer-range estimate seems to be based on Iranian claims and assumptions about an improved version, not on full-scale operational tests.[39]

U.S. experts believe that the Shahab-3 missile still has a nominal range of 1,300 kilometers. Iran, however, has claimed that the Shahab-3 had a range of 2,000 kilometers (1,250 miles). Nasser Maleki, the head of Iran's aerospace industry, stated on October 7, 2004, that "very certainly we are going to improve our Shahab-3 and all of our other missiles." Tehran then claimed in November that the Shahab-3 could reach targets up to 2,000 kilometers away, presumably allowing the missiles to be deployed a greater distance away from Israel's air force and Jericho-2 ballistic missiles.[40]

IRGC political bureau chief Yadollah Javani stated in September 2004 that the modified Shahab—sometimes called the Shahab-3A or Shahab-3M—could be used to attack Israel's Dimona nuclear reactor.[41] Iran performed another test on October 20, 2004, and Iran's defense minister, Ali Shamkhani, claimed it was part of an operational exercise. On November 9, 2004, he claimed that Iran was now capable of mass-producing the Shahab-3 and that it reserved the option of preemptive strikes in defense of its nuclear sites. Shamkhani claimed shortly after that the Shahab-3 now had a range of more than 2,000 kilometers.[42]

One leading German expert, Robert H. Schmucker, stresses the uncertainty of any current estimates and notes that range-payload trade-offs would be critical. He puts the range for the regular Shahab-3 at 820 kilometers with a 1.3-ton payload and 1,100 kilometers with a 0.7-ton payload. An analysis by John Pike of Global Security also points out that missiles—like combat aircraft—can make trade-offs between range and payload. For example, the Nodong-B has a range of 1,560 kilometers with a 760-kilogram warhead and 1,350 kilometers with a 1,158- kilogram warhead.[43]

Schmucker thinks that an improved Shahab could use a combination of a lighter aluminum airframe, light-weight guidance, reduced payload, increased propellant load, and increased burn time to increase range. He notes that little is really known about the improved Shahab-3, but he estimates that its maximum range would still be 2,000 kilometers, that a 0.7–0.8-ton warhead would limit its range to 1,500 kilometers, and that a 0.8–0.9–1.0-ton warhead would reduce it to 1,200 kilometers. A 1.2-ton warhead would limit it to around 850 kilometers. Schmucker thinks Iran may have drawn on Russian technology from the R-21 and R-27. Photos of the system also show progressive changes in cable duct position, fins, and length in 2004 and 2005.[44]

The differences in range estimates may be a matter of Iranian propaganda, but a number of experts believe that Iran's claims refer to the modified Shahab-3D or the Shahab-3M and not the regular Shahab-3. There are reports that such modified versions use solid fuel and could have a range of up to 2,000 kilometers. The standard Shahab-3 reportedly remains in production, but the improved Shahab is now called the Shahab-3M.[45]

Much also depends on the missile warhead. In 2004, Secretary of State Colin Powell accused Iran of modifying its Shahab-3 to carry a nuclear warhead, based on documents the U.S. government had received from a "walk-in" source. While experts argued that the information was yet to be confirmed, others claimed that Iran had obtained "a new nosecone" for its Shahab-3 missile.[46] In addition, other U.S. officials claimed that the source of the information provided "tens of thousands of pages of Farsi-language computer files" on Iranian attempts to modify the Shahab-3 missile to deliver a "black box," which U.S. officials believed "almost certainly" referred to a nuclear warhead. The documents were said to include diagrams and test results, weight, detonation height, and shape, but not warhead designs.[47]

Media reporting indicates that the United States was able to examine drawings on a stolen laptop from Iran and found that Iran had developed 18 different ways to adapt the size, weight, and diameter of the new nosecone on its Shahab-3 missile. It was also reported, however, that Iran's effort to expand the nosecone would not work and that it did not have the technological capabilities to adapt nuclear weapons to its Shahab-3 missile. U.S. nuclear experts claimed that one reason for the failure was that the project "wasn't done by the A-team of Iran's program."[48]

Some experts believe that new "bottleneck" warhead tested in 2004 was for the Shahab-3M, and makes it more accurate and capable of air-burst detonations, which could be used to spread chemical weapons more effectively. Others believe a smaller warhead has increased the missile's range.

As for other aspects of performance, it is again easy to be precise but difficult to be correct. One source, for example, reports that the Shahab-3 has a CEP of 190 meters and carries a 750–989–1,158-kilogram warhead. The same source reports that the Shahab-3 has a height of 16 meters, a stage mass of 15,092 kilograms, a dry mass of 1,780–2,180 kilograms, and a propellant mass of 12,912 kilograms. In terms of propelling ability, its thrust is between 26,760 and 26,600 kilograms-force, its burn time is 110 seconds, and it has an effective Isp of 226 and a drag loss of 45 seconds. According to this source, the Shahab-3 possesses one thrust chamber. Its fuel is TM-185, and its oxidizer is the AK 271.[49]

High levels of accuracy are possible, but this remains to be seen. If the system uses older guidance technology and warhead separation methods, its CEP could be anywhere from 1,000 to 4,000 meters. If it uses newer technology, such as some of the most advanced Chinese technology, it could have a CEP as low as 190–800 meters. In any case, such CEP data are engineering estimates based on the ratios from a perfectly located target.

This means real-world missile accuracy and reliability cannot be measured using technical terms like circular error of probability even if they apply to a fully mature and deployed missile. The definition of the term is based on the assumption that the missile can be perfectly targeted at launch and performs perfectly through its final guidance phase. CEP is then somewhat arbitrarily defined as the accuracy of 50 percent of the systems launched in terms of distance from a central point on the target. True performance can be derived only by observing reliability under operational conditions and correlating actual point of impact to a known aim point.

Schmucker notes, for example, that the operational CEP of the improved Shahab-3 is likely to be around 3 kilometers, but the maximum deviation could be 11 kilometers.[50] In short, the unclassified estimates of the Shahab-3's accuracy and reliability available from public sources are matters of speculation, and no unclassified source has credibility in describing the missile's performance in real-world, war-fighting terms.

This is not a casual problem, as actual weaponization of a warhead requires extraordinarily sophisticated systems to detonate the warhead at the desired height of burst and to reliably disseminate the munitions or agent. Even the most sophisticated conventional submunitions are little more than area weapons if the missile accuracy has errors in excess of 250–500 meters, and a unitary conventional explosive warhead without terminal guidance is little more that a psychological or terror weapon almost regardless of its accuracy.

The effective delivery of chemical agents by spreading the agent or the use of submunitions generally requires accuracies of less than 1,000 meters to achieve lethality against even large point targets. Systems with biological weapons are inherently area weapons, but a 1,000-kilogram nominal warhead can carry so little agent that accuracies of less than 1,000 meters again become undesirable. Nuclear weapons require far less accuracy, particularly if a "dirty" groundburst can be targeted within a reliable fallout area. There are limits, however. For example, a regular fission weapon of some 20 kilotons requires accuracies under 2,500–3,000 meters for some kinds of targets like sheltered airfields or large energy facilities.

What is clear is that the Shahab could carry a well-designed nuclear weapon well over 1,000 kilometers, and Iran may have access to such designs. As noted earlier, the Shahab-3 missile tested in its final stages in 2003 and in ways that indicate it has a range of 2,000 kilometers, enough to reach the Gulf and Israel. A.Q. Khan sold a Chinese nuclear warhead design to Libya with a mass of as little as 500 kilograms and one meter in diameter. It is highly probable such designs were sold to Iran as well.

Mobility and Deployment

The Shahab-3 is mobile, but requires numerous launching support vehicles for propellant transport and loading and power besides its transport-erector-launcher.[51] It is also slow in setting up, taking several hours to prepare for launch.[52] Its deployment status is highly uncertain.

Some reports have claimed that the Shahab-3 was operational as early as 1999, that development of the Shahab-3 was completed in June 2003 and that it underwent "final" tests on July 7, 2003. However, the Shahab-3 underwent only nine tests from inception through late 2003, and only four of them could be considered successful in terms of basic system performance. The missile's design characteristics also continued to evolve during these tests. A CIA report to Congress dated November 10, 2003, indicated that upgrading of the Shahab-3 was still under way, and some sources indicated that Iran was seeking a range of 1,600 kilometers (944 miles).

There is an argument among experts as to whether the system has been tested often enough to be truly operational. The CIA reported in 2004 that Iran had "some" operational Shahab-3s with a range of 1,300 kilometers. Some experts feel the missile has since become fully operational and that Iran already possesses 25–100 Shahab-3's in its inventory.[53] Iranian opposition sources have claimed that Iran has 300 such missiles. According to other sources, the IRGC operated six missile batteries in the spring of 2006, and was redeploying them within a 35-kilometer radius of their main command and control center every 24 hours because of the risk of U.S. or Israeli attack. The main operating forces were deployed in the west in Kermanshah and Hamadan provinces with reserve batteries further east in Fars and Esfahan provinces.[54]

A substantial number of experts, however, believe the Shahab-3 may be in deployment, but only in "showpiece" or "test-bed" units using conventional warheads and with performance Iran cannot accurately predict.

Shahab-3A/3M/3D/IRIS

In October 2004, the Mujahedin-e Khalq claimed that Iran was developing an improved version of the Shahab with a 2,400-kilometer range (1,500 miles). The MEK has an uncertain record of accuracy in making such claims, and these claims could not be confirmed. Mortezar Ramandi, an official in the Iranian delegation to the UN, denied that Iran was developing a missile with a range of more than 2,000 kilometers (1,250 miles).[55] This new but unconfirmed range for the Shahab-3 may have marked a significant change in Iran's technological capability, as some experts believe Iran switched the fuel source from liquid fuel to solid. The possible existence of a Shahab-3 with a solid fuel source created yet another variant of the Shahab-3 series—the Shahab-3D, or IRIS missile.

The development of a solid fuel source might enable the Shahab-3D to enter into space and serve as a satellite launch vehicle. Perfecting solid fuel technology would also move Iran's missile systems a long way toward the successful creation of a long-range intercontinental ballistic missile, or LRICBM, which is what the Shahab-5 and Shahab-6 are intended to accomplish.[56]

If there is an IRIS launch vehicle, it apparently consists of the Nodong/Shahab-3 first stage with a bulbous front section ultimately designed to carry the IRIS second-stage solid motor, as well as a communications satellite or scientific payload.[57] The IRIS solid fuel missile itself may be the third-stage portion of the North Korean Taep'o-dong 1.[58]

The Shahab-3D is unable to launch a large satellite probe into space by itself, and it is possible that it is a test for the second- and third-stage portions of the upcoming IRBM Ghadr designs and the LRICBM Shahab-5 and Shahab-6.[59]

No test flights of the Shahab-3D have been recorded on video, but it is believed that they have taken place at a space launch facility.[60] The following timeline shows the reported tests of the Shahab-3D/IRIS:

- **July 22, 1998:** First test flight (explodes 100 seconds after takeoff).
- **July 15, 2000:** First successful test flight (range of 850 kilometers, or 528 miles).
- **September 21, 2000:** Unsuccessful test flight (explodes shortly after take off).
- **May 23, 2002:** Successful test flight.
- **July 2002:** Unsuccessful test flight (missile did not function properly).
- **June 2003:** Successful test flight. Iran declares this was the final test flight before deployment.
- **August 11, 2004:** Successful test flight of the Shahab-3M. The missile now has the bottleneck warhead
- **October 20, 2004:** Another successful test flight of Shahab-3M. Iran now claims the modified missile has a range of 2,000 km.[61]

Shahab-4

Iran seems to be developing much larger designs with greater range-payload using a variety of local, North Korean, Chinese, and Russian technical inputs. These missiles have been called the Sahab-4, Sahab-5, and Sahab-6. As of early 2006, none were being produced, and the exact nature of the programs remained speculative.

Some experts believe the Shahab-4 has an approximate range of between 2,200 and 2,800 kilometers. Various experts have claimed that it is based on the North Korean Nodong-2, the three-stage Taep'o-dong-1 missile, the Russian SSN-6 SERB, or even some aspects of the Russian SS-4, but it has a modern digital guidance package rather than the 2,000–3,000 meter CEP of early missiles like the SS-4.

Russian firms are believed to have sold Iran special steels for missile development, test equipment, shielding for guidance packages, and other technology. Iran's Shahid Hemmet Industrial Group is reported to have contracts with the Russian Central Aerohydrodynamic Institute, Rosvoorouzhenie, the Bauman Institute, and Polyus. It is also possible that Iran has obtained some technology from Pakistan.

One source has provided a precise estimate of some performance characteristics of the Shahab-4. These include an estimated height of 25 meters, a diameter of 1.3 meters, and a launch weight of 22,000 kilograms. In terms of propelling ability, its thrust is estimated to be around 26,000 kilograms-force, and its burn time around 293 seconds. It is said to be a two or three stage rocket with three thrust chambers, one for each stage. Its fuel for the first stage is heptyl, and its oxidizer is the IRFNA.[62]

Iran has sent mixed signals. In October 2003, Iran claimed it was abandoning its Shahab-4 program, saying that the expected increase in range (from its current range of 2,200 (1,367 miles) to 3,000 kilometers (1,864 miles)) would cause too much global tension.[63] Some speculate that Iran may scraped its Shahab-4 because it either was not innovative and large enough and/or to avoid controversy. Some Iranians have claimed that the reason for creating a missile like the Shahab-4 was for satellite launches. However, the IRIS/Shahab-3D, with its solid fuel source, has shown potential for space launches. The improved range and bottleneck warhead design offered by the Shahab-3M (which began testing in August 2004) may make the Shahab-4 simply not worth the effort or controversy.[64]

According to German press reports, however, Iran is moving ahead with its development of the Shahab-4. In February 2006, the German news agency cited "Western intelligence services" as declaring that Iran had successfully tested the Shahab-4 missile with a range of 2,200 kilometers (1,367 miles) on January 17, 2006, and that the test was announced on Iranian television several days later by the commander of the Islamic Revolutionary Guards Corps.[65] These reports remain unverifiable.

Shahab-5 and Shahab-6

Israeli intelligence has reported that Iran is attempting to create a Shahab-5 and a Shahab-6, with a 3,000–5,000-kilometer (1,864–3,107 miles) range. The missiles would be based on the North Korean Taep'o-dong-2 and would be three-stage rockets. If completed, the Shahab-5 and the Shahab-6 would take Iran into the realm of limited range ICBMs and enable it to target the eastern seaboard of the United States. The Shahab-5 and Shahab-6 would possess a solid fuel third stage for space entry and liquid fuel for the first-stage take units.

It is alleged that Russian aerospace engineers are aiding the Iranians. It is believed that Iranian engineers will employ a version of Russia's storable liquid propellant, RD-216, in the missile's first stage. The RD-216 is an Energomash engine originally used on the Skean/SS-5/R-14 IRBM, Saddler/SS-7/R-16 ICBM, and Sasin/R-26 ICBM missiles used in the Cold War. These reports remain uncertain, and Israeli media and official sources have repeatedly exaggerated the nature and speed of Iranian efforts.[66]

Neither the Shahab-5 nor the Shahab-6 has been tested or constructed. Although no description of the Shahab-6 is available, extrapolations for the Shahab-5 have been made based on the North Korean Taep'o-dong-2. The Shahab-5 has an approximate range of between 4,000 and 4,300 kilometers (2,485–2,671 miles). It has an unknown CEP, and its warhead capacity is between 700 and 1,000 kilograms. It has a height of 32 meters, a diameter of 2.2 meters, and a launch weight of 80,000–85,000 kilograms.

In terms of propelling ability, some experts estimate its thrust to be 31,260 kilograms-force, and its burn time to be 330 seconds. The Shahab-5 is a three-stage rocket that possesses six thrust chambers, four for stage one and one for each of the two remaining stages. The Shahab-5 and Shahab-6 would be considered long-range ICBMs.[67]

As of January 2006, Iran had not completed its plans for these missiles, and it had none in its inventory. In February 2006, however, German press reports claimed that the Federal German Intelligence Service (BND) estimated that it was possible for Iran to acquire the Shahab-5 as early as 2007 with a range of 3,000–5,000 kilometers (1,864–3,107 miles).[68] These estimates, however, are speculative and remain unconfirmed.

Ghadr 101 and Ghadr 110

The uncertainties surrounding Iran's solid fuel problem and the existence or nonexistence of the Shahab-3 are compounded by reports of a separate missile development program. The Iranian exile group NCRI (National Council of Resistance in Iran) claimed in December 2004 that the Ghadr 101 and Ghadr 110 were new missile types that used solid fuel and were, in fact, IRBMs. Their existence has never been confirmed, and conflicting reports make an exact description difficult.

At the time, U.S. experts indicated that the Ghadr was actually the same as the Shahab-3A/Shahab-M/Shahab-4, which seemed to correspond with the thinking of some Israeli experts who felt that Iran was extending the range/payload of the Shahab-3, and that reports of both the Gadr and Shahab-4 were actually describing the Shahab-3A/3M. [69]

In May 2005, Iran tested a solid fuel motor for what some experts came to call the Shahab-3D, possibly increasing the range to 2,500 kilometers, making space entry possible and setting the stage for the Shahab-5 and Shahab-6, which are three-stage rockets resembling ICBMs.[70] The test showed that Iran had developed some aspects of a successful long-range, solid-fuel missile design, but did not show how Iran intended to use such capabilities.

In March 2006, the NCRI again claimed that Iran was moving forward with the Ghadr solid-fuel IRBM. It also claimed that Iran had scrapped the Shahab-4 because of test failures and performance limitations. It reported that Iran had substantial North Korean technical support for the Ghadr, and that the missile was 70 percent complete and had a range of 3,000 kilometers. One Israeli expert thought that the NCRI was confusing a solid-state second stage for the liquid-fueled Shahab-4 with a separate missile.[71]

Work by Robert Schmucker indicates that Iran is working on solid-fueled systems, building on its experience with solid-fuel artillery rockets like its Fateh 110A1 and with Chinese support in developing solid-fuel propulsion and guidance. The Fateh, however, is a relatively primitive system with strap-down gyro guidance that is not suited for a long-range ballistic missile.[72]

As is the case with longer-range variants of the Shahab, it is probably wise to assume that Iran is seeking to develop options for both solid- and liquid-fueled IRBMs, and will seek high range-payloads to ensure it can deliver effective CBRN payloads even if it cannot produce efficient nuclear weapons. It is equally wise to wait for systems to reach maturity before reacting to vague possibilities rather than real-world Iranian capabilities.

Raduga KH-55 Granat/KH-55/AS-15 Kent

The Raduga KH-55 Granat is a Ukrainian/Soviet-made armed nuclear cruise missile first tested in 1978 and completed in 1984.[73] The Russian missile carries a 200-kiloton nuclear warhead; it has a range of 2,500–3,000 kilometers. It has a theoretical CEP of about 150 meters and a speed of Mach 0.48–0.77. Its guidance system is reported to combine inertial-Doppler navigation and position correction based on in-flight comparison of terrain in the assigned regions with images stored in the memory of an onboard computer. It was designed to deliver a high-yield nuclear weapon against fixed area targets and has little value delivering conventional warheads. Although it was originally designed to be carried by a large bomber, and its weight makes it a marginal payload for either Iran's Su-24s or F-14As, it has land- and ship-launch capability. It can also be adapted to use a much larger nuclear or other CBRN warhead by cutting its range, and it might be a system that Iran can reverse-engineer for production.[74]

Russian president Boris Yeltsin made manufacture of the missile illegal in 1992.[75] Still, the Ukraine had 1,612 of the missiles in stock at the end of 1991, and it agreed to give 575 of them to Russia and scrap the rest.[76] The plans to give the missiles to Russia in the late 1990s proved troublesome, however, and an organization was able to forge documents listing 20 missiles as being sold to Russia, while in fact 12 seem to have been distributed to Iran and 6 to China (the other 2 are unaccounted for).[77] It was estimated that the missiles were smuggled to Iran in 2001.[78]

Ukrainian officials confirmed the illegal sale on March 18, 2005, but the Chinese and Iranian governments were silent regarding the matter. While some U.S. officials downplayed the transaction, the U.S. State Department expressed concern that the missiles could give each state a technological boost.[79] The missiles did not contain warheads at the time of their sale, and they had passed their service life in 1995 and were in need of maintenance.[80] It is feared, however, that Iran could learn from the cruise missiles' technology to improve their own missile program and that the missiles could be fitted to match Iran's Su-24 strike aircraft.[81]

ALTERNATIVE DELIVERY OPTIONS AND COUNTERTHREATS

Iran has several alternatives for delivering its WMDs in addition to its missile program. First, Iran can use its existing air force assets to delivery CBRN weapons. Second, as was described in chapter 3 (table 3.1), Iran can use its asymmetric warfare capabilities and the covert assets available to the IRGC and its intelligence services to carry out WMD attacks against U.S. assets in the region, neighboring states, or energy routes. Third, Iran can use proxy groups such as Hezbollah to attack targets in the Middle East and beyond. Fourth, Iran can smuggle CBRN devices into target cities, U.S. forces, or neighboring states' military and energy sites.

Air Force

The Iranian Air Force is still numerically strong, but most of its equipment is aging, worn, and has limited mission capability. It has some

52,000 men, 37,000 in the air force per se and 15,000 in the air defense force, which operates Iran's land-based air defenses. It has more than 300 combat aircraft in its inventory (the IISS estimates 306).

Many of these aircraft are either not operational or cannot be sustained in extended air combat. This includes 50 percent to 60 percent of Iran's U.S.- and French-supplied aircraft and some 20 to 30 percent of its Russian- and Chinese-supplied aircraft. It has nine fighter ground attack squadrons with 162–186 aircraft; seven fighter squadrons, with 70–74 aircraft, a reconnaissance unit with 4–8 aircraft, and a number of transport aircraft, helicopters, and special purpose aircraft. It operates most of Iraq's land-based air defenses, including some 150 I Hawks, 45 HQ-21s, 10 SA-5s, 30 Rapiers, and additional forces equipped with light surface-to-air missiles.

The Iranian air force is headquartered in Tehran with training, administration, and logistics branches, as well as a major central Air Defense Operations Center. It has a political directorate and a small naval coordination staff. It has three major regional headquarters: Northern Zone (Badl Sar), Central Zone (Hamaden), and Southern Zone (Bushehr). Each regional zone seems to control a major air defense sector with subordinate air bases and facilities. The key air defense subzones and related bases in the Northern Zone are at Badl Sar, Mashhad, and Shahabad Kord. The subzones and bases in the Central Zone are at Hamadan and Dezful, and the subzones and bases in the Southern Zone are at Bushehr, Bandar Abbas, and Jask. Iran has large combat air bases at Mehrabad, Tabriz, Hamadan, Dezful, Bushehr, Shiraz, Esfahan, and Bandar Abbas. It has smaller bases at least at 11 other locations. Shiraz provides interceptor training and is the main base for transport aircraft.

As is the case with most aspects of its military forces, estimates of Iran's exact air strength differ by source. The IISS estimates that the air force has 18 main combat squadrons. These include nine fighter ground-attack squadrons, with 4/55–65 U.S.-supplied F-4D/E and 4/55–65 F-5E/FII, and 1/27–30 Soviet-supplied Su-24 aircraft. Iran had 7 Su-25K and 24 Mirage F-1 Iraqi aircraft it seized during the Gulf War, some of which may be operational. Some reports indicate that Iran has ordered an unknown number of TU-22M-3 "Backfire C" long-range strategic bombers from either Russia or the Ukraine.[82] Although such discussions seem to have taken place, no purchases or deliveries can be confirmed.

Iran had seven air defense squadrons, with 2/20–25 F-5B, 60 U.S.-supplied F-14, 2/25–30 Russian/Iraqi-supplied MiG-29, and 1/25–35 Chinese-supplied F-7M aircraft.[83] The Iranian air force had a small reconnaissance squadron with 3–8 RF-4Es. It has 5 C-130H MP maritime reconnaissance aircraft and 1 RC-130 and other intelligence/reconnaissance aircraft, together with large numbers of transports and helicopters.

Most Iranian squadrons can perform both air defense and attack missions, regardless of their principal mission—although this is not true of Iran's F-14 (air defense) and Su-24 (strike/attack) units. Iran's F-14s, however, were, designed as dual-capable aircraft and have not been able to use their Phoenix air-to-air missiles since the early 1980s. Iran has claimed that it is modernizing its F-14s by equipping them with I-Hawk missiles adapted to the air-to-air role, but it is far from clear that this is the case or that such adaptations can have more than limited effectiveness. In practice, this means that Iran might well use the F-14s in nuclear strike missions. They are capable of long-range, high payload missions, and would require minimal adaptation to carry and release a nuclear weapon.[84]

As a result, Iran has a large number of attack and air defense aircraft that could carry a small to medium-sized nuclear weapon long distances, particularly since most such strikes are likely to be low-altitude, one-way missions. (These were the mission profiles in both NATO and Warsaw Pact theater nuclear strike plans.) Several might conceivably be modified as drones or the equivalent of "cruise missiles" using autopilots, on-board computers, and add-on GPS.

Iran also has some indigenous capability to make combat aircraft and drones. Iran has been developing three new attack aircraft. The indigenous design and specifics of one of the fighters in development, the Shafagh, were unveiled at the Iran airshow in 2002. Engineers hope to have a prototype by 2008, although it is unclear what the production numbers will be and what the real-world timetable for deployment may be.[85] Only limited data are available on the other two fighters in development, the Saeghe and the Azarakhsh, other than they have been reportedly derived from the F-5F. Claims have been made that the Azarakhsh is in low-rate production and has had operational weapons tests. There are also some indications that Iran is experimenting with composites of the Azarakhsh and is seeking to give it locally modified beyond-visual-range radar for air-to-air combat.[86]

The Islamic Revolutionary Guards Corps (Pasdaran)

The Islamic Revolutionary Guards Corps contribute some 120,000 men to Iran's forces and have substantial capability for asymmetric warfare and covert operations. It operates most of Iran's surface-to-surface missiles, and it would probably have custody over deployed nuclear weapons and most or all other CBRN weapons, and would operate Iran's nuclear-armed missile forces if they are deployed.

The Air Branch

The air branch of the IRGC is believed to operate Iran's three Shahab-3 IRBM units, and it may have had custody of its chemical weapons and any biological weapons. While the actual operational status of the Shahab-3 remains uncertain; Iran's supreme leader, Ayatollah Ali Khamenei, announced in 2003 that Shahab-3 missiles had been delivered to the Islamic Revolutionary Guards Corps. In addition, six Shahab-3s were displayed in Tehran during a military parade in September 2003.[87]

The IRGC also has some air elements. It is not clear what combat formations exist within the IRGC, but the IRGC may operate Iran's 10 EMB-312 Tucanos.[88] It seems to operate many of Iran's 45 PC-7 trainers, as well as some Pakistani-made trainers at a training school near Mushak, although the school may be run by the regular air force. It has also claimed to manufacture gliders for use in unconventional warfare. These are unlikely delivery platforms but could carry small numbers of weapons.[89]

The Naval Branch

The IRGC also has a naval branch with some 20,000 men. According to the IISS, this figure includes Iran's marines of some 5,000 men and a combat strength of one brigade. Other sources show this force subordinated to the navy. Such a force could deliver small nuclear weapons or other CBRN weapons into ports, oil and desalination facilities, and operational areas in the Gulf and Gulf of Oman.

The naval branch has bases in the Gulf, many near key shipping channels and some near the Strait of Hormuz. These include facilities at Al-Farsiyah, Halul (an oil platform), Sirri, Abu Musa, Bandaer-e Abbas, Khorramshahr, and Larak. It also controls Iran's coastal defense forces, including naval guns and an HY-3 Seersucker land-based anti-ship missile unit deployed in 5–7 sites along the Gulf coast.

The naval branch's forces can carry out extensive raids against Gulf shipping and carry out regular amphibious exercises with the land branch of the IRGC against objectives like islands in the Gulf. They also could conduct raids against Saudi Arabia or other countries on the southern Gulf coast. They give Iran a major capability for asymmetric warfare. The Guards also seem to work closely with Iranian intelligence and to be represented unofficially in some embassies, Iranian businesses and purchasing offices, and other foreign fronts.

The naval branch has at least 40 light patrol boats, 10 Houdong guided missile patrol boats armed with C-802 anti-ship missiles, and a battery of HY-2 Seersucker land-based anti-ship missiles. Some of these systems could be modified to carry a small CBRN weapon, although they are scarcely optimal delivery platforms because of their limited-range payload and unsuitable sensor/guidance platforms for the mission.

Proxy and Covert CBRN Operations

Other elements of the IRGC could support proxy or covert use of CBRN weapons. They run some training camps inside Iran for outside "volunteers." Some Guards still seem to be deployed in Lebanon and actively involved in training and arming Hezbollah, other anti-Israeli groups, and other elements.[90] The IRGC has been responsible for major arms shipments to Hezbollah, including large numbers of AT-3 anti-tank guided missiles, long-range rockets, and some Iranian-made Mohajer UAVs.[91]

According to some reports, the Fajr 5 has a range of 75 kilometers (46.60 miles) with a payload of 200 kilograms. Iran seems to have sent arms to various Palestinian movements, including some shiploads of arms to the Palestinian Authority.[92]

The IRGC has a complex structure that is both political and military. It has separate organizational elements for its land, naval, and air units, which include both military and paramilitary units. The Basij and the tribal units of the Pasdaran are subordinated to its land unit command, although the commander of the Basij often seems to report directly to the commander-in-chief and minister of the Pasdaran and through him to the Leader of the Islamic Revolution.

The IRGC has close ties to the foreign operations branch of Iran's Ministry of Intelligence and Security (MOIS), particularly through the IRGC's Quds force. The Ministry of Intelligence and Security was established in 1983 and has an extensive network of offices in Iranian embassies. It is often difficult to separate the activities of the IRGC, MOIS, and the Foreign Ministry, and many seem to be integrated operations managed by a ministerial committee called the Special Operations Council that includes the Leader of the Islamic Revolution, the president, the minister of Intelligence and Security, and other members of the Supreme Council for National Defense.[93]

The Quds Forces

The IRGC has a large intelligence operations and unconventional warfare component. Roughly 5,000 of the men in the IRGC are assigned to the unconventional warfare mission. The IRGC has the equivalent of one Special Forces "division," plus additional smaller formations, and these forces are given special priority in terms of training and equipment. The IRGC also has a special Quds force that plays a major role in enabling Iran to conduct unconventional warfare overseas using various foreign movements as proxies.[94]

The budget for the Quds force is classified and is not reflected in the general budget. It is controlled directly by Ayatollah Khamenei. The Quds force operates primarily outside Iran's borders, although it has bases both inside and outside of Iran. The Quds troops are divided into specific groups or "corps" for each country or area in which they operate. There are directorates for Iraq; Lebanon, Palestine, and Jordan; Afghanistan, Pakistan, and India; Turkey and the Arabian Peninsula; the Asiatic republics of the FSU; Western Nations (Europe and North America); and North Africa (Egypt, Tunisia, Algeria, Sudan, and Morocco).

The Quds has offices or "sections" in many Iranian embassies, which are closed to most embassy staff. It is not clear whether these are integrated with Iranian intelligence operations, or that the ambassador in such embassies has control of, or detailed knowledge of, operations by the Quds staff. However, as noted above, there are indications that most operations are coordinated between the IRGC and offices within the Iranian Foreign Ministry and the Ministry of Intelligence and Security. There are separate operational organizations in Lebanon, Turkey, Pakistan, and several North African countries. There also are indications that such elements may have participated in the bombings of the Israeli embassy in Argentina in 1992 and the Jewish Community Center in Buenos Aires in 1994—although Iran has strongly denied this.[95]

The Quds force seems to control many of Iran's training camps for unconventional warfare, extremists, and terrorists both in Iran and in countries like the Sudan and Lebanon. It has at least four major training facilities in Iran. The Quds forces have a main training center at Imam Ali University for Army Officers, based in the Sa'dabad Palace in northern Tehran. There troops are trained to carry out military and terrorist operations and are indoctrinated in ideology. Other training camps are located in the Qom, Tabriz, and Mashhad governates and in Lebanon and the Sudan. These include the Al Nasr camp in northwest Iran for training Iraqi Shi'ites and Iraqi and Turkish Kurds, and a camp near Mashhad for training Afghan and Tajik revolutionaries. The Quds seems to help operate the Manzariyah training center near Qom, which recruits from foreign students enrolled in the religious seminary and which seems to have trained some Bahraini extremists. Some foreigners are reported to have received training in demolition and sabotage at an IRGC facility near Esfahan; airport infiltration at a facility near Mashad and Shiraz; and underwater warfare at an IRGC facility at Bandar Abbas.[96]

The IRGC's Role in Iran's Industries

The IRGC plays a major role in Iran's military industries. Its lead role in Iran's efforts to acquire surface-to-surface missiles and weapons of mass destruction give it growing experience with advanced military technology. As a result, the IRGC is believed to be the branch of Iran's forces that plays the largest role in Iran's military industries.[97] It also operates all of Iran's Scuds, controls most of its chemical and biological weapons, and provides the military leadership for missile production and the production of all weapons of mass destruction.

The Basij and Other Paramilitary Forces

The rest of Iran's paramilitary and internal security forces seem to have relatively little capability in such missions. The Basij (Mobilization of the Oppressed) is a popular reserve force of about 90,000 men with an active and reserve strength of up to 300,000 and a mobilization capacity of nearly 1,000,000 men. It is controlled by the IRGC and consists largely of youths, men who have completed military service, and the elderly.

Iran also has 45,000–60,000 men in the Ministry of Interior serving as police and border guards, equipped with light utility vehicles, light patrol aircraft (Cessna 185/310 and AB-205 and AB-206s), 90 coastal patrol craft, and 40 harbor patrol craft.

ASSESSING IRAN'S DELIVERY OPTIONS

There is no way to know Iran's plans relative to missiles, long-range aircraft, and covert/proxy use. Clearly, however, Iran has, made a major commitment to developing and deploying long-range surface-to-surface missiles. And it may eventually have enough nuclear weapons to use them as shorter-range tactical weapons. That possibility is so remote at this time, however, that it does not seem to merit detailed analysis.

Aside from the Scud, Iranian programs are too transitional or too early in their development to allow any precise estimate of their nuclear capability. The ranges, payloads, and accuracies quoted for all missiles except the Scud are engineering estimates based on nominal performance criteria. This method of estimation has produced drastic and consistent errors for more than half a century. Hard data based on telemetry and actual tests are the only reliable sources of such data. Yet even these sources often do not produce trustworthy data on operational accuracy and reliability unless tied to multiple tests and enough information to be sure of the aim point.

It is important to note that Iran faces much the same uncertainties in many aspects of developing its testing and designing missiles and warheads, and it will continue to do so until it has a comprehensive set of operational test data based on its missiles and the behavior of its warheads. Even then, there will probably be a significant risk that any given missile launch will be at least a partial failure and could impact far from its target. CEP is always nominal and based on a perfectly functioning system. Even then, it makes no effort to predict where the 50 percent of the missiles that fall outside the CEP actually go.

Warhead and bomb design also are major problems. It is one thing to create a nuclear device, or even a bomb, and another to create a reliable and effective nuclear warhead. Such a device has to be safe and reliable, and—for most uses that have predictable and controllable nuclear weapons effects—have arming and detonation that allow precise control of the height of burst. Making even a small, efficient bomb is still a state-of-the-art exercise in design, engineering, and manufacturing. A missile warhead requires far more skill. The leak of Chinese designs may help, as may other technology transfers, but Iran would want great assurance that such designs would function as planned. Up to a point, a design's performance can be simulated by using non-fissile material, by testing specially configured conventional warheads, by conducting static or even underground tests, and by testing bombs configured to give missile warhead design data. Concealment and nonfissile testing of nuclear missile warheads is possible and could be highly effective in some ways, but would not be without risk.

That said, ballistic and cruise missile systems offer the highest probability of successful penetration, although Israel has deployed the Arrow antiballistic missile (ABM) and can use its Patriot missile for cruise missile defense. The United States also has the Patriot, as well as a sea-based cruise missile and limited ABM defenses, and is developing much more advanced theater ABMs. Because of their limited footprint and coverage in any given area, however, such defenses might be partially countered by firing a volley of missiles at the same time.. Only one missile would need to be nuclear-armed, and Iran could fire unarmed missiles first to determine how effective the defenses were.

The use of aircraft is often ignored but presents complex trade-offs. Such systems may be easier to detect and defend against, but they also offer more reliability and control. Iran has only a limited number of

aircraft with high-range payloads, but it has a large number of aircraft it could launch on one-way ferry missions. Iran practiced multi-
ple-attack or swarming techniques to suppress U.S. Navy defenses in
exercises during the time of the shah. Such techniques have limited effectiveness against today's more capable defenses, but could still have
some value.

The risk of any mix of such attacks would still be high and compounded by the near certainty of retaliation. U.S., Saudi, Israeli, and
other regional sensors would also detect any Iranian ballistic missile
launch, and an alert force might well track a cruise missile at least back
to Iranian territory. The use of missiles or aircraft to deliver CBRN
weapons may not be easy to defend against, but would clearly impli-
cate Iran in the attacks. If such a system were nuclear-armed, it would
be more than a license to escalate; it would be a license for massive retaliation with nuclear weapons.

It is unclear how the United States would retaliate under these conditions. The minimal demand would probably be for unconditional
surrender, reinforced by immediate U.S. military action. The Israeli
reaction is more speculative, but it seems doubtful that Israel would
take any chances in such an existential war. From an Israeli perspective, a nuclear attack by Iran might well be seen as total war and one in
which Israel could not afford not to send the most drastic signal possible to other nations in the region. The end result might well be thermonuclear groundbursts on all of Iran's major cities. If so, the damage
would be far greater than the damage caused by the smaller nuclear
weapons shown in table 8.1, and it would be compounded by the
long-term killing effects of massive amounts of fallout.

As has been discussed, this possibility might make the use of covert,
remote, or proxy options seem more desirable. Iran's role would be
far harder to detect, which would complicate the exercise of retaliatory options. The problem, however, is that it would take far more than
mere "plausible deniability" to deter nations like the United States or
Israel or America's regional allies from demanding an immediate response. A total "black" operation is always difficult, and the lack of a
clear trace back to Iran would probably be irrelevant in a war or serious crisis. The threshold of any nuclear attack is simply too high for

further risk taking or restraint. Even an attack that initially seemed to succeed in obfuscating Iran as a source, or succeed in using a "false flag," would create the risk of future discovery. Memories, to put it mildly, would be long, and the response would probably be equally grim.

Notes

[1] "Iran Heading towards Conflict," *Jane's Intelligence Digest*, November 12, 2004.

[2] Bill Gertz, "U.S. Told of Iranian Effort to Create Nuclear Warhead," *Washington Times*, December 2, 2004, p. 3.

[3] Dafna Linzer, "Iran Is Judged 10 Years from Nuclear Bomb," *Washington Post*, August 2, 1005, sec. A-1.

[4] Abraham Rabinovich, "Iran Boasts Dimona Now 'Within Range,'" *Washington Times*, August 24, 2004.

[5] Director of Central Intelligence, *Unclassified Report to Congress on the Acquisition of Technology Relating to Weapons of Mass Destruction and Advanced Conventional Munitions, 1 July Through 31 December 2003*, CIA, available at http://www.cia.gov/cia/reports/721_reports/july_dec2003.htm.

[6] John R. Bolton, "Iran's Continuing Pursuit of Weapons of Mass Destruction" (testimony before the U.S. House International Relations Subcommittee on the Middle East and Central Asia, June 24, 2004, available at http://www.state.gov/t/us/rm/33909.htm).

[7] Lowell E. Jacoby, "Current and Projected National Security Threats to the United States" (statement for the record by the director of the Defense Intelligence Agency [DIA] to the U.S. Senate Armed Services Committee, March 17, 2005).

[8] "Iran Enhances Existing Weaponry by Optimizing Shahab-3 Ballistic Missile," *Jane's Missiles and Rockets*, January 20, 2004.

[9] "U.S. Consultancy Claims Iran Has Built Underground Missile Factories," *Jane's Missiles and Rockets*, December 8, 2005.

[10] GlobalSecurity.org, "Iran: Missiles," available at http://www.globalsecurity.org/wmd/world/iran/missile.htm.

[11] Federation of American Scientists, "SCUD-B/Shahab-1," December 1, 2005, available at http://www.fas.org/nuke/guide/iran/missile/shahab-1.htm.

[12] Ibid.

[13] Kenneth Katzman, "Iran's Long Range Missile Capabilities," *Executive Summary of the Report of the Commission to Assess the Ballistic Missile Threat to*

the United States, Appendix 3: Unclassified Working Papers, Commission to Assess the Ballistic Missile Threat to the United States, July 15, 1998, available at http://www.globalsecurity.org/wmd/library/report/1998/rumsfeld/pt2_katz.htm.

[14] Ibid.

[15] Ibid.

[16] Ibid.

[17] Ibid.

[18] Paul Beaver, "Iran's Shahab-3 IRBM 'Ready for Production,'" *Jane's Missiles and Rockets*, June 1, 1998.

[19] International Institute for Strategic Studies (IISS), *The Military Balance 2005–2006* (Washington, D.C.: IISS, 2005).

[20] Federation of American Scientists, "Shahab-2," December 1, 2005, available at http://www.fas.org/nuke/guide/iran/missile/shahab-2.htm.

[21] GlobalSecurity.org, "Iran: Missiles."

[22] Kenneth Katzman, "Iran's Long Range Missile Capabilities."

[23] Beaver, "Iran's Shahab-3 IRBM 'Ready for Production."

[24] Katzman, "Iran's Long Range Missile Capabilities."

[25] Ibid.

[26] "Flashpoints: Iran," *Jane's Defence Weekly*, March 4, 1995, p. 18.

[27] "Iran Says Shahab-3 Missile Entirely Iranian, Production Ongoing," Agence France-Presse, May 5, 2005.

[28] Katzman, "Iran's Long Range Missile Capabilities."

[29] Ibid.

[30] "Iran Tests Shahab-3 Ballistic Missile," *Jane's Missiles and Rockets*, August 1, 1998.

[31] GlobalSecurity.org, "Shahab 3/Zelzal 3," available at http://www.globalsecurity.org/wmd/world/iran/shahab-3.htm.

[32] David Isby, "Shahab-3 Enters Production," *Jane's Missiles and Rockets*, November 26, 2001.

[33] Ed Blanche, "Shahab-3 Ready for Service, Says Iran," *Jane's Missiles and Rockets*, July 23, 2003.

[34] "Shahab-3/Zelzal 3," GlobalSecurity.org, available at http://www.globalsecurity.org/wmd/world/iran/shahab-3.htm

[35] Farhad Pouladi, "Iran Vows to Continue Nuclear Drive at All Costs," Agence France-Presse, September 22, 2004.

[36] "Iran 'Tests New Missile Engine,'" BBC News, May 31, 2005, available at http://news.bbc.co.uk/2/hi/middle_east/4596295.stm.

[37] Robert H. Schmucker, "Iran and Its Regional Environment," Schmucker Technologies, Pease Research Institute, Frankfurt, March 27, 2006, http://www.hsfk.de, and http://www.hsfk.de/static.php?id=3929&language=de.

[38] For further details on the history and nature of the Shahab and Iran's programs, see Andrew Feickert, *Missile Survey: Ballistic and Cruise Missiles of Selected Foreign Countries*, Congressional Research Service, RL30427, (regularly updated); the work of Kenneth Katzman, also of the Congressional Research Service; the "Missile Overview" section of the Iran Profile of the NTI (http://www.nti.org/e_research/profiles/Iran/Missiles/; and the work of Global Security, including http://www.globalsecurity.org/wmd/world/iran/shahab-3.htm.

[39] Ed Blanche, "Iran Claims Shahab-3 Range Now 2,000km," *Jane's Missiles and Rockets*, November 1, 2004.

[40] "Iran Boasts Shahab-3 Is in Mass Production," *Jane's Missiles and Rockets*, November 19, 2004.

[41] "Iran Threatens to Abandon the NPT," *Jane's Islamic Affairs Analyst*, September 29, 2004

[42] Douglas Jehl, "Iran Reportedly Hides Work on a Long-Range Missile," *New York Times*, December 2, 2004.

[43] "Iran: Missiles Development," GlobalSecurity.org, available at http://www.globalsecurity.org/wmd/world/iran/missile-development.htm.

[44] See the work of Robert H. Schmucker, "The Shahab Missile and Iran's Delivery System Capabilities" (briefing, conference on a nuclear Iran, James Shasha Institute for International Seminars, Jerusalem, May 30–June 2, 2005); and Schmucker, "Iran and Its Regional Environment."

[45] International Institute for Strategic Studies (IISS), *Iran's Strategic Weapons Programmes: A Net Assessment*, IISS Strategic Dossier (London: IISS, 2005), p. 102.

[46] Sonni Efron, Tyler Marshall, and Bob Drogin, "Powell's Talk of Arms Has Fallout," *Los Angeles Times*, November 19, 2004.

[47] Carla Anne Robbins, "U.S. Gives Briefing on Iranian Missile to Nuclear Agency," *Wall Street Journal*, July 27, 2005, p.3.

[48] Dafna Linzer, "Strong Leads and Dead Ends in Nuclear Case against Iran," *Washington Post*, February 8, 2006, sec. A-1.

[49] "Shahab-3," Federation of American Scientists, December 1, 2005, available at http://www.fas.org/nuke/guide/iran/missile/shahab-3.htm.

[50] Schmucker, "The Shahab Missile and Iran's Delivery System Capabilities," and "Iran and Its Regional Environment."

[51] "Shahab-3D," Federation of American Scientists, December 1, 2005, available at http://www.fas.org/nuke/guide/iran/missile/shahab-3d.htm.

[52] Doug Richardson, "Iran is Developing an IRBM, Claims Resistance Group," *Jane's Rockets and Missiles*, December 14, 2004.

[53] "Iran: Missiles" GlobalSecurity.org, available at http://www.global security.org/wmd/world/iran/missile.htm

[54] "Iran Moves Its Shahab 3 Units," *Jane's Missiles and Rockets,* April 1, 2006.

[55] Douglas Jehl, "Iran Is Said to Work on New Missile," *International Herald Tribune*, December 2, 2004, p. 7.

[56] GlobalSecurity.org, "Iran: Missiles Development."

[57] Federation of American Scientists, "Shahab-3D."

[58] GlobalSecurity.org, "Iran: Missiles Development."

[59] Federation of American Scientists, "Shahab-3D."

[60] Ibid.

[61] IISS, *Iran's Strategic Weapons Programmes.*

[62] "Shahab-4," Federation of American Scientists, December 1, 2005, available at http://www.fas.org/nuke/guide/iran/missile/shahab-4.htm.

[63] Richardson, "Iran Is Developing an IRBM, Claims Resistance Group."

[64] Federation of American Scientists, "Shahab-4."

[65] "Western Intelligence Confirms Iranian Missile Developments—German Report," BBC Monitoring International Reports, February 6, 2006, available through Lexus Nexus.

[66] Federation of American Scientists, "Shahab-5," December 1, 2005, available at http://www.fas.org/nuke/guide/iran/missile/shahab-5.htm.

[67] Federation of American Scientists, "Shahab-4."

[68] "Western Intelligence Confirms Iranian Missile Developments," BBC Monitoring.

[69] Andrew Koch, "Tehran Altering Ballistic Missile," *Jane's Defence Weekly*, December 8, 2004.

[70] "Iran Tests Shahab-3 Motor."

[71] Robin Hughes, "Iranian Resistance Group Alleges Tehran Is Developing New Medium-Range Missile," *Jane's Defence Weekly*, March 22, 2006.

[72] Schmucker, "Iran and Its Regional Environment."

[73] "KH-55 Granat," Federation of American Scientists, available at http://www.fas.org/nuke/guide/russia/bomber/as-15.htm.

[74] See http://www.globalsecurity.org/wmd/world/russia/as-15-specs.htm, http://www.globalsecurity.org/wmd/world/russia/kh-55.htm, and http://www.globalsecurity.org/wmd/world/iran/x-55.htm.

[75] Ibid.

[76] "Cruise Missile Row Rocks Ukraine," BBC News, March 18, 2005, available at http://news.bbc.co.uk/2/hi/europe/4361505.stm.

[77] Bill Gertz, "Missiles Sold to China and Iran," Washington Times, April 6, 2005, available at http://washingtontimes.com/national/20050405-115803-7960r.htm.

[78] Ibid.

[79] Paul Kerr, "Ukraine Admits Missile Transfers," Arms Control Today 35, no. 4 (May 2005) available at http://www.armscontrol.org/act/2005_05/Ukraine.asp.

[80] "Ukraine Investigates Supply of Missiles to China and Iran," Jane's Missiles and Rockets, May 1 2005.

[81] "18 Cruise Missiles Were Smuggled to Iran, China," Associated Press, March 18, 2005.

[82] "Iran," Jane's Sentinel Security Assessment: The Gulf States, October 7, 2004, available at http://sentinel.janes.com/.

[83] The range of aircraft numbers shown reflects the broad uncertainties affecting the number of Iran's aircraft that are operational in any realistic sense. Many of the aircraft counted, however, cannot engage in sustained combat sorties in an extended air campaign. The numbers are drawn largely from interviews; Jane's Intelligence Review, Special Report No. 6, May 1995; "Iran," Jane's Sentinel Security Assessment: The Gulf States, various editions; International Institute for Strategic Studies, "Iran," Military Balance, various editions; Andrew Rathmell, The Changing Balance in the Gulf, Whitehall Papers 38 (London: Royal United Services Institute, 1996); Andrew Rathmell, "Iran's Rearmament: How Great a Threat?" Jane's Intelligence Review, July 1994, pp. 317–322; Jane's World Air Forces (CD-ROM).

[84] Wall Street Journal, February 10, 1995, p. 19; Washington Times, February 10, 1995, sec. A19.

[85] "2002–2003," Jane's All the World's Aircraft, pp. 259–263.

[86] Robert Hewson, "Iran's New Combat Aircraft Waits in the Wings," Jane's Defence Weekly, November 20, 2002, p. 15; "2002–2003," Jane's All the World's Aircraft.

[87] "Iran Enhances Existing Weaponry by Optimizing Shahab-3 Ballistic Missile."

[88] Reports that the Iranian Revolutionary Guards Corps (IRGC) is operating F-7 fighters do not seem to be correct.

[89] Reuters, June 12, 1996, 17:33.

[90] Riad Kahwaji and Barabara Opall-Rome, "Hizbollah: Iran's Battle Lab," *Defense News*, December 13, 2004, pp. 1, 6.

[91] Amir Taheir, "The Mullah's Playground," *Wall Street Journal*, December 7, 2004, sec. A-10.

[92] The estimates of such holdings of rockets are now in the thousands, but the numbers are very uncertain. Dollar estimates of what are significant arms shipments are little more than analytic rubbish, based on cost methods that border on the absurd, but significant shipments are known to have taken place.

[93] See *Time* (March 21, 1994, pp. 50–54; November 11, 1996, pp. 78–82); *Washington Post* (November 21, 1993, sec. A-1; August 22, 1994, sec. A-17; October 28, 1994, sec. A-17; November 27, 1994, sec. A-30; April 11, 1997, sec. A-1; April 14, 1997, sec. A-1); *Los Angeles Times* (November 3, 1994, secs. A-1, A-12); Deutsche Presse-Agentur (April 17, 1997, 11:02); Reuters (April 16, 1997, BC cycle; April 17, 1997, BC cycle); *European* (April 17, 1997, p. 13); *Guardian* (Manchester) (October 30, 1993, p. 13; August 24, 1996, p. 16; April 16, 1997, p. 10); *New York Times* (April 11, 1997, sec. A-1); Associated Press (April 14, 1997, 18:37); *Jane's Defence Weekly* (June 5, 1996, p. 15); Agence France-Presse (April 15, 1997, 15:13); BBC News (April 14, 1997, ME/D2892/MED); Deustcher Depeschen via ADN (April 12, 1997, 07:43); *Washington Times* (April 11, 1997, sec. A-22).

[94] The reader should be aware that much of the information relating to the Quds is highly uncertain. Also see, however, the article from the Jordanian publication *Al-Hadath*, FBIS-NES-96-108, May 27, 1996, p. 9, and *Al-Sharq Al-Awsat*, FBIS-NES-96-110, June 5, 1996, pp. 1, 4; A. J. Venter, "Iran Still Exporting Terrorism," *Jane's Intelligence Review*, November, 1997, pp. 511–516.

[95] *New York Times*, May 17, 1998, sec. A-15; *Washington Times*, May 17, 1998, sec. A-13; *Washington Post*, May 21, 1998, sec. A-29.

[96] Venter, "Iran Still Exporting Terrorism."

[97] For typical reporting by officers of the IRGC on this issue, see the comments of its acting commander in chief, Brigadier General Seyyed Rahim Safavi, speaking to reporters during IRGC week (December 20–26, 1995), FBIS-NES-95-250, December 25, 1995, IRNA 1406 GMT.

CHAPTER TEN

IRAN'S OPTIONS AND POTENTIAL RESPONSES

There is no way to know what strategy Iran will choose in the future or how the international community will respond. Iran's possible efforts to acquire nuclear weapons are an ongoing test of the entire process of arms control and the ability to limit nuclear proliferation. At the same time, they raise critical issues about how Iran might use such weapons and about the security of the Gulf region—an area with more than 60 percent of the world's proven conventional oil reserves and some 37 percent of its gas.

Iranian acquisition of nuclear weapons is not simply a struggle over issues of national prestige or "rights." It has a major potential impact on regional stability and future war-fighting. If Iran does acquire nuclear weapons, it is possible that it will use them largely as a passive deterrent and means of defense. It is also possible, however, that Iran will use them to put direct or indirect pressure on its neighbors in order to achieve goals it could not achieve without the explicit or tacit threat of weapons of mass destruction.

Iran's possession of nuclear weapons, or of highly lethal biological weapons for that matter, would change the military map of the region. It would almost certainly lead to contingency planning by other nuclear powers to attack Iran—certainly Israel and possibly Pakistan and India. Such planning for potentially "existential" conflicts takes place when there is a possibility, even if there is no probability.

U.S. and allied forces in the Gulf would have to plan for nuclear war or the risk of nuclear escalation, and for preventive, preemptive, deterrent, and retaliatory options. Iran would target cities, key civilian facilities, and military targets with nuclear weapons and be targeted in return. The risk of misunderstandings, misperceptions, and miscalculations would be significant in a crisis or war both before any use of nuclear weapons and during the transattack and conflict termination phases.

At the same time, the previous chapters have shown that it can be difficult to stop a truly dedicated Iran with either military operations or steps like sanctions. Such actions might well simply push Iran into more concealment and to more drastic options or alternatives like biological weapons. This does not mean that military operations or sanctions cannot be effective, by slowing Iran's efforts or even halting them if political conditions in Iran should change. It does mean that no single set of actions to halt Iran can be decisive if Iran is determined to continue and willing to pay the cost.

THE UNCERTAIN FUTURE OF IRAN'S WMD CAPABILITIES

It is far from clear whether Iran will stop its pursuit of nuclear weapons, and it may be only a matter of time before it acquires nuclear weapons. However, it is very unclear what kind of a nuclear power Iran is or will seek to be. No plans have ever surfaced as to the number and type of weapons it is seeking to produce or the nature of its delivery forces.

Iran might be content to simply develop its technology to the point it could rapidly build a nuclear weapon. It might choose to create an undeclared deterrent and limit its weapons numbers and avoid a nuclear test. It might test and create a stockpile, but not openly deploy nuclear-armed missiles or aircraft. However, it also might create an overt nuclear force. Each option would lead to a different response from Saudi Arabia and Iran's other neighbors, as well as from Israel and the United States—creating different kinds of arms races, patterns of deterrence, and risks in the process.

Iran's Options for Riding Out Military Strikes or Coercive Diplomacy

Iran can pursue a wide range of nuclear weapons development options–many of which could be effective even if Iran was subject to many forms of preemptive attack. Iran could:

- Simply carry out enough ambiguous activity to convince outside nations it has an active nuclear weapons effort, seeking to use the threat of development to create some degree of nuclear ambiguity.

- Pause long enough to convince the international community that it has complied with EU3 and UN demands, while creating new dispersed facilities and improving concealment and deception.

- Pause most efforts, but push forward with more advanced centrifuge development and possible laser isotope separation. Accelerate its efforts to acquire boosted or thermonuclear weapons. Leapfrog a pause in activity by having acquired more advanced production capabilities and more lethal weapons requiring less fissile material when large-scale activity resumes.

- Carry out a low-level research and development effort that was covert enough to steadily move it towards a breakout capability to rapidly create weapons production capabilities, but not actually build production facilities. Maintain ambiguity by using small redundant efforts, canceling efforts when uncovered, or pausing when acute pressure came from the outside. Develop truly advanced centrifuges or LIS facilities, and complete bomb design and simulation, before beginning development of production facilities, two particularly attractive options.

- Covertly develop a highly dispersed set of small and redundant production facilities, combining covert facilities like small "folded centrifuge" operations with sheltered or underground facilities. Slowly acquire actual production capability and begin stockpiling.

- Rely on covert simulation to test bomb designs and their weaponization. Test a fractional weapon underground under the cover of an earthquake. Conduct an overt surface test as proof of its nuclear capability.

- Appear to cancel most of its ambiguous activities and wait until its civil nuclear reactor and technology program advances to the point that it is no longer dependent on outside supply. Use some of its power reactors to obtain plutonium. Use compliance with the NPT to proliferate.

- Assemble a limited number of nuclear devices without any public statement—such a "bomb in the basement" strategy could allow sudden testing to prove its existence, be used in surprise attacks, and be linked to covert attack strategies or carried to the level of weaponization necessary for use in a missile warhead or bomb.

- Deploy its Shahab missiles with conventional warheads and create a launch-on-warning/launch-under-attack (LOW/LUA) capability mixed with sheltering and mobility. Arm the missiles with weapons of mass destruction once this capability is ready. Alternatively, covertly arm some missiles as soon as the Shahab missiles and warheads are ready and/or seek at least limited missile defenses like the SA-400. Combine Shahab forces with air units and sea-based cruise missile units to create survivable and redundant forces. Either announce nuclear capability once a survivable/retaliatory force is in being or rely on nuclear ambiguity.

- Stop at fission weapons, or go on to develop "boosted" and true thermonuclear weapons.

- Stop building up a force at the level of minimal assured deterrence. Participate in an open-ended arms race. Seek "parity" with other regional powers like Israel—at least in terms of weapons numbers.

- Rely on an area targeting capability or develop a point target capability as well.

- Deploy its Shahab missiles as conventionally armed missiles and give them mobility so as to hide them, or organize them with suitable warning and command and control systems so they can launch on warning (LOW) or launch under attack (LUA). "Instantly" convert part of its air force to an LOW or LUA capability simply by arming it with nuclear weapons and putting it on alert—even a few nuclear deployments of this kind could act as a powerful deterrent to both Israel and the United States, and do serious damage to any Gulf state or major Gulf energy facility.

- Deploy satellites to improve targeting, damage assessment, and C4I (command, control, communications, computers, and intelligence) capabilities.

- Develop small weapons and/or radiological weapons for possible covert delivery or use by extremist and/or proxy organizations. Use the threat of transfer as a further deterrent, execute strikes in ways where deniability of responsibility has some credibility, or use actual transfer to aid in attacks or for retaliatory purposes.

The "CBR" Option, with or without the "N"

It is impossible to dismiss the possibility that Iran could respond to any decision to give up nuclear weapons by developing and producing advanced biological weapons, or that it may already have biological and nuclear efforts going on in parallel. It might also choose to develop and use "radiological weapons." These weapons might take three forms—all of which would interact with Iran's potential use of chemical and biological weapons.

- The first would be to use a "dirty weapon" using fissile material with contaminated or low enrichment levels that would have limited heat and blast effects but still produce yields of 3 to 5 kilotons, and that would effectively poison a city if detonated near the ground. Such a device would reduce some of the manufacturing and design problems inherent in creating clean or efficient nuclear weapons.

- The second would be to use a weapon that had not been tested, that was believed to be unreliable, or that was on an inaccurate missile and detonate it near the ground so that the radiation effects would compensate for a failure to reach design efficiency or accuracy of the delivery system.

- The third would be to use radioactive material in micropowder or liquid form as a terror or unconventional weapon. It would be very difficult to get substantial lethality from the use of radioactive material, and such a weapon would be less efficient than biological weapons in terms of weight and lethality. It would, however, have the capacity to contaminate a key area and to create panic.

The United States and Russia have rejected radiological weapons because they have the ability to precisely control the yield from their nuclear weapons. But the option might be attractive to Iran. As is the case with chemical and biological weapons, even the prospect of Iran's acquiring any such nuclear weapons has increased its ability to intimidate its neighbors.

Iran could deliver chemical, biological, or nuclear weapons on any of its fighter-bombers, use covert delivery means, or use its missiles. It could use its Scuds and some types of antiship missiles to deliver such warheads relatively short distances. Its Shahab-3 missiles could probably reach virtually all of the targets in Gulf countries, including many Saudi cities on the Red Sea coast and in western Saudi Arabia.

As has been discussed earlier, Iran's Shahab-3s are probably too inaccurate and their payload too limited to be effective in delivering conventional weapons. This does not mean that conventionally armed Shahab missiles could not be used as terror weapons, or weapons of intimidation, but they could only have a major military impact–even against area targets–if they were armed with warheads carrying weapons of mass destruction. Moreover, Saudi Arabia faces the possibility of an Iranian transfer of WMDs to some anti-Saudi extremist group or proxy. These currently do not seem to be probable scenarios, but Saudi Arabia is worried.

IRAN'S UNCERTAIN NUCLEAR WAR-FIGHTING DOCTRINE AND CAPABILITIES

As has been discussed throughout this analysis, few meaningful data are available on Iranian nuclear doctrine and targeting, and it is uncertain that any current plans would even be relevant in the future. The same is true of Iran's plans to limit the vulnerability of its weapons and facilities–and whether it would try to create a launch-on-warning or launch-under-attack capability. It is easy to speculate at length about what Iran would do with nuclear weapons. It is impossible, however, to determine how aggressively Iran would exploit that capability in terms of threatening or intimidating its neighbors, or putting pressure on the West. Lacking meaningful data, one can only try to guess at Iran's war-fighting doctrine and actions using weapons of mass destruction.

The Risk of Iranian Proliferation without Meaningful Planning

It is quite possible that Iran has not yet looked far enough beyond its nuclear weapons acquisition efforts to work out detailed plans for possession. There is no way to know if Iran would choose a relatively stable model of deterrence or if it would aggressively exploit its possession politically. It is equally difficult to guess whether Iran would develop an aggressive doctrine for use, consider developing a LOW/LUA capability, or reserve the use of a nuclear weapon as a last resort.[1]

As for war-fighting capability, any working nuclear device Iran is likely to develop will be sufficient to destroy any hardened target, area target, or city in the Middle East if the delivery vehicle is accurate enough. Nuclear weapons do, however, differ sharply in their effects as they grow in size and if Iran had to rely on inaccurate delivery systems it not only would have to target area targets like cities and major energy facilities; it might have to either use multiple strikes or develop more advanced and higher-yield nuclear weapons like "boosted weapons." Alternatively, it might rely on groundbursts and fallout.

Iran's nuclear efforts will also interact heavily with the progress Iran makes in biological and chemical weapons programs and its efforts to improve its delivery capabilities. By the time Iran has significant nuclear capability, it may have significant missile, cruise missile, and long-range strike aircraft capability—although it may not have cruise missiles capable of carrying a nuclear weapon. It also may have rebuilt much of its conventional capabilities to the point where it has significant war-fighting capabilities.

The Challenges of Actual Possession

As the previous chapters have discussed, Iran will encounter certain practical problems regardless of which weapons of mass destruction it develops and deploys:

- Unless Iran acquires satellites it will have limited dynamic targeting capability and limited ability to assess the impact of any strikes it launches. Even if it does acquire satellites, it will experience serious problems in trying to assess damage and its target

and escalatory options in the event of either a chemical and biological strike or nuclear fallout.

- It would take a major surface-testing effort to be certain of the reliability and yield of its weapons designs, and testing of actual bombs
  and warheads to know the success of its weaponization effort—although a nuclear device could be tested using noncritical materials
  to determine that its explosive and triggering systems functioned.

- Quite aside from theoretical accuracy problems, long-range missiles are subject to some loss of accuracy depending on the vector
  they are fired in, as well weather conditions. Combined with targeting, weapons design, and other accuracy problems—plus reliability problems—a significant number of Iranian strikes might
  miss their targets and some might hit unintended targets.

- Past tests have shown that efforts to apply chemical and biological lethality data based on laboratory or limited human testing
  simply do not provide anything approaching an accurate picture
  of area lethality. Nominal lethality data can be wrong by more
  than an order of magnitude. The impact of nuclear strikes on
  large, semi-hard, area targets is very hard to predict. So is the effect of unusual winds and other weather conditions.

- Iran's C4I systems might not be adequate and survivable enough
  to maintain cohesive control over Iranian weapons and launch
  forces. Any reliance on launch on warning or launch under attack
  virtually precludes such control, and could trigger Iranian action
  based on false alarms or serious misunderstanding of the developing
  tactical situation. If Iran was preempted or subject to a first strike, its
  ability to characterize the result could be equally uncertain.

- Iran might well have comparable problems with characterizing
  enemy responses and retaliatory strikes once exchanges begin.

- For all these reasons, Iran's command and control might have to
  operate on the basis of grossly inadequate information in both
  planning operations and conducting them. The "fog of war" might
  well be exceptionally dense.

What is clear is that if Iran acquired a working nuclear device, the
perceived military balance in the region would change suddenly and

radically. Iran is likely to acquire such weapons at about the same time it acquires MRBMs, and this would be a volatile combination. Iran could then destroy any hardened target, area target, or city within the range of its delivery systems.

Iran's southern Gulf neighbors are extremely vulnerable to attacks on a few cities, and even one successful nuclear attack might force a fundamental restructuring of their politics and/or economy. They are effectively "one bomb" countries. The same is true of Israel, although it has limited missile defenses and is steadily improving them, and could launch a massive retaliatory nuclear-armed missile strike against virtually all of Iran's cities.

OUTSIDE HELP TO IRAN'S WMD PROGRAM

Any discussion of Iran's CBRN and missile programs is not complete without discussing the role of outside powers. Some of the most important technologies that Iran uses, particularly in its nuclear and missile programs, were acquired from foreign sources. Previous chapters have shown just how important foreign technology, equipment, and expertise have been to Tehran's WMD and missile programs.

In its effort to develop its nuclear capabilities, Iran at times sought the help of other countries such as Russia. At other times, Iran worked hard to acquire the technology covertly through legitimate institutions and the open market in Europe, Russia, and, before the revolution, even the United States. It also attempted to acquire expertise through the black market. In the case of Pakistan, most of the evidence points to the fact that Iran was approached by the A.Q. Khan network in 1987 and given the designs of centrifuges (P-1 and probably P-2).

Regardless of the ways in which Tehran attempted to adapt new technologies, there is little doubt that its nuclear and missile programs—and to a lesser extent its CBW programs—have relied heavily on foreign help and expertise. In 2001, the U.S. Department of Defense cited Iran as one of the major concerns in international proliferation, declaring that "Iran, with foreign assistance, is buying and developing longer-range missiles, already has chemical weapons, and is seeking nuclear and biological capabilities."[2]

Iranian Efforts to Acquire Technology and Expertise

A European assessment by British, French, German, and Belgian intelligence services, dubbed an "early warning," was leaked to the press following Tehran's decision to resume its nuclear research in January 2006. The estimate reportedly concluded that "in addition to sensitive goods Iran continues to intensively seek the technology and know-how for military applications of all kinds." According to the *Guardian,* Iran was working on acquiring such technology through "an extensive web of front companies, official bodies, academic institutes, and middlemen dedicated to obtaining—in western Europe and in the former Soviet Union—the expertise, training, and equipment for nuclear programmes, missile development, and biological and chemical weapons arsenals."[3]

The leaked document added that Iran was using "middlemen" in Azerbaijan and Armenia to collect expertise in nuclear and missile technology in states of the former Soviet Union (FSU). According to the *Guardian,* the document listed more than 200 front companies, government offices, and academic institutions engaged in "weapons research" In the FSU.[4]

The Role of Pakistan

Pakistan helped Iran advance its nuclear research, but there is no evidence to suggest that the Pakistani government was directly involved. It was revealed, however, that the A.Q. Khan network played an instrumental role in advancing Tehran's nuclear research efforts. Although it remains unconfirmed, U.S. officials have accused Dr. Khan of providing the Iranians with the design and components of the P-2 centrifuge.

The investigation by U.S., French, Japanese, British, and Russian scientists into the source of highly enriched uranium contamination at Iranian nuclear sites proved that it came from equipment Iran bought from Pakistan during the 1980s and the 1990s. One official involved in this investigation concluded that "the biggest smoking gun that everyone was waving is now eliminated with these conclusions." Another official was quoted by the *Washington Post* as saying "the contamination issue is revolved."[5]

In early 2005, Pakistan provided the IAEA with equipment to compare to that found at nuclear sites in Iran. As of August 2005, both the IAEA and the U.S. administration refused to comment on the findings of the comparison.[6] Many experts, however, believe that Pakistan was the source of some of the centrifuge designs and perhaps equipment. On August 20, 2005, IAEA diplomats declared that the traces of highly enriched uranium on centrifuges in Natanz were not from Iranian domestic experiment, but rather from equipment provided by Pakistan. The Iranian government confirmed that "the source of contamination was not related to Iran . . . . We are sure that source is not internal."[7]

The Iranian exile group NCRI claimed that A.Q. Khan had actually delivered a small quantity of highly enriched uranium to Iran, but said that the amount was too small to produce nuclear weapons.[8] According to a September 2005 report by the IAEA, inspections found traces of weapons-grade uranium on equipment that was imported from Pakistan. According to press reports, the equipment was bought on the black market—presumably from the A.Q. Khan network. The IAEA report qualified these findings, however, stating that "it is still not possible at this time to establish a definite conclusion" about the other traces that were not yet enriched.[9]

It is important to know what help Pakistan offered to Iran, but it is also important to know that the HEU contamination did not come from Iran's own uranium enrichment program—which would have meant evidence of a nuclear program. This represents one uncertainty in understanding Iran's nuclear capabilities. No one outside Pakistan has been able to talk to A.Q. Khan about the type of help he provided to Tehran because of resistance by the Musharaf government. President Pervez Musharaf was concerned that giving IAEA, U.S., or European inspectors access to Khan could jeopardize Pakistan's own national security.

On March 10, 2005, however, the Pakistani government admitted that its nuclear scientist had sold Iran crucial components needed for enrichment. Pakistan's minister of information, Rashid Ahmed, said that A.Q. Khan "gave some centrifuges to Iran . . . . He helped Iran in his personal capacity, and the Pakistani government had nothing to do with it . . . . Yes, we supplied Iran the centrifuge system. Yes, Dr. Qadeer [Khan] gave Iran this technology.[10]

It was also reported that Bukhary Sayed Tahir, an alleged salesman in the A.Q. Khan network, had admitted to selling Iran three advanced centrifuges in the mid-1990s. The United States fears that these models can be used to manufacture thousands of P-2 centrifuges, which can move Iran's nuclear research beyond where it is believed to be now. This reported transaction also seems to contradict Iran's claims that the 1987 offer from A.Q. Khan provided it with the drawings of the P-2 designs but not the models. U.S. intelligence, however, believes that the claims by Tahir are uncertain, as they contradicted his previous statements as well as claims by other people in the Khan network who were involved in the offer to Iran.[11]

The extent of Pakistan's help to Iran is yet to be fully known. Even if the IAEA inspectors were granted complete access, it is unlikely that they could gather enough information to understand the full extent and history of the network's help. In addition, it remains uncertain how Iran used the help and equipment it received from Pakistan—to advance its nuclear research efforts or to weaponize its fissile materials.

The Role of Russia

Russia's relationship with Iran has a complex history. Current relations and Russian attitudes toward Iranian proliferation are equally intricate. Viktor Mizin, an official in the Russian Ministry of Foreign Affairs, summarized the thinking in Russia concerning Iran as follows:

> To understand Russian attitudes toward Iran, it is important to distinguish three major groups in the Russian political elite. The first could be termed proliferation zealots or proponents. These are the people who exchange a flurry of memos with the U.S. government and who formulate official Russian positions on nonproliferation, including the Iran case, which basically do not differ much from the official American approach as described by U.S. National Security Advisor Sandy Berger.
>
> Then, there are the people who manufacture armaments, and they could be called neutrals. Finally, the last group opposes any kind of export control or non-proliferation. They view such regimes as some sort of sly ruse devised by the U.S. government under the pressure of U.S. companies to squeeze out Russian armament makers from lucrative world markets. While the first group, the zealots or proponents, is engaged in endless consultation with Americans and signs all kinds of papers, the third group is constantly undermining the regime Russia signed on to.

It is also important to understand the difference in U.S. and Russian approaches to proliferation concerns. While certain people in Russia pay lip service to the politically correct notion that proliferation is dangerous, if one looks at the countries that are known as "rogue states" (in official Russian parlance, Moscow rejects the notion of rogue states), all of those countries are former clients of the Soviet Union: North Korea, Libya, Iraq, and others. And unlike the situation faced by the United States, the deployment of any ballistic missiles does not threaten Russian troops stationed abroad. There is also no political community in Russia—like in the United States—strong enough to influence the voting in the Parliament.

That is why one always hears very politically correct words from Russian political scientists about the concerns that Iran is developing missile capabilities. No one in the Russian political elite is seriously considering the threat of this development. For example, it was the same case with Saudi Arabia developing an IRBM potential.

Iran remains a very important market for the remnants of the Russian military industry. The collapse of the economy in Russia literally prods the best of Russian industry (the most technologically saturated companies), which have now lost state government procurement orders, literally to search for clients abroad. Russia officially considers the Bushehr reactor deal, for example, legitimate because Iran is under IAEA safeguards. [12]

In January 1995, Iran signed an $800 million contract with the Russian Ministry of Atomic Energy to complete reactors at Bushehr. This included a 1,000-megawatt reactor plant. It was scheduled to be completed in 2005, but the revelation in 2002 about Iran's uranium enrichment facility at Natanz and heavy water reactor at Arak led to further scrutiny of Iran's nuclear program. Russian president Vlamimir Putin promised the United States and the EU3 that Moscow would not provide Iran with the reactor unless it complied with the IAEA safeguards. The concern, however, is that Iran would use the technology and the reactors provided by Russia to advance its "covert" nuclear program.[13]

In spite of the perceived concealment activities by Iran, however, Moscow and Tehran signed a fuel supply deal in early 2005 that paved the way for Bushehr to come on-line in late 2006. In June 2005, President Putin said that Russia would continue its nuclear cooperation with Iran's new president, Mahmoud Ahmadinejad. In addition, the head of the Russian Atomic Energy Agency, Alexander Rumyantsev, announced that "Tehran intends to build another six nuclear reactors," and that Russia would be willing to help.[14]

Russian engineers continue their work on the Bushehr reactor. The Iranian-Russian negotiations regarding the Bushehr reactor and uranium enrichment continued through the referral of Iran to the United Nations Security Council. The United States, the EU3, the IAEA, and the UN secretary general have publicly backed the Russian plan, but privately, officials in France, Germany, the UK, and the United States have voiced skepticism about its chances of success. Many officials in Russia have expressed a determination to stop Iran from acquiring nuclear capabilities at all cost. They argue that it is not in the Russian Federation's interests to have a nuclear-armed Iran 165 kilometers from its border.[15]

These concerns were reflected in both Russia's willingness to report Iran to the UN Security Council and the many negotiations Moscow held with Tehran. In addition to its role in the Bushehr reactor, Russia led the negotiations in convincing Iran to abandon its uranium enrichment program. During March 2006, Russia and Iran held several meetings regarding Iranian enrichment experiments. Iran refused most of the deals that were offered by Russia, including a proposal presented on March 6, 2006. That proposal would have required Iran to put a moratorium on the production of enriched uranium on an industrial scale, but allowed it to carry on a small-scale "research and development" program. The United States, Europe, and many nonproliferation experts expressed their opposition to this deal. They argued that if Iran is able to enrich uranium on a small scale, it is only a matter of time before it moves to produce it at "industrial scale."[16]

The Role of North Korea

The history of North Korean help to Iran's nuclear and missile program is long and complex. As noted earlier, North Korea has been a major supplier of missile technology to Iran. Recently, scrutiny of the two countries by the international community may have limited the cooperation. Intelligence estimates in the summer of 2005, however, accused North Korea of helping Iran's nuclear program even during the IAEA inspections. An intelligence report was quoted by Reuters in July 2005 as follows:

> In the late 1990s, cooperation began between the two countries, which focused on nuclear (research and development) . . . . There has been a significant improvement in relations between Iran and North Korea over the past few months . . . [including a] special course to provide technological and practical information to outstanding students . . . . This nuclear cooperation between the two countries has apparently increased significantly during the past year as seen in the arrival of an academic delegation from North Korea in Iran and the existence of this special course . . . . It seems Iran is taking another step to promote its military nuclear project by exploiting North Korea's extensive technological information in the nuclear sphere.[17]

Some experts argued that the report was plausible even though its credibility was in question. As one IAEA expert described the report, "It is credible. No one would be surprised if this was true." Other experts went further to argue that the North Korean regime could replace the A.Q. Khan network as a major proliferator of nuclear technology to Iran.[18]

More recently, it was also reported that Western intelligence services were concerned about possible North Korean sales of plutonium to Iran, which could fast-track Iranian nuclear developments. Intelligence agencies point to the IAEA's discovery of the delivery of 1.7 tons of slightly enriched uranium hexafluoride. Press reports claimed that Iran and North Korea were in negotiations about an offer to exchange Iranian oil and gas shipments for plutonium from Pyongyang. The concern was over the revelation that North Korea was estimated to have produced 43–53 kilograms of plutonium, enough to use domestically and sell the rest to Iran. The negotiations reportedly were taking place directly between the IRGC and the North Korean regime.[19]

Other press reports have revealed evidence of North Korean help in building underground bunkers in Tehran to protect important nuclear sites. A North Korean team of scientists and experts visited Tehran in 2005 at the request of the IRGC to conduct a feasibility study of building underground facilities to house nuclear sites. London's *Daily Telegraph* quoted "Western intelligence" reports as saying that the North Korean plan was to construct several bunkers each with a space of 1,000–2,500 square meters (covering a total area of 10,000 square meters). Each bunker would be big enough to house the equipment needed to produce weapons-grade uranium.[20]

North Korea has also helped Iran develop its missile arsenal, as chapter 9 showed. Iran's Shahab program is highly dependent on North Korean-designed missiles such as the Scud-B, Scud-C, Nodong-1, Taep'o-dong-1, and Taep'o-dong-2. The later two are more worrisome, as they have a range of 3,000–6,000 kilometers (1,864–3,728 miles), which means they can reach beyond the Middle East. It has also been reported that Iran financed North Korea's missile program in exchange for the missile technology and the option to buy finished missiles. Although most observers agree that Iran's Shahab-4 and Shahab-5 are not yet operational, advances in North Korean missile technology can increase the pace of development of these ICBM.

The Role of China

Observers contend that China was Iran's main supplier of nuclear-related technologies during the 1980s. Some of those technologies included a small electromagnetic isotope separation (EMIS) machine and a 30-kilowatt-thermal research reactor. In addition, the United States claimed that China helped Tehran in building up its uranium mining capacity, fuel fabrication and uranium purification programs, and zirconium tube production. The United States did not believe, however, that Beijing provided Tehran with a nuclear weapons design.[21]

In the early 1990s, it was revealed that China had been helping Iran for nearly a decade. The help included training Iranian nuclear scientists, supplying Tehran with two "mini" research reactors, and providing the equipment used in electromagnetic isotope separation enrichment of weapons-grade uranium. These revelations and their implications have often played a major role in discussions between the Chinese and the Americans.[22]

In 1997, Beijing agreed to halt its nuclear cooperation with Tehran, including a uranium conversion project that the United States feared would provide Iran with the know-how to produce uranium hexafluoride (UF_6) or uranium dioxide (UO_2)—materials used in manufacturing weapons-grade plutonium. In addition, in 1998 China implemented new export controls that covered the export of dual-use equipment, and the United States concluded in 2001 that "China appears to be living up to its 1997 commitments."[23]

While the Chinese government may have kept its commitments, Chinese companies have been accused by the United States of helping Iran. In December 2005, the U.S. State Department sanctioned six Chinese companies along with one Australian and two Indian firms. The United States called the sanctions "an important and effective tool in constraining Iran's efforts to develop missile and WMD capabilities." U.S. sanctions against key Chinese companies such as China North Industries Group (Norinco) and China National Aero-Technology Import & Export prompted the Chinese government to state, "We are strongly dissatisfied with and firmly apposed to the U.S. government sanctioning Chinese companies . . . . [China] has always adopted a serious and responsible attitude on the anti-proliferation issue and has adopted a series of effective measures to strengthen export management control."[24]

In September 2005, the Iranian opposition group NCRI—the National Council of Resistance of Iran–issued the following statement about Iran's centrifuge enrichment program: "The first phase involves the manufacture of 5,000 machines. Some two-thirds have been manufactured, tested and [are] ready to be installed . . . . They have managed to smuggle centrifuges from China, to Dubai, to Tehran . . . in the last two years."[25] These allegations remain unconfirmed, however, particularly those regarding the number of centrifuges. Some believe that Iran may have the design for the centrifuges, but many experts believe that the Iranian nuclear research does not have the capabilities yet to manufacture that many centrifuge machines. It is equally important to note that the IAEA inspections plus technical difficulties encountered may well have delayed Iranian efforts.

POSSIBLE ECONOMIC SANCTIONS

Economic sanctions are often used when diplomatic solutions fail in order to prevent the exercise of a military option. Many experts, however, believe that sanctions have become what Jeffrey Schott calls a "way station" to the use of military force.[26]

Sanctions have been imposed in numerous cases. Economic sanctions, however, have a poor success record. A study by the Institute for International Economics (IIE) estimated that there were 115 cases of economic sanctions between 1914 and 1990. However, only 40 cases (35 percent) were deemed successful. When the United States was part of the sanctions coalition, the impact on the success rate was modest. At times the involvement of the United States improved the rate, but at other times it actually hurt the rate of success.[27]

In addition, over time, the success ratio for economic sanctions is declining. For example, the success rate for cases between 1914 and 1945 was 50 percent; between 1945 and 1969, 44 percent; and between 1970 and 1989, 26 percent.[28]

The declining success rate of economic sanctions is due to several reasons:

- First, sanctions are often violated through smuggling and backdoor deals to benefit the ruling elite while hurting the general population.

- Second, with a globalized economy, countries under sanctions have alternatives. While some countries abide by sanctions many nations and companies are willing to trade and violate imposed restrictions to advance their economic and commercial interests.

- Third, sanctions are highly politicized, and this gives other nations the reasons to violate them. Political rivalries between nations often drive some to utilize sanctions to advance national strategic, military, and commercial interests.

- Fourth, technology and capital markets are widely available, making it possible for nations to import from third parties. For example, even if the United States stops the export of its computer chips to a nation, the same product or a close substitute exists elsewhere and can be easily imported.

That said, sanctions can be useful diplomatic tools, without resorting to a military option, to pressure nations to change their policies or at least come to the bargaining table. Economic sanctions, arms embargo, trade restrictions, private divestments, and diplomatic pressures worked to end apartheid in South Africa. The United Nations Security Council the United Nations General Assembly, and the Organization of African Unity, supported by key European powers like France and the UK, and the United States forced the South African government to end apartheid. Although they took a long time to be effective, the sanctions worked once they were adopted by key trading partners and had an effect on many aspects of the South African economy.

In the case of Iran, it is too early to predict whether the UN Security Council will impose sanctions, or the nature of any sanctions, or their effectiveness. It is also uncertain if Iran's key trading partners on the Security Council would allow broad export and import sanctions or even targeted sanctions on certain sectors. China and Russia have said that they would oppose any sanctions proposed by the Security Council; many attribute their opposition to their commercial and trade interests with Iran. France and Britain have sent mixed messages about their willingness to go along with an economic sanctions regime. That leaves the United States out of the five permanent members of the Security Council as fully supporting punitive measures against Iran.

A European diplomat has described deciding on the sanctions as "most difficult debate ever." The difficulty for Europe is that "sanctions would hurt the people in Iran, not the elite. If we were to talk about sanctions, then maybe they would be targeted on certain people. But I repeat, we have not raised the options of sanctions."[29]

Iran's strategy is to use this ambivalence among the European nations and use its trade and energy leverage with other powers to stop the Security Council from imposing sanctions against it. In addition, Iranian officials have argued that if the United States and the EU impose sanctions against Iran, Western economies will suffer more than Iran's.

That argument is partially true, but it also depends on the type of sanctions. The Security Council has several options that could exert pressure on the Iranian government—each with different enforcement mechanisms, but none that are without consequences.

The Nature of Effective Economic Sanctions

Far too often, economic sanctions are levied to serve immediate political or national interests without taking into account the long-term strategic implications. For economic sanctions to be effective they must be tailored and targeted to achieve their objective and their repercussions must be understood.

Experts also argue that the objective of sanctions must be "modest" if they are to achieve their goals in a reasonable time period. There are no risk-free options or violation-proof sanctions, but the chances of success of economic sanctions can be vastly improved by having well-defined objectives. The goal of the UN Security Council in the case of Iran is to prevent the Iranian government from acquiring nuclear weapons capabilities. If the debate drifts toward regime change, however, or stopping Iran's support of proxy groups, it is likely to divide the international community and diminish the chances that the sanctions will succeed. In addition, if the sanctions turn out to weaken the economic well-being of the Iranian population, the sanctions will likely defeat their purpose.

Iraq is a good case in point. The UN sanctions levied against Iraq following its invasion of Kuwait in 1990 were intended to stop the regime of Saddam Hussein from importing weapons technology, but most of the burden fell on the Iraqi population. The Iraqi regime was able to use the oil-for-food program to build palaces, while at the same time blaming the sanctions for the worsening standards of living for Iraqi citizens and using the suffering of the population as information warfare to gather sympathy for its cause. In addition, oil was smuggled and sold on the black market solely to benefit the regime. Thus while the sanctions may have achieved one of their goals—to stop Iraq from rebuilding its military and WMD capabilities—some argue that the costs of the sanctions may have outweighed their benefits in the grand strategic sense.

It is equally important to note that sanctions could well fail to achieve their objective of stopping Iran from acquiring nuclear capabilities. Despite the economic and diplomatic costs of sanctions, nations can feel that the benefits to their national security interests outweigh those costs. For example, sanctions did not stop India and Pakistan from acquiring nuclear weapons because of their perception that their national security was threatened.[30] The sanctions on both countries have been lifted and they are now accepted as nuclear powers.

The Difficulty of Enforcing Sanctions

One key difficulty in enforcing economic sanctions on Iran is that Iran's economy is more of a command economy than a free market. Some estimate that the government controls nearly 80 percent of the total economy. Experts argue that the absence of a vibrant private sector means there is no strong business class that could pressure the government to comply with Security Council demands so that sanctions could be lifted.[31]

Another equally important aspect of Iran's economy is that while energy exports might be important to the economy, total net trade is only a small portion of Iran's total gross domestic product (GDP). In 2005, Iran's total real GDP was $551.6 billion, of which 1 percent was net exports (current account balance). Iran exported an estimated $55.42 billion (10 percent of its GDP) and imported an estimated $42.5 billion (8 percent of GDP).[32]

The difficulty lies, however, not only in the size of Iran's net trade, but in the diversity of its trading partners. Its key exporting partners are Japan, 18.4 percent; China, 9.7 percent; Italy, 6 percent; South Africa, 5.8 percent; South Korea, 5.4 percent; Taiwan, 4.6 percent; Turkey, 4.4 percent; and Netherlands, 4 percent. Its key importing partners are Germany, 12.8 percent; France, 8.3 percent; Italy, 7.7 percent; China, 7.2 percent; the UAE, 7.2 percent; South Korea. 6.1 percent; and Russia, 5.4 percent.[33]

As these percentages show, Russian and China are not the only major players. Table 10.1 shows Iran's key trading partners between 2000 and 2004. Iran trades with virtually every country in the world. Its largest trading region is Asia. This is due largely to Iran's oil exports, but also to geographic proximity and lower costs. The table also shows that exports and imports are growing, and that Iran's dependence on international trade is steadily increasing. Iran's imports doubled from $14.3 billion in 2000 to $38.25 billion in 2004. The value of its exports increased at a slightly lower rate, from $25.0 billion in 2000 to nearly $41.0 billion in 2004.

Table 10.1
Iran's Key Trading Partners, 2000–2004
(in U.S. millions)

	Exports					Imports				
	2000	2001	2002	2003	2004	2000	2001	2002	2003	2004
Key Countries[a]										
China (PRC)	1,612	2,203	2,133	3,014	3,961	565	887	1,046	2,550	2,762
France	960	670	720	1,078	1,614	617	1,109	1,318	2,598	3,186
Germany	478	330	273	292	443	1,504	1,807	3,777	3,318	4,900
Greece	1,079	879	415	882	1,296	10	19	8	12	23
India	428	462	241	241	333	254	561	717	937	1,253
Italy	2,032	1,920	1,620	1,946	2,452	856	996	1,389	2,442	2,962
Japan	4,869	4,561	4,311	6,764	7,515	684	787	714	1,236	1,231
Netherlands	989	206	620	1,171	1,655	270	346	308	465	715
Russia	49	31	45	56	101	920	914	874	1,451	2,081
South Korea	2,175	1,908	1,214	1,677	2,214	737	958	894	1,956	2,348
South Africa	1,167	1,027	917	1,238	2,357	103	73	36	44	59
Turkey	742	763	837	1,692	1,783	233	291	369	587	891
United Kingdom	46	39	49	45	72	510	666	769	852	897
United States	159	135	148	152	142	94	74	68	109	94

(continued)

Developing Regions[b]	11,230	10,278	8,746	12,796	17,538	6,893	8,841	9,744	16,018	19,809
Middle East	398	432	425	471	1,234	1,290	2,015	2,704	3,467	4,068
Africa	1,600	1,314	1,204	1,392	2,779	208	153	119	153	159
Asia	8,065	7,400	5,928	8,797	11,201	2,462	3,219	3,740	7,289	8,730
Europe	1,110	1,115	1,173	2,114	2,313	1,988	2,133	2,132	3,973	5,367
W. Hemisphere	57	17	16	22	11	945	1,321	1,049	1,136	1,485
Industrial Countries	12,285	10,297	9,469	14,192	17,169	7,356	8,715	12,468	14,474	18,284
Others[c]	3,376	3,643	3,874	4,696	6,214	97	135	114	127	164
Total[d]	26,891	24,219	22,090	31,683	40,921	14,347	17,690	22,324	30,619	38,257

Source: Adapted from International Monetary Fund (IMF), Direction of Trade Statistics Yearbook 2005 (Washington, D.C.: IMF, 2005).

Note: Due to rounding off, numbers do not always add up exactly.

[a] These countries are Iran's major trading partners and/or permanent members of the United Nations Security Council.

[b] These include subregions that are considered developing by the IMF.

[c] "Others" are those referred to by the IMF as "Countries/Areas ns," which includes trade whose origin or destination is "not specified."

[d] The total is the sum of Developing Regions, Industrial Countries, and Others.

All the permanent UN Security Council members have strong trade ties with Iran with the exception of the United States. In volume, nearly all of Iran's exports and imports with China, the UK, France, and Russia at least doubled between 2000 and 2004:

- **China**: exports to Iran increased by 159 percent and imports from Iran grew by 389 percent.

- **France**: exports to Iran increased by 68 percent and imports from Iran grew by 416 percent.

- **Russia**: exports to Iran increased by 106 percent and imports from Iran grew by 126 percent.

- **UK**: exports to Iran increased by 57 percent and imports from Iran grew by 76 percent.

- **United States**: exports to Iran declined by 11 percent and imports from Iran remained the same.

Enforcing economic sanctions would mean ensuring that all of these key trading partners stop trading with Iran. If the sanctions target Iranian imports of goods and services, then it means removing key markets for many of these economies. That may complicate the dynamics of enforcing such sanctions. So might sanctions that target Iranian energy exports. In 2005, China, for example, imported 0.30 million barrels per day (mmbpd), or roughly 5 percent) of its oil needs, from Iran.

Some have argued that China's interests go beyond its immediate energy demands, given that Chinese energy demand is estimated to grow at 14 percent between 2005 and 2007 and reach 7.9 mmbpd in 2007, according to the EIA. To secure energy supplies, China Sinopec has been active and successful in obtaining energy deals and investment opportunities in the Gulf. For example, Sinopec may sign a major agreement worth $100 billion regarding Iran's Yadavaran oil field.[34] If signed, the arrangement would involve China's purchase of 10 million tons of liquefied natural gas per year for the next century.[35]

Observers point to the fact that China stopped the passage of UN Security Council sanctions against Sudan because of China's oil interest. China is seen as not willing to agree to any economic sanctions that affect Iran's energy exports. The same applies for other Security

Council members such as Russia, although Russia's motivation is not energy security per se. Russia has maintained a long-term commercial and military relationship with Tehran. Moscow has also been in negotiations to build the Bushehr reactor. Losing that contract would mean a loss to Russia's economy. Other European powers are heavily invested in Iran's energy sector, including major French, Italian, and British energy firms. For example, the British firm Total signed a $2 billion contract with Iran to develop liquefied natural gas.[36]

These trade and commercial interests complicate the choice of sanctions even further. There is always the incentive to cheat or "free ride." Even if countries believe in stopping Iran from acquiring nuclear capabilities, it is unclear if they want to pay for it in domestic political terms. Trade relations are local political issues as much as they are global phenomena. Countries must be convinced of the danger in order to impose sanctions and give up access to markets. In the case of Iran, countries imposing the sanctions have to realize two key things: (1) Iran is a threat to their national security and international peace; and (2) sanctions will prevent Iran from acquiring WMD capabilities, which can have an impact on their vital interests.

At times, long-term strategic interests come ahead of economics. For example, regional powers such as Saudi Arabia and Egypt are unlikely to support a sanctions regime against Iran. While Iran's trade with the region has more than doubled in the last four years (Iran's exports to the Middle East increased by 260 percent and its imports from the region increased by 215 percent), what may prevent the region from agreeing to economic sanctions against Iran goes beyond their commercial and trade interests.

As noted earlier, although regional powers are concerned about the threat of proliferation, they argue that the United States and the UN must adopt a single standard in dealing with the region. A WMD-free Middle East, they argue, must include Israel, Pakistan, and India. This reaction is partly to increase the pressure on Israel and partly because of concern about further escalation of WMD proliferation in the Middle East to other states.[37]

Other countries in the region that are not major trading partners with Iran, have by and large the same trading partners as Iran. Iran can import goods, and they may in fact defy the sanctions against Iran. Certainly, some nations in the region did comply with the UN sanctions against Iraq during the 1990s. Many, however, did not enforce the oil-for-food program and allowed Iraq to use their territories as smuggling routes for sanctioned goods and markets for its oil.

These difficulties of enforcing sanctions bring up another important element in crafting effective economic sanctions: sanctions must be universal. Although the United States has long maintained sanctions against Iran, table 10.1 shows that Tehran has maintained strong trading relations with many countries in the EU, Asia, and the Middle East.

The Nature of U.S. Sanctions against Iran

The United States has maintained sanctions against Iran since the revolution and the seizure of American hostages on November 4, 1979. It also has extended and strengthened the sanctions several times. President Bill Clinton signed two executive orders in March and May 1995 banning U.S. companies and their foreign subsidiaries from doing business with Iran or financing projects in Iran's petroleum sector.[38] .

U.S. economic sanctions against Iran were strengthened further in the Iran-Libya Sanctions Act (ILSA) that was passed by the U.S. Congress in August 1996 and was extended for five years in July 2001. The act imposes sanctions of up to $20 million annually on any company investing in Iran's gas and oil sector. The Clinton administration reinforced the sanctions again in 1997 by prohibiting all U.S. nationals from investing in Iran. In March 2000, the United States allowed for importation of Iranian carpets, caviar, pistachios, and dried fruits into the United States, but did not relax the sanctions against other products or direct investment in Iran. The sanctions were extended by President George W. Bush in March 2003, who cited Iran's support for international terrorism .[39]

Still, even though U.S.-imposed sanctions have stopped U.S. companies from investing in Iran's energy industry, many multinational companies have invested in that industry since the passing of ILSA in 1996. The penalties under ILSA that target foreign companies were opposed by many countries that had energy interests in Iran. The EU, for example, passed a resolution in 1996 directing European companies not to comply with the U.S. sanctions regime.[40] It is estimated that since ILSA's passage, Iran has attracted $30 billion of foreign direct investment in its oil and gas sectors.

The United States has investigated Italian, Russian, Japanese, Canadian, French, and Malaysian companies regarding their investment in Iran's energy industry. It is believed, however, that penalties under ILSA have not been imposed on any foreign or U.S. company. [41] Experts question the cost of U.S. sanctions against Iran and doubt their success. The United States imposed the sanctions against Iran for several reasons—high among them to stop Iran from pursuing CBRN capabilities, to end its support of proxy groups that are attacking Israel, and to end incitement against the United States. A quarter century later, the sanctions have not achieved any of their goals—partly because of the lack of meaningful enforcement mechanisms and partly because they were not universally accepted and enforced.

The U.S.-imposed sanctions may have stopped Iran from importing spare parts for its American-made conventional weapons, but they have not deterred it from importing other weapons, building missile systems, advancing its nuclear research program, and continuing to fund proxy groups. Although some of the lack of foreign direct investment in Iran's gas and oil industries has been the result of U.S. sanctions, much of Iran's aging infrastructure is due to self-inflicted wounds. Iranian bureaucracy and lack of meaningful plans to attract foreign direct investment to its oil and gas sectors have prevented Iran from upgrading its infrastructure and expanding its capacity.

Iran may be able to offer better deals in the future. The rise in global oil demand and the surge in the price of oil increased the government's oil revenues, as shown in figure 10.1. For example, between 2002 and 2005 Iran's oil revenues in constant dollars doubled. Extra revenues can be used to rebuild its energy infrastructure, but they can also be used to recapitalize its conventional military forces and even its WMD and missile programs.

Figure 10.1 also shows that Iran can sell its oil to willing buyers at market prices. Oil and gas are global commodities, and are bought in an open market. Sanctions by the United States would have little impact on Iran's oil revenues or on Iran's overall production and export capacities.

Figure 10.1
Iran's Net Oil Export Revenues, 1971–2007
(in $billions)

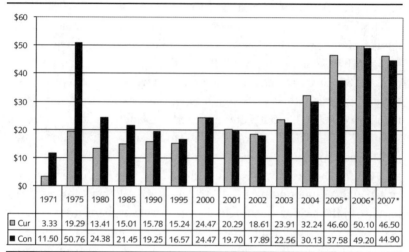

	1971	1975	1980	1985	1990	1995	2000	2001	2002	2003	2004	2005*	2006*	2007*
▢ Cur	3.33	19.29	13.41	15.01	15.78	15.24	24.47	20.29	18.61	23.91	32.24	46.60	50.10	46.50
■ Con	11.50	50.76	24.38	21.45	19.25	16.57	24.47	19.70	17.89	22.56	30.13	37.58	49.20	44.90

Source: Energy Information Administration (EIA), "OPEC Revenues Fact Sheet,"
    several editions, http://www.eia.doe.gov.
Note: Cur = Current dollars; Con = Constant dollars.
*Figures for 2005, 2006, and 2007 are projected total oil revenues.

In summary, past U.S. sanctions against Iran have had some impact on Iran's economy. They certainly have prevented U.S. foreign direct investment from flowing into the Iranian energy sector, and they have contributed to slowing the rate of expansion of its oil and gas production capacity. Other factors, however, have contributed far more to the economic problems Iran is suffering.

- First, its command economy continues to prevent the rise of a vibrant private sector that can drive and attract investment, offer employment, and provide the stability of a middle class. The government continues to be the largest employer, investor, and consumer in Iran.

- Second, Iranian foreign investment laws are dated. They have many protectionist characteristics that have prevented many necessary investments from flowing into the Iranian economy, particularly its energy sector.

- Third, Iran's banking systems and lending mechanisms are rigid and not able to keep up with the growth in the global economy and Iranian domestic investment needs.

- Finally, despite diversification and privatization efforts, Iran continues to rely heavily on oil exports. In 2005, oil accounted for 80–90 percent of Iran's export earnings and 40–50 percent of the government's budget.[42]

The Problems of Oil Sanctions

For sanctions against Iran to be effective, they must target the most important export commodities—oil and gas. Iran is the second-largest oil producer after Saudi Arabia and holds the world's fourth-largest pool of proven oil reserves (approximately 126 billion barrels or 10 percent of the world's total). Yet its production dropped by more than a third from a peak of over 6.0 mmbpd in 1974 to about 4.1 mmbpd in 2005.[43]

One implication of targeted economic sanctions against Iran's oil and gas sectors is a further diminution of its upstream and downstream infrastructure. Iran's domestic energy demands are growing at high rates. Between 2003 and 2010, the International Energy Agency (IEA) projects Iran's primary energy demand to grow by 3.4 percent a year, its demand for power generation and water desalination to increase by 4.1 percent a year, its demand for transport fuel to grow by 3.1 percent a year, and its electricity generation to grow by 4.9 percent a year.[44]

Figure 10.2 shows the trends in Iran's oil production and exports. Years of political isolation, recurring wars, and U.S. sanctions have deprived the Iranian oil sector of needed investment. Iran's share of total world oil trade peaked at 17.2 percent in 1972, then declined to 2.6 percent in 1980, but has since recouped to roughly 5 percent. Iranian oil exports declined even further since the revolution. In 1975, Iran exported 4.88 mmbpd; in 2005, it exported roughly 2.63 mmbpd (3 percent of total world exports).

According to the IEA, Iran's net oil exports are estimated to reach 2.8 mmbpd in 2010, 3.6 mmbpd in 2020, and 4.4 mmbpd in 2030. This would represent an average increase of 1.9 percent per year from its 2.7 mmbpd in 2004 (the EIA estimates that Iran's oil exports in 2004 were 2.55 mmbpd).[45]

Regardless of the exact number, cutting 5 percent of the world's oil supply might well increase the price per barrel by more that 5 percent if one takes into account the possibility of market panics, political or military miscalculations, and the fear of sustaining these sanctions.

Figure 10.2
Iran's Oil Production and Exports, 1971–2006
(in million barrels per day)

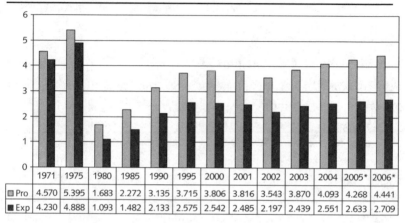

	1971	1975	1980	1985	1990	1995	2000	2001	2002	2003	2004	2005*	2006*
Pro	4.570	5.395	1.683	2.272	3.135	3.715	3.806	3.816	3.543	3.870	4.093	4.268	4.441
Exp	4.230	4.888	1.093	1.482	2.133	2.575	2.542	2.485	2.197	2.439	2.551	2.633	2.709

Source: Energy Information Administration (EIA), "Oil Export Revenues Fact
    Sheet," 2005, http://www.eia.doe.gov.
Note: Pro = Production; Exp = Exports.
* Figures for 2005 and 2006 are projected levels.

Given the tightness of the global energy market, Iran's oil exports remain an important element in keeping oil prices at moderate levels. Total world oil supply is barely meeting total world oil demand. According to the U.S. Energy Information Administration (EIA), on average, the world consumed 83.10 mmbpd compared to a total world oil supply of 83.97 mmbpd in 2005.

Some have argued that the United States is not importing oil from Iran, and that the impact of disrupting Iran's oil supply will not affect U.S. energy demands. These arguments are largely specious. First, even if the United States is not directly importing oil from the Islamic Republic, the U.S. economy is highly dependent on energy-intensive imports that come from Asia. Cutting Iranian exports to Taiwan, South Korea, Japan, or China is likely to have an indirect effect on the U.S. and global economy. Second, temporary disruption or, even worse, sustained cutoff of Iranian oil exports will increase the price per barrel of oil for everyone in the world, including the United States. Third, high oil prices can have devastating effect on the global economy and, in turn, on the U.S. economy.

Equally important, the world oil market will have excess demand without a viable way to replace Iranian production. With the exception of Saudi Arabia, world oil producers do not have surplus capacity. During past shortages, Saudi Arabia played the swing producer to replace Iraqi, Venezuelan, Nigerian, or U.S. production decreases. The Kingdom, however, has a surplus production capacity of roughly 1.5 mmbpd (with plans to reach 2.5 by 2009), but this is simply not enough to replace 4.0 mmbpd of production capacity.

Other experts have argued that industrialized countries can minimize the damage of any supply shortages by using the crude reserves that the United States and other International Energy Agency members have. It is estimated that IEA members hold 1.48 billion barrels of oil in their emergency stocks, equivalent to 2.4 mmbpd for 600 days.[46] In addition, Saudi Arabia has an estimated 1.5 mmbpd of surplus capacity. These additions (3.9 mmbpd) can certainly compensate for disruptions of Iran's oil exports, but the real question is how sustainable those additions are. The emergency stocks are limited and will run out in two years, and for Saudi Arabia to produce at capacity with no cushion can cause market unease.

There have been some studies of the impact of cutting Iranian oil exports. Virtually all predict that the price per barrel of oil might exceed $100 if Iran stopped its energy exports. One study predicted that the price per barrel could reach $131 if Iran stopped oil production.[47] Other energy experts have estimated that even if Iran cut its production by a small amount, given the tightness of the oil market the price per barrel of oil could exceed $100.[48]

Reaching or exceeding the $100 per barrel price mark—even for very short periods—could play a major psychological role in driving the energy market even further toward panic and further increases in energy prices. However, these attempts to project into the future are more "guesstimates" than perfect forecasts. Energy analyses and projections about the impact of supply shortages are uncertain at best. It is even more unpredictable when one tries to judge the impact of hypothetical sanctions without knowing the reaction of the Iranian government, the global energy market response, or the response of other oil and gas exporters.

Some Israeli experts have argued that the only effective sanctioning regime is a total embargo on Iran's oil trade. The author of the proposal, Aluf Benn, was quoted as follows: "No country is dependent in its energy requests, its energy demands, upon Iran. [But] the Iranian oil industry, for instance, they need to export oil not only for the cash, but also to get back refined oil products like gasoline and other products because they don't have enough refinery capacity."[49]

It is one thing to impose an oil embargo; it is another thing to enforce it. As noted earlier, the damage to Iran may not be high enough to cause a change of heart with regard to its nuclear research. The government in Tehran can violate sanctions with smuggling, use the money to advance its military and nuclear programs, and blame the world for the economic suffering of its population.

Iran can also carry out its own "sanctions" by launching an oil embargo. An oil embargo seems an unlikely choice for the UN Security Council, given the consequences and the national interest of key member states. But Iran might choose to cut off its oil supply in response to other types of sanctions. Iranian officials have argued that they do not need the West, but that the West needs their energy exports. Iran can also shoot itself in the foot by cutting off 80 to 90 percent of its export revenues, but in such uncharted territories all options are on the table. Given the intricate nature of diplomacy at the Security Council and the fragile internal political dynamics in Iran, even non-desirable options may become viable—including acting irrationally.

Iranian officials have left potential oil embargos or disrupting energy supply through the Strait of Hormuz on the table. A member of Iran's parliament, Mohammad Nabi Rudaki, who serves on the parliament's National Security and Foreign Policy committee, put it this way: "Oil is exported from Iran and the Persian Gulf territorial states to Europe and America, and East Asia; the Strait of Hormuz, the Persian Gulf and, in case of a referral or an air or economic embargo, not even one drop of oil will be exported from this region. . . . the Islamic Republic of Iran is able to hinder oil exportation from the coast of the Persian Gulf and our own oil if Europe fails to handle the nuclear case wisely and imposes unfair economic sanctions on Iran."[50]

Refined Products Sanctions

The traditional economy of Iran (e.g., carpets, caviar, pistachios) is another unlikely area for sanctions, as such sanctions would largely affect farmers and small businesses without major implications on the Iranian government. Such sectors are also self-sustained, because they are not dependent on imports.

Other sectors, however, are highly dependent on imports and would be more affected by economic sanctions. Sectors such as industry, for example, play a major role in Iran's economy. It is estimated that 43.3 percent of Iran's GDP is dependent on industry, 44.9 percent on services, and 11.8 percent on agriculture.[51] Security Council members would find it hard to justify the use of sanctions against agricultural products—except for dual-use technologies and fertilizers that can be used in the production of WMD—but industrial sanctions might be a different story.

Iran's heavier industries that rely on imports of refined products would suffer from economic sanctions. Iran's dependence on imports of gasoline has surged since 1982 due the damage to the refineries during the Iran-Iraq War, mismanagement of the refineries, and the lack of foreign investment in the refinery sector. According to the IEA, Iran's refining sector is inefficient. For example, only 13 percent of the refinery output is gasoline—which is estimated to be half of what European refineries produce.[52]

In 2004, Iran imported an estimated 0.160 million barrels a day of oil equivalent of gasoline (40 percent of its domestic consumption). Iran's dependence on gasoline import steadily increased in 2005 and 2006. Iran imported an estimated 0.170 mmbpd of gasoline (41 percent of its domestic consumption) in 2005, and is projected to import 0.196 mmbpd (43 percent of its domestic consumption) in 2006. It is noteworthy that 60 percent of Iran's gasoline is imported from Europe, 15 percent from India, and the rest from elsewhere (Middle East and Asia).[53]

These trends are likely to continue. Iran's domestic demand for gasoline is estimated to increase at approximately 9 percent per year, and the costs of gasoline imports are also steadily increasing. For example, Iran paid an estimated $2.5–$3.0 billion for its gas imports in 2004 and an estimated $4.5 billion in 2005.[54] Other experts, however, estimate that the cost of importing refined products was as high a $10 billion in 2005.[55] This figure is likely to include jet fuels, diesel, residual oil, kerosene, and other products.

Iran's dependence on gasoline imports is unlikely to change in the near future. It is estimated that Iran is planning to spend $16 billion between 2003 and 2030 to expand its refinery capacity from 1.5 mmbpd in 2004 to 1.7 mmbpd in 2010, 2.2 mmbpd in 2020, and 2.6 mmbpd in 2030. However, its total energy demand and consumption of refined products are also estimated to increase at higher rates.[56]

Sanctioning exports of refined products to Iran would certainly have an impact on the Iranian economy, but the effectiveness of such a sanctions regime would be uncertain. Iran can get around the imposed sanctions through unofficial deals and smuggling. In addition, Iran is enjoying high oil revenues and may well use them to fast-track its plans to expand refining capacity. Tehran might use such deals to attract foreign companies and to further complicate a UN Security Council resolution, as some of those contracts might go to Chinese, Russian, French, German, and British firms.

Travel Restrictions

Some have argued that the first round of sanctions against Iran should target Iranian officials directly. This would include restricting Iranian officials, including the president, Mahmoud Ahmadinejad, as well as other top officials and clerics, from traveling outside Iran.

These sanctions would have little impact on the general population. And although they might affect the mobility of Iranian officials, their impact would be limited. Travel sanctions are difficult to enforce outside the EU and the United States. Their impact could be further complicated if Iranian officials were prevented from attending UN meetings in the United States or the EU. Middle Eastern and Asian countries might find it hard to comply with these travel restrictions—given the fragile strategic situation in the region.

If the goal is to send a message to the Iranian government and the world that the international community does not approve of Iran's nuclear weapons, then such sanctions might do that. It is questionable, however, whether travel restrictions would change the attitudes or actions of the Iranian government or the attitudes of the Iranian public toward acquiring nuclear technology. Iran's nuclear research program does not depend on the ability of the Iranian president to visit Paris. Thus the impact of such sanctions would be symbolic in the case of Iran.

The historical precedents also are not reassuring. For example, the EU has maintained travel restrictions and financial sanctions against Zimbabwe. The targeted sanctions included travel bans, an oil embargo, and freezing of financial assets of President Robert Mugabe and 100 other senior Zimbabwean officials. The ban has been extended several times since its inception in February 2002 and is expected to run out in February 2007. These extensions make the point that either these travel restrictions did not work or they need a long time to work.

Financial Sanctions

Travel restrictions and financial sanctions combined are an option that might have more effect. This may, in fact, be the set of sanctions that would arouse the least amount of resistance by Security Council members. Most of the Iranian financial assets being held in the West belong to the government or the ruling elite of Iran. The combination of travel restrictions and freezing assets held in Westerns banks can have the least impact on the general population and apply the maximum amount of pressure on the ruling elites.

Although U.S. capital markets have been closed to the Iranian government since the revolution, Iran had alternative sources. Iran relies on loans particularly from European and Asian banks to finance domestic projects in its energy sector.[57] For example, Iran's shipbuilding and car manufacturing sectors are growing faster than Iranian domestic financial institutions, and those industries have relied on European banks for investment loans. A number of European banks stopped doing business with Tehran, but many others continue to finance projects in Iran, including major European banks such as HSBC, BNP Paribas, Deutsche Bank, Commerzbank, Standard Chartered, and Royal Bank of Scotland. Observers have argued that targeting loans from European banks can have major impact on Iran's economy, particularly since the Iranian capital market is still small and key industries in Iran cannot survive without investment loans from the outside.[58]

Another way to target Iranian finances is to freeze Iranian assets in European and Asian banks. Iran's financial assets in the United States have been frozen since the revolution, but Tehran has a significant amount of financial assets in European financial institutions. There are no reliable estimates as to the size of Iran's hard currency deposits. It is safe to assume, however, that it is a large amount, given the recent surge in oil prices. Some estimates put it at $36 billion in 2005.

The significance of this can be seen through the reaction of the Iranian government following the IAEA's referral of Iran's case to the UN Security Council. In January 2006, the governor of Iran's central bank announced that Iran had started transferring its assets out of European banks. It is unclear where the funds have been moved, but there are indications and initial admission that they may have been transferred to Southeast Asia.[59]

It has also been reported that Iranian government figures have started to move their money from European financial institutions to Dubai, Hong Kong, Malaysia, Beirut, and Singapore. Iranian officials were quoted as saying that as much as $8 billion was moved out of Europe.[60]

Sanctions can reach beyond European financial institutions to include Asian banks and international NGOs such as the World Bank and the International Monetary Fund. This will drain another key source of financial support to the Iranian government. For example, in May 2005, the World Bank approved loans to Iran in the amounts of $344 million to support the Caspian provinces in managing scare water resources, $200 million for rebuilding following the Bam earthquake in October 2004, and $359 million to the government of Iran to improve housing, sanitation, and access to clean water in Ahvaz and Shiraz.[61] These loans are focused on humanitarian projects, but that does not mean that they cannot be delayed to force Iran back to the bargaining table.

The global economy offers many options to Iran, and enforcing such sanctions is not perfect. Iran is not confined to European private and central banks or international organizations to finance its domestic projects. If Iran does build enough incentives for foreign direct investment, no amount of sanctions can stop the flow of money into the country, particularly in its energy sector.

All of these scenarios are hypothetical at this point. It is unclear if the UN Security Council will actually agree to impose financial restrictions on Iran. In addition, no one can fully predict the response of the Iranian government, the ruling elite in Iran, or the Iranian general population. Clearly, freezing money and restricting the travel of key regime figures is far less disagreeable to some UN Security Council members than preventing investment in Iran's energy sector and causing further tightness in the global energy market. It is also clear that these restrictions might put more pressure on the regime than any broad economic sanctions that have direct implications on the Iranian population.

Arms Embargo

Another type of sanctions is an embargo on conventional arms imports. While Iran produces some small arms and even missiles, its indigenous military industrial complex is not yet able to produce most heavy arms at industrial levels. Iran imports most of its conventional military weapons, and much of its present weaponry is worn or obsolete.

Iran has not obtained significant amounts of U.S. or Western European arms since 1980 or, indeed, significant amounts of modern arms from any of its other suppliers at the time of the shah. Most of its deliveries during 1988–1992 were relatively low-grade weapons, although Russia did supply some modern armor and aircraft. Iran then faced major financial problems until the mid-1990s and could not obtain resupply or new weapons from most Western states.

Iran was a major importer of other Western systems during the Iran-Iraq War. However, Iran did not carry out a major arms import effort once the Iran-Iraq War was over and it received the backlog of arms imports from the orders it placed during the war. Figure 10.3 shows the drastic decline in Iranian arms deliveries from 1993 to 2004. According to unclassified U.S. intelligence estimates, Iran received roughly $2.6 billion of new arms deliveries between 1993 and 1996, $1.9 billion between 1997 and 2000, and only $500 between 2001 and 2004. This represents an 81 percent decline in Iran's overall arms deliveries.

Figure 10.3
Arms Deliveries to Iran by Supplier, 1993–2004
(in $U.S.millions)

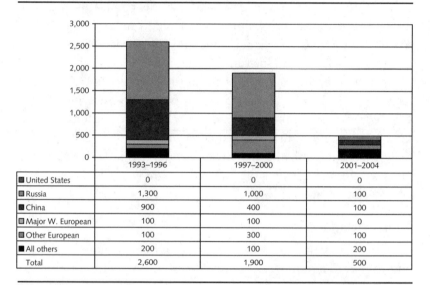

	1993–1996	1997–2000	2001–2004
■ United States	0	0	0
▨ Russia	1,300	1,000	100
■ China	900	400	100
▨ Major W. European	100	100	0
▨ Other European	100	300	100
■ All others	200	100	200
Total	2,600	1,900	500

Sources: Richard F. Grimmett, *Conventional Arms Transfers to Developing Nations, 1997–2004*, Congressional Reference Service, August 29, 2005; and Richard F. Grimmett, *Conventional Arms Transfers to Developing Nations, 1993–2000*, Congressional Reference Service, August 16, 2001.

The trends in Iran's new arms agreements are similar. As figure 10.4 shows, Iran's *new* arms agreements have been on the decline. Between 1993 and 1996, Iran signed $1.2 billion of new agreements; this rose slightly to $1.5 billion between 1997 and 2000, but then declined to $800 million between 2001 and 2004.

It is important to understand where Iranian arms are coming from and how this might affect the behavior of China and Russia. As figures 10.3 and 10.4 show, Iran has received arms from a variety of sources, including China, Russia, and "other" Europeans. Although they have not been active in selling Iran new weapons since 2001, between 1997 and 2000 Western European nations delivered $100 million of arms transfers to Iran, and signed agreements to supply an additional $100 million of new arms. It is unclear if the latter have already been transferred to Iran. If not, these weapon deliveries can be held back and used as leverage against Iran.

Figure 10.4
New Arms Agreements with Iran by Supplier, 1993–2004
(in $U.S.millions)

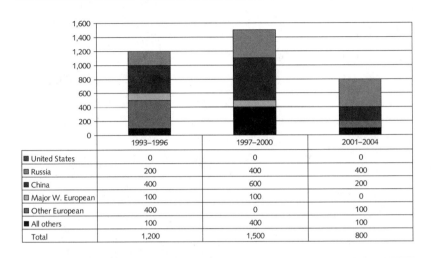

	1993–1996	1997–2000	2001–2004
■ United States	0	0	0
■ Russia	200	400	400
■ China	400	600	200
▫ Major W. European	100	100	0
■ Other European	400	0	100
■ All others	100	400	100
Total	1,200	1,500	800

Sources: Richard F. Grimmett, *Conventional Arms Transfers to Developing Nations, 1997–2004*, Congressional Reference Service, August 29, 2005; and Richard F. Grimmett, *Conventional Arms Transfers to Developing Nations, 1993–2000*, Congressional Reference Service, August 16, 2001.

China has been the second-largest supplier of arms to Iran. During the 1990s, China delivered approximately $1.3 billion of arms to Iran, and signed agreements for an additional $1 billion. From 2001 to 2004, China transferred $100 million of new weapons to the Iranians. In addition, China is estimated to hold $200 million of new agreements and can be used to pressure Iran on the nuclear issue, but it remains uncertain what type of leverage China could use against Iran.

Russia remains the largest exporter of arms to Iran. During the 1990s, Russia transferred $2.3 billion of new arms and signed $600 million of new arms deals with Iran. From 2001 to 2004, Russia delivered $100 million of arms and signed agreements to supply Iran with an estimated $400 million of new arms. As is the case with China, it remains unclear how Russia will deal with Iran and how much, or if, it will use its close ties and deals to influence Iran's decisionmakers to comply with the Security Council's demands.

The Iranian-Russian relationship is deep and may not change even if it is proved that Iran has developed nuclear weapons. In addition to its help to Iran's nuclear program and investment in its energy sectors, Russia is a major exporter of conventional weapons to Iran. This was true during the era of the Soviet Union and continued after its collapse. In 1999, Viktor Mizin, an official in the Russian Ministry of Foreign Affairs, described the importance of Iran as an arms importer:

> Iran is . . . a very important market for Russian conventional armaments, and as it is well known, this issue slowed Russian adherence to the Wassenaar Arrangement. Many arms experts in Russia believe that Iran is another untapped market for Russian weapons, and therefore there is no rational basis for ending arms sales to this country, even after fulfillment of current contracts as was agreed in bilateral U.S.-Russian talks. These experts now consider Iran, since the death of Ayatollah Khomeini, just another country that actually has ceased supporting terrorist activity and is no less democratic than some U.S. allies in the Middle East. These feelings are quite widely shared by the Russian political elite.[62]

During 2005, Russia exported more than $6.1 billion of new arms and received $23 billion of new orders. This accounted for a large portion of the Russian economy. Iran's exact share of these arms exports is not known, but Iran signed an agreement with Russia to buy Tor-M1 surface-to-air missiles at an estimated cost of $700 million. The decision to sell the antiaircraft missiles was criticized by the United States, Israel, and the European Union. Moscow, however, argued that there was no reason not to fulfill the contract it signed with Tehran in December 2005.[63]

Whether Russia and China agree to sanctions are important uncertainties. It is also important to remember that it is one thing to recommend a conventional arms embargo and another thing to enforce it. On the one hand, Iran needs these imports to upgrade its aging military weapons. On the other hand, given its missiles and asymmetric capabilities, it is not as reliant as it used to be on arms imports for its "strategic" and security goals.

Finally, the United States has imposed an arms embargo against Iran since the revolution. Also, the above data show that Western

European nations have contributed relatively little to Iran's arms re-capitalization. Nevertheless, Iran found alternative sources to meet its military needs. The effectiveness of their procurement and their importance to Iran's overall strategic posture and military needs, however, are not as important as the fact that these exporting economies would find it hard to give up such a customer. For many of these exporting countries, the decision to support sanctions will be as much economic as it is strategic.

The Uncertain Effect of Economic Sanctions

There is no point in paying the cost of sanctions against Iran unless their value outweighs that cost and they achieve their strategic objectives. Sanctions may become self-inflicted wounds to the powers imposing them far more than they might stop Iran from achieving nuclear capabilities. As noted earlier, there are countless examples where broad economic sanctions failed to achieve their purposes.

Sanctions can fail because of a lack of collation to enforce them, Iranian smuggling of sanctioned goods, or Iranian defiance despite the effect of such sanctions on the Iranian economy. Iran can ride out the sanctions and still develop its nuclear capabilities, in which case even a military option might become useless in stopping Iran from obtaining an atom bomb.

Even if the sanctions are enforced without smuggling and do have a major impact on the Iranian economy, Iran is not without options. Although Iran has certainly received help from the outside, as previous chapters have shown, the nature of Iran's nuclear research program is still too uncertain and it is unclear how much Iran has already gained in terms of importing CBRN technology. As important, no one fully knows how advanced Iran's "indigenous" nuclear research program is. Iranian nuclear experts may be at a "point of no return," in which case there is little that outside help can offer.

Another important element in judging the effectiveness of sanctions is not who would abide by them but who would not. Rogue states, namely North Korea, are unlikely to be deterred by any sanctions. If sanctions are imposed against Iran, new help might come from the North Korean regime to develop Iran's nuclear program, sell Tehran a nuclear bomb, and/or sell Iran more advanced missiles.

The nature of the regime in Iran is unlikely to be changed by sanctions, and economic restrictions may in fact help the regime consolidate its power. The Iranian people seem to support Iran's bid for nuclear power, both civilian and military. Despite the conventional wisdom in the United States, the Iranian public may not be as "anti-American" as others in the Middle East, but they are not "pro-American" either.

Iran's effort to achieve nuclear capabilities has become a matter of national pride. The idea that Iran has a special place on the world stage is supported by the majority of Iranians. Economic sanctions imposed by the UN Security Council are unlikely to change this widely held view. Despite their disagreements with some current domestic policies, Iranians see the Islamic Republic as the legacy of the Persian civilization that must become a regional superpower.

That being said, sanctions may become the only short-term option that could still have an impact—if their objective is practical and they are targeted well enough to persuade Iran to bargain. In summary, the UNSC has the following options, which can be exercised individually or in combinations:

- Impose financial sanctions against official Iranian assets, freezing government officials' capital, and restrict Iranian government officials' travels. Stop all loans from European, Asian, and Middle Eastern banks.

- Target certain trading partners. In particular, stop all trade between Iran and North Korea to stop the transfer of weapons, missiles, or nuclear technology.

- Continue the U.S. arms embargo and strengthen it to include Russian, Chinese, and European sanctions against any conventional military exports to Iran.

- Strengthen inspections of Iranian imports to stop the importation of any sensitive dual-use technologies or devices. This would mean intrusive inspections at the source and would require robust intelligence.

- Impose a total embargo on Iranian imports of refined products. This would mean cutting off all European and Indian exports of gasoline, jet fuels, and other refined products to Iran.

■ Stop all shipment of machineries from Germany, Italy, Russia, and France to Iran's heavy industry.

None of these options is perfect, and none is guaranteed to achieve its goal, but the combination of these can enhance the pressure against the Iranian government. The previous sections have outlined the consequences of each of these options in detail. They could be defied by the Iranians. They could also cause further escalation to a conventional or asymmetric attacks, or WMD conflict.

It must also be understood that sanctions can be combined with military force. The United States can choose to conduct surgical air and missile strikes against known or new Iranian nuclear and missile sites, and hope that they can delay Iranian nuclear program. Military strikes are unlikely to be supported by the Security Council and may break up the "coalition," including the EU3, Russia, and China. However, if Iran decides to defy UN-imposed sanctions and move toward further development of its nuclear program, then the outlook of the Security Council may change. As the following section will show, there are several military options, but Iran is not without retaliatory options either.

POSSIBLE MILITARY OPTIONS

Official U.S. policy toward Iran's nuclear enrichment program is to leave all options on the table and emphasize diplomatic activity through the EU3 and the UN. Vice President Richard Cheney reiterated the United States' policy on March 7, 2006:

> The Iranian regime needs to know that if it stays on its present course, the international community is prepared to impose meaningful consequences. For our part, the United States is keeping all options on the table in addressing the irresponsible conduct of the regime .... And we join other nations in sending that regime a clear message: We will not allow Iran to have nuclear weapons.[64]

Other United States officials reiterated the same message about preventive military options. During a presentation on the U.S. national security strategy in March 2006, the national security adviser, Stephen J. Hadley, stated that Iran poses a grave threat to the United States' national security: "We face no greater challenge from a single country than from Iran . . . . The doctrine of preemption remains sound . . . . We do not rule out the use of force before an attack occurs."[65]

The United States' estimates of timelines for Iran's nuclear and missile efforts also allow at least several years in which to build an international consensus behind sanctions and diplomatic pressure, and a consensus behind military options if diplomacy fails.

The United States would also have the potential advantage of finding any Iranian "smoking gun," improving its targeting and strike options, and being able to strike targets in which Iran had invested much larger assets. The fact Iran can exploit time as a weapon in which to proliferate does not mean that the United States cannot exploit time as a weapon with which to strike Iran.

The Problem of Targeting

There are no risk-free military options for the United States or neighboring states. Tehran's known nuclear research facilities are dispersed around the country and are generally large with new construction always in progress. Many key sites are underground, and there may be many others that are unknown or are not identifiable. IAEA inspections have identified at least 18 sites, but others argue that there might be more than 70.[66]

There is a range of views regarding what can be achieved by targeting Iranian nuclear sites. For example, former Pentagon adviser Richard Perle has stated that a one-night strike with B-2 bombers by United States could devastate Iran's nuclear program. Gary Bernsten, a former CIA operative, however, declared that "this is a huge system of facilities . . . . This is not going to be a small sort of engagement. We are probably going to have to destroy 30 facilities in 30 locations. Or at least 15." However, Bernsten added, "we can take care of it in a couple of days with air strikes and they wouldn't be able to stop us."[67]

Iran, however, has had a quarter of a century to learn from the experience of Iraq in 1981. It may have constructed redundant sites and underground facilities, and it has built in high levels of protection around at least some of its known nuclear research centers. Others have argued that Iranian nuclear sites may have been deliberately built near populated areas or in facilities with many other "legitimate" purposes so the United States would be confronted with the problem of collateral damage or being charged with having hit an "innocent target." The previous chapters have also strongly suggested that many of Iran's research, development, and production activities are almost certainly modular and can be rapidly moved to new sites, including tunnels, caves, and other hardened facilities.

U.S. officials have publicly identified key nuclear research sites that may have been placed underground to shield them against airborne assaults. For example, the United States identified the Parchin military complex, located south of Tehran, as a "probable" location for nuclear weaponization research.[68] This site alone has many sections, hundreds of bunkers, and several tunnels. The site is also being used to manufacture conventional armaments and missiles.[69] Parchin is one possible target for attack, but the evidence linking it to military nuclear weapons manufacturing was ambiguous. The site has civilian and conventional military use. The IAEA's initial assessment was that Parchin was not linked to nuclear weapons manufacturing, but most agree that there was no definitive proof that this was the case.

As noted, Iran has increased its protection of sites against possible U.S. or Israeli air strikes. It has been reported that the Islamic Revolutionary Guards Corps launched a program to build a defense infrastructure to protect Iran's nuclear research facilities. The program was recommended by the Nuclear Control Center of Iran and endorsed by Iran's Supreme Leader, Ali Khamenei.[70]

This program, reportedly coordinated with North Korea, is to build underground halls and tunnels at the cost of "hundreds of millions of dollars." Some key sites such as Esfahan and Natanz are high on the list of facilities to protect. The logistic defense infrastructure would include natural barriers (tunnels into mountains and cliffs) and manufactured barricades (concrete ceilings and multiple floors), as well as camouflage activities around key sites. The construction, a joint venture between Iranian and North Korean companies, was estimated to be completed by June 1, 2006.[71]

That said, this does not mean the United States cannot target much or most of Iran's capabilities or does not have much better targeting intelligence than outsiders can estimate. One great danger in open-sourced analysis is that it cannot be based upon anything other than guesses about the quality targeting intelligence. In addition, it cannot provide a meaningful picture of what the United States or other potential attackers know at the classified level. It is also dangerous, if not irresponsible, for analysts with no empirical training and experience in targeting and modern weapons effects to make sweeping judgments about strike options. They simply lack basic professional competence and even minimal credibility.

Options also do not need to be limited to known targets or nuclear targets. A power as large as the United States could strike at possible targets as well. The problem with a shell game is that it virtually provokes strikes at all the shells.

The United States also could strike at a wide range of critical Iranian military facilities, including missile production facilities. Most are soft targets, and their loss would be extremely costly to Iran. Even if many of Iran's nuclear facilities did survive U.S. strikes, Iran would be faced with either complying with the EU3 and UN terms or taking much broader military losses—losses its aging and limited forces can ill afford.

More generally, the United States could cripple Iran's economy by striking at major domestic gas production and distribution facilities, refineries, and electric power generators. Iran may have a lever in terms of suspending its oil exports, but the Iranian economy has a highly fragile infrastructure and selective strikes could paralyze a great deal of Iran's economic activity outside the oil sector in ways that would put intense pressure on Iran to both suspend its nuclear activity and export at maximum rates to fund its economic recovery. There are no rules that would preclude the United States from immediate restrikes or restrikes over time. If the United States chose to strike at the necessary level of intensity, it could use conventional weapons to cripple Iran's ability to function as a nation in a matter of days with attacks limited to several hundred aim points.

Iranian Defense against U.S. Strikes

Iran would find it difficult to defend against U.S. forces using cruise missiles, stealth aircraft, and stand-off precision weapons, and equipped with a mix of vastly superior air combat assets and the intelligence, surveillance, and reconnaissance assets necessary to strike and restrike Iranian targets in near real time.

For example, each U.S. B-2A Spirit stealth bomber could carry eight 4,500-pound enhanced BLU-28 satellite-guided bunker-busting bombs—potentially enough to strike one hardened Iranian site per sortie. Such bombers could operate flying from Diego Garcia in the Indian Ocean, RAF Fairford in Gloucestershire, and Whiteman USAF base in Missouri.[72]

The United States also has a wide range of other hard-target killers, many of which are in development or classified. Systems that are known to be deployed include the BLU-109 Have Void "bunker busters," a "dumb bomb" with a maximum penetration capability of 4 to 6 feet of reinforced concrete. An aircraft must overfly the target and launch the weapon with great precision to achieve serious penetration capability.[73] It can be fitted with precision guidance and converted to a guided glide bomb. The joint direct attack munition (JDAM) GBU-31 version has a nominal range of 15 kilometers with a circular error probable, or CEP, of 13 meters in the Global Positioning System (GPS)-aided INS (Inertial Navigation System) modes of operation and 30 meters in the INS-only modes of operation.[74]

More advanced systems include the BLU-116 Advanced Unitary Penetrator (AUP), GBU-24 C/B (USAF), or GBU-24 D/B (Navy), which has about three times the penetration capability of the BLU-109.[75] It is not clear whether the United States has deployed the AGM-130C with an advanced earth-penetrating/hard-target kill system. The AGM-130 Surface Attack Guided Munition was developed to be integrated into the F-15E, so it could carry two such missiles, one on each inboard store station. It is a retargetable, precision-guided standoff weapon using inertial navigation aided by GPS satellites and has a 15–40 NM range.[76]

It is not clear such weapons could destroy all of Iran's most hardened underground sites, although it seems likely that the BLU-28 could do serious damage at a minimum. Much depends on the accuracy of reports that Iran has undertaken a massive tunneling project, with some 10,000 square meters of underground halls and tunnels branching off from each hall for hundreds of meters. Iran is reported to be drawing on North Korean expertise and to have created a separate corporation (Shahid Rajaei Company) for such tunneling and hardening efforts under the IRGC, with extensive activity already under way in Natanz and Esfahan. The facilities are said to make extensive use of blast-proof doors, extensive divider walls, hardened ceilings, 20-centimeter-thick concrete walls, and double concrete ceilings with earth fill between layers to defeat earth penetrators.[77] Such passive defenses could have a major effect, but reports of such activity are often premature, or exaggerated, or report far higher construction standards than are actually used.

At the same time, the B-2A could be used to deliver large numbers of precision-guided 500-pound bombs against dispersed surface targets or a mix of light and heavy precision-guided weapons. Submarines and surface ships could deliver cruise missiles for such strikes, and conventional strike aircraft and bombers could deliver standoff weapons against most of Iran's suspect facilities without suffering a high risk of serious attrition. The challenge would be to properly determine what targets and aim points were actually valuable, not to inflict high levels of damage.

Iran has "quantity," but its air defenses have little "quality." It has assigned some 12,000 to 15,000 men in its air force to land-based air defense functions, including at least 8,000 regulars and 4,000 IRGC personnel. It is not possible to distinguish clearly between the major air defense weapons holdings of the regular air force and the IRGC, but the air force appears to operate most major surface-to-air missile systems.

Total holdings seem to include 30 Improved Hawk fire units (12 battalions/150-plus launchers), 45–55 SA-2 and HQ-2J/23 (CSA-1) launchers (Chinese-made equivalents of the SA-2), and possibly 25 SA-6 launchers. The air force also has three Soviet-made long-range SA-5 units with a total of 10–15 launchers—enough for six sites. Iran has developed and deployed its own domestically manufactured surface-to-air missile (SAM), dubbed the Shahab Thaqeb. The SAM requires a four-wheeled trailer for deployment and closely resembles the R440 SAM.[78]

Iran's holdings of lighter air defense weapons include five Rapier squadrons with 30 Rapier fire units, 5–10 Chinese FM-80 launchers, 10–15 Tigercat fire units, and a few RBS-70s. Iran also holds large numbers of man-portable SA-7s, HN-5s, and SA-14s, plus about 2,000 anti-aircraft guns—including some Vulcans and 50–60 radar-guided and self-propelled ZSU-23-4 weapons.[79] It is not clear which of these weapons were operated by the army, the IRGC, or the air force. The IRGC clearly had larger numbers of manportable surface-to-air launchers, including some Stingers that it had obtained from Afghanistan. It almost certainly has a number of other light air defense guns as well.

There are no authoritative data on how Iran now deploys its land-based air defenses, but it seems to have deployed its new SA-5s to cover its major ports, oil facilities, and Tehran. It seems to have concentrated its Improved Hawks and Soviet- and Chinese-made SA-2s around Tehran, Esfahan, Shiraz, Bandar Abbas, Kharg Island, Bushehr, Bandar Khomeini, Ahvaz, Dezful, Kermanshah, Hamadan, and Tabriz.

Although Iran has made some progress in improving and updating its weapons, sensors, and electronic warfare capability, and has learned much from Iraq's efforts to defeat U.S. enforcement of the "no-fly zones" from 1992 to 2003, its current defenses are outdated and poorly integrated. All of its major systems are based on technology that is more than 35 years old, and all are vulnerable to U.S active and passive countermeasures.

Iran's air defense forces are too widely spaced to provide more than limited air defense for key bases and facilities, and many lack the missile launcher strength to be fully effective. This is particularly true of Iran's SA-5 sites, which provide long-range, medium-to-high altitude coverage of key coastal installations. Too few launchers are scattered over too wide an area to prevent relatively rapid suppression. Iran also lacks the low-altitude radar coverage, overall radar net, command and control assets, sensors, resistance to sophisticated jamming and electronic countermeasures, and systems integration capability necessary to create an effective air defense net.

Iran's land-based air defenses must operate largely in the point defense mode. Iran lacks the battle management systems and its data links are not fast and effective enough to allow it to take maximum advantage of the overlapping coverage of some of its missile systems—a problem further complicated by the difficulties of trying to net different systems supplied by Britain, China, Russia, and the United States. Iran's missiles and sensors are most effective at high-to-medium altitudes against aircraft with limited penetrating and jamming capability.

This situation may change in the future, however, and improvements in Iran's land-based air defenses could be a factor in the timing of any U.S. or Israeli strikes. Iran purchased 20 Russian 9K331 Tor-M1 (SA-15 Gauntlet) self-propelled surface-to-air missiles in December 2005.[80] Global Security indicates that this is a modern short-range missile with the capability to simultaneously attack two targets using a relatively high-powered and jam-resistant radar, and has "electronic beam control and vertically launched missiles able to maintain high speed and maneuverability inside an entire engagement envelope."[81] It is said to be capable of detecting targets at a distance of 25 kilometers and attacking them at a maximum distance of 12 kilometers. For what it is worth, Russian sources claim that Tor is much more efficient than similar systems like France's Crotale and Britain's Rapier.

The basic combat formation is a firing battery consisting of four TLARs and the Rangir battery command post. The TLAR (transporter, launcher, and radar) carries eight ready missiles stored in two containers holding four missiles each. It is claimed to have an effective range of 1,500 to 12,000 meters against targets flying at altitudes between 10 and 6,000 meters. The maximum maneuvering load factor limit on the weapon is said to be 30 "Gs."[82] It should be noted that Russian manufacturer claims are no less exaggerated than those of European and U.S. manufacturers.

Delivery dates ranging between 2006 and 2009 have been reported, but the Tor is too range-limited to have a major impact on U.S. stealth attack capability, although its real-world performance against cruise missiles still has to be determined. It might have more point-defense lethality against regular Israeli and U.S. strike fighters like the F-15 and F-16 using precision-guided bombs, but it would be lethal against such aircraft with standoff air-to-surface missiles only if it could be deployed in the flight path in ways that were not detected before the attack profile was determined.

Iran also announced in February 2006 (along with several other weapons and military exercise announcements that seemed timed to try to deter U.S. or Israeli military action) that it was mass-producing a new manportable, low-altitude, short-range air defense missile called the Mithaq-2.[83] It was said to be electronic-warfare and IR (infrared)-flare resistant, and seemed to be based on the Chinese QW-1 Vanguard. If it is based on the QW-1, it is an IR-homing missile introduced in the mid-1990s. It may, however, be a variant of the QW-2 with an improved IR seeker. China claims it has an effective range of 500–5,000 meters at target altitudes of 30–4,000 meters. The maximum maneuvering load factor limit on the weapon is said to be 30 Gs. In spite of Iranian claims, it does not seem superior to the Russian SA-14s already in Iran's inventory, and it is too short-ranged to have more than a minimal deterrent effect.[84]

Some reports indicate that Iran is seeking to buy more modern Soviet SA-300 missiles and to use Russian systems to modernize its entire air defense system. Acquiring, deploying, and bringing such systems to a high degree of readiness would substantially improve Iranian capabilities. A report in *Jane's* claims that Iran is building surface-to-air missile defense zones around its nuclear facilities that will use a single battery of S-300PMU (SA-10) missiles to defend the Bushehr reactor and that it will deploy the S-300V (SA-12b) to provide wide-area defense coverage of other targets, which it will mix with the ToR-M1 to provide low-altitude point defense.

This is a logical approach for Iran to take for improving its defenses, and it has sought to purchase the S-300 in the past. The SA-10 is reported to be able to intercept aircraft at a maximum slant range of 32,000 to 43,200 meters and a maximum effective defense perimeter of 150 kilometers (90 miles). The minimum effective interception altitude is claimed to be 10 meters.

One variant of the missile is reported to have some ballistic missile defense (BMD) capability and be able to engage ballistic missile targets at ranges of up to 40 kilometers (25 miles). Each battery is said to have a load of 32 missile rounds on its launchers, a battery deployment time as low as five minutes, and the ability to fire three missiles per second. A standard battery consists of an 83M6E2 command post, up to six 90Zh6E2 air defense missile complexes, 48N6E2 air defense missiles, and technical support facilities.[85]

If Iran were to get the S-300V (SA-12a and SA-12b), it would get a system with far more advanced computer systems and sensors, electronic warfare capabilities, and significant point defense capabilities against ballistic missiles than it currently has. A Russian S-300V brigade has the following components: 9M82 SA-12b Giant missiles (two per launcher) and TELAR, 9M83 SA-12a Gladiator missiles (four per launcher), and TELAR, Giant, and Gladiator launcher/loader vehicles, 9S15 Bill

Board Surveillance Radar system, 9S19 High Screen Sector Radar system, 9S32 Grill Pan Guidance Radar system, and 9S457 Command Station. The SA-12a is a dual-role antimissile and antiaircraft missile with a maximum range of between 75 and 90 kilometers. The SA-12b GIANT missile is configured as an anti-tactical ballistic missile (ATBM) with a longer maximum range of between 100 and 200 kilometers. Each unit can detect up to 200 targets, track as many as 70 targets, and designate 24 of the targets to the brigade's four Grill Pan radar systems for engagement.[86]

It seems doubtful, however, that Iran has operational S-300PMU systems, has taken delivery on such units, or has even been able to buy them from Russia. It is also unclear that Russia has sold Iran S-300V systems or plans to. In February 2006, the Russian minister of defense flatly denied any such sales had taken place.[87] Even if such systems are delivered, their real-world performance will be uncertain. In the past, Russia has also been careful to control some critical aspects of its weapons exports and sell degraded export versions.

Iran's air forces are only marginally better able to survive in air-to-air combat than Iraq's were before 2003. Iran's command and control system has serious limitations in terms of secure communications, vulnerability to advanced electronic warfare, netting, and digital data transfer. According to the IISS, Iran still has five operational P-3MP Orion aircraft and may have made its captured Iraqi IL-76 Candid AEW aircraft operational. These assets would give it airborne warning and command and control capability, but these are obsolescent to obsolete systems and are likely to be highly vulnerable to electronic warfare and countermeasures and to long-range attack, even with Iranian modifications and updates. There are some reports Iran may be seeking to make a version of the Russian AN-140 AEW aircraft but these could not be deployed much before 2015.[88]

Iran's air defense aircraft consist of a maximum operational strength of two squadrons of 25 export versions of the MiG-29A and two squadrons of 25–30 F-14As. The export version of the MiG-29A has significant avionics limitations and vulnerability to countermeasures, and it is not clear that Iran has any operational Phoenix air-to-air missiles for its F-14As or that it has successfully modified its Improved Hawk missiles for air-to-air combat. The AWG-9 radar on the F-14 has significant long-distance sensor capability in a permissive environment, but is a U.S.-made system in a nearly 30-year-old configuration that is now vulnerable to countermeasures.

Iran might risk using its fighters and AEW aircraft against an Israeli strike. It seems doubtful that Israel could support a long-range attack unit with the air defense and electronic assets necessary to provide anything like the air defense and air defense suppression assets that would support a U.S. strike. A U.S. strike could almost certainly destroy any Iranian effort to use fighters, however, and destroy enough Iranian surface-to-air missile defenses to create a secure corridor for penetrating into Iran and against key Iranian installations. The United States could then maintain such a corridor indefinitely with restrikes.

Iranian Retaliation against U.S. Strikes

This does not mean it would be easy or desirable for the United States to exercise its military options. U.S. forces are preoccupied in Iraq, and the lack of security in Iraq makes a full military attack against Iran all too unlikely. U.S. military options are not risk-free, and the consequences of U.S. strikes are enormous. Tehran has several retaliatory options:

- Retaliate against U.S. forces in Iraq and Afghanistan overtly, using Shahab-3 missiles armed with CBR warheads.

- Use proxy groups, including Abu Musab al-Zarqawi and Moqtada Sadr in Iraq, to intensify the insurgency and escalate the attacks against U.S. forces and Iraqi security forces.

- Turn the Shi'ite majority in Iraq against the U.S. presence so that they demand that U.S. forces to leave.

- Attack the U.S. homeland using suicide bombers from proxy groups or deliver CBR weapons to al-Qa'ida to use against the United States.

- Use its asymmetric capabilities to attack U.S. interests in the region, including soft targets (e.g., embassies, commercial centers, and American citizens).

- Attack U.S. naval forces stationed in the Gulf with antiship missiles, asymmetric warfare, and mines.

- Attack Israel with missiles, possibly with CBR warheads.

- Given Iran's strategic location near the Strait of Hormuz, as shown in map 10.1, it retaliate against energy targets in the Gulf and temporarily shut off the flow of oil from the Strait of Hormuz.

- Stop all of its oil and gas shipments to increase the price of oil and inflict damage on the global and U.S. economies.

Iran has close relations with many Iraqi Shi'ites, particularly Shi'ite political parties and militias. Some Iraqi groups have warned against U.S. military strikes against their neighbors. For example, Moqtada Sadr pledged that he and his militia, the Mahdi army, would come to the aid of Iran in the case of a military strike by the United States against Tehran. According to Sadr, Iran asked him what his position would be if Iran was attacked by the United States, and he pledged that the Mahdi army would help any Arab or neighboring country if it was attacked.[89] Both the U.S. and British ministers of defense have complained that Iran is actively supporting various militias in Iraq, has supplied advanced triggering and motion detector systems for improvised explosive devices (IEDs), and is using elements of the al-Quds force to train death squads and militias.[90]

Many observers argue that a military strike against Iran can add to the chaos in Iraq and may further complicate the U.S. position there. While the consequences of U.S. military attacks against Iran remain unclear; the Shi'ite majority in Iraq can (1) as the United States to leave Iraq, (2) sanction militia groups to directly attack U.S. forces, and/or (3) turn the new Iraqi security and military forces against U.S. forces.[91]

As has been discussed earlier, Iran has extensive forces suited to asymmetric warfare. These include not only the Revolutionary Guards and elements of the al-Quds force under the Directorate of the Islamic Revolutionary Guards Corps, but also elements of the foreign intelligence directorate in the Ministry of Intelligence and Security (Vezarat-e-Ettela'at va Amniat-e Keshvar, or VEVAK).[92]

The Iranian surface navy is highly vulnerable, but Iran could position land-based anti-ship missile where it could strike at tanker traffic. Mobile firing elements using systems like the HY-2/C-201 Silkworm or Seerseeker (Raad) have ranges of 90 to 100 kilometers and have proved difficult to detect and kill in the past.[93] Iran is reported to have

Map 10.1   Strait of Hormuz

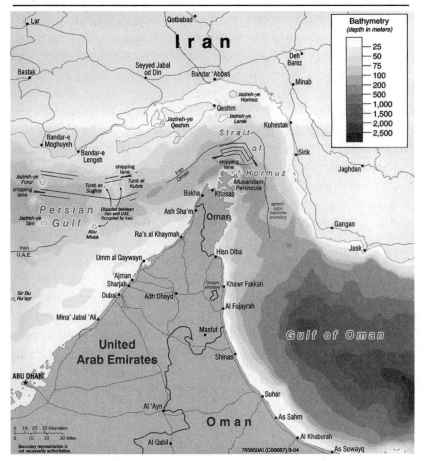

Source: CIA, Map of Strait of Hormuz, 2004, available at http://www.lib
.utexas.edu/maps/middle_east_and_asia/iran_pol01.jpg.

the capability to make or assemble such missiles, modify and upgrade
them, have roughly 100 systems in stock, and have 8–10 mobile missile
launchers. These are reported to be deployed near the Strait of Hormuz, but may actually be in a number of different locations.[94]

Iran also has three relatively effective Kilo-class submarines, which
can use long-range wire-guided torpedoes or release mines. (Reports
that Iran has advanced "bottom" mines with sensors that release and
activate them as they sense ships passing overhead are uncertain.)

The naval branch of the IRGC is reported to have up to 20,000 men.
They operate 10 Hudong missile patrol boats with C-801K (8–42

kilometers) and C-802 (42–120 kilometers) sea-skimming anti-ship missiles.[95] The Iranian air force has airborne variants of these systems.

The naval branch also has additional C-14 high-speed catamarans, each of which has C-701 antiship missiles, and additional North Korean missile boats. They operate some 50 additional patrol boats, including 40 Bohammar Marine boats. Many are so small they are difficult to detect with shipborne radars. These can be armed with recoilless rifles, rocket-propelled grenades (RPGs), and small arms to attack or harass ships in or near the Gulf and raid or attack offshore facilities. They can conduct suicide attacks or release floating mines covertly in shipping lanes or near key facilities. Iran can use any commercial ship to release free-floating mines for the same purpose.[96]

Iran made claims in the spring of 2006 that it was testing more advanced weapons for such forces. These included a sonar-evading underwater missile (possibly a torpedo) that IRGC Rear Admiral Ali Fadavi claimed no enemy warship could detect and "no warship could escape because of its high velocity." Iran also claimed to be testing a new missile called the Kowsar—with a very large warhead and extremely high speed to attack "big ships and submarines"—that it claimed could evade radar and antimissile missiles. Although such tests may have actually taken place, Iran has made so many grossly exaggerated claims about its weapons developments in the past that it seems they are designed more to try to deter U.S. military action and/or reassure the Iranian public than to describe serious real-world capabilities.[97]

In any case, Iran could not close the Strait of Hormuz or halt tanker traffic, and its submarines and much of its IRGC forces would probably be destroyed in a matter of days if they become operational. It could, however, conduct a series of raids to threaten and disrupt Gulf traffic and/or strike at offshore and shore facilities in the southern Gulf or at Iraqi oil facilities in the Gulf. Even sporadic random strikes would create a high-risk premium and potential panic in oil markets. Iran could potentially destabilize part of Afghanistan and use Hezbollah and Syria to threaten Israel.

Iran can also use its IRGC asymmetric warfare assets to attack U.S. interests in the region. Iranian officials do not hide the fact that they would use asymmetric attacks against U.S. interests. For example, a brigadier general in the IRGC and the commander of the "Lovers of

Martyrdom Garrison," Mohammad-Reza Jaafari, once threatened U.S. interests with suicide operations if the United States were to attack Iran:

> Now that America is after gaining allies against the righteous Islamic Republic and wants to attack our sanctities, members of the martyrdom-seeking garrisons across the world have been put on alert so that if the Islamic Republic of Iran receives the smallest threat, the American and Israeli strategic interests will be burnt down everywhere.
>
> The only tool against the enemy that we have with which we can become victorious are martyrdom-seeking operations and, God willing, our possession of faithful, brave, trained and zealous persons will give us the upper hand in the battlefield.
>
> . . . Upon receiving their orders, our martyrdom-seeking forces will be uncontrollable and a guerrilla war may go on in various places for years to come. . . . America and any other power cannot win in the unbalanced war against us.[98]

Iran could seek to create an alliance with extremist movements like al-Qa'ida in spite of these groups' hostility to Shi'ites. It can seek to exploit Arab and Muslim anger against U.S. ties to Israel and the invasion of Iraq on a global level. It can also try to exploit European and others' concerns that the United States might be repeating its miscalculation of the threat posed by Iraq and striking without adequate cause. Unless Iran is far more egregious in its noncompliance, or the United States can find a definitive smoking gun to prove Iran is proliferating, Iran would be certain to have some success in such efforts.

Iran's energy resources are another potential weapon. Shutting off exports would hurt Iran deeply but would have an impact on global markets. As Iraq found, energy deals also can sharply weaken support even for diplomatic options, and Russia and China might well oppose any kind of U.S. military strike, regardless of the level of justification the United States could advance at the time.

U.S. Military Options

If the United States does choose to respond militarily, it has several major types of military and strategic options. Each of these options might have many of the following broad characteristics, although it should be stressed that these are only rough outlines of U.S. options and are purely speculative and illustrative points. They are more warnings than recommendations, and they are not based on any inside knowledge of actual U.S. war plans, and calculations. Those who argue strongly for and against such options should note, however, that the United States could act in many different ways. There are no rules or certainties, however, that such attacks could not succeed or that they would.

Demonstrative, coercive, or deterrent strikes:

- Conduct a few cruise missile or stealth strikes simply as a demonstration or warning of the seriousness of U.S. intentions if Iran does not comply with the terms of the EU3 or the UN.

- Hit at least one high-value target recognized by the IAEA and the EU3 to show credibility of threat to Iran and minimize international criticism.

- Strike at new sites and activities to show Iran that it cannot ignore the UN or the EU3 and secretly proceed with or expand its efforts.

- Carry out carrier-base attacks, which would not require using territory of any Gulf ally.

- International reaction would be a problem regardless of the level of U.S. action.

- Actions might trigger Iranian counteraction in Iraq, Afghanistan, and dealings with Hezbollah.

Limited U.S. attacks:

- Limited strike would probably take 16–20 Cruise missile and strike sorties. (Total sorties in Gulf and area would probably have to total 100 or more, including escorts, enablers, and refuelers.)

- Might be able to combine B-2s and carrier-based aircraft and sea-launched cruise missiles. Might well need land base(s) in the Gulf for staging, refueling, and recovery.

- Goal would be to critically damage or destroy at least 2–3 of most costly and major facilities.

- Hit at high-value targets recognized by the IAEA and the EU3 to show credibility to Iran and minimize international criticism.

- Might strike at new sites and activities to show Iran that it cannot secretly proceed with or expand its efforts by ignoring the UN or EU3.

- Might slow down Iran if used stealth aircraft to strike at hard and underground targets, but the impact over time would probably still be more demonstrative than crippling.

- Hitting hard and underground targets could easily require multiple strikes during mission and follow-on restrikes to be effective.

- Battle damage would be a significant problem, particularly for large buildings and underground facilities.

- Size and effectiveness would depend very heavily on the quality of U.S. intelligence and suitability of given ordnance, as well as the time the United States sought to inflict a given effect.

- Iran's technology base would survive; the same would be true of much of equipment even in facilities hit with strikes. Little impact, if any, on pool of scientists and experts.

- Iranian response in terms of proliferation could vary sharply and unpredictably: Deter and delay vs. mobilize and provoke.

- Likely to produce cosmetic Iranian change in behavior at best. Would probably make Iran disperse program even more and drive it to deep underground facilities. Might provoke Iran to implement (more) active biological warfare program.

- Any oil embargo is likely to be demonstrative.

- Would probably trigger Iranian counteraction in Iraq, Afghanistan, and dealings with Hezbollah.

- International reaction could be a serious problem; the United States might well face the same level of political problems as if it had launched a comprehensive strike on Iranian facilities.

Major U.S. attacks on Iranian CBRN and major missile targets:

- 200–600 cruise missiles and strike sorties; would have to be at least a matching number of escorts, enablers, and refuelers. Period of attacks could extend from 3 to 10 days.

- Hit all suspect facilities for nuclear, missile, BW, and related C4IBM.

- Knock out key surface-to-air missile sites and radars for future freedom of action.

- Would need to combine B-2s, carrier-based aircraft, and sea-launched cruise missiles, and used of land base(s) in the Gulf for staging, refueling, and recovery.

- Threaten to strike extensively at Iranian capabilities for asymmetric warfare and to threaten tanker traffic, facilities in the Gulf, and neighboring states.

- At least 7–10 days to fully execute and validate.

- Goal would be to critically damage or destroy at least 70–80 percent of the most costly and major facilities.

- Hit at all high-value targets recognized by the IAEA and EU3 to show credibility to Iran and minimize international criticism, but also hit possible or suspected sites as well.

- Strike at all known new sites and activities to show Iran that it cannot secretly proceed with or expand its efforts, unless hold back some targets as hostages to the future.

- Impact over time would probably be crippling, but Iran might still covertly assemble some nuclear device and could not halt Iranian biological weapons effort.

- Hitting hard and underground targets could easily require multiple strikes during mission and follow-on restrikes to be effective.

- Battle damage would be a significant problem, particularly for large buildings and underground facilities.

- Size and effectiveness would depend very heavily on the quality of U.S. intelligence and suitability of given ordnance, as well as the time the United States sought to inflict a given effect.

- Much of Iran's technology base would still survive; the same would be true of many equipment items, even in facilities hit with strikes. Some impact, if any, on pool of scientists and experts.

- Iranian response in terms of proliferation could vary sharply and unpredictably: Deter and delay vs. mobilize and provoke.

- A truly serious strike may be enough of a deterrent to change Iranian behavior, particularly if coupled with the threat of follow-on strikes in the future. It still, however, could as easily produce only a cosmetic change in behavior at best. Iran might still disperse its program even more, and shift to multiple, small, deep underground facilities.

- Might well provoke Iran to implement (more) active biological warfare program.

- An oil embargo might be serious.

- Even if it tried to, the Iranian government could probably not prevent some elements in Iranian forces and intelligence from seeking to use Iraq, Afghanistan, terrorist support, and Hezbollah to hit back at the United States and its allies; it probably would not try.

- International reaction would be a serious problem, but the United States might well face the same level of political problems as if it had launched a small strike on Iranian facilities.

Major U.S. attacks on military and related civilian targets:

- Conduct 1,000–2,500 cruise missiles and strike sorties.

- Hit all suspect facilities for nuclear, missile, BW, and C4IBM, and potentially "technology base" targets, including universities and dual-use facilities.

- Strike extensively at Iranian capabilities for asymmetric warfare and to threaten tanker traffic, facilities in the Gulf, and neighboring states or else threaten to do so if Iran should deploy for such action.

- Would require a major portion of total U.S. global assets. Need to combine B-2s, other bombers, and carrier-based aircraft and sea-launched cruise missiles. Would need land base(s) in the Gulf for staging, refueling, and recovery. Staging out of Diego Garcia in the Indian Ocean would be highly desirable.

- Would probably take several weeks to two months to fully execute and validate.

- Goal would be to critically damage or destroy 70–80-plus percent of the most costly and major CBRN, missile, and other delivery systems; key conventional air and naval strike assets; and major military production facilities.

- Hit at all high-value targets recognized by IAEA and EU3 to show credibility to Iran and minimize international criticism, but also hit possible sites as well.

- Strike at all known new sites and activities to show Iran cannot secretly proceed with or expand its efforts, unless hold back some targets as hostages to the future.

- Hitting hard and underground targets could easily require multiple strikes during mission and follow-on restrikes to be effective.

- Impact over time would probably be crippling, but Iran might still covertly assemble some nuclear device, and the attacks could not halt Iranian biological weapons effort.

- Battle damage would be a significant problem, particularly for large buildings and underground facilities.

- Size and effectiveness would depend very heavily on the quality of U.S. intelligence and suitability of given ordnance, as well as the time the United States sought to inflict a given effect.

- Much of Iran's technology base would survive, as would many equipment items even in facilities hit with strikes. Some impact, if any, on pool of scientists and experts.

- Iran's response in terms of proliferation could vary sharply and unpredictably: Deter and delay vs. mobilize and provoke.

- Such a series of strikes might be enough of a deterrent to change Iranian behavior, particularly if coupled with the threat of follow-on strikes in the future. It still, however, could as easily produce only a cosmetic Iranian change in behavior at best. Iran might still disperse its program even more, and shift to multiple, small, deep underground facilities.

- Might well provoke Iran to implement (more) active biological warfare program.

- An oil embargo might be serious.

- Even if it tried to, Iranian government could probably not prevent some elements in Iranian forces and intelligence from seeking to use Iraq, Afghanistan, support of terrorism, and Hezbollah to hit back at the United States and its allies; it probably would not try.
- International reaction would be a serious problem.

Delay and then strike:

- The United States could execute any of the above options and wait until Iran provided proof it was proliferating. Such a "smoking gun" would create a much greater chance of allied support and international tolerance or consensus.
- Iran will have committed major resources and created considerably higher-value targets
- The counter risk is an unanticipated Iranian breakout; some form of Iranian launch-on-warning (LOW), launch-under-attack (LUA), or survivable "ride-out" capability.
- Iranian dispersal and sheltering may be much better than a strategy of "breakout," LOW, LUA, or a survivable "ride-out."
- Iran might have biological weapons as a countermeasure.
- Allied and regional reactions would be uncertain. Time tends to breed tolerance of proliferation.

Ride out Iranian proliferation:

- Announce or quietly demonstrate U.S. nuclear targeting of Iran's military and CBRN facilities and cities.
- Deploy antiballistic and cruise missile defenses, and sell such defenses to Gulf and neighboring states.
- Signal U.S. conventional option to cripple Iran by destroying its power generation, gas, and refinery facilities.
- Provide U.S. guarantees of extended deterrence to the Gulf states.
- Tacitly accept Saudi Arabia's acquisition of nuclear weapons and long-range strike capabilities.
- Maintain a preventive/preemptive option at constant combat readiness. Act without warning.

- Encourage Israel to openly declare its strike options as a deterrent.
- Announce doctrine that any use by Iran of biological weapons will lead to nuclear retaliation against it.

The "ride-out" option is one that many commentators need to consider in more depth. Unless it finds evidence of an imminent Iranian threat—which at this point might well require Iran to find some outside source of nuclear weapons or weapons-grade material—the United States may well simply choose to wait. Patience is not always a virtue, but it has never been labeled a mortal sin.

The Consequences of an Israeli Strike

Some military experts in Israel have said that Iranian rhetoric calling for the destruction of Israel is more a smokescreen and excuse for creating an Iranian nuclear monopoly in the Gulf than a sign of any serious willingness or desire to engage Israel. Others have said the opposite. Yet even if Iran's nuclear ambitions are mainly centered on the U.S. presence in the Gulf and in other Muslim and Arab states, this may not deter preventive or preemptive action in dealing with an existential threat, where one or two nuclear ground bursts centered on Tel Aviv and Haifa could virtually destroy Israel as a state.

A number of Israeli officers, officials, and experts have said that Israel must not permit Iran to acquire nuclear capabilities, regardless of Tehran's motivations. Some have called for preemptive strikes by Israel. Ephraim Inbar, the director of the Begin-Sadat Center for International Affairs at Israel's Bar-Ilan University, said, "For self-defense, we must act in a pre-emptive mode."[99]

According to Israeli military officials quoted in press reports in January 2006, the Israeli Defense Forces had received orders to prepare for a military strike against Iranian nuclear sites by March 2006.[100] It is unclear what type of military strikes Israel might choose if it decides to respond preemptively. Some have argued that Israel could declare its nuclear weapons and establish a mutually assured destruction strategy for deterrence. While the impact of an Israeli declaration remains uncertain, it is likely to have little impact on Israel's strategic posture in the region, as most states already factor Israel's nuclear weapons into their strategic thinking.

Some experts argue that Israel does not have viable military options, that it does not have U.S. targeting capability and simply cannot generate and sustain the necessary number of attack sorties. Some argue that Israel might do little more than drive Iranian activity further underground, provoke even more Iranian activity, make it impossible for diplomatic and UN pressure to work, and turn Israel into a real rather than proxy or secondary target.

No doubt such a strike would face problems. The Israelis do not have conventional ballistic missiles or land-based and sea-based cruise missiles suited for such a mission. The shortest flight routes would be 1,500–1,700 kilometers through Jordan and Iraq, 1,900–2,100 kilometers through Saudi Arabia, and 2,600–2,800 kilometers in a loop through Turkey.[101]

All such missions would probably be detected relatively quickly by the radars in the countries involved, and very-low-altitude penetration profiles would lead to serious range and payload problems. The countries overflown would have to either react or risk losing credibility by claiming surprise. An overflight of Iraq would be seen in the region as having to have been approved by the United States. Iran would almost certainly see Jordanian, Turkish, and/or Saudi tolerance of such an IAF strike as a hostile act. It might well claim a U.S. "green light" in any case in an effort to mobilize hostile Arab and Muslim (and possibly world) reactions.

Israel has configured its F-15s and F-16s for long-range strikes, and it has refueling capability. It is doubtful, however, that it has enough refueling capability to do more than send a strike force that would have to defend itself without a significant fighter escort or support from electronic warfare aircraft. Its strike aircraft would probably need close to maximum payloads to achieve the necessary level of damage against most targets suspected of WMD activity, although any given structure could be destroyed with one to three weapons. (This would include the main Bushehr reactor enclosure, but its real-world potential value to an Iranian nuclear program is limited compared to more dispersed and/or hardened targets).

The IAF's mix of standoff precision-guided missiles—such as the Harpoon or Popeye—might not have the required lethality with conventional warheads. (Wildly differing reports exist about the range of the Popeye, which is deployed in the United States as the Have Nap missile. The base system has a range of around 60–70 kilometers. Popeye II has a range of 150 kilometers. Reports have appeared about improved "turbo" versions with ranges of 200–350 kilometers.) [102] There have even been reports of air or submarine-launched versions with ranges of 1,500 kilometers. (One report notes that "Israel is reported to possess a 200-kilogram nuclear warhead, containing 6 kilograms of plutonium, that could be mounted on cruise missiles.")[103]

This would greatly increase Israeli survivability and penetration capability. However, multiple strikes on the dispersed buildings and entries in a number of facilities would be necessary to ensure adequate damage without restrikes. Restrikes would require repeated penetration into Arab air space and do not seem to be feasible planning criteria for Israeli commanders to use.

Much has been made of Israel's purchase of 500 BLU-109 Have Void "bunker busters," but considerable caution is needed about such reports. These are 2,000-pound weapons that are far less effective against deeply buried targets than the much larger U.S. weapons described earlier. The standard version is a "dumb bomb" with a maximum penetration capability of 4 to 6 feet of reinforced concrete. An aircraft must overfly the target and launch the weapon with great precision to achieve serious penetration capability.[104]

It is possible to fit the weapon with precision guidance and convert it to a guided glide bomb, and the United States may have sold such a version to Israel and Israel may have modified them. The joint direct attack munition (JDAM) GBU-31 can be fitted to the bomb to give it a nominal range of 15 kilometers with a CEP of 13 meters in the GPS-aided INS (Inertial Navigation System) modes of operation and 30 meters in the INS-only modes of operation.[105] Open source reporting, however, does not provide any data on such capabilities.

It is also possible that Israel actually purchased the BLU-116 Advanced Unitary Penetrator (AUP), GBU-24 C/B (USAF), or GBU-24 D/B (Navy) which has about three times the penetration capability of the BLU-109.[106]

At least limited refueling would be required, and backup refueling and recovery would be an issue.

Many have compared Israel's current military options vis-à-vis Iran to its 1981 attack against Iraq's Osiraq reactor and have noted that the conditions are very different. For example, Peter Brookes, a military expert, has asserted that Israel has several options, including satellite-guided JDAM (joint direct attack munition) bombs, cruise missiles on submarines, and Special Operation Forces. But he also argued that Iran's nuclear facilities are "much tougher" to target than Iraq's reactor, given the nature of the Iranian nuclear facilities and the strategic balance in the region.[107]

Still, these are problems to be solved, not insuperable barriers. Israel has the capabilities to carry out at last one set of air strikes, and senior U.S. officials have warned about this capability. Vice President Richard Cheney suggested on January 20, 2005, that, "Given the fact that Iran has a stated policy that [its] objective is the destruction of Israel, the Israelis might well decide to act first, and let the rest of the world worry about cleaning up the diplomatic mess afterwards."[108]

General Moshe Ya'alon, the Israeli chief of staff, was quoted in August 2004 as saying that Iran must not be permitted to acquire nuclear weapons. He added that Israel must not rely on the rest of the world to stop Iran from going nuclear, because a nuclear Iran would change the Middle East where "moderate States would become more extreme."[109] General Ya'alon also indicated that Israel might conduct such attacks without using its aircraft, triggering a wide range of speculation about Israeli and U.S. covert operatives and Special Forces conducting such strikes.

Israel may have specially designed or adapted weapons for such strikes, and it bought 500 bunker buster bombs from the United States in February 2005. Experts have speculated whether the purchase was a power projection move or whether Israel was in fact planning to use these conventional bombs against Iranian nuclear sites. These speculations were further exacerbated when Israeli Chief of Staff, Lt. General Dan Halutz, when asked in 2005 how far Israel would go to stop Iran's nuclear program, said "2,000 kilometers."[110]

Brigadier General Shlomo Brom a 30-year veteran of the Israel Defense Forces, has argued that Israel's capabilities may not be enough to inflict sufficient damage on Iran's nuclear program:

. . . any Israeli attack on an Iranian nuclear target would be a very complex operation in which a relatively large number of attack aircraft and support aircraft (interceptors, ECM aircraft, refuelers, and rescue aircraft) would participate. The conclusion is that Israel could attack only a few Iranian targets and not as part of a sustainable operation over time, but as a one-time surprise operation.

Even if Israel had the attack capabilities needed for the destruction of all the elements of the Iranian nuclear program, it is doubtful whether Israel has the kind of intelligence needed to be certain that all the necessary elements of the program were traced and destroyed fully. Israel has good photographic coverage of Iran with the Ofeq series of reconnaissance satellites, but being so distant from Iran, one can assume that other kinds of intelligence coverage are rather partial and weak.

Covert action demands different kinds of operational capabilities and intelligence. There is no indication that Israel has capabilities of covert operations in Iran. The recent information about the development of the Iranian program indicated that it reached a status of being independent of external assistance. Moreover, the assistance Iran got was mostly from Pakistan, another place which is not a traditional area of operations for the Israeli secret services, like Europe or South America. It seems that there is no real potential for covert Israeli operations against the Iranian Nuclear program.[111]

As is the case with a U.S. strike, Iran has the capabilities to strike back. In fact, it has threatened retaliation if attacked by Israel. Iran's foreign minister, Manouchehr Mottaki, reportedly said in 2004 that an attack by Israel or the United States would have "severe consequences," and he threatened that Iran would retaliate "by all means" at its disposal. Mottaki added: "Iran does not think that the Zionist regime is in a condition to engage in such a dangerous venture and they know how severe the possible Iranian response will be to its possible audacity . . . . Suffice it to say that the Zionist regime, if they attack, will regret it."[112]

Iran has several options for responding to an Israeli attack:

- Multiple launches of Shahab-3 missiles, including the possibility of using CBR warheads, against Tel Aviv, Israeli military and civilian centers, and suspected Israeli nuclear weapons sites.

- Escalating the conflict by using proxy groups such Hezbollah or Hamas to attack Israel proper with suicide bombings, covert CBR attacks, and missile attacks from southern Lebanon and Syria.

- Covert attacks against Israeli interests by its intelligence and IRGC assets. These could include low-level bombings against Israeli embassies, Jewish centers, and other Israeli assets outside and inside Israel.

In addition, any Israeli military option would have to include an air strike. This would seriously complicate Israel's fragile relations with Jordan and could provoke Saudi Arabia to respond. An Israeli strike against Iranian nuclear facilities could also strengthen the Iranian regime's stance on moving toward nuclear capabilities and drive many neighboring states to support Iran's bid for nuclear weapons. The United States will be seen as having given the "green light" for such Israeli strikes, which could lead to further escalation of the Iraqi insurgency, increase the threat of asymmetric attacks against U.S. interests and allies in the region, or, even worse, be used as a justification for urging and carrying out attacks against the U.S. homeland with CBR weapons by proxy groups or through an alliance with groups such as al-Qa'ida.

On the other hand, Israeli officials have expressed the concern that Iran's acquisition of nuclear weapons and the means to deliver them could spark further proliferation in the region. This would spread WMD capabilities around the Middle East and greatly increase the threat of CBRN attacks against Israel and the entire region.[113] Waiting also has its penalties.

STRATEGIC IMPLICATIONS

It may be years, or as much as a decade, before all of the implications surrounding Iran's possible efforts to acquire nuclear weapons become clear. As the previous chapters have shown, the strategic implications of whether Iran has a nuclear device are only part of the story. There are many different ways in which Iran can proliferate, deploy nuclear-armed or other CBRN weapons, and use them to deter, intimidate, and strike against other nations. All have only one thing in common: they are all provocative and dangerous—both to any nation Iran may choose to try to influence and target, and to Iran itself.

Iran's options for war-fighting, and the possible response, have already been described in detail. One final point needs to be raised, however. Even Iranian ambiguity will probably lead Israel and the United States—and possibly India, Pakistan, and Russia—to develop nuclear options to deter or retaliate against Iran. Restraint does not have to stop at the first convincing Iranian threat to use nuclear or highly lethal biological weapons, but it could do so. Any actual use by Iran of such weapons is likely to provoke a nuclear response, possibly targeted on Iran's cities and general population. Iran's effort to limit or control the game will probably end at the first ground zero.

Iranian ambiguity also may trigger efforts by Saudi Arabia and Egypt to become nuclear powers. They might show restraint if the United States could provide convincing ballistic and cruise missile defenses and the same form of extended deterrence it once provided to Germany during the Cold War. But, these options are speculative and do not yet exist. Saudi Arabia has already said that it has examined nuclear options and rejected them, but this is no certainty and inevitably depends on Iranian action.

The end result is the prospect of a far more threatening mix of CBRN capabilities in the Gulf region and the areas that most models project as the main source of world oil and gas exports beyond 2015. It is also the threat of more polarization between Sunni and Shi'ite and broader regional tensions and actions spilling out of the confrontation over Iran's nuclear activities. None of these prospects are pleasant.

Notes

[1] For interesting insights into possible scenarios and their implications, see Anthony H. Cordesman, "Terrorism and the Threat from Weapons of Mass Destruction in the Middle East: The Problem of Paradigm Shift," working draft, CSIS, October 17, 1996; Brad Roberts, *Terrorism with Chemical and Biological Weapons, Calibrating Risks and Responses* (Alexandria, Va.: Chemical and Biological Weapons Control Institute, 1997); Shai Feldman, *Nuclear Weapons and Arms Control in the Middle East* (Cambridge, Mass.: MIT Press, 1997).

[2] Office of the Secretary of Defense, *Proliferation: Threat and Response,* U.S. Department of Defense, 2001, p. 1, available at http://www.defenselink .milpubs/ptr20010110.pdf.

[3] Ian Cobain and Ian Traynor, "Secret Services Say Iran Is Trying to Assemble a Nuclear Missile," *Guardian* (Manchester), January 4, 2006, available at http://www.guardian.co.uk/iran/story/0,12858,1677542,00.html.

[4] Ian Cobain and Ian Traynor, "Intelligence Report Claims Nuclear Market Thriving," *Guardian* (Manchester), January 4, 2006, available at http://www.guardian.co.uk/iran/story/0,12858,1677554,00.html.

[5] Dafna Linzer, "No Proof Found of Iran Arms Program," *Washington Post*, August 23, 2005, sec. A-1.

[6] "UN Findings Support Iran Nuke Claims," Associated Press, August 20, 2005.

[7] Ibid.

[8] Robin Wright and Keith B. Richburg, "Powell Says Iran Is Pursuing Bomb," *Washington Post*, November 18, 2004, sec. A-1.

[9] George Jahn, "U.N. Report Says Iran Has Produced Tons of Gas Needed for Uranium Enrichment," Associated Press, September 2, 2005.

[10] "Iran Bought Centrifuges, Pakistan Says," Associate Press, March 10, 2005.

[11] Dafna Linzer, "Strong Leads and Dead Ends in Nuclear Case against Iran," *Washington Post*, February 8, 2006, sec. A-1.

[12] Viktor Mizin, Ministry of Foreign Affairs, Russia (remarks, 7th Carnegie International Nonproliferation Conference, Carnegie Endowment for International Peace, Washington, D.C., January 11–12, 1999, http://www.carnegie endowment.org/files/Repairing_12.pdf).

[13] Robin Gedye, "Iran's Nuclear History," *Daily Telegraph* (London), October 9, 2003, available at http://www.telegraph.co.uk/news/main.jhtml?xml=/news/2003/09/10/wiran210.xml&sSheet=/news/2003/09/10/ixnewstop.html.

[14] "Russia Wants to Build More Nuke Reactors for Iran," Reuters, June 28, 2005.

[15] "Russia Hosts Iranians for Key Talks on Nuclear Row," Reuters, February 19, 2006.

[16] William J. Broad, "Small-Scale Atomic Research By Iran Is Risky, Experts Say," *New York Times*, March 8, 2006, p. 14.

[17] Louis Charbonneau, "N. Korea Provides Nuclear Aid to Iran—Intel Reports," Reuters, July 6, 2005.

[18] Ibid.

[19] Michael Sheridan, "North Korea's Plutonium Attracts Iran," *Sunday Times* (London), January 29, 2006, available at http://www.timesonline.co.uk/article/0,,2089-2014464,00.html.

[20] Con Coughlin, "North Korea to Help Iran Dig Secret Missile Bunkers," *Daily Telegraph* (London), December 6, 2005, available at http://www.telegraph.co.uk/news/main.jhtml?xml=/news/2005/06/12/wnkor12.xml.

[21] David Albright, "An Iranian Bomb," *Bulletin of the Atomic Scientists* 51, no. 4 (July/August 1995): 20–26.

[22] Joseph Cirincione, Jon Wolfsthal, and Miriam Rajkumar, *Deadly Arsenals: Nuclear, Biological, and Chemical Threats,* 2nd ed. (Washington, D.C.: Carnegie Endowment for International Peace, July 2005), p. 303.

[23] Office of the Secretary of Defense, *Proliferation: Threat and Response,* p. 36.

[24] Dan Bilefsky and David E. Sanger, "Europeans Criticize U.S. Sanctions as Potential Risk to Iran Talk," *New York Times,* December 29, 2005.

[25] "Opp Group Says Iran Moving towards Uranium Enrichment," *Daily Times* (Lahore, Pakistan), September 14, 2005, available at http://www.dailytimes.com.pk/default.asp?page=story_14-9-2005_pg4_17.

[26] Jeffrey J. Schott, "U.S. Economic Sanctions: Good Intentions, Bad Execution" (testimony before the Committee on International Relations, U.S. House of Representatives, June 3, 1998).

[27] Gary Clyde Hufbauer, Jeffrey J. Schott, and Kimberly Ann Elliott, *Economic Sanctions Reconsidered,* 3rd ed. (Washington D.C.: Institute for International Economics, forthcoming), available at http://www.iie.com/publications/papers/paper.cfm?ResearchID=342.

[28] Ibid.

[29] Judy Dempsey, "Hint of Iran Sanctions Tugs at Trade Ties," *International Herald Tribune,* January 11, 2006.

[30] Schott, "U.S. Economic Sanctions: Good Intentions, Bad Execution."

[31] Daniel Altman, "Quandary over Iran Sanctions," *International Herald Tribune,* January 24, 2006.

[32] CIA, "Iran," *The World Factbook,* January 2006, available at http://www.cia.gov/cia/publications/factbook/index.html.

[33] Ibid.

[34] Chris Baltimore, "China, Russia Would Fight Iran Oil Sanctions," Reuters, January 18, 2006.

[35] Peter Goodman, "China Rushes toward Oil Pact with Iran," *Washington Post,* February 18, 2006, sec. D-01.

[36] Dempsey, "Hint of Iran Sanctions Tugs at Trade Ties."

[37] Hassan M. Fattah, "Gulf States Join Call for Tougher Action toward Iran," New York Times, February 1, 2006.

[38] Energy Information Administration (EIA), "Global Energy Sanction," Country Analysis Briefs, July 2004, available at http://www.eia.doe.gov.

[39] Ibid.

[40] Ibid.

[41] Ibid.

[42] EIA, "Iran," Country Analysis Briefs, January 2006, available at http://www.eia.doe.gov/emeu/cabs/Iran/pdf.pdf.

[43] EIA, "World Crude Oil Production (Including Least Condensate), 1997–Present," International Petroleum Monthly (IPM), July 2005, available at http://www.eia.doe.gov/emeu/ipsr/t11a.xls.

[44] International Energy Agency (IEA), World Energy Outlook 2005, Middle East and North Africa Insights (Paris: Organization for Economic Cooperation and Development (OECD)/IEA, 2005), p. 568.

[45] Ibid.

[46] Brad Foss and George Jahn, "Iran Sanctions Could Drive Past $100," Associated Press, January 22, 2006.

[47] John Zarocostas, "Skyrocketing Oil Costs Feared in Nuke Standoff," Washington Times, January 24, 2005, p. 11.

[48] Foss and Jahn, "Iran Sanctions Could Drive Past $100."

[49] Jeffery Donovan, "Iran: Diplomatic Efforts on Possible Sanctions Intensify (Part 1)," Radio Free Europe/Radio Liberty (RFE/RL), January 18, 2006, available at http://www.rferl.org/featuresarticle/2006/01/36423915-CFFA-4C02-817F-59C491C90B73.html.

[50] Bill Samii, "Iran: Military Options Considered as Nuclear Crisis Escalates," RFE/RL, February 1, 2006, available at http://www.rferl.org/featuresarticle/2006/02/7a07b21a-8799-4ff3-85da-f4caee452f48.html.

[51] CIA, "Iran." World Factbook.

[52] IEA, World Energy Outlook 2005, Middle East and North Africa Insights, p. 361.

[53] EIA, "Iran," Country Analysis Briefs, January 2006.

[54] Ibid.

[55] Daniel Altman, "Quandary over Iran Sanctions," International Herald Tribune, January 24, 2006.

[56] IEA, World Energy Outlook 2005, Middle East and North Africa Insights, p. 568.

[57] Christian Oliver and Alireza Ronaghi, "Iran's Powerful Bazaar Braced for Atomic Storm," Reuters, February 7, 2006.

[58] Christian Oliver, "Iran Bravado on UN Sanction May Ring Hollow," Reuters, February 1, 2006.

[59] Nazila Fathi and Andrew E. Kramer, "With Threat of Sanctions, Iran Protects Some Assets," New York Times, January 21, 2006, p. 5.

[60] "Iran Denies Shifting Assets in Europe," Gulf Daily News (Manama, Bahrain), January 20, 2006, available at http://www.gulf-daily-news.com/Story.asp?Article=133050&Sn=BUSI&IssueID=28306.

[61] World Bank, "Iran," available at http://web.worldbank.org/wbsite/external/countries/menaext/iranextn/0,,menuPK:312962~pagePK:141159~piPK:141110~theSitePK:312943,00.html.

[62] Viktor Mizin (remarks, Carnegie Endowment for International Peace 7th Carnegie International Non-proliferation Conference, January 11–12, 1999), available at http://www.carnegieendowment.org/files/Repairing_12.pdf.

[63] "Iran Report," RFE/RL 9, no. 5, February 17, 2006.

[64] Steven R. Weisman, "Cheney Warns Of 'Consequences' For Iran On Nuclear Issue," New York Times, March 8, 2006.

[65] Peter S. Canellos, "As a Threat from Iran Increases, US May Lack Preemptive Options," Boston Globe, March 21, 2006.

[66] Peter Brookes, "Iran: Our Military Options," New York Post, January 23, 2006.

[67] Yigal Grayeff, "US Could Wipe Out Iran Nukes in 2 Days," Jerusalem Post, March 21, 2006.

[68] T. Orszaq-Land, "Iran Threatens to Abandon the NPT," Jane's Islamic Affairs Analyst, October 1, 2004.

[69] David Albright and Corey Hinderstein, "Parchin: Possible Nuclear Weapons–Related Site in Iran," Institute for Science and International Security, Issue Brief, September 15, 2004, available at http://www.isis-online.org/publications/iran/parchin.html.

[70] Robin Hughes, "Tehran Takes Steps to Protect Nuclear Facilities," Jane's Defence Weekly, January 25, 2006.

[71] Ibid.

[72] Global Security reports that the Guided Bomb Unit-28 (GBU-28) bomb was developed in 1991. It can penetrate hardened targets before exploding, and is capable of penetrating 100 feet of earth or 20 feet of concrete. The GBU-28 is laser-guided and uses an 8-inch artillery tube as the bomb body. It is fitted

with GBU-27 LGB kits and is 14.5 inches in diameter and almost 19 feet long. The operator illuminates a target with a laser designator, and then the munition guides to a spot of laser energy reflected from the target. Global Security notes that the bomb is nominally a 5,000-pound bomb, but may actually weigh 4,700 pounds.

F-117s dropped two weapons during the Gulf War. The bomb was modified after the conflict, and F-15s used the weapon in Kosovo. It is not clear that the B-2 or U.S. aircraft would now use this weapon. The Hard and Deeply Buried Target Defeat System (HDBTDS) program has made major progress in recent years.

The fuzing of the weapon is believed to have been improved and possibly some aspects of its penetration capability. It has been tested against rock as well as soil. Global Security indicates that the Guided Bomb Unit-28C/B, also known as BLU-122 or Enhanced Paveway III, provides an improved aerial delivery capability for the BLU-113 P3I warhead, and possesses a Global Positioning System (GPS)-aided laser guidance capability with improved lethality, survivability, and penetration over the 28B/B weapons system, and is compatible with F-15E and B-2A aircraft platforms. See http://www.globalsecurity.org/military/systems/munitions/gbu-28.htm.

The B-2 Spirit bomber has also tested simulated nuclear earth penetrator modifications of the B61-11. See http://www.globalsecurity.org/wmd/library/news/usa/1998/n19980326_980417.html.

[73] See http://www.globalsecurity.org/military/systems/munitions/blu-109-specs.htm.

[74] See http://www.globalsecurity.org/military/systems/munitions/jdam.htm.

[75] See http://www.globalsecurity.org/military/systems/munitions/blu-116.htm.

[76] See http://www.globalsecurity.org/military/systems/munitions/agm-130.htm.

[77] Hughes, "Tehran Takes Steps to Protect Nuclear Facilities."

[78] "Iran Reveals Shahab Thaqeb SAM Details," *Jane's Defence Weekly,* September 4, 2002.

[79] Based on interviews with British and U.S. experts; Anthony H. Cordesman, *Iran and Iraq: The Threat from the Northern Gulf* (Boulder: Westview Press, 1994); Anthony H. Cordesman and Ahmed S. Hashim, *Iran: The Dilemmas of Dual Containment* (Boulder: Westview Press, 1997); International Institute for Strategic Studies (IISS), *Iran's Strategic Weapons Programmes: A Net Assessment,* IISS Strategic Dossier, various editions; "Iran," *Jane's Sentinel Security Assessments: The Gulf States,* various editions; United States Naval Institute (USNI) database; Anoushiravan Ehteshami, "Iran's National Strategy," *International Defense Review* 4 (1994): 29–37; Military Technology, *World Defense Almanac: The Balance of Military Power* 17, no. 1 (1993): 139–142; working data

from the Jaffee Center for Strategic Studies; Andrew Rathmell, "Iran's Rearmament: How Great a Threat?" *Jane's Intelligence Review*, July 1994, pp. 317–322; Ahmed Hashim, "The Crisis of the Iranian State," *Adelphi Paper 296* (London: IISS, July 1995), pp. 7–30, 50–70; Andrew Rathmell, *The Changing Military Balance in the Gulf*, Whitehall Series (London: Royal United Services Institute for Defence and Security Studies [RUSI], 1996), pp. 9–23; Michael Eisenstadt, *Iranian Military Power, Capabilities and Intentions* (Washington, D.C.: Washington Institute for Near East Policy, 1996), pp. 9–65; and Anoushiravan Enreshami, "Iran Strives to Regain Military Might," *International Defense Review* 7 (1996): 22–26.

[80] Alon Ben David, "Iran Launches New Surface to Air Missile Production," *Jane's Defence Weekly*, February 15, 2006.

[81] See http://www.globalsecurity.org/military/world/russia/sa-15.htm.

[82] Ibid.; "Russia May Deliver Iranian Tor-M1s Earlier Than Expected," *Jane's Missiles and Rockets*, February 1, 2006.

[83] Lyubov Provina, "Russian Arms Sale to Iran Draws US Scrutiny," Defense News.com, December 12, 2005; Alon Ben David, "Iran Launches New Surface to Air Missile Production," *Jane's Defence Weekly*, February 15, 2006.

[84] For full details, see http://www.globalsecurity.org/military/world/china/qw-1.htm.

[85] Reuters, January 5, 1997, 7:00:32 PST; http://www.globalsecurity.org/military/world/russia/s-300pmu2.htm; http://www.globalsecurity.org/military/world/russia/s-300pmu.htm.

[86] See http://www.globalsecurity.org/military/world/russia/s-300v.htm.

[87] "No S-300 deal with Iran, says Russian defense minister," *Jane's Missiles and Rockets*, March 1, 2006.

[88] Michael Knights, "Iran's Conventional Forces Remain Key to Deterring Potential Threats," *Jane's Intelligence Review*, February 1, 2006.

[89] Ellen Knickmeyer and Omar Fekeiki, "Iraqi Shi'ite Cleric Pledges to Defend Iran," *Washington Post*, January 24, 2006, sec. A-13.

[90] Robin Hughes, "Rumsfeld alleges IRGC Al Qods Infiltrating Iraq," *Jane's Defence Weekly*, March 15, 2006.

[91] Knickmeyer and Fekeiki, "Iraqi Shi'ite Cleric Pledges to Defend Iran."

[92] Michael Knights, "Deterrence by Punishment Could Offer Last Resort Option for Iran," *Jane's Intelligence Review*, April 1, 2006.

[93] This would require remote targeting. Surface radar coverage of a large ship from a ground-mounted radar is about 26–32 nautical miles.

[94] It is unclear what version of the missile Iran has and what modifications it may have made. China made a wide range of variants of the system. Global Security describes them as follows (http://www.globalsecurity.org/military/world/china/c-201.htm):

- HY-2A terminal guidance radar of the prototype missile was modified into a passive infrared target seeker that effectively raised the concealment and anti-jamming capabilities of the missile. The interception performance of this missile within guidance range can realize omnidirectional attacks on ship targets at sea.

- HY-2B conical scanning terminal guidance radar of the prototype missile was modified to an advanced monopulse system radar that improved its resistance to sea waves interference and various forms of electronic jamming.

- HY-2C terminal guidance radar of the prototype missile was modified into a television-equipped target seeker that was able to effectively raise the concealment and anti-jamming capabilities of the missile as well as increase its hit probability.

- HY-2G uses a high precision radio altimeter so that the level flight altitude of the missile can be lowered to 30–50 meters, raising penetration capabilities. The basic HY-2 uses active radar homing, while the HY-2G adds a radio altimeter to permit a lower penetration altitude.

[95] See http://www.globalsecurity.org/military/world/china/c-802.htm.

[96] IISS, *Military Balance, 2005–2006*; Knights, "Deterrence by Punishment Could Offer Last Resort Option for Iran."

[97] Al Akbar Dareini, "Iran Rolls Out Yet Another Missile," *Chicago Tribune*, April 4, 2006; "Iran Says Has Tested 2nd Missile," CNN.com, April 4, 2006; Ali Ronaghi, "Iran Says Fires Sonar-evading, Underwater Missile," Washingtonpost.com, April 2, 2006, 1:03 PM.

[98] "Iran Suicide Bombers to 'Burn Down' U.S. Interest," Iran Focus, February 13, 2006, available at http://www.iranfocus.com/modules/news/article.php?storyid=5753.

[99] Orszaq-Land, "Iran Threatens to Abandon the NPT."

[100] "Iran Report," RFE/RL 9, no. 2, January 23, 2006.

[101] For further discussion, see Knights, "Iran's Conventional Forces Remain Key to Deterring Potential Threats"; Paul Rogers, "Iran: Consequences of a War," briefing paper, Oxford Research Group, February 2006, available at www.oxfordresearchgroup.uk.

[102] See http://www.globalsecurity.org/wmd/world/israel/popeye-t.htm.

[103] Ibid.

[104] See http://www.globalsecurity.org/military/systems/munitions/blu-109-specs.htm.

[105] See http://www.globalsecurity.org/military/systems/munitions/jdam.htm.

[106] See http://www.globalsecurity.org/military/systems/munitions/blu-116.htm.

[107] Peter Brookes, "Iran: Our Military Options," *New York Post*, January 23, 2006.

[108] Jim VandeHei, "Cheney Warns of Iran as a Nuclear Threat," *Washington Post*, January 21, 2005, sec. A-2.

[109] Abraham Rabinovich, "Iran Boasts Dimona Now 'within Range,'" *Washington Times*, August 24, 2004.

[110] Kenneth R. Timmerman, "The Crisis Has Begun," *Washington Times*, January 7, 2006.

[111] Shlomo Brom, "Is the Begin Doctrine Still a Viable Option for Israel?" in *Getting Ready for a Nuclear Iran*, ed. Henry Sokolski and Patrick Clawson (Carlisle, Pa.: Strategic Studies Institute, October 2005).

[112] Ewen MacAskill and Simon Tisdall, "Iran's Message to the West: Back Off or We Retaliate," *Guardian* (Manchester), February 2, 2006, available at http://www.guardian.co.uk/iran/story/0,1700266,00.html.

[113] Tom Carter, "Tehran Nukes a Global Threat, Israeli Warns," *Washington Times*, December 7, 2004.

ABOUT THE AUTHORS

Anthony H. Cordesman holds the Arleigh A. Burke Chair in Strategy at CSIS. He is also a national security analyst for ABC News and a frequent commentator on National Public Radio and the BBC. His television commentary has been prominently featured during the Iraq War, the conflict in Kosovo, the fighting in Afghanistan, and the Gulf War.

Prior to CSIS, Cordesman served in numerous government positions, including as national security assistant to Senator John McCain of the Senate Armed Services Committee, as director of intelligence assessment in the Office of the Secretary of Defense, as civilian assistant to the deputy secretary of defense, and as director of policy and planning for resource applications at the Department of Energy. He has also served in the State Department and on NATO International Staff and has had many foreign assignments, including posts in Lebanon, Egypt, and Iran, with extensive work in Saudi Arabia and the Gulf.

Cordesman is the author of more than 40 books on U.S. security policy, energy policy, and the Middle East, as well as a four-volume series on the lessons of modern war. His most recent books include *The Changing Dynamics of Energy in the Middle East*, with Khalid R. Al-Rodhan (Praeger/CSIS, 2006); *The Global Oil Market: Risks and Uncertainties*, with Khalid R. Al-Rodhan (CSIS, 2006); *The Challenge of Biological Terrorism* (CSIS, 2005); *Iraqi Security Forces: A Strategy for Success* (Praeger/CSIS, 2005); *The Israeli-Palestinian War: Escalating to Nowhere* (Praeger/CSIS, 2005); *National Security in Saudi Arabia: Threats, Responses, and Challenges*, with Nawaf Obaid (Praeger/CSIS,

2005); *Iran's Developing Military Capabilities* (CSIS, 2005); *The War after the War: Strategic Lessons of Iraq and Afghanistan* (CSIS, 2004); *The Military Balance in the Middle East* (Praeger/CSIS, 2004); *Energy Developments in the Middle East* (Praeger/CSIS, 2004); and *The Iraq War: Strategy, Tactics, and Military Lessons* (Praeger/CSIS, 2003).

Khalid R. Al-Rodhan is research fellow with the Office of the Arleigh A. Burke Chair in Strategy at CSIS, where his research focuses on the military balance in the Middle East; Saudi Arabia's national security; Iran's nuclear capabilities; internal security and intelligence apparatuses of the Gulf states; counterterrorism; WMD proliferation; energy modeling; Middle Eastern energy policy; and global energy security.

Before joining CSIS, Al-Rodhan worked in investment banking and the financial markets, where among his various positions he was a research analyst at FDO Partners/Revere Street Capital Management in Cambridge, Massachusetts. He earned a B.A./M.A. in economics-mathematics, as well as a B.A. in international relations, from Boston University. He also earned an M.A. and finished the Ph.D. coursework in international economics at Georgetown University, where he is enrolled in doctoral studies in international relations.

Al-Rodhan is the author of strategic net assessment studies on the Middle East, military strategy, and energy policy, and his work is widely quoted in the press. He is the coauthor of several books with Anthony Cordesman, including *The Global Oil Market: Risks and Uncertainties* (CSIS, 2006); *The Changing Dynamics of Energy in the Middle East* (Praeger/CSIS, 2006); and *Gulf Military Forces in an Era of Asymmetric War* (Praeger/CSIS, forthcoming).